JEWELLERY

JEWELLERY

AN HISTORICAL SURVEY
OF BRITISH STYLES AND JEWELS

NANCY ARMSTRONG

LUTTERWORTH PRESS · GUILDFORD AND LONDON

First published 1973

ISBN 0 7188 1977 2

*Printed in Great Britain
by Ebenezer Baylis and Son Limited
The Trinity Press, Worcester, and London*

Sitting in the 'bus
in the sunless cavern
between Mount Royal
and C & A Modes . . .

Sitting in the 'bus
(is it Honiton lace in those windows?)
I appreciate
that the Angel is Dusty.
Whisking the feather duster
with the pink bamboo handle,
over the cob-web corners of my mind,
I consider the merits
of putting water on the floor
so that the dust
stays
pestled and mortared
by the talcum-powdered physical contact
of our communicating intellects.
When the 'bus moves
out of the sunless cavern,
the dust rises,
stirred up by the gale
from the exhausting manifold.

The dust settles,
seeps into my shoes.
I must remember to leave
my ticket.
But I shall keep
my Dusty Angel.

Dusty Angel
R. J. H.
1945

Contents

CONTENTS

Acknowledgments

Author's Acknowledgments

I should like to thank the various people, private collectors, jewellery shops and companies, and public organizations who have so generously helped me with the illustrations for this book, and the various museums and libraries whose patient staffs I have badgered. The people who have answered my letters so patiently are really too numerous to list, but it is heart-warming to see all their painstaking replies which have helped me so much.

I would, however, like to pick out by name several individuals whose help has been far beyond the scope of their normal duties: Miss Susan Hare of the Worshipful Company of Goldsmiths who has been an inspiration for years and has consistently given me scholarly help; Miss Clare Snowden and Miss Susan Farmer of De Beers Consolidated Mines Ltd. who have helped in every possible way with illustrations and information; Mrs. Winifred Ward whose loving guidance I have followed for many years with gratitude; Marcus Armstrong, my younger son, who has been completely uncomplaining at the disruption of our home life for months; and Miss Jenny Overton, my Editor, who has so charmingly controlled my every action, and without whose guidance there would have been no book.

N.J.A.

Copyright and Illustration Acknowledgments

The author and the publishers would like to thank Mr. Kevin Crossley-Holland and Macmillan & Co. Ltd. for permission to quote the seventeen lines from Mr. Crossley-Holland's translation of *Beowulf*, published in 1968, and here appearing on page 33.

They also wish to express their gratitude to all who have granted permission for the taking, use and reproduction of illustrations: in particular the Trustees of the Ashmolean Museum at Oxford for the colour plate facing page 34; N. Bloom & Son for the colour plates facing pages 162 and 243, and for Figures 27, 28, 29, 37, 38, 44, 47, 52, 57, 59, 70 and 71; the Trustees of the British Museum for Figures 5, 6, 7 and 33; Messrs. Cairncross of Perth for Figure 56; Cameo Corner for Figures 39, 46, 48, 50, 54; De Beers Consolidated Mines Ltd. for Figures 60, 61, 62, 63, 64, 65, 66 and 67; the Syndics of the Fitzwilliam Museum at Cambridge for Figure 24; Fox Photos Ltd. for Figure 14; the Worshipful Company of Goldsmiths for the colour plate facing page 51 and for Figures 3, 4, 10, 11, 12, 13, 58 and 69; Andrew Grima Ltd. for the colour plate facing page 252 and for Figure 72; H.M.S.O. for Figures 35 and 36; the Trustees of the London Museum for the colour plate facing page 115; the Trustees of the National Portrait Gallery for the colour plate facing page 146 and Figures 16, 17 and 31; the Trustees of the Sir John Soane Museum for Figure 34; the authorities of Stonyhurst College for Figure 15; the Trustees of the Victoria and Albert Museum for the colour plates facing pages 98, 195 and 226 and for Figures 1, 2, 8, 9, 18, 19, 25, 30, 42, 43, 45, 49, 53 and 68; Wartski Jewellers Ltd. for Figure 40; Wedgwood and Co. Ltd. for Figure 41; the Dean and Chapter of Westminster Abbey for Figure 26; and the owners of private collections who have given most generous and courteous help. Illustrations reproduced by permission of H.M.S.O. and the Trustees of the Victoria and Albert Museum are Crown Copyright. Mr. E. G. Bishop kindly took a number of photographs especially for this book, including Figures 29, 44, 47, 51, 52, 59, 70 and 71.

List of Illustrations

Introduction

JEWELLERY DESIGN is based on the developments in the history of art and its creation ranks as high as any other form of decorative art the world has known. For centuries, world-wide, the accent was on male ownership, more recently on female, but in contemporary society the balance is reasonably even.

One should establish here, at the very beginning, that although the word "jewel" is commonly used nowadays to mean a gemstone, it may also be applied—as it is throughout this book—to signify any piece of jeweller's work made to be worn as personal decoration. A jewel can quite well contain no gemstones at all.

Because of the importance of superstition and of belief about the magical and medicinal qualities of gemstones, which had an immense effect on the craft for thousands of years, the opening chapter has been devoted to this; and because the progress of the craft in the British Isles was inevitably affected by the traditions and styles of mainland Europe, a second chapter sketches in the succession of the ancient civilizations and the rise, decline and fall of the Roman Empire, with the subsequent establishment of the Byzantine civilization and the later Carolingian attempt to revive the western Empire of classical Rome.

Jewellery in England has been much influenced by the Worshipful Company of Goldsmiths, with their unbroken record of overseeing the craft of gold-, silver- and jewellery-making for over six hundred years; a tradition no other country can emulate. It seemed only fair to devote a chapter to the Goldsmiths, partly in sheer gratitude for the way in which they have kept national standards impeccably high, and partly because the historical events out of which and against which the Company grew were so very interesting.

The greater part of the rest of the book is devoted to the progression of jewellery in Britain, and attempts to set its development in the context of historical events and political and social changes, and to remark on the more influential of the changes in the other decorative arts. It has been impossible to do more than sketch and indicate so many things that deserved fuller mention.

Our knowledge of the early years of the craft derives largely from wills, inventories and effigies—so much was lost at the Reformation, or was melted down and re-made because of changes in fashion, civil disturbances, and so on. With the sixteenth century we find in addition paintings and a few historic pieces still displayed in museums and galleries, leaving us unhappily aware of the great wealth that has been lost or destroyed. Georgian and Victorian jewellery is, however, readily available, and one can still examine it in the quality shops; and the jewellery of the early twentieth century

I

often now lies fallow in some half-forgotten jewel-case. The changing styles throughout were related to the developments in the other arts—painting, sculpture, architecture—and sifting the one will often reveal the bones of the other. But whereas the other arts are, in the main, academic, jewellery has an extra dimension: it is wholly personal. Jewels, in general, were made to adorn, to lure, to decorate, with the extra draw of intrinsic value into the bargain.

Many jewellery books either concentrate on a single period, or take the history of jewellery in a broad sweep which finishes abruptly at the end of the nineteenth century. But any study of British styles and jewels must include comment on the present-day work; there has been a renaissance in the craft in the last quarter-century, and more jewels are now being created which are individual, brilliantly designed, and unerringly made than at any other period in our history. It is an intensely exciting time—but there is a real danger that the ordinary person, the man in the street, is unaware of this. Yet it is he or she who is the patron of today. In the past patronage lay in the hands of the great—the rulers, the popes, the lords and the churchmen. The extent of their influence was such that the chapters which deal, for example, with the jewellery of the sixteenth and seventeenth centuries are very closely tied to the actions and characters of the Tudor and Stuart monarchs. Henry VIII's hold, for instance, was so firm that every piece of jewellery imported into England had to be shown to him before it could be marketed; thus he was sure of getting all the finest work for his own collection. The sumptuary laws of the past restricted the kind of jewels men and women might wear, according to their social standing. All this is gone, and we can be glad of it. The relative affluence and freedom of the present day means that anyone with an interest in jewellery can indulge it happily.

The difference is partly due to the spread of education. The fuller and broader education of the present day, the new emphasis on tolerance, leaves everyone free to make his or her own decisions over taste. It is, of course, important to learn from the past, and to be able to sift what is good from what is unworthy and to pick out good contemporary design, as opposed to mere styling; but it is tragic that so many of us still revere the past to such an extent that we ignore the present. The habit of buying and selling through antique shops grew up soon after the Second World War, partly out of sheer economic necessity—people had to sell their small personal treasures to help eke out their incomes—and partly out of nostalgia for a safe and gracious-seeming past—people bought things which reminded them of the old days, refusing to look ahead into a future which then seemed even more dismal and depressing than the war just over. Surely these times are now long past? Yet people seem to cling to the habit of buying antiques, rather than considering contemporary work, deciding for themselves, and buying for the future. Quality antiques are best seen in the stately homes for which they were originally designed; the patrons of those early periods, commissioning from the finest contemporary artists, bought new furniture, new paintings, new artefacts to adorn the new masterpieces of architecture—they looked forward, not back, though many of them had the highest reverence for the styles of the past and the old traditions from which the new work (new to them, treasured antiques to us) had grown and flowered.

The jewels that are being created here today are scintillating in their beauty, personal, individual, with their emphasis on the natural crystalline formation of the stone, supreme craftsmanship and extreme honesty. It is surely up to us to learn about them, buy them, commission them. So many people seem to feel that their opinions are of no interest or importance, yet their appreciation and criticism are vital to the continuing vigorous development of the arts. How many of the people who go to an exhibition write afterwards to the artist, sculptor or craftsman to comment on his work? An artist can come to feel that he is working in a vacuum, sealed off from the rest of the world. It is surely our duty to communicate with creative people—even if it is merely a cook who has taken trouble over some special dish; a word of appreciation is invaluable. An artist may work for years to create sufficient material for a worthwhile show, and yet meet with perfect silence; for him that is a disaster. Even if one cannot afford to commission work from a contemporary craftsman, one can surely afford a postage stamp, an entrance fee, the price of a catalogue. One need not, and should not, look to the past for all that is good, any more than one need, or should, always look abroad. It is all too easy to indulge in pride in the past and its achievements, and like so many other countries throughout the world, we have good reason to be proud of it; yet with the vitality and the beauty of the contemporary jewellery being created here and now, we can have pride both in the past and, especially, in the present. It is a heart-warming reality.

NANCY J. ARMSTRONG
March 1973

CHAPTER ONE

A Background of Belief

Introduction—The Development of Astrology—The Virtues of Gemstones: Amulets and Talismans; Early Lapidary Texts; Biblical References; Later Lapidaries—The Survival of Superstition

Introduction

Would you accept an opal as a gift? Most women, if offered one, would refuse. Not all women, but eleven out of twelve. However beautiful the stone, even if it suited their way of life or the clothes they liked to wear, eleven out of twelve would probably refuse. Why? Because the opal was not their birthstone, and so they felt it was unlucky. "*Isn't* it unlucky?" they might well say vaguely, on being questioned further. "I always thought it was. I really can't afford any more bad luck after all these things that have happened to me lately, I'm afraid. No, I really don't want to tempt Fate at present." This type of remark is heard again and again by jewellers, although we are living in the latter half of the twentieth century A.D. A belief in fate, or luck, still influences people's lives today. It has done so since the beginning of time. Such a belief cannot be dissected or disproved, for it is intangible—a state of mind, like religious faith, which cannot be tested by reliable scientific means.

Until the mid-nineteenth century, religion, science and magic were as intricately interwoven as the threads of a Flemish tapestry. They are still closely affiliated. In some parts of the world it is impossible, even today, to separate religious practice and belief from the practice of, and faith in, magic; and even now a person unversed in science is apt to regard a scientist or a doctor as a magician.

It is impossible to offer a simple and satisfying definition of "magic"; but the impulse to believe in the power of magic seems to have sprung originally from deep reverence for, and fear of, the forces of the natural world, and indeed the universe beyond it—the sky with sun, moon and stars, and the earth with its changing seasons. Men the world over, and from the earliest times, recognized the essential relationship between the natural world and their own well-being, for their well-being was centred in the crops on which they fed and with which they could trade.

The Development of Astrology

The history of mankind seems to have begun with nomadic tribes wandering about the earth. By the fourth millennium B.C., these tribes were beginning to develop permanent settlements, choosing sites where both water and salt were available. The earliest village and urban civilizations of which we have found traces are in river regions: in the Indus valley; along the Hwang-Ho, the great "Yellow River"; along the Nile; and in the area between the lower courses of the Tigris and the Euphrates in western Asia which came to be called Mesopotamia, "the land between the rivers".

The earliest settlers in Mesopotamia of whom we have any real knowledge are the Sumerians, whose language is the oldest written language in existence. By the third millennium B.C., they had developed a considerable culture. In about 2350 B.C. Sumer was conquered by Sargon, a Semitic king who had established himself as ruler over Akkad, a town in northern Mesopotamia. The dynasty which he founded ruled tranquilly for about a hundred years, its kings being accepted by the Sumerians in the south as well as the Akkadians in the north, until a barbarian tribe, the Guti, came storming in from the east, split up the empire, and destroyed the kingship and city of Akkad. The Guti, however, were overthrown in their turn, in about 2130 B.C., by a man called Ur-Nammu, who united the country under the rule of the city of Ur. His dynasty lasted another hundred years, eventually crumbling under the effects of famine and invasion; it was another two hundred and fifty years before the great Hammurabi of Babylon re-united the country (*circa* 1770 B.C.), established a dynasty that lasted for one hundred and fifty-five years, and created a new empire. His reign was to be the classical period of the Old Babylonian civilization.

It was the people of ancient Mesopotamia who initiated the study of astrology—that is, the art or science of forecasting events on earth by observation of the sun, the moon, the planets, and the fixed stars. They believed that the terrestrial world, in which they lived, and the celestial world of the heavens, which their priests studied, were interdependent. From a detailed study of the skies the astrologers could thus predict the fortunes of the state.

The Mesopotamian astrologers of the third millennium B.C. saw that the sun, the moon and the planets appear to move within a narrow band of the heavens: the belt of sky which spreads to either side of the sun's path, and which the Greeks were to name the Zodiac. (The Greek name means "circle of Animals", and derives from the fact that the greater number of the constellations crossed by this path are the animal ones.) It is believed to have been the Mesopotamian priests who first grouped the fixed stars into constellations representing the goat, the serpent, and so on; they who first divided the belt of sky into twelve signs (bearing the same names as the twelve constellations that lie within it)—one of the earliest known portrayals of Scorpio is from a Babylonian boundary stone of the tenth century B.C.; they who associated each sign with a particular part of the body—the stinging Scorpion ruling the sex organs; they too who first associated the planets with particular metals. (The Zodiacal signs appear on the clock which is shown in Fig. 14.) A whole series of systems of divination, prophylactic magic and exorcism arose from the complicated workings of the early astrologers as they tried to calculate the exact connections between the heavenly bodies and the lives of men on earth. The Assyrians conquered the Babylonians in the first millennium B.C., but the religious beliefs of both peoples were essentially the same, and the conquerors honoured the temples of Babylon and their great stores of astrological and astronomical texts.

6

More than half the extant Assyrian documents, in fact, are astrological presages or magical incantations.

The study of astrology had spread east from Babylonia into Asia Minor, Syria, India and, eventually, China, by about the sixth century B.C. At about the same time it began to gain ground in Egypt, though whereas the Babylonians were mostly concerned with their earthly lives and how to protect them, the Egyptians' main concern was the hereafter and how to prepare for life after death.

The cult spread also to the Hebraic culture. The Book of Daniel, for example, describes how Nebuchadnezzar, King of Babylon, besieged and took Jerusalem, and carried off to his palace a number of clever, well-born young men "whom they might teach the learning and the tongue of the Chaldeans" (Chaldea being another name for the Babylonian lands); among these young Jews, trained up in the king's palace, were four famous men—the prophet Daniel, and the three who were to come unscathed from the fiery furnace, Shadrach, Meshach and Abed-nego. When Nebuchadnezzar examined the young men at the end of three years, he found that these four were "ten times better than all the magicians and astrologers that were in his realm". Troubled by terrible dreams, he sent for "the magicians and the astrologers, and the sorcerers, and the Chaldeans"; so did the regent Belshazzar when he saw the writing on the wall ("The king cried aloud to bring in the astrologers, the Chaldeans and the soothsayers"): but in neither case could magicians, astrologers, soothsayers or Chaldeans offer any useful interpretation; that was left to the prophet Daniel, who put them very firmly in their place. But in spite of the shown triumph of the man of God over the Babylonian astrologers, and in spite of the warnings of the Hebrew prophets, neither the practices nor belief in them could be stamped out.

Most important of all, astrology spread to the Hellenic culture; thus, eventually, to Roman, Islamic and Christian. By the fourth century B.C. the Greeks had made tremendous advances in the scientific study of astronomy and geometry. They absorbed the Babylonian faith in astrology, and adapted it to their own styles of belief, coming to believe, in fact, that the pattern of the skies did not simply predict events on earth, but influenced and caused them. No one can now be sure where Greek accuracy and Mesopotamian enterprise overlapped, but there seems to be no doubt that it was the Greeks who gave astrology its pronounced individual flavour. The Mesopotamians had studied the skies in order to provide for the safety and well-being of the state, and of its head, the king, whose actions and decisions were of vital concern to his subjects, but the Greeks, famed for their rationality, were also highly individual, they cared about the personal destiny of each man—or at least, of each man who could afford to pay the astrologer's fee. The casting of horoscopes, which depends on zodiacal calculations, spread and flourished (the earliest surviving book on the practice dates from the Egypt of the second century B.C.). The Romans' efficiency and discipline were frequently balanced by passionate superstition ("Beware the Ides of March"), and the casting of horoscopes eventually became a part of the normal pattern of Roman life as well.

By the time of Christ's birth, belief in astrology had become an accepted and natural part of men's way of thinking, and condemnation, whether by scholars and statesmen (Cicero, for instance) or the early Christian councils, made very little difference to the ordinary man.

7

The Virtues of Gemstones

AMULETS AND TALISMANS

Magic is essentially a practical affair. A man employs its arts for his own benefit, to impose his own will on the forces of nature, by use of the proper and potent ceremonies and rituals of the magician's craft—the repeating of the exact words of the spell, the performing of the exact actions of the rite, the mixing of the exact ingredients of the potion, the precise drawing of the required magical sign, the precise engraving of the required talisman. It was inevitable that the practices of magic and the science of astrology would get mixed up together: the astrologer who warns of coming disaster, the priest who prays God may prevent (or send) it, and the magician who casts the spell to check (or cause) it, are closely allied.

Amulets are objects which are believed to have special powers to protect or help the bearer. They may be man-made: the Christian Church, in spite of its condemnation of primitive magical amulets—created according to the appointed ritual, and at a favourable astrological time—permitted, and eventually promoted, the wearing of medallions with a religious inscription, the carrying of reliquaries containing, perhaps, a fragment of some saint's finger-nail, the making of holy images, exactly as it adapted pagan decorations into the Christian iconography. Such things were familiar to the people, and held in awe by them; they could be used to pave the way gently to higher understanding.

But there are also natural amulets: plants, for instance; a bear's claw, a rabbit's foot; and, of course, precious stones. The earliest cuneiform writings show evidence of the popular belief in the magical properties of gems. People came to believe that particular stones had particular powers, just as they believed that the planets and the fixed stars had power over the lives of earthly men. At a time when the skies' pattern was favourable to the future wearer, a stone was engraved with the sign, or sigil, of the appropriate planet; this was a precious talisman, treasured by its owner. (The word "talisman" derives from Arabic, and may be loosely translated as "the influence of the heavenly bodies upon the universe".) The Egyptians attributed particular stones and minerals to each day of their thirty-day month as well.

EARLY LAPIDARY TEXTS

One of the earliest known works on mineralogy is the lapidary of Theophrastus, *On Stones*, written in about 315 B.C. (this may be only a fragment of a longer work). It shows the characteristic Greek interest in medicine. Theophrastus attributes medicinal properties to particular stones, a practice which leads naturally to the wearing of stones as healing amulets. The Egyptians went further; the Hermetic texts, which came from Egypt, are full of elaborate medical astrology. The supposed "author" of these texts was Thoth, the Egyptian god who was the patron of all the arts that depended on the written word—medicine, for one, astronomy for a second, and magic for a third—and who became identified with the Greek god Hermes. The basic concept underlying them is the familiar one of the interdependence of the universe, whose parts are linked together by the laws of sympathy and antipathy. The god Hermes-Thoth revealed to men the operation of these laws, which could thus be used for healing.

8

The Egyptians selected three dozen bright stars whose risings were separated by intervals of ten days, thus designing a huge heavenly clock. Each star influenced its own particular period of time. These came to be called the *Decans* stars, and the twelve signs of the Zodiac were each sub-divided into three decanates. Ailments were assigned to the proper planet or decanate. Certain stones and plants were linked by the laws of sympathy with each decanate; you diagnosed your ailment, gathered the appropriate herb—at the appropriate time—repeated the appointed prayers or incantation in the appointed way, engraved the appropriate sigil on the appropriate stone, bound herb and talisman together, donned them, and waited for a cure. Magic, medicine, and astrology were here thoroughly mixed up, as inter-related as the universe itself.

In direct contrast to Theophrastus and to the Hermetic texts was the vast *Historiae Naturalis XXXVII* ("Natural History in Thirty-Seven Books"), written by Pliny the Elder (A.D. 23/24–79), which appeared in A.D. 77. Pliny wrote as a traditional man of science—a character which did not, however, prevent his including manifold examples of the infinite wonders of the natural world, with such marvels as unicorns, nereids, and mouthless men. In Books XXXIII–XXXVII he deals with mineralogy and metals, quoting only a few instances of the magical qualities of stones, with heavy overtones of scepticism.

None the less, the belief persisted. One extremely important book, the *Kyranides*, written about two hundred years earlier—a tentative date is 100 B.C.—was to influence medicine and literature and iconography right through to the Middle Ages. One version, *Kirani Kyranides et ad eas Rhyatini Koronides*, was printed as late as A.D. 1638. The Prologue to the early Greek text states that the first book was the work of Cyranus, King of Persia, the second that of Harpocration of Alexandria, and the third, dealing with natural virtues divided according to sympathies and antipathies, of Hermes. It is an extraordinary medley of Babylonian astrology, Mithraic rites, Jewish religious belief and practice, Greek festivals and Greek medicine. Among its many legends was that of the pelican: the mother bird laid her eggs in her nest, hatched the baby chicks, and cared for them, but they grew quarrelsome and selfish and tried her patience to such a degree that one day her control snapped and she stamped them to death; convulsed with remorse, she pecked at her own breast, and the great drops of blood that fell on to the chicks revived them—but she paid for their lives with her own. The Christian craftsmen adapted this tale to illustrate the redemption of man through Christ crucified, and many a pelican-in-her-piety loving cup, many a precious personal jewel, elaborated on the theme. The *Kyranides* was also the source of the popular belief in the virtues of the toadstone (in actual fact, a brownish-grey trap-rock):

> "The earth-toad, called *saccos*, whose breath is poisonous, has a stone in the marrow of its head. If you take it when the moon is waning, put it in a linen cloth for forty days, and then cut it from the cloth and take the stone, you will have a powerful amulet. Hung at the girdle it cures dropsy and the spleen, as I myself have proved."
> (III, lxvii)   (De Mély, *Les Lapidaires Grecs*, 1893)

Failing this, one could try the serpent-stone cure quoted by Philostratus in his *Life of Apollonius of Tyana*, III, 8:

"They say, indeed, that the heads of dragons contain brilliant stones of all colours, which have marvellous properties . . . After the snake has been hung up and exorcized with laurel smoke that it may vomit forth the stone, pronounce the words 'By the God Who created thee, Whom thou justly adorest with thy double tongue, if thou wilt give me the stone, I will do thee no harm, but will send thee back to thine own home.' And when it has given up the stone, take a piece of silk and keep it as a treasure. And if it refuses, take a knife and split its head, and you will find the stone, such as many other animals have, possessing natural virtues."

The wonder-working stone was said to be absorbent, and was thus valued as a cure for dropsy and rheumatism.

An important Hellenistic lapidary is that ascribed to Damigeron. Some fragments of the original Greek texts were preserved in the second book of the medical collections of Aetius (*vide* Rose, *Hermes*, 1875, IX, pp. 471–91; De Mély also cites this), but the whole text survives only in a Latin translation, which Rose ascribes to the first, and Beck to the fifth or sixth, century A.D. This has been published by Abel from a fourteenth-century manuscript in the Bibliothèque Nationale, thought to be unique; Joan Evans, however, has found an earlier manuscript among the Hatton MSS at the Bodleian in Oxford, which differs on some important points from the French one. The Damigeron lapidary was the principal source of a famous medieval text, that of Marbode, Bishop of Rennes.

BIBLICAL REFERENCES

The lapidaries of later Christian writing demonstrate a continuing belief in the virtues of gemstones, adapted to serve a new iconography and illustrating the interdependence of the natural world, where men struggled to save their souls, and the supernatural world, with God enthroned among His saints and angels.

One of the best-known early religious references to the ritual significance of precious stones comes in the Old Testament, in the 28th chapter of Exodus. God is giving Moses instructions for the making of the breastplate to be worn by Aaron the High Priest (translations vary in their interpretations of which stones were to be used; the quotation given here is taken from the King James Bible of A.D. 1611, at which time lapidaries were still being written; though not as accurate as a modern translation, it is a better illustration of the splendid image envisaged by the post-Renaissance scholars):

"And these are the garments which they shall make; a breastplate, and an ephod, and a robe, and a broidered coat, a mitre and a girdle."

The ephod was a sleeveless garment, made of two pieces joined by straps at the shoulders, with a girdle tied about the waist. Aaron's was to be made of gold, blue, purple, scarlet and fine linen. On each shoulder-piece he was to wear an onyx set in gold, engraved with the names of the twelve tribes of Israel—six on each. Then came the breastplate:

"Thou shalt make the breastplate of judgment with cunning work . . . of gold, of blue, and of purple, and of scarlet, and of fine twined linen, shalt thou make it. Foursquare it shall be being doubled; a span shall be the length thereof, and a span shall be the breadth thereof. And thou shalt set in it settings of stones, even four rows of stones: the first row shall be a sardius, a topaz, and a carbuncle: this shall be the first row. And the second row shall be an emerald, a sapphire and a diamond. And the third row a ligure, an agate and an amethyst. And the fourth row a beryl, and an onyx, and a jasper: they shall be set in gold in their inclosings. And the stones shall be with the names of the children of Israel, twelve, according to their names, like the engravings of a signet; every one with his name shall they be according to the twelve tribes."

The breastplate was fastened to the ephod with gold rings, gold chains and blue ribbon, and "the Urim and the Thummim" were to be put in it so that they lay upon Aaron's heart when he went in before the Lord; unfortunately we do not know what these were. (The other garments—the robe, the coat, the mitre and the girdle—were far simpler; they were made from fine embroidered linen. God added finally that the priests must wear linen breeches under all this bright magnificence, and that these must reach from loin to thigh.)

This breastplate became one of the great symbols of Christian literature. The twelve stones were associated with twelve virtues (truth, honesty, and so on), which made up the exemplar of the perfect man. On the day of Atonement, the High Priest—Aaron's successor—asked God to forgive the nation's sins; there was an ancient Jewish tradition that if forgiveness were granted, all the stones in the breastplate shone brightly; if it were withheld, they became first dulled, then black. Several medieval authors of note commented on this belief, including such scholars as the Venerable Bede, Amatus of Monte Cassino, and Hugues of the Abbey of St Victor. In one of his edicts to the bishops, Pope Gregory the Great (*circa* A.D. 540–604) linked the gemstones of the breastplate to the Nine Orders of Angels: sard to the Seraphim, topaz to the Cherubim, jasper to the Thrones, chrysolite to the Dominations, onyx to the Principalities, beryl to the Powers, sapphire to the Virtues, carbuncle to the Archangels, and emerald to the Angels.

The New Jerusalem, too, was walled about with precious stones, guarded with angels, and inscribed with the names of the twelve tribes of Israel: the Church could point to the evidence of St. John, in the Book of Revelation: the city of his vision blazed like a precious stone, clear as crystal (the translation is again from the King James Bible of A.D. 1611):

"And the building of the wall of it was of jasper: and the city was pure gold, like unto clear glass. And the foundations of the wall of the city were garnished with all manner of precious stones. The first foundation was jasper; the second, sapphire; the third, a chalcedony; the fourth, an emerald; the fifth, sardonyx; the sixth, sardius; the seventh, chrysolite; the eighth, beryl; the ninth, a topaz; the tenth, a chrysoprasus; the eleventh, a jacinth; and the twelfth, an amethyst. And the twelve gates were twelve pearls; every several gate was of one pearl: and the street of the city was pure gold, as it were transparent glass."

The fortune-tellers were left outside, with murderers, fornicators, and other sinners.

LATER LAPIDARIES

In the early centuries of the Christian era, lapidaries fell into two main categories: those which assigned magical and medical properties to stones and metals, and those which concentrated on magic and astrology. The gap between the two categories gradually widened, until by about the twelfth century A.D. the Christian lapidaries were basically medicinal, and the astrological ones had drifted to the East.

The Christian lapidaries of the Middle Ages were more closely derived from classical sources than any other type of medieval literature excepting ecclesiastical law; when Marbode, Bishop of Rennes from A.D. 1067 to 1081, wrote his Latin lapidary, for example, which was to be one of the most famous of the Middle Ages texts, his principal source was the pre-Christian Hellenistic lapidary of Damigeron, already mentioned. As a result of this, lapidaries were not greatly affected by the Early Renaissance advances in classical scholarship; indeed, their number was actually to increase during the sixteenth century.

About a hundred medieval lapidaries still survive, thirty-two of them being in Great Britain. Among these is an especially interesting one (A.D. 1513), the property of the Worshipful Company of Goldsmiths, which is founded on Marbode's work, and thus owes a great deal to Damigeron. A page from this lapidary is reproduced facing page 51.

The first English printed book containing lapidary material came out in 1582. This was *Batman uppon Bartholeme, his book De Proprietatibus Rerum*, printed by Thomas East of Paul's Wharf, London. It is far from original, but forever comforting. Diamonds, for example, are:

> "to resist poyson and witchecrafte; to put away feare, to give victorie in contention, to help them that be lunatike or phrantike."

One rather wonders if the victim had become lunatic and frantic because of the revolting potions he was forced to take.

All these lapidaries describe the virtues of gemstones and metals, and their medicinal properties—whether worn as amulets or ground up and taken internally. The Goldsmiths' Lapidary tells how God gave the diamond great virtues and graces:

> "It giveth to a man that beareth it strength and virtue, and keepeth him from grievance, meetings and temptations and from venom. Also it keepeth the bones and the members whole. It doth away any wrath and lechery. It enricheth him that beareth him, enricheth in value and in good. The diamond is most worth to be holden upon for witless men and for defence against enemies. For that beareth it shall the more love God. It keepeth the seed of a man within the womb of his wife, it helpeth the child and keepeth all his members."

The symbolic qualities of gemstones are stressed over and over: their purity, translucence and beauty should inspire men to lead lives that are similarly pure and unsullied. Indubitably the stars which God in His Wisdom had set in the heavens had a direct influence upon gems, and gems in their turn had implicit powers. Medieval references laying any stress on the monetary value of stones are virtually non-existent. A gem was valued for its religious, magical and medicinal virtues, not for its intrinsic worth. A rich man of the Middle Ages would, it is true, be expected to pay well for the stone of his choice, and would expect to get a fine specimen in return, but monetary value was a purely secondary consideration. Many such stones, purchased for their talismanic properties, were not even displayed; a talisman was a personal thing, often kept completely secret, and worn on a chain about the neck so that it was completely hidden by one's clothing.

The coming of the Renaissance in the fifteenth century was, however, to have a profound effect on the design of jewellery. There was a shift of emphasis: appearance and display became of enormous importance. Many big and apparently meaningless jewels were made for the great and wealthy men of the time, as well as many beautiful and individual works of art that were rich with personal significance. The increase of interest in the study of classical antiquity affected jewellers as it did all who were engaged in the decorative arts. The techniques of classical metalworking were not revived (though they were to be resurrected later, during the Neo-Classical period of the eighteenth and early nineteenth centuries), and so the "classical" style had to be expressed through the general design of the jewel, and through the engraving of stone or setting (one of the closest links between the classical past and the Renaissance was the use of engraved symbols). A jewel was designed to be seen, to decorate, to impress, not to be hidden away under a man's shirt.

In spite of the Renaissance shift of emphasis and the gradual advance of scientific scholarship, lapidaries continued to be written until the end of the seventeenth century. Belief in the implicit magical properties of gemstones lingered on a while longer, but by the end of the eighteenth century critical and scientific experiment had tested all the old beliefs and found them to be little more than a cobweb of tradition criss-crossed with superstition.

The Survival of Superstition

And yet eleven women out of twelve would probably refuse an opal. Why? There is one historical reason which is entirely practical. In the past, a stone-cutter who lost or damaged any stone which was entrusted to his keeping, had to compensate the owner in full. The rare opal is not formed like the majority of gemstones—it is much easier to fracture or to scratch; and as a result, cutting and mounting it was a hazardous responsibility. There are other reasons too: old superstitions, tales, stories, incidents from the past. The medievals believed that it could cure eye troubles (the name derives from the Greek *opthalmos*, "the eye") and even make its wearer invisible—so it quickly became the patron stone of thieves. Until the nineteenth century, the stones were held in awe because of their scarcity, and were set in the crowns and jewels of rulers; then, during the Victorian age, superb deposits of opal were found in Australia. Queen Victoria, who was excellent at promoting exports from the emergent countries of the British Empire, had many jewels set for her with Australian opals, and regularly gave gifts of jewellery to her splendid and far-flung relatives, so that the magnificent Empire stones were advertised over much of the world. The Australian black opal was not discovered until 1905, four years after her death, so the Queen never saw this type, but she had a choice of about fourteen other varieties which were spread across a wide spectrum. Her daughter-in-law, Alexandra, was of a very different calibre, and did not care for opals at all; when she became Queen Consort, all her mother-in-law's parures of opals and diamonds were hastily reset for her with rubies. The ladies of the court naturally followed her example, and perhaps friends commiserated: "What frightful bad luck having to have all your opals reset . . ."

There are other reasons, too, for the "bad luck" connotation. Few people know them all, many people know none, they just have a feeling that opals are unlucky, and nothing and no one can shift this belief.

For superstition lives on: and sadly, over the last hundred years or so, the trade has developed a great many new commercial gimmicks. Charms are still for sale: not a hound's tooth these days, or the stone from the horn of a toad ("Guaranteed to cure dropsy and spleen if taken when the moon is waning"), but a gold model of a London bus tinkling with its fellows as shrilly as ice cubes stirred in a crystal cocktail jug; just as popular, and just as pointless. Every jeweller's shop has a list of birthstones and Zodiac charms which are honour-bound to benefit the wearer. In August 1913 there was a convocation of jewellers in Kansas City, U.S.A., and there, among other weighty matters, the question of which birthstone and which astrological sign should be applied to which period of days was finally settled once and for all, world-wide; Mab Wilson subsequently reported that every man there had agreed that it was "all nonsense anyway", "laughing heartily and crossing his fingers behind his back".

Two hundred years of scientific enlightenment are really nothing when compared with the period of time—thousands and thousands of years—that superstitions have been as much a part of life as eating and sleeping.

CHAPTER TWO

A Background of Events

Introduction—The Discovery of Metals—The Ancient Civilizations—
Caesar to Charlemagne—Early Enamelling Techniques—Gemstones in
Early European Jewellery: Settings

Introduction

Very few of the people who walk through the Victoria and Albert Museum in
London are aware of the value of the early Church plate exhibited there. They stroll
disinterestedly through these galleries, gazing with far more interest at the silver from
the sixteenth, seventeenth, eighteenth and nineteenth centuries which is displayed
further on. Here they can relate the exhibits to the pieces of silver they have at home—
yet the sixteenth-century apostle spoons, the seventeenth-century porringers, the
eighteenth-century coffee pots, were made in eras when silver, though valuable, was
relatively commonplace, whereas the pieces of early Church plate date from a time when
it was far rarer, far more valuable. Until the explorers of the mid-sixteenth century
opened up their routes to the treasure mines of the New World, where supplies seemed inexhaustible, silver and gold had to be wrested from the earth speck by speck and
painful grain by grain. They were more precious to the people of those early times than
we can nowadays comprehend. This is Diodorus Siculus, a Greek historian writing in
the first century B.C.:

> "Nature herself makes it clear that the production of gold is laborious, the guarding
> of it difficult, the zest for it very great, and its use balanced between pleasure and
> pain."

The Discovery of Metals

So far as we can tell the first metals known to the men of prehistoric times were those
which may be found in the "free" state—grains and nuggets of pure metal washed
down in the beds of rivers. We do not know which they discovered first: perhaps gold,
perhaps copper. It is estimated, at any rate, that they knew these two "free" metals
well before the fourth millennium B.C.; and it is also thought that they knew meteoritic
iron, which some ancient civilizations valued above gold. The Sumerians were to call it
"the metal of heaven", believing that the gods had flung it down from the skies, and the
Incas "sweat of the sun".

Gold is so ductile and malleable that in its pure state it has no utilitarian value at all; one cannot, for instance, make a useful gold hammer or a sharp gold hunting knife. Prehistoric men valued it none the less, for its brightness and beauty, and used it for decoration and adornment. Copper is also ductile, but even in the pure state it can be worked and used for weapons, pots, and so on; and some time before 4000 B.C. men discovered that copper nuggets could be hammered into shape. The metal-working trade was under way.

Around the same time the metalworkers discovered two new techniques: how to melt copper and cast it into crude shapes, and how to smelt—that is, to heat copper-bearing ore and separate the pure metal. Men armed with stone tools began to mine the ore, digging out horizontal shafts and tracking the veins back into the rock. Mining and smelting are thought to have begun in Western Asia and spread slowly out to Mesopotamia, Egypt, India, and other parts of the ancient world. Copper takes its name from Cyprus where they were smelting copper ore by about 3000 B.C.; the deposits there were so great and so valuable that control of the island passed successively from the Egyptians via the Phoenicians, the Greeks, and the Persians to the Romans, who drew almost the whole of their supplies from there, calling the ore *aes cyprium*, "ore of Cyprus". The Trojan civilization on the coast of Asia Minor was a great disseminator of metalworking skills and in the five hundred years of its trading history, Trojan traders spread west as well as east; by 2000 B.C. they had reached west to Portugal and north to present-day Austria.

We do not know who first discovered the virtues of mixing and fusing metals to produce an alloy with special characteristics, such as greater hardness or increased strength. We do, however, know that the great alloy of the ancient world was bronze, and that even before men consciously made bronze by alloying smelted copper and smelted tin (which was not *deliberately* smelted until about 1500 B.C.) they were making fortuitous bronze alloys which occurred when they smelted copper from ores which also contained tin. Bronze was known in the Aegean by about 2000 B.C., and within the next six or seven centuries its use had spread right across Europe and Asia, from Ireland to China.

Nor do we know when men first discovered silver (which is found in the "free" state as well as in ore), but it seems likely that the discovery antedated 3000 B.C. By 2500 B.C. the Sumerian craftsmen of Mesopotamia were working gold, silver, electrum (a natural alloy of the two), copper, lead (smelted from its ores) and bronze. By 200 B.C. workers were refining lead to extract silver, which is often present in lead ore.

Gold, silver, electrum, copper: they are all decorative metals, and the early metal-workers experimented with their ornamental use. Many of the jewellery techniques which are still in use today were being employed before 2500 B.C.—inlay, for example, *repoussé* work, soldering and riveting and granulation. Some of these workers were slaves, but others were free craftsmen who made their way from settlement to settlement, making, mending, bartering products, trading raw materials. Soon more sophisticated traders, like the famous Phoenicians, were travelling along the coasts of Europe, trading metals and metal artefacts along with other goods.

If copper was the first great utilitarian metal, iron was the second. For thousands of years it was of extreme rarity; then somehow, somewhere—probably in the regions of

Asia Minor where the Hittites were then settled—metalworkers discovered how to smelt iron from its ores and to forge the resulting metal. By about 1200 B.C. the Hittites were on the move, perhaps driven out by invaders; they took their craft with them and it spread out across the ancient world. At about the same time, men discovered that if they heated wrought iron in a bed of charcoal, it hardened; without realizing it, they had created carburized steel. Within three hundred years, by about 800 B.C., they made another discovery, this time of supreme importance: if a carburized blade were heated and then plunged into cold water, it became both harder and stronger. Copper and bronze were displaced as man's principal utilitarian metals, and iron set firmly in their place.

The Ancient Civilizations

We owe all our knowledge of the early civilizations to the archaeologists, and especially to their tomb discoveries. Almost all the early exhibits that one sees in museums today survived for one of two main reasons: either they were deliberately hidden, or they were buried in the tomb of their original owner. All the early civilizations, whether in Asia or Africa, the Americas or Europe, shared this custom of supplying funeral offerings and tomb furnishings to accompany their great men on the journey to the afterlife, and their jewels and household vessels were sometimes remarkably similar.

Some of the finds are enormous, others relatively simple. The Royal Tombs of Ur (*circa* 2600 B.C.) contained a wonderful variety of treasures, including jewels whose workmanship is of exceptional quality: fine pure gold, paper-thin, embossed (that is, adorned with a design which is raised in relief from the reverse side) and *repoussé* (that is, crisply finished off on the face), the glittering mass occasionally punctuated with lapis lazuli. There are examples at the British Museum in London, as well as at Baghdad and the University of Pennsylvania. The Egyptian treasures from the tomb of Tutankhamun, dating from the fourteenth century B.C., are superb, and include jewels sculpted from pure gold sheet and inlaid with lapis lazuli, cornelian, turquoises and glass pastes in brilliant colours. The work is sculptural in form and heavily symbolic in its motifs, and is full of colour, with the rich stones carved or polished *en cabochon* (that is, having a rounded surface which is not faceted—gemstones were not cut with facets until the time of the Renaissance), and the pastes glowingly deep in tone.

In the main, the earliest surviving items discovered by the archaeologists are made of gold (silver has corroded to dust), and there are only a few gemstones. Such gems as *are* used are either placed like punctuation points, breaking up a mass of glitter to give some semblance of form, or have some talismanic significance.

In the nineteenth century A.D. a German parson told his small son the legend of Troy—a story so old that thousands of boys before him had heard and studied it. Heinrich Schliemann, however, believed every word; grown to manhood, he equipped an expedition and took himself off to Asia Minor, to the grassy site where he decided the fabled city had stood. Here he dug down regardless, in a fashion which would appal any modern archaeologist, completely missing the Homeric Troy, whose remains lay hidden in the upper strata, and uncovering a city of immense antiquity, and a treasure of gold jewellery and gold and silver plate which he named the "Treasure of Priam", after the king who had ruled during the Trojan Wars—Schliemann was convinced that he had found the Homeric city. The huge hoard of jewels included bracelets, earrings, beads, and diadems or pectorals, the largest made of nearly a hundred gold chains edged with tiny scales, and featured chain-work and gold filigree, very sophisticated and feminine in design.

Schliemann wanted, naturally, to go on digging, but the Ottoman Government made difficulties (they felt they should have got a greater share of the treasure), so he sailed across to Mycenae in Greece, where there were some ruins so old that Pausanias, a traveller of the second century A.D., mentioned them in his guide to the Greek sights. He began digging there too, and in 1876 uncovered the shaft graves, in which was found a vast treasure of gold, silver, bronze and ivory, including diadems, pectorals, hairpins, bracelets, pendants, signet rings and finger-rings, and a few earrings, many of them embossed with beast and flower motifs.

Evans's subsequent excavations at Knossos, on the island of Crete, were to reveal still more of the magnificence of the Bronze Age cultures of the Aegean civilization. It had apparently come into being in Crete, towards the end of the third millennium B.C., and though it owed much to the older civilizations of Egypt and Mesopotamia, had a character and splendour and originality of its own. The first civilization to flower in Europe, it spread out across the Aegean Sea, through the islands, to the mainland of Greece, and in about 1400 B.C. the centre of its power shifted, it seems, from Knossos to Mycenae on the mainland; it continued to spread and pollinate, along the coasts of Asia Minor, into Cyprus, even into southern Italy. Schliemann's discoveries, and the findings and patient scholarship of the archaeologists who came after him, thus showed that a high and flourishing civilization had existed in the Aegean long before new invaders came swarming into the Greek peninsula, to settle there and, in time, to raise a civilization of their own, so great that its memory would last into our own time, obliterating, for three thousand years, knowledge of the culture that had preceded it. These were the people we call the Greeks.

We do not know when the Greek invaders first entered the Aegean, though some authorities think they first appeared there at the beginning of the second millennium B.C. and that the last wave washed through Greece in about 1100 B.C. It is, however, certain that by the sixth century B.C. they had established a civilization which was the artistic centre of the Mediterranean world. Sadly, little of their early metalwork has come down to us. The artists of classical Greece seem to have been far more interested in stone and marble sculpture portraying their contemporaries, or their gods in familiar contemporary human form, than in decoration, display or symbolism. Many of the extant Greek vessels and pieces of jewellery are of pure sculptural form, echoing in miniature the severe "classic" simplicity of their stone and marble sculpture. (Some authorities say they preferred silver to gold, believing it had a natural affinity with the moon.)

By the middle of the fourth century B.C. the small independent Greek city-states were threatened by the power of Persia, and in 338 B.C. all but Sparta leagued together under the leadership of Philip of Macedon, in the hope of thrusting back the Persians and of protecting their own independence. Philip died two years later, but was succeeded by his son, Alexander—who had once, on hearing of his father's victories, remarked to his friends, "What will there be left for you and me to do when we are grown up?" He found plenty, however: first invading Persia, he then marched on through Asia Minor, Palestine and Egypt, doubled back and struck out southward into Mesopotamia, and then thrust on eastward, creating an empire that reached from India in the east to Scythia in the north, south to the Persian Gulf and west through Egypt, and founding towns that spread Greek civilization throughout Asia. He was only thirty-two when he died, in Babylon, in June 323 B.C. The seven years of his victorious campaigns had two significant effects on jewellery and metalwork. First of all, he sent back large quantities of gold to Greece—having taken an expert mining prospector with him on the campaigns—and second, more gradually, men began to develop a hunger for luxury and display. The old designs, light and delicate and elegant, gave way to a bolder, heavier, oriental look. Metalworkers began to experiment with new ideas. Soon gemstones appeared, also from the East, and colour became a dominant feature for the first time. Indigenous stones had been used before this for seals; now, however, they were set as bezels for rings. Garnets, agates, emeralds: the range of stones increased. Some were plain, others cut *en cabochon* and polished, still others engraved to create either an intaglio, with the design carved out of the surface, or a cameo, with the design standing up from the background. (The Cretan civilization had produced beautiful intaglio seal rings, and the early Greeks had inherited the technique; cameo-cutting they developed rather later, in the Hellenistic period.) Portrayals of female heads, set in gold, became fashionable, especially for earrings and necklaces. Other favourite motifs, which were to recur throughout the history of European jewellery, were flowers, animals, insects, sea-horses and snakes.

A new turning-point in the history of metals had occurred rather earlier than this, in the reign of one of the kings of Lydia (the kingdom lay in Asia Minor, but its exact boundaries are no longer known) whose name was to become a synonym for wealth. This was Croesus (*circa* 560–*circa* 540 B.C.), a king so rich that he offered a huge gift of gold—at least seven and a half thousand pounds in weight—at the shrine of Apollo in Delphi. Unlike Midas and some of the other fabled rulers of the ancient world whose histories belong to legend rather than fact, Croesus was real enough, a man of great historical importance who had the intelligence to look beyond the boundaries of his own kingdom, and to recognize the importance of trade between states and of a stable regulated economy. It is said to have been he who introduced the first authoritative state coinage: coins of pure gold and silver, each marked on the obverse with a royal device. For the first time a state took real control of its economy, and of the production of gold and silver. Seen in retrospect, these innovations mark a definite dividing point in the history of precious metals: the radical division between use for decoration and display, and use for coinage and trading.

It was about fifty years after the reign of Croesus that the citizens of Rome, descendents of wandering Indo-European tribes who had settled in the Tiber region of Italy, thrust back their Etruscan neighbours and rulers and formed their own republican government (the traditional date is 509 B.C.). In the struggles that followed Rome gradually increased her power. By 265 B.C. she ruled all Italy; by 146 B.C. the whole of the western Mediterranean; by 49 B.C., when Caesar crossed the Rubicon to make himself master of the Roman Empire, she was the supreme power in the civilized world;

and by A.D. 116, when the Emperor Trajan had finished his annexing, she ruled Spain, Gaul, almost all Britain, Italy herself, Europe west of the Rhine and south of the Danube, Dacia, Moesia, and Thracia which bounded the western shores of the Black Sea, Greece, Asia Minor, Armenia, Assyria, Mesopotamia, Syria, Palestine, Egypt and the northern shores of Africa.

Roman jewellery was affected by four separate trends of influence, their importance altering with the spreading of her Empire. First, Etruscan: the metalworkers of Etruria north and west of Rome had developed the techniques of filigree and granulation to a pitch of perfection that has never been surpassed, working with fine gold wire and with minute gold grains, fused and soldered to the backgrounds. Their *repoussé* decoration was also extremely fine. Among the motifs they used were sphinxes, lions, pomegranates and lotuses. Secondly, Greek, as she traded with Greece and gradually absorbed Greek culture and techniques. Thirdly, oriental, from the Eastern civilizations. And fourthly, the "barbaric" styles of the north, including the Celtic.

The Celts were a group of tribes sharing a common language and a common skill in metalwork. They spread slowly across Central Europe during the first millennium B.C., becoming established across a great northern swathe of the continent and in the offshore islands, reaching from Ireland to the Balkans. The Roman invasions drove them back for a time, but they continued to practise their craft, both within the confines of the Empire and in the distant places that lay beyond Roman control—Ireland, for example, was never subdued by the legions. In their decorative art—and it was definitely decorative rather than narrative—the Celts used the ancient animal motifs traditional among their people, the heads being beast-masks rather than naturalistic portraiture, the bodies linked and woven in fantastic designs, in a non-representational treatment whose complex patterns of whorls and coils (Fig. 1) eventually became stylized as abstract and geometrical.

Caesar to Charlemagne

In 46 B.C. Julius Caesar returned to Rome in triumph and made himself master of the State, which he immediately began to reform, thus alienating and alarming some of the most powerful men in Rome; in March 44 B.C. a band of conspirators cut him down. There were two possible successors, Antony and Octavian; in the war that followed, Octavian won, becoming the ruler of Rome and her Empire in 31 B.C. and reigning as *Augustus*, the Illustrious One, for nearly half a century, until his death in A.D. 14. By the end of his reign the Empire was so rich that coinage valued at £385,000,000 was in circulation—and much of it was gold.

The gold or silver coins of this time were struck bearing the emblem of the town in which they had been minted; thus any town whose emblem has been found on a Roman coin of this period possessed a mint, at any rate for some time. Unfortunately there is no real record of how many towns had mints in the early decades A.D., but recent discoveries indicate that there were mint towns in Gaul and the Germanic countries as well as principal mints in Alexandria and Rome. Because it was vital to protect the currency, mints were generally located in protected cities where there was a strong military establishment. The Romans suppressed, for example, the indigenous

British mints (though reproduction coins seem to have been cast in Britain even during the period of full Roman control) and supplied their own coinage from their mints at Trier, Lyons and Arles.

The goldsmiths of the Roman Empire were free men of citizen status, not slaves, a fact which itself shows that they were of standing in the community and that the importance of their craft was recognized. The ornaments created at this period were made of gold, silver or electrum, the natural alloy of the two (the name is also applied to an alloy of copper, zinc and nickel). Earrings, necklaces and bracelets were worn; rings, too, and clasps; and an ornament which has no modern equivalent, the bractate, a decorative disc of beaten metal, about the same shape and size as a large coin, sometimes set with gemstones, with a metal loop at the top so that it could be sewn on to a garment. Amulets were very popular; the Romans were a superstitious race. Cameo-cutting and intaglio-cutting were developed to a high degree of fineness.

The decline and fall of Rome from its Augustan glory was a gradual process, paralleled by the gradual rise and spread of Christianity. By the year A.D. 313, when Christianity was officially recognized throughout the Roman Empire by the Edict of Milan, the threat to Rome was growing plain. Her boundaries were so widely set that it would take a massive, loyal and disciplined force to hold them; but she no longer had enough men to keep back the barbarian tribes beyond, on and within her northern frontiers. (Some of them even had the impertinence to march on Rome and there complain about the Roman tax-collectors.) In A.D. 323 the Emperor Constantine therefore decided to shift the Imperial capital to the East. He chose Byzantium, on the Bosphorus, and there raised a great new city which was named after him, Constantinople. On his death in A.D. 337, his sons divided the Empire between them, one setting up his administration in Constantinople and ruling the east, the other returning to Rome to try to rule the west. The Empire was broken in two, and never recovered its mighty ancient unity.

All across Europe the barbarian tribes came swarming: Picts and Scots, Teutons and Vandals, Ostrogoths, Visigoths, Franks and Lombards. In A.D. 402 the Emperor of the West fled from Rome to Ravenna, the fortified sea-port at the head of the Adriatic; eight years later Alaric and a Visigoth host attacked and took Rome herself; and a quarter of a century after that Attila and his Huns sacked Constantinople and levied an annual tribute of 700 pounds of gold (the inhabitants evidently found this easy to pay, for within the next few years he tripled it). In A.D. 475 the last Emperor of the West was deposed, symbolizing the fact that all the riches of the western empire lay open to the plunderers, but the eastern empire survived, paying off the barbarian hordes when need be, and was in fact to last a thousand years—it was A.D. 1453 before the Turks finally sacked it.

During the first centuries of those thousand years, however, when Constantinople was the principal city of the Mediterranean and, in spite of the claims of the Bishop of Rome (and the occasional claims of the Bishop of Jerusalem) the centre of Christianity, the people of the Byzantine Empire lived under the constant threat of attack—a threat that was to increase in intensity after the founding of Islam by the prophet Mohammed in the early seventh century. The most celebrated of her emperors was the Greek, Justinian (A.D. 521–565) whose empire almost encircled the

Mediterranean. Deciding to centralize the imperial power, and aware of the possibility of barbarian attack, he restricted the gold and silver mints to Byzantium herself, Rome, Carthage and Ravenna (acquired in A.D. 539, and made, by reason of its commanding position, the capital of the Eastern Empire's European possessions).

Most of the early Byzantine work was later melted down, both for the intrinsic value of its metal and stones (they used emeralds and pearls as well as lapis lazuli, amethysts, rose agate and enamels) and because of changes in fashion; there is, however, a sixth-century mosaic at San Vitale in Ravenna which shows Justinian in a circular crown of gemstones set in horizontal rows, with a huge fibula clasping his cloak on the right shoulder, and his empress, Theodora, in a jewelled diadem, with pendants, long dangling earrings, a necklace of emeralds and gold, and a great collar embroidered with gold, gemstones, and pearls. The goldsmiths' craftsmanship went to glorify the Imperial power, hedged about with all the stiff jewelled ceremonious ritual of a sacred institution, and to glorify the Church herself, with her embossed gold reliquaries, gospel covers, and chalices adorned with gold filigree.

The number of mints fluctuated under Justinian's successors, but in the late seventh and early eighth centuries was reduced, both because of the need to centralize power at Constantinople, and because the Islamic conquests were swallowing up the old Byzantine territories in North Africa and the eastern Mediterranean. After the mid-eighth century, no Byzantine coins seem to have been minted in Italy. What then became of the metalworkers, trained in the Imperial tradition, craftsmen who had absorbed the eastern styles and techniques and skills? Fortunately for them a new patron arose, a new European colossus: Charlemagne, King of the Franks.

Charlemagne, who acceded in A.D. 771, was resolved to re-unite the West in a new Roman Empire. Rome herself had, after all, survived the destruction of the old empire, survived even the looting and burning of the barbarians. Her bishops had managed, just, to hold on to her independence; and the greatest of them all, Gregory, elected in A.D. 590 (he was most unwilling to serve, feeling that his true vocation was to convert the heathen English) had by the time of his death in A.D. 604 been officially recognized by the Christians of western Europe as the head of the Church.

It was one of Gregory's successors, Pope Leo, who, holding that supreme power, himself crowned Charlemagne Emperor of the Romans and honoured him with the old Roman title that dated back eight hundred years: *Augustus*. We do not know what regalia Charlemagne wore for that crowning in St. Peter's on Christmas Day, A.D. 800, but the great imperial crown in the regalia of the Holy Roman Empire, ante-dating A.D. 1024 (it is now in Vienna) is said to have been based on Charlemagne's. Made, as all crowns were to be for several centuries, of simple round-headed plates of 21-carat gold hinged together—eight of them, the number symbolic of infinity—it is covered with deeply glowing polished gemstones, pearls and enamels. The single arch symbolizes sovereignty, the cross of Christianity predominating, and the shape reflects the ground plan of his octagonal Palace Chapel at Aachen, created to show the grandeur of the Empire of the West, and containing a simple hinged throne in the Tribune (the gallery at the western end), the whole designed in imitation of classical Roman architecture.

When Charlemagne moved the capital of the Empire to Aachen (Aix-la-Chapelle) in the year of his crowning, he changed the course of the jewellers' craft, for many a moneyer and metalworker moved to northern Europe, bringing his advanced Byzantine techniques, his coin-minting skills, his feeling for sculptural forms, his eastern sense of colour, to Charlemagne's Rhineland.

The East has always been associated with brilliant blazing colour, and the love of colour which burns up in Carolingian jewels was to influence European jewellery for a thousand years, yielding at last to the bright crystalline glittering diamonds of the eighteenth-century work; the metalworkers of the Germanic countries, supreme in their craft, were to dominate the scene for almost as long, though styles and motifs changed with the shifts of cultural and political power. In his move to Aachen, Charlemagne made a conscious effort to re-create the traditional Imperial style, working deliberately towards a Roman Renaissance.

Classical, Byzantine and barbarian influences all affected the Carolingian Court, as one can see from contemporary architecture, sculpture and decorative art. Charlemagne is said, for instance, to have been so impressed by the Church of San Vitale in Ravenna, completed by the Byzantine Emperor Justinian and consecrated in A.D. 547, that he used it as the model for his Chapel in Aachen; and among the many splendid works of art produced by the Imperial workshops one may cite as a single example the Gospel Book of Godescalc, written in gold and silver on purple parchment like the great Imperial manuscripts of Constantinople. This is doubly remarkable when one realizes that Charlemagne had to work hard late in life to learn to read and write, he was by inclination a warrior and an administrator rather than a natural patron of learning and the arts.

Carolingian jewels often incorporate cameos and intaglios from classical times. A fine example of this practice, though rather later in period (it is early thirteenth century) is the Schaffhausen Onyx, now in the Musée de Tous-les-Saints: a most beautiful pendant jewel incorporating an antique cameo set in gold and rubies.

Unlike their classical prototypes, however, with their coherence and control and feeling for space, Carolingian jewels are crowded and full of colour. The lavish goldwork is rich with surface interest, finely executed and vibrant with light; the Byzantine enamelling glows with Imperial splendour; and the eastern gemstones shine with a richness of their own.

Early Enamelling Techniques

Enamel is powdered glass which is fused by heat on to a surface or into a mould. The earliest of the enamelling techniques was *cloisonné*, later overtaken by *champlevé*, which was in turn overtaken by *basse-taille*. Although each type went out of fashion for a while, none was ever completely dropped, and by the year A.D. 1600 all three were in use. There are examples of enamelwork in the jewellery of the Egyptian and Cretan civilizations, and the Celts were famed for it.

Cloisonné enamelling can be likened to the veneering of furniture. Let us suppose that a classical goldsmith is making a brooch. He has completed the basic gold artefact which he is going to enamel. He marks the lines of his design on the smooth surface of the metal. Then, following these lines, he solders into place thin strips of gold, making cells, or *cloisons*—cuplike compartments which will hold the separate curls or blobs of colour. He then places the coloured enamel powder in the cells and fires the piece. The enamel liquifies and fuses to its cells. When cool, it is polished, so that the surface of the hardened enamel is level with the walls of the cells; and gradually the entire pattern is built up with tiny bowls of colour in a tracery of spider-fine gold lines.

Champlevé enamelling, on the other hand, is built *down* into the surface of the article which is being decorated. Again the goldsmith completes his artefact and marks his design on the surface. Then he scoops out the lines of the design, making little compartments for the enamels. The filling, firing and cooling processes follow as before; and again the piece is finally polished so that the enamels and the metal surface are uniform in height. This enamelling technique is rather like furniture inlaying.

Baisse-taille enamelling is very similar in technique to *champlevé*, but the enamels used are translucent. To get an effect of heightened light and shade, the smith cuts the grooves of his design to varying depths. A translucent blue enamel, for instance, looks light and clear in a shallow groove, dark and glowing in a deeper one. This technique was not practised by the Byzantine craftsmen, but was apparently developed in Italy during the fourteenth century A.D.

Niello work, however, is very old indeed, and was known to Bronze Age civilizations. It is a form of decoration which was much employed in Europe until the seventeenth century, but which is mainly found nowadays in the East, in Burma, Malaysia and Thailand. It is very similar in technique to *champlevé* enamelling, but a powder composed of an alloy of silver, copper, sulphur and borax is used instead of powdered glass. The smith engraves his design on the surface of his piece, spreads the alloy over it, fires the piece, allows it to cool, and then polishes it, so that the black *niello* design is revealed brilliantly, engraved on shining silver or gold. Jewellery decorated with *niello* (Figs. 6 and 7, for example) has a masculine aura of richness and mystery.

Gemstones in Early European Jewellery

Many of the stones used in early European jewellery have flaws (technically named "inclusions") which look simply dreadful to modern eyes; but until the end of the seventeenth century, when a jeweller discovered the "brilliant" cut which revealed the full beauty of the diamond, no one seems to have worried greatly about a gemstone's clarity. Although stones which were relatively clear were naturally preferable, men valued them for their magical power, their colour or their size, rather than their fineness. If a jeweller did decide to cut a stone, he probably restricted himself to a simple table-cut: that is, he sliced off one side, and set the stone with the cut side uppermost. Very little was known about mineralogy in pre-Renaissance days, and still less about refraction and reflection of light, so attempts to cut a gemstone might well be disastrous.

Polishing a stone, however, with powder ground down from a stone harder than itself was a different matter. By doing this the jeweller could achieve a smooth surface, smooth edges and a uniform shape; whereas if he tried to cut it, he might shatter it into splinters. Polishing and engraving—another sure and tried technique which was unlikely to damage the stone—were much safer than cutting.

Thus the gemstones set in jewellery of the Carolingian period are polished or engraved stones, mined in Europe, the Middle East or India, believed to have magical or medicinal power, and with a depth of rich and glowing colour. There were rubies from India; garnets from Bohemia; lapis lazuli and sapphires (the latter's name being applied to the former); emeralds, amethysts, beryl and aquamarine; amber, the fossilized resin of the ancient forests, which had been known and valued since the beginning of recorded time: turquoises and cornelians, both of which the Egyptians too had gathered; pearls and jet, for which the Romans had had a great liking: all of these were gems which were relatively easy to find, or which could be mined in fairly shallow workings.

And, of course, there were diamonds. Diamonds have always been famed for their hardness and cutting power, and take their name from the Greek *adamas* which means "unconquerable". In their early history they seem to have been used to tip tools for engraving, to cut marble, even to edge swords and scimitars, rather than for ornament. Being so hard and difficult to cut, the gem came to represent power and strength, but not beauty (an uncut diamond has a slight opaque skin which makes it look like a piece of washing soda) and was worn for its symbolic qualities rather than its shine, until, in the sixteenth and seventeenth centuries A.D., craftsmen learned to cut it correctly and release its fire; then at last its beauty too was acknowledged.

There is an ancient story which shows that the men of early India were well aware of diamonds' hardness and cutting qualities. A man of wealth and power would collect a handful of small diamonds, and then his servants would spread a piece of thick cloth or leather, or even lead, on the ground—about a yard square—scatter the diamonds on this, and roll it all up rather like a Swiss roll, with solid diamonds as the jam and cream infilling. A labourer would then be employed to smash this roll with a hammer for days, weeks, even months, continually turning the bundle. Men knew that a diamond would shatter if it was struck in the right place at the right angle; they did not know the exact point, but reasoned that if one struck the roll of diamonds long enough there was a good chance that one of the blows would strike one of the gems at that precise place. Eventually the labourer was paid off and the roll unwound. Thousands of diamond slivers lay among the dust, sparkling with light, and deadly dangerous; brute force and sheer ignorance had cloven the diamonds' planes again and again to needle proportions. The next act was to take one's scimitars and daggers, heat them in glowing embers until they were almost at melting point, and then draw them quickly through the little pile of shimmering diamond needles. These would penetrate the almost molten metal; and next day, when they had cooled and hardened, these blades would be the deadliest weapons known, with a cutting edge of sparkling diamond.

The rulers and their henchmen who owned these terrible weapons became envied and feared across the East; and the diamonds themselves came to represent total power and strength. When the medieval European monarchs laid down their sumptuary laws, decreeing which gemstones and which garments might be worn by each social class, diamonds were among the foremost gemstones they restricted. No poaching on the king's preserves! This tradition lingered on, even when the diamond had come to be considered simply as a fashionable gem, costly and brilliant, no longer symbolic of kingly authority, no longer regarded as the stone of ruler and conqueror; none the less, it was, and is, still held to be supreme among stones.

SETTINGS

In the main there were two styles of setting for the gemstones used in early jewellery: the box setting and the collet. In the former, the jeweller made a small metal box without a lid, placed the gemstone inside, and hammered the metal edges carefully down to hold it in place. A collet set is very similar, but the sides of the box were cut down so that more of the stone might be seen, and claws were sometimes incorporated for the sake of safety. Each gemstone was, of course, individually set.

CHAPTER THREE

The Offshore Islands

Introduction—Metal Supplies in the British Isles and Ireland: England; Wales; Ireland; Scotland—Historical Background—Designs and Artefacts of Dark Age Britain—Celtic Ireland—Church Patronage: the Spread of Christianity; Church Craftsmen—Early English Enamelled Jewels: the Alfred Jewel; the Minster Lovell Jewel

Introduction

For many centuries after the birth of Christ the British Isles were merely offshore islands, of little or no consequence. The jewellery created or worn in Britain from the Roman invasions until the advent of the Norman conquerors is often considered dull. Dull because of its lack of faceted stones. Dull because so much of what survives is damaged. Dull because many of us know little of the history of the centuries that lay between the Romans and the Normans: how the people lived, whom they worshipped, and what influences affected their work. That thousand-year stretch of time began with Celtic and Roman influence; by the time it drew to a close, Teutonic, Scandinavian and even Byzantine trends had made their mark on the work of the craftsmen of these islands.

Metal Supplies in the British Isles and Ireland

ENGLAND

Mining was already established in Britain at the time of the Roman occupation, and the competent Romans developed it and organized it all across the southern half of the country. With their passion for efficient water-works they had a great need of lead, and found Britain an excellent source of supplies. Lead mines were developed in North Wales and in the Tamar Valley north of the present-day city of Plymouth. Tin mines were already being worked in Cornwall, which seems also to have been the principal source of such small amounts of silver as were then found in Britain.

Silver in the "free" state has never been found in quantity in England, but a steady small amount has been mined, mainly in the West Country; its extraction being well organized over the centuries. No one now knows what proportion of the silver produced in Britain in earlier times was a by-product of the refining of copper or lead (by Norman times lead was being used for roofing, and it is interesting to speculate what proportion of the lead roofs built by the Norman and Plantagenet workmen were shot through with gleaming silver), and what proportion mined "free".

We know very little about mining and smelting in England in the Dark Ages—how much silver was mined and refined here? And at what periods? Did the Saxon metal-workers, for instance—who seem to have been scattered fairly evenly over England, judging from the coins and artefacts that have been found (though there is a rather blank space in the South Midlands)—melt down the coins and the hoarded treasures of earlier periods, or mine their own, or even bring in supplies? If so, where from? One may choose, as a single example of a silver artefact made in Dark Age England, the **Trewhiddle Chalice**, found hidden in the earth about seventeen feet below ground, near St. Austell in Cornwall in 1744. It is 5½ inches (140 mm) high, with a bowl 4 inches (100 mm) across, and is unfortunately in very bad condition. A considerable amount of money was found with it, and some broken jewellery and a silver scourge, which goes to suggest that it may have been looted from some pillaged monastery, though when, again, we do not know. In spite of its condition, it is cherished as one of the earliest surviving English examples of metalwork, and dates from some time during the second half of the ninth century A.D.

WALES

A good deal of the silver used in Britain in the first millennium A.D. was mined in Wales, and so too was a little gold. Quite a few silver treasures have been discovered hidden in Welsh soil; we cannot say for certain that they were made *in situ* from Welsh silver, but this is a distinct possibility. There are some interesting examples of silver and jewels in the National Museum of Wales in Cardiff; and amongst other Welsh treasures is the **Mostyn Harp**, a tiny nine-stringed silver instrument which is only 4 inches (100 mm) high. Elizabeth I, always ready with a penetrating eye for gain, became interested in the possibilities of Welsh silver-mining, and brought in some foreign experts to advise her. So glowing were their reports that she immediately claimed that all mines were Royal property, cancelling a decree issued by her predecessor, Edward I, to the effect that anyone might dig for precious metals on condition that he compensated the owner of the land for any damage (a later decree, issued in 1426 early in the reign of Henry VI, had permitted the owner of the land to claim a twentieth part of the mined metals). Fortunately for Queen Elizabeth, and fortunately perhaps for the advisers too, they were proved right. In 1575 the silver mines established near Aberystwyth produced exactly double the entire English turnover of that year. (Several hundred years later, in the reign of Elizabeth II, the lead mine at Millclose in Derbyshire, which had been producing a few thousand ounces of silver each year, finally closed down.)

It is heartening to know that Elizabeth II, like every other British Royal bride in the twentieth century, was married with a ring fashioned from Welsh gold, the metal being dug from a small mine between Barmouth and Dolgelly. A little gold is still found in Wales, though regular mining on a commercial scale has now stopped. Anyone at all can still, however, apply for a permit—the cost is very low—and set up as a goldminer in Wales.

IRELAND

In pre-Roman times copper was mined in Ireland, and when the traders had opened up routes to tin supplies overseas the Irish metalworkers were able to produce true bronze as well; even before this, however, they had made copper-based alloys which were similar to bronze. Gold was also mined there in the Wicklow mountains.

Great treasures have been found in Ireland. The National Museum in Dublin has a splendid hoard of gold ornaments dating from 2000 B.C. onwards, together with silver from a later period—the fifth century A.D.—and bronze artefacts. Among the greatest of these treasures is the **Ardagh Chalice**, generally considered to date from the eighth century A.D. It is made of silver, beautifully and delicately enriched with gold filigree and enamels, and is one of Ireland's greatest historical works of art. The "Chalice" is more properly a ministerial cup, of the kind used until about the thirteenth century A.D. The priest at Mass consecrated the wine in a small priest's cup and poured some of this consecrated wine into a large two-handled ministerial cup, containing more wine, which was taken to the communicants by the deacons. The use of the ministerial cup eventually died out, the priest's cup alone being used in Masses of a later date, but a small number of examples survive on the continent of Europe (there are none, however, in England). The extant cups are very fine and lavishly decorated, the one found at Ardagh in 1868 being one of the finest of them all. Celtic missionaries were to play an important part in the evangelization of Scotland and England, so it seems probable that this type of Cup was familiar to the devout of both islands.

SCOTLAND

Whereas the Irish had the advantage of a long settled period in which to develop the metalworkers' craft and the other allied arts that were to flower into her great Dark Ages civilization, the tribes of Caledonia were continually harried by raiders, pirates and invaders from across the North Sea. Far fewer artefacts from the first millennia before and after the birth of Christ, have been found in Scotland, and those which have survived seem to date from the eighth and ninth centuries A.D. and look very Irish in origin. (One must remember the blood links between the two countries; Scotland even took its name from an Irish tribe, the Scoti from the north-eastern corner of Ireland, who conquered and settled the south-western corner of Caledonia; it was to these people that the Irish evangelist Columba came in the late sixth century A.D.)

There were, however, silver mines on the east coast of Scotland, and slowly, as the country took shape and settled, and towns were established along the eastern coast, silversmiths set up there, from Wick down to Edinburgh, and established a reputation as craftsmen. In the sixteenth century James V developed gold mining in Scotland, and it is believed that all the metal used by John Mosman in remaking and enlarging the Scottish Regalia came from his own native soil. (Mosman obtained 56 ounces (over 1·5 kg) of gold in 1540, with which to remake and enlarge the Royal Crown, and also made a 35-ounce (1 kg) crown for Mary of Guise, the King's wife, and enlarged other pieces of the Regalia.)

Historical Background

The Romans first invaded Britain in 55 B.C., when two legions led by Julius Caesar, landed in Kent; they were driven back but returned again in the following year with a greater force, fought their way through to the Thames, and burned the Belgic chieftain's camp. The Belgic tribes (of mixed Celtic/Teutonic stock), then established in the south-east of the island, were the newest settlers, but before them had come the Gaelic Celts, and before them still others, the small dark folk, the "Little People", whom the iron-bearing Celts had driven back into the west. Ninety years after that expedition the Romans came again, in full force, to annex Britain, and by A.D. 80 the legions had driven the Celts back into the far north of Caledonia and even subjugated the wild hill tribes of Wales. The southern part of the island was to lie at relative peace under Roman rule for about three hundred and fifty years.

By the beginning of the fourth century A.D., however, danger was already threatening Roman Britain: the Picts raiding across Hadrian's Wall, the Scoti gathering strength in Ireland, the Saxons raiding across the North Sea. The Teutonic conquest of Gaul early in the fifth century cut Britain off from Rome altogether. The Roman troops had been withdrawn; the Romano-British settlements must fend now for themselves until new civil and military appointments could be made from Rome—and that day never came. The Romano-British civilization lasted a few decades longer, but in the latter part of the fifth century the European raiders, driven perhaps by hunger, perhaps by the pressure of the migrating tribes who were spreading westward across Europe from Asia, now crossed the North Sea not merely to plunder, but to settle, to stay. "The barbarians drive us into the sea," the Britons wrote in appeal to Rome, "and the sea drives us back to the barbarians." But there was no help from Rome.

The Jutes, who came from the jutting north-west corner of Europe, settled in Kent and around the Isle of Wight. The Anglo-Saxons—great fighters, whose name, it is thought, derived from *seax*, a short sword, their national weapon—settled in the eastern part of the country (giving their name to East Anglia) and across a vast area of the central regions. A line drawn from Bristol to Oxford, south-east to London, south-west to Bournemouth, and thus back to Bristol, would give a rough outline of their territory. The British-Romano-Celtic peoples, gradually coalescing, were forced back into the West Country, Wales, the wild Lake District, and the south-west corner of Scotland. They won, it seems, a few more decades of truce, until the Anglo-Saxons advanced again and seized a great tract of land stretching from sea to sea across the north country; this they made into the kingdom of Northumbria. By the end of the sixth century, the Welsh mountains, the Scottish Highlands, and the Devon-Cornwall peninsula were still "British", in precarious isolation from one another; the rest was England, the land of the Angles, with the various tribal communities grouped in their separate communities within it: Kent, East Anglia, Wessex, Bernicia, Deira, Mercia.

Late in the eighth century, however, a new threat arose. Pirates came raiding across the North Sea to harry the eastern coast, much as the Angles and Saxons and Jutes had themselves done long before. In A.D. 793 they sacked Lindisfarne off the Northumbrian coast; the following year they were seen off Jarrow; and in A.D. 802, rounding the far north coast of the island, they sacked the Christian settlement at Iona, off the western coast of Scotland, slaughtered the monks, and storming on south, raided the rich shrines and holy places of Ireland.

While Charlemagne lived and held his great empire, the Vikings held back from mainland Europe, confining themselves to raiding and plundering the far coasts and the offshore islands, but after his death and the gradual slackening of Imperial power, every spring brought them pillaging and burning. They sacked Utrecht and Paris, they thrust inland to Charlemagne's Imperial capital at Aachen, they swept into the Mediterranean and clear across it to threaten Byzantium. By A.D. 870 Northumbria, East Anglia and Mercia had all fallen to the Scandinavians, and it seemed only a matter of time before they gobbled up the last English kingdom: Wessex.

In 871, however, a new king succeeded to the leadership of the West Saxons, a young and devout man called Alfred. After seven years of struggle and unceasing patient effort, when his kingdom seemed to be at its last gasp, the merest tallow dip about to be extinguished, he rallied his men one more time and met the Danish army on the downs above Bratton. Unbelievably, he won—drove the Danes back to their camp, besieged them there, and compelled them at last to lay down their arms. The defeated Danish king agreed to be baptised; Alfred stood godfather. The last Christian kingdom in England was still an independent entity.

Alfred made peace in the true creative sense of the word. The Danish settlers drew back into the north and east of England, and, sometime after this, probably in A.D. 886, he made a treaty with the Danish King, defining the frontier between their territories (along the Lea, the Ouse and Watling Street) and setting out the terms on which Danish settlers and Englishmen should now live alongside one another. With Mercia and the other peoples not already directly subject to the Danes accepting him as suzerain (the Welsh, however, held back, still hostile), Alfred re-organized the army, built ships, raised fortified burghs, re-established a culture which had collapsed in ruin under the constant pressure of raids and war, drove back the force from the Danish mainland which continued to threaten the coasts; by the time of his death in A.D. 899 he had created a strong Christian kingdom well equipped to maintain its independence.

Designs and Artefacts of Dark Age Britain

When the Dark Ages began, Britain had been under Roman domination for four hundred years, and classical traditions lingered long after the legions had been withdrawn. Some work had been created by indigenous craftsmen during the long period of Romano-British civilization, interpreting the classical style in terms of their own traditions; other Graeco/Roman artefacts were imported from the Mediterranean. Especially notable is the influence of Roman coins and mosaics. There is, for example, a sixth-century bractate in the Ashmolean Museum in Oxford whose design derives from a Roman coin, and a number of saucer-shaped *fibulae* with mosaic patterns. The Celtic liking for curves, scrolls, curling foliage and linear decoration seems to have married happily enough with a Graeco/Roman sculptural simplicity and quiet controlled use of colour—throughout the centuries of their history the Celtic craftsmen displayed a remarkable aptitude for adapting new ideas to serve their own highly individual style.

Fresh influences came with the migrating tribes from northern Europe who thrust

31

back the Romano-British peoples in the fifth and sixth centuries A.D. and settled in Britain, bringing with them their own cultures and their own techniques; and they in turn were to be affected by the gradual spread of oriental influence from the Asian migrations, one of the impulses which had helped to dislodge them from their earlier settlements and send them travelling westward. The Huns, bands of terrifying horsemen from the Asiatic steppes, had made their first attack on Europe in the late fourth century. When they came storming out through the Caucasus Mountains, there in their path, north of the Black Sea, were the settlements of the Goths. With the Huns pressing them onward, the Goths too began to move westward, hurrying across the Danube; the attack on the Roman Empire was soon to begin, the barbarians swarming down into Gaul and Italy and Spain. After the first outbursts of pillaging and battle, there was a lull of about two hundred years, before the Huns came again, in organized force, under their great leader Attila in two great conquering swoops across Europe; it took defeat at Châlons in A.D. 451 to check them (Romans and their Gothic conquerors uniting with Franks and Burgundians against the common enemy) and Attila's death two years later to scatter them; they settled at last—most of them in a region that was to be called Hungary—and were slowly absorbed into the shifting European pattern of peoples.

The Eastern styles of design travelled gradually along the tracks of the Great Migrations, reaching Britain in about the sixth century A.D. The same designs of griffins, eagles and leopards which were adapted and conventionalized by Celtic and Anglo-Saxon craftsmen have been found in the Treasure of the Oxus, now in the British Museum, supposedly a temple hoard of the fifth or fourth century B.C.—many of the items having cast animal-head terminals, especially the bracelets which are pennanular in form (a broken circle) and which are thought to be forerunners of the Celtic torcs of Western Europe—and in the Treasure of Petrossa, a hoard from the fourth century A.D., found near Bucharest (this contained samples of the new style of garnet-decoration, with thin slices of garnet set in cells like enamels, which spread across Europe from the third to the eighth centuries A.D.). These design motifs gradually became debased, until at last they were merely stylized adaptations filling in spaces; by A.D. 1000, they had been reduced to nothing more than interlaced patterns of lines.

The technique of inlaying metal with garnets and pastes (that is, glass substitutes for true gemstones), samples of which were found in the Petrossa Treasure, is called *verroterie cloisonné*, and is believed to have originated in Egypt in the twelfth century B.C. It had reached Kent, where the Jutes had settled, in the sixth century A.D., and the Kentish metalworkers created some splendid pieces in this style. There were strong ties between the Jutish tribes of Kent and the people of the Rhineland where, two hundred years later, Charlemagne was to set up his new Imperial court, and where Mediterranean craftsmen, many of them trained in the Byzantine school of elaborate enamelled splendour, were to settle, grafting their own style of work on to indigenous traditions.

The **Kingston Brooch** is the most famous example of Kentish work of this period and style. It was found in a woman's grave at Kingston Down in Kent in 1771 and is now in the City of Liverpool Museum. The jewel is a *fibula*, made of two circular plates joined at the rim, a pin being fixed to the back plate, and is about 3¼ inches (over 80 mm) in diameter, weighing 6¼ ounces (about 170 g). The slightly convex facing plate is divided into a multitude of tiny compartments or *cloisons*, studded with garnets, pastes, lapis lazuli and ivory bosses, the whole jewel being interlaced with beaded, pearled and braided gold wire, creating the effect of a colourful mosaic.

The Jutes and the Saxons had brought their own craftsmen with them to Britain, but as their tribal settlements became established they no doubt absorbed British craftsmen as well, trained in the old traditions of classical Rome and of the Celts. They had a liking for display and loved heavy gold jewels and splendid armaments. Some of the metal may perhaps have been mined in England; quite possibly it was melted down from Romano-British plunder. The finest of the Saxon hoards, and by far the most famous, is undoubtedly the Sutton Hoo ship burial treasure, found in 1939 near Woodbridge in Suffolk and now on view at the British Museum. It contained the richest artefacts ever yet dug from English soil. Amongst a great mass of other pieces lay a sceptre, a shield, musical instruments, bowls and spoons, a sword with a jewelled gold pommel and hilt, and literally heaps of gold jewellery—a great gold buckle, heavy curved clasps, a purse-lid (Fig. 5) with thirty-seven Merovingian gold coins, and many personal jewels. The majority of the gold pieces are decorated with garnets: there are, in all, over four thousand individually cut stones, most of them backed by patterned gold foil and fitted into gold cells built up on a base plate in the *cloisonné* technique which had been brought to a high pitch of craftsmanship by the Kentish workers. In addition there are decorations of inset chequers of blue-and-white or red-and-white *millefiori* glass—this is the first known example of the use of *millefiori* in Germanic jewellery. The designs are zoomorphic, with the interlaced elements showing knotted animals twisting and coiling to bite one another's heads and tails, and the intricate and rhythmic patterning which spread all across north-western Europe, from Celtic Ireland to Scandinavia, and which is believed to have stemmed originally from the Middle East. This was a chieftain's grave, and they buried his treasures with him as the Geats buried Beowulf:

> "*Then the Geats built a barrow on a headland—*
> *it was high and broad, visible from far*
> *to all seafarers; in ten days they built the beacon*
> *for that courageous man; and they constructed*
> *as noble an enclosure as wise men*
> *could devise, to enshrine the ashes.*
> *They buried rings and brooches in the barrow,*
> *all those adornments that brave men*
> *had brought out from the hoard after Beowulf died.*
> *They bequeathed the gleaming gold, treasures of men,*
> *to the earth, and there it still remains,*
> *as useless to men as it was before . . .*
> *Thus the Geats, his hearth-companions,*
> *grieved over the death of their lord;*
> *they said that of all the kings on earth*
> *he was the kindest, the most gentle,*
> *the most just to his people, the most eager for fame.*"
> (*Beowulf*, from the translation by Kevin Crossley-Holland,
> Macmillan & Co. Ltd., 1968)

Thus the hearth-companions buried their lord who had lived with them in the common hall, whom they had known as well as any blood-brother, and with whom they had gone to fight, shoulder to shoulder. He had lived among them, a man among men, not a being set apart like a Byzantine Emperor, and when he died they set about him his own treasures, that he might go honourably into death.

Celtic Ireland

Britain had fallen to the invaders, and her arts and crafts were to be disrupted by plundering, raiding, invasion and struggle, and affected by the new styles and influences of each succeeding wave, but Ireland, serenely apart, was to develop during the Dark Ages into a country of paramount importance, a source of religious and artistic strength. Scholars flocked to her universities at Armagh and Durrow (her students were even learning Greek, which was not to be revived in Europe for hundreds of years). Her artists developed the techniques of manuscript-illumination to a pitch of perfection and refinement never seen before and not yet seen since. The same strong linear style, the same rich and varied ornament, were lavished on all the arts. Celtic ornament may be recognized by its intricate interlacing: never-ending lines plaited and folded up and

The Alfred Jewel: one of the most outstanding enamelled jewels of the Early English period, this is believed to date from the late ninth century A.D. It is just under 2½ inches (63.5 mm) long and 1¼ inches (32 mm) wide, and is made of gold richly decorated with *cloisonné* enamels. The Jewel is thought to have been commissioned by Alfred I as an *aestel*—that is, a decorative terminal for one of the pointers which were used by readers and copyers when following a manuscript; the King is known to have sent an *aestel* worth fifty manacuses to each bishopric in his kingdom, with his translation of Gregory I's *Liber Regulae Pastoralis*. The upper illustration shows the socket of rich gold wirework and granulation into which a rod could have been fitted, and the lower the flat back which could have rested on a manuscript. The enamelled design, which is protected by a slice of rock crystal set in a wide band of gold filigree, is thought to be a symbolic representation of Sight (it may be compared with the image of Sight on the ninth-century Anglo-Saxon brooch shown in Fig. 6). The elaborate design engraved on the back is reminiscent of contemporary Celtic Irish manuscript decoration in its full and fluid detail. The inscription which is cut around the Jewel reads ✠ AELFRED MEC HEHT GEWYRCAN (which may be translated as ALFRED ORDERED ME TO BE MADE), and this, together with its richness and elegance, suggests that it may have been created in the workshops of the King's craftsmen. The Jewel was found in 1693, near Athelney in Somerset, and may have been hidden during the Dissolution of the Monasteries in the sixteenth century. It is now in the Ashmolean Museum at Oxford.

By courtesy of the Trustees of the Ashmolean Museum

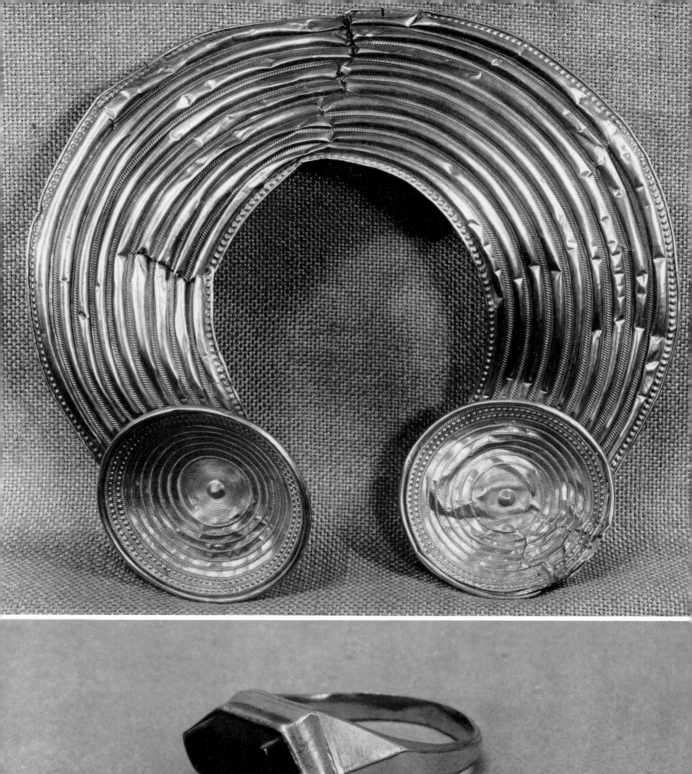

over until the eye, following the convolutions, becomes confused and lost. Each different series of patterns is framed in a geometric compartment with very strong outlines, sometimes raised, sometimes depressed. At its finest, Celtic work is fluent and tranquil, its generous fluid lines balanced by the intricacy of its detail, its strong geometric forms balanced by its lyrical freshness. Spiny monsters and long-billed birds are recurring images, created in miniature with fine flowing lines, and linked with other distinctively Celtic motifs—the trumpet and the spiral. The Celtic craftsman did not rely on gemstones for effect, but rather on the treatment and texturing of the metal itself, with chasing, engraving, and filigree work.

One of the most magnificent examples of Celtic Irish work is the **Tara Brooch**, made in the early part of the eighth century and now at the National Museum in Dublin; it was found on a beach near Bettystown in 1850, and was to inspire a great mass of Victorian imitations. This is a ring-brooch with a long pin to hold the folds of the wearer's garment, and is made from bronze, heavily gilt, rich with gold filigree interlacing in compartments, decorated with *niello* work, and incorporating a few studs of amber and paste. Many of the decorative designs which it bears both on front and back parallel the illuminations of the Book of Kells—a supremely beautiful illuminated manuscript dating from the eighth or ninth century A.D., now in Trinity College,

Fig. 1: this magnificent gold collar was found at Shannongrove in County Limerick, Eire, and was made in the seventh century B.C. It is $11\frac{1}{2}$ inches (290 mm) across, and $3\frac{3}{4}$ inches (95 mm) at its widest point. As it is designed to be worn around the neck and resting across the shoulders, with the golden discs fully displayed, it is gently curved to fit the body. The gold is very thin (it would otherwise have been impossible for the craftsman to work it into such sophisticated undulations); basically simple, the collar is made to look far richer by the meticulous application of gold granules of differing sizes. The blaze of shimmering gold seems to contemporary eyes to be more in keeping with Eastern Mediterranean splendour, reflecting the rays of the hot sun, than with a misty Celtic Ireland. It shows the controlled curving beauty of the "barbaric" style for which the Celts were famed, and their equally famous craftsmanship.

Fig. 2: nothing could be a greater contrast to the Celtic collar than this ring, silvergilt set with a "stone" of blue glass. It dates from the fourteenth or fifteenth centuries A.D., and its simplicity and angular lines denote that the focus of interest is the bezel itself rather than the setting. This stone was clearly valued for its colour, and probably also for supposed magical powers. The design is such that the ring could be worn either on a man's finger or a woman's thumb, and although it lacks an engraved motto it is similar in style to the medieval "posy" rings.

By courtesy of the Trustees of the Victoria and Albert Museum

Dublin—with its birds' head terminals, interlaced monsters, and engraved spirals.

Celtic brooches of about the same period have also been found in Scotland, among them the **Hunterston Brooch** which is now in the National Museum of Antiquities in Edinburgh. Though not perhaps as fine as the Tara Brooch, it is more personal, for inscribed on the reverse are the names of two of the former owners: *MAELBRITHA* and *OLFRITI*.

The golden age of Irish Celtic art was during the seventh and eighth centuries A.D., before the Vikings fell on Ireland. During this period Celtic influence fanned out across the mainland of Europe and down into Britain, via the Irish missionaries and their Anglo-Saxon disciples. Some of the finest craftsmen in Europe were to train at the monastery of St. Gall in Switzerland, named after the Irish saint who founded it in A.D. 613, and the Irish and Saxon scholars were to play their own part in Charlemagne's attempt to revive Christian culture and craftsmanship within his new Empire.

Church Patronage

THE SPREAD OF CHRISTIANITY

The influence of the spread of Christianity was to be as important as any of the migratory influences, for the establishment of the Church, gradual and tenuous though it was, encouraged the growth of a gentler culture, a revival of craftsmanship and learning as adjuncts to the worship of God, cruelly disrupted by the Danish invasions but fostered anew by Alfred of Wessex.

The Romans had introduced the worship of their own gods into Britain, but had permitted the worship of native gods where this did not encourage insurrection against the might of Rome. In the long decay of the Empire, Christianity had spread slowly among the conquerors and among their subject peoples. When the legions withdrew, the Christian Faith survived here and there among the British-Celtic peoples, and as they were pressed back into the north and west by the invasions of the barbarian Angles and Saxons and Jutes, they took the Faith with them. In the far north and far west of the island, and in Ireland across the sea, Christians and pagans lived for a time, side by side, in threatened freedom.

Then, in the spring of A.D. 597, carrying a silver cross before them, Augustine and his missionary monks landed in Kent (it took them nearly a year to get up the courage to cross to that barbaric place). The Jutish king was converted, and thirty years later, when his daughter was sent north to marry the King of Northumbria, she took with her Paulinus, her chaplain. He preached to the Northumbrians—an especially brave act since a few years earlier they had slaughtered the Christians of Wales—and he converted them in thousands.

That first mission was ultimately to fail, but other monks came: the Celtic evangelists spread out from Patrick's Ireland and Columba's Iona, across Scotland and down into Northumbria again; Roman and Frankish missionaries preached the Faith in Wessex. By the middle of the seventh century, all England but the Isle of Wight and the Weald was Christianized. A Northumbrian abbot named Wilfred converted Sussex. The Celtic Aidan spent seven years journeying through Northumbria. Cuthbert, whose cross pendant may still be seen in the cathedral museum at Durham, meditated on

Lindisfarne for hours at a time. Bede the scholar studied at Jarrow. Wilfred, later Bishop of York, evangelized Sussex and, in A.D. 664, gathered all the rulers and church-men of the north at Whitby, where the Synod finally agreed to accept the authority and follow the ritual of Rome; Celtic Christianity was subordinated to Roman authority, and the English were united in a new and unprecedented way. As the people came to understand and appreciate the Christian religion, they began first to build churches, then to decorate and beautify them. In the north they raised great Celtic crosses, to gather round for open-air worship. Some of the high crosses erected to commemorate those who had died, or to mark a holy place, are still extant: the Ruthwell Cross, for instance, the Bewcastle Cross, the Reculver Cross, all dating from about A.D. 700. They are carved with leaf scrolls, birds and beasts, and human figures portrayed with great tenderness.

When the Vikings came raiding towards the end of the eighth century, they naturally attacked the sources of the greatest wealth: they plundered the monasteries, they burned the churches, they slaughtered the monks and priests. From the destruction of Cuthbert's church at Lindisfarne in A.D. 793 until Alfred secured his kingdom almost a century later, English Christianity was in dire peril; and even Alfred only gave it a breathing space. After his death (*circa* A.D. 899) England had a century of relative peace in which to build, before the Norsemen struck again. Ethelred, proverbially Unready, could not hold them back, and in A.D. 1012 they sacked Canterbury.

CHURCH CRAFTSMEN

With the firm establishment of Christianity in Britain, and the gradual development of Royal authority, came the introduction of new spheres of influence: those of the kings and of the Church. Fortunately the Church patronized and encouraged the craftsmen who were to beautify her monasteries, churches and cathedrals. The reliquaries and the vessels were generally made of gold or silver-gilt, often incorporating gemstones as well. The rich fabrics of the vestments worn by bishops and priests were decorated with pearls, pastes, gemstones and enamels. Many of the monks were them-selves skilled craftsmen. Apart from the famed monkish illuminators, there were wood-carvers, sculptors and metalworkers among them; and skilled embroiderers among their sister-religious, the nuns. The great religious foundation at Ely was founded in A.D. 673 by Etheldreda, daughter of the King of East Anglia and wife of the King of Northumbria; she became its first abbess, and there were at least two goldsmiths— Brednothus and Elsinus—among the abbots who succeeded her. (By a curious chance her name came eventually to be synonymous with cheap and shoddy work; the people of medieval England honoured her as St. Audrey, and held a great yearly fair at which were sold inexpensive trinkets—of "St. Audrey" quality, people said; it is from this that we get the word "tawdry".) The monastery of St. Albans was founded by a Mercian king in A.D. 793; Richard, one of its abbots, was a goldsmith, and the abbey became famed for fine goldsmiths' work, known far and wide—to such an extent that the King of Denmark invited a monk from there named Ankere to go and work for him. But probably the most famous of all the craftsmen monks was St. Dunstan (*circa* A.D. 909– 988), now the patron saint of goldsmiths; his career and achievements are described in more detail in the next chapter.

Early English Enamelled Jewels

By pure chance several enigmatic enamelled jewels made in the Early English period have been discovered in past centuries; Figs. 6 and 7 show, for instance, the Fuller Brooch and the Strickland Brooch—both ninth-century Anglo-Saxon work, silver inlaid with *niello*. Two of the most outstanding discoveries were the Alfred Jewel and the Minster Lovell Jewel. The questions about their actual function have never been fully answered, but a most scholarly piece of detective work has been put forward by Joan R. Clarke and David A. Hinton for the Ashmolean Museum, Oxford, where the jewels are in safe-keeping. Their findings point to a close connection between the two jewels in style, date and function; it even appears that they might have been made by the same craftsman.

The jewels were probably commissioned by Alfred the Great who succeeded his brother as King of Wessex in A.D. 871. It seems likely that they were richly decorative terminals for *aestels*. Alfred was resolved to raise the standards of learning and scholarship in his kingdom, and to that end translated into the vernacular a number of manuscripts—"some books," he said, "which may be most necessary for men to know". Among these was the *Liber Regulae Pastoralis* of Pope Gregory the Great. Alfred is believed to have translated this some time after 890. In his Preface he stated that he would present a copy of his translation to every see in his realm, together with a valuable *aestel*:

> "I turned it into English, and to every Bishopric in my kingdom will I send one; and in each there is an aestel which is worth fifty manacuses; and in God's name I command that no man remove the aestel from the book."

We do not know for certain what an *aestel* was, but it seems likely from a translation note which was written into Alfred's Preface at a later date that it meant a pointer or rod. These pointers were used by readers or copyers, so that they could follow a text without dirtying the manuscript with greasy fingermarks. Both jewels have obvious sockets into which a slender stick (perhaps of carved ivory?) could be fitted, and one side of each is flat—suitable to rest on a manuscript—and is not enriched with enamel. Both are small, colourful and richly decorated, being made of gold enriched with *cloisonné* enamelling in different colours.

The **Alfred Jewel** is illustrated facing page 34. It was found in 1693 in Newton Park near North Petherton in Somerset, four miles from Athelney. Alfred hid from his enemies in the Athelney marshes in 878, before re-gathering his forces and winning his great victory over the Danes; he is said to have founded a monastery there in thanksgiving. The Abbot of Athelney helped him with his translation of Pope Gregory's work, and it therefore seems probable that the jewel was the terminal from the abbot's *aestel*. The jewel is pear-shaped, and is just under $2\frac{1}{2}$ inches (about 62 mm) long and $1\frac{1}{4}$ inches (about 30 mm) wide. It is made of gold, with a rich design in *cloisonné* enamel showing a male figure seated on a stool and carrying in each hand a stem which blossoms into a flower above his shoulder. This figure is almost certainly a symbolic representation of one of the five senses: Sight. It is protected by a slice of rock crystal set in a wide band of gold filigree, around which are cut the words

✠ AELFRED MEC HEHT GEWYRCAN

which may be translated as *Alfred ordered me to be made*. The socket is formed of an animal's head made of rich gold wirework and granules. The gemstone eyes have been lost. The back is flat, and is engraved with an elaborate design reminiscent of contemporary Irish manuscript decoration.

The **Minster Lovell Jewel** was found near Witney in Oxfordshire just over a hundred years ago, and given to the Ashmolean shortly afterwards. It is smaller and simpler than the Alfred Jewel, and is circular in shape—about ¾ inch (18 mm) across—with a socket extending another ½ inch (12·5 mm). The design shows geometric sections on a dark blue background. Only four colours of enamel are used (in the Alfred there are five); but the framework of rich gold granulated work is as splendid as that of the Alfred.

The technique of using filigree and granulated gold with *cloisonné* enamelling is characteristic of jewels made for the governing class, and stems from the Mediterranean; the simpler techniques of gilt-bronze work were developed by the governed, rather than the governing. This is one of the arguments for holding that the Alfred and Minster Lovell Jewels were made in the royal workshops.

It is probable that both jewels were hidden or lost during the dissolution of the monasteries in the sixteenth century. Their survival drives one mad with thinking how much other beautiful work has been lost.

The Worshipful Company of Goldsmiths

FROM ST. DUNSTAN TO THE PRESENT DAY

Introduction—St. Dunstan and his England—The Worshipful Company of Goldsmiths: The Development of Guilds; The Medieval Goldsmiths; The Coin of the Realm, The Trial of the Pyx; Assaying and Hallmarking, The "Touch" and the First Hallmarks, Assaying Today, Hallmarking Today—Substitutes for Gold and Silver—Platinum—Craftsmanship from the Middle Ages to the Present Day

Introduction

The Worshipful Company of Goldsmiths was incorporated in A.D. 1327, but the history of the craft stretches back well beyond that, past the voluntary banding together of craftsmen from which the guilds developed, to the metalworkers of Saxon England; and pre-eminent among them, the statesman and craftsman who was to become the goldsmiths' patron saint: Dunstan.

St. Dunstan and his England

In the Bodleian Library at Oxford there is a tenth-century manuscript incorporating an outline drawing of considerable interest. This shows Christ, seated centrally, with flowing draperies and a coloured halo. He is looking unemotionally out of the drawing towards a spot well over the viewer's left shoulder. In drawing his eyes, the artist was clearly influenced by the Byzantine style.

On the right of the illustration is a tiny little monk, half-kneeling, half-lying at Christ's feet. The few simple lines evoke the image of a roly-poly, middle-aged, tonsured man, a fraction of the size of Christ, crouching there just as one sees Man between Christ's feet in the Sutherland tapestry in Coventry Cathedral. Just above this little figure is a prayer which reads:

> *"Dunstanum memet clemens rogo Christe tuere*
> *Tenarias me non sinas sorbsisse procellas."*

The plea may be translated:

> *"Me, Dunstan, in thy mercy, O Christ, protect,*
> *Suffer not the whirlpools of Hell to swallow me up."*

Right at the top of the illustration is another inscription (which was added later), explaining that the scene is a self-portrait of Dunstan.

Dunstan was born in about A.D. 909, near the great monastery of Glastonbury at Baltonsborough in the West Country. He died in A.D. 988 as Archbishop of Canterbury. The intervening seventy-nine years were filled with incident; they fell in the turbulent period of history that followed Alfred's defeat of the Danes, when the English were trying to rebuild a Christian society and to maintain its defence against the pirates and plunderers.

His name, Dunstan, is believed to be derived from the Anglo-Saxon *dún*, meaning "firm", "strong" (many place names derive from *dun*, "a fortified mound"), and *stán*, meaning "a stone", "a rock". He truly proved again and again, throughout his difficult life, that he was "as firm as a rock".

Although he was to rise to the highest ecclesiastical honour in England, he came reluctantly into the Church. Unlike many young men of the period, who went into a monastery straight from childhood, he resisted the strange pull of faith until he was twenty-seven.

Heorstan and Cynedryda, Dunstan's parents, were of noble standing. At the time of their son's birth, the King of the West Saxons was Alfred's son, Edward the Elder. Edward fought a series of campaigns to extend the boundaries of his kingdom, and by the time of his death in 925, almost all southern and central England was united under him; even the Welsh kings acknowledged his supremacy, and he had formed an alliance with the King of the Scots, who was welding together a kingdom from the Pictish and Scottish peoples.

Edward's eldest son, Athelstan, succeeded to this inheritance, and immediately began to enrich it, taking Danish North-humberland under his direct rule, exacting tribute from the Welsh kings, and marrying off his sisters to the rulers of Europe. In A.D. 937 the King of the Picts and Scots made a rash attempt to invade England, with allies from the kingdom of Strathclyde in south-west Scotland, and from Ireland and the Western Isles; Athelstan trounced them soundly.

Aldhelm, Dunstan's uncle, was Archbishop of Canterbury during Athelstan's reign. It was he who introduced Dunstan into the king's court, and, as time went by, promoted his career, until young Dunstan found that one of his duties was "to play harp music to lull the king to sleep after the pleasures and fatigues of the chase". The position was much sought after and very difficult to hold, with countless jealous rivals on all sides, and honest young Dunstan, who was never devious in his life, was soon ousted. Various people at court accused him of practising "the forbidden arts", and in the end persuaded the king to discharge him.

So Dunstan had to make his way home again, no doubt concerned that he had lost his post at court but extremely glad to get away from the evil and envious people there. His troubles, however, were by no means at an end. As he travelled homeward, he was set upon, beaten up, and finally thrown down a well and left for dead. Some passers-by heard his weak cries for help, rescued him and took him to the Bishop of Winchester for safety. Bishop Alfheah cared for him, and invited him to enter the monastic order there, but Dunstan could not bring himself to such a final decision. When he was fit to travel, he continued on his way to Glastonbury. But there his health finally broke down, and he was extremely ill for a long time, vowing that when and if he recovered, he would, after all, become a monk. In due time he did so; he went back to the Bishop of Winchester and took his vows, and then entered the monastic community at Glastonbury.

Glastonbury lay in Somerset, islanded in marshes. It was reputed to be the oldest place of Christian worship in England, and one of the most important abbeys in the kingdom was built there. Here Dunstan occupied a cell which was five feet long by two and a half feet broad, with a roof no higher than a man; here he worked and prayed; and here, according to his clerical biographer, Osbern, the Devil came to plague him. This is the tale by which most people remember Dunstan:

> "But the Devil, lest he might seem to commiserate the poverty of him whom in former times he had not suffered to live in a palace, now strives to drive him from his cell. The crafty one accordingly, having concealed himself under the image of a man in the gloom of the evening, seeks the young man's cell, and leaning on the window with his head stretched forward sees him occupied with some smith's work, and enquires of him what work he is engaged upon. But Dunstan, paying no attention to his wiles, now suffering his importunity fixed his attention on the work he was being questioned about.
>
> Meanwhile the Devil, conversing in a wily manner, introduces the name of women, recalls his luxuries to his encumbrance, and puts religion before him in a ridiculous way.
>
> But the Christian champion, understanding what he means, puts in the fire the tongs with which he held the iron, and with closed lips prays to Christ; and when he perceives that the end of the tongs were at white heat, inflamed with a holy rage he quickly snatches them from the fire, and seizes the frightful face with the pincers and drags the monster inside.
>
> Dunstan, standing, gathered up all his strength, when he whom he held broke away the hands that were holding him (the wall being knocked down), crying out with a savage yell 'Oh what has that bald-pated fellow done? Oh what has he done?' (for Dunstan had thin though beautiful hair) and such-like things he cried concerning him."

This translation, a literal one made from the original Latin, is of great interest, because it makes it clear that Dunstan grasped the Devil's whole face between his pincers and dragged his whole body into the cell. Re-tellings generally state that Dunstan gripped the Devil by the nose alone, for this is the manner in which the incident is portrayed in the stained glass of Wells Cathedral, the Bodleian Library at Oxford, and Mayfield Church in Sussex, and in the old doggerel,

> *"He seized the Devil by the nose,*
> *With red-hot tongs to make him roar,*
> *Till he could be heard ten miles and more."*

Perhaps the illustrators thought the scene would look more dramatic that way. But they were wrong.

It was while he was at Glastonbury that Dunstan developed his love of the arts: music, writing and illuminating manuscripts, making crosses and censers and chalices. Later in his life he was to cast some famous bells for Canterbury Cathedral, and the

Anglo-Saxon pocket sundial there is attributed to him. During his years at Glastonbury the king and his court are said to have visited the abbey often, sometimes bringing with them foreign embassies.

In A.D. 939 Athelstan died and was succeeded by his brother, Edmund. There was, inevitably, a general Danish uprising which he suppressed. Mindful of the constant Scottish threat, he also seized Strathclyde, and there set up a king who was bound in alliance to him. It was Edmund who, in A.D. 940, appointed Dunstan Abbot of Glastonbury. There is a legend that he did so because he was once hunting stag near Cheddar Gorge, and would have plunged to his death there, had not Dunstan intervened to save his life.

From then on Dunstan became a real force in the monastic world. A true churchman and scholar, he also served the kings of England as counsellor in affairs of state. Edmund died in 946, killed by an outlaw in a brawl in his own royal hall, and was succeeded by his brother, Edred (who in his turn put down the usual Danish rising). By the time Edred died, in 955, the greater part of England, from the Forth river to the south coast, was ruled by the house of Wessex—which, however, now produced an adolescent king, Edmund's son Edwig. According to a later monkish chronicler, the young king grew bored at the feast that followed his crowning—so bored that he insulted his lords and counsellors by going off to amuse himself with a young cousin, a girl named Elfgifu. Abbot Dunstan followed him and dragged him back to the hall. Edwig subsequently married the girl, an action which, far from pacifying Dunstan and his fellow churchmen, had the opposite effect, since the Church forbade marriages within certain degrees of kinship. In the quarrel that followed Dunstan was exiled and went to study at Bladinium Abbey near Ghent in Flanders, but came triumphantly home again when the nobles of the north and central regions of England set up Edgar, the king's brother, in Edwig's place; the Archbishop of Canterbury took courage from this, forcibly separated Edwig and Elfgifu, and dispatched the luckless girl beyond the Channel; and in 959, when Edwig died, Edgar succeeded to the whole kingdom. He was a man of very different make from his brother, and had, moreover, welded Dunstan and the Church to his side.

In the year after his accession, Edgar made Dunstan Archbishop of Canterbury. It is said to have been Dunstan who crowned the young king at Bath, with a crown he made himself, and who composed for that occasion a special service, binding the king to his people, anointing him as the chosen ruler under God. (Perhaps, if the chronicler's tale about Edwig is true, Dunstan was determined to have a seemly affair this time.) The new archbishop encouraged scholarship, learning, the decorative arts. He became the first of the great ecclesiastical statesmen: the first king's counsellor who was a sworn man of peace rather than a warrior. Under him the two great reformers, Ethelwold and Oswald, rebuilt churches and restored the strict monastic rule of celibacy and self-denial in a number of monasteries. Ethelwold was made Bishop of Winchester, Oswald Bishop of Worcester (Dunstan himself had earlier held the bishoprics of Worcester and London), and both of them drove out the secular canons at their cathedrals and brought in monks to fill their places; an example which Dunstan himself did not follow, tolerating the secular canons of Canterbury. But he worked tirelessly for the unification of the country, and at first it seemed, no doubt, that God had blessed the work. Edgar is said to have ceded Lothian (the plain that stretches

43

from the Tweed to the Forth) to Kenneth, King of the Scots and Picts, in return for a promise of allegiance; such a gift pacified the north and for a time at least, enabled Celts and English to live in neighbourly peace.

England was growing into a rich and stable place: the arts flourished; craftsmen were encouraged; towns were appointed where reliable money could be minted, proper contracts made, law-suits heard and judgment given, and the trade of the market-place carried on under proper supervision—Winchester, for instance, had eight mints, a court which met weekly, a guildhall and proper rules for checking weights and measures, by the second quarter of the century.

But in 975 Edgar died. He left two sons, Edward and Ethelred; there was a quarrel over the succession, complicated by a religious split; the elder boy was crowned, but murdered four years later, and the succession fell on his brother Ethelred, a spoilt, inconstant and devious man, who was unfortunately long-lived into the bargain. Dunstan was present at his christening in 969, and prophesied disaster when the baby wet the font; he was perfectly right. Ethelred's heedless cruelty drove the Danish settlers of northern England to call to their kin from across the North Sea, who were already swooping gladly down to plunder the rich kingdom. A generation of destruction culminated in the sack of Canterbury and the murder of Dunstan's successor, the holy Alphege, who refused to appeal for ransom lest the price of his freedom were wrung from the poor. The following year Ethelred fled abroad, leaving his kingdom in the hands of the Danish king Sweyn. For three years his elder son Edmund Ironside put up a gallant fight against Sweyn's successor, Canute, battling across southern England as Alfred had done long before; but in 1016 he died and his exhausted kingdom accepted Canute as king. The great Dane, ruler of Denmark and England, and conqueror of Norway, re-established law and order. His death in 1035 laid England open to a new power struggle, which was eventually resolved in 1042 when the English chose Edward as their king. This most devout man, nicknamed the Confessor, was Ethelred's youngest son, and had been brought up in Normandy. He filled his court with Normans and, though he married a Saxon girl, was too devout to give her a child; in spite of the brief and gallant efforts of his successor and brother-in-law, Harold the Saxon, the kingdom fell in 1066 to the last foreign race to invade her successfully: the Normans under Duke William.

But Dunstan, though he foresaw disaster, did not live to see its actual shape. His death in 988 left the young King Ethelred truly "Unready"—the name is derived from the Anglo-Saxon *raed*, meaning "counsel"—and was a contributory factor in leaving the realm open to the invaders. His countrymen mourned him deeply, and it is proof of the esteem in which he was universally held that he was canonized very shortly after his death. Many churches in London and the provinces were dedicated to him, and he became the patron saint of the goldsmiths. At Goldsmiths Hall in the City of London the greatest yearly festival is still St. Dunstan's Day (May 19), and among their records, dating back as far as the fourteenth century, are some which illuminate the rules for the observance of this great day. The shops were closed, the Ordinances of the Company were read, and the new wardens took office. The Livery went in procession from Goldsmiths Hall to St. Paul's, where candles were lighted, bells were rung, and a service held. After that they all returned to the hall to dine in state; later in the evening they held another service at the church of St. John Zachary (destroyed in the Great Fire of London in 1666).

Ceremonies today at Goldsmiths Hall take place on a Wednesday, so St. Dunstan's Day is celebrated on the nearest Wednesday to May 19. On that day the officers of the Company renew their oaths of allegiance, and the date-letter for the hallmarking of gold and silver (described in more detail on pages 48–56) is changed, the old one being destroyed. Sadly there is no longer a special goldsmiths' service at St. Paul's; a service is, however, held at St. Mary Woolnoth, at the end of Lombard Street, about a week after St. Dunstan's Day, in remembrance of Sir Martin Bowes (d. 1566), who had the honour of being Prime Warden for the incredible total of thirteen times—eight times more than any other person—(he was Master of the Mint as well) though he was not himself a practising goldsmith. At this service the newly elected Prime Warden reads the Lesson.

The great staircase in Goldsmiths Hall divides at a half-landing. Today, as one walks up its broad but shallow steps, there in front of one, within an architectural niche, is the gilded statue of St. Dunstan, originally made in about 1680 for the Worshipful Company's barge and shown in Fig. 10. He stands there as archbishop and as saint, but above all as the overseer of all the many diverse activities of the Hall. Most of the other objects associated with him and owned by the company have unhappily been destroyed; there used to be a set of Flanders tapestries showing scenes from his life, a silver statue studded with gems, even a window dedicated to him in St. Paul's—but time has swept them away. Everything is gone now except this gilded statue in Goldsmiths Hall, his patronage of the goldsmiths, and an untarnished reputation. It is enough.

The Worshipful Company of Goldsmiths

THE DEVELOPMENT OF GUILDS

Craft guilds and trade guilds grew out of the voluntary banding together of craftsmen and merchants, to promote the well-being of their fellow-members, to maintain proper standards of workmanship and to secure a monopoly of trading. Religious guilds also flourished under the Norman and Plantagenet kings (their activities ranging from the giving of alms to the upkeep of bridges), and even the secular guilds were strongly imbued with charity and religious observance. The development of the craft guilds, whose members were granted by the king the monopoly of working and trading in their particular field, gradually ate away the authority of the merchant guild, whose members were granted the right to trade freely within a particular town; by the fourteenth century they were fully established in England, and by the fifteenth century the term "mystery", from the Latin *ministerium*, "craft", was beginning to replace the older Saxon-rooted term "guild"; it was then, in 1462, that the Goldsmiths were granted the title "The Wardens and Commonalty of the Mystery of Goldsmiths of the City of London".

The impulse to form into a group for mutual help was a natural one, particularly in turbulent times when the state could barely protect its people, let alone provide for them in sickness and old age. We know that the Saxons banded together into fraternities whose members were bound to help one another; surviving ordinances from the first half of the eleventh century show that members met periodically, contributed to a common fund, were fined for misconduct, prayed for their dead and so on. Although no direct connection can be shown, lacking full historical records, it seems perfectly possible that the character of the craft guilds and the merchant guilds developed from the traditions of these earlier fraternities.

THE MEDIEVAL GOLDSMITHS

The goldsmiths of Norman and Plantagenet England did not merely work in gold, as their name suggests. Since earliest times, the possession of gold and silver artefacts has been regarded as a mark of wealth, prestige and power; they were centrepieces, proudly displayed at court or in church, their fineness, beauty, weight and solidity the outward and visible signs of their owner's importance. Because silver tarnishes, solid silver artefacts were often given a thin surface coating of gold. The craftsman made his silver cup, for instance, and then took a small bowl in which he mixed pure molten gold and mercury until he had a frothy cream which was lavishly—and quickly—applied over the whole surface of the cup, flowing into every crevice; the mercury quickly evaporated, leaving a thin protective film of gold. Thus the metalworker worked in both the costly metals, but because gold was the richer of the two, and because his silver artefacts were so often gilded (a precautionary measure, which was especially necessary for silver vessels used for food and drink, *not* an attempt to defraud the customer), he was simply called a "goldsmith".

The medieval goldsmiths were held in particularly high repute, for the nature of their craft involved them in other activities beyond caring for their members' welfare, maintaining high standards of craftsmanship, and undertaking charitable works; in the course of their history, they came also to be appointed to check the coin of the realm, and to test and approve, with special hallmarks, the standard of precious metals and artefacts, thus protecting craft and patron alike and equally, and preventing anyone from bringing into disrepute either the trading of precious metals, or the coinage—a vital factor in establishing and maintaining a settled and assured society.

THE COIN OF THE REALM

The ancient method of minting coins, which lasted in England until the seventeenth century, was extremely simple. The moneyer needed two dies: one, the obverse die, was set in his anvil, and the other, the reverse die, in his punch. He made his "blanks" either by casting them or simply by making blobs of metal. Pure gold and pure silver coins have been struck at certain periods, but in general ancient coins were alloyed with copper, partly because of the need to conserve the precious metals and partly because the use of an alloy made the coin more durable. The blank was heated and placed on the anvil, so that it lay on the obverse die; the punch, with the reverse die embedded in its head, was set in place, and struck sharply with a hammer; and that was that. In a well-conducted mint the coin was then weighed to check that it was up to standard, but until proper controls were established the weight and quality could vary considerably, and the impending collapse of any empire or power was generally heralded by the debasement of its coinage.

With the departure of the Roman military forces, the controlled supply of gold and silver coins in Britain came to an end, though the local powers struggled on, striking small copper coins, examples of which still survive. In or about A.D. 561, when the Christian Frankish princess Bertha married Ethelbert of Kent, she brought with her a chaplain who minted gold coin at Canterbury: it was the beginning of a long tradition of ecclesiastical minting. London had a mint early in the seventh century and retained it for about a hundred years, and by A.D. 650 there was a mint in York too; but in the eighth century, minting dropped considerably, especially south of the Humber. The early Saxon mints seem to have been controlled by the ecclesiastics, by merchants or traders—rarely by the princes and kings. In the latter half of the eighth century, however, Offa, King of Mercia (A.D. 757–796) struck his famous silver penny, a sturdy reliable coin which bore his name and portrait on the obverse and the moneyer's name on the reverse. During the ninth century the kings of Kent, Wessex and East Anglia were all striking their own silver pennies, and so too was the Archbishop of Canterbury; and in the tenth, Athelstan made the first attempt to standardize the coinage, declaring that a single coinage should be current throughout the realm, that all dies must be supplied by the London die-makers, that mints must be located in towns, and that only certain towns might have them. The ordinances of the Council of Greatley (A.D. 928) listed the towns where coins might be struck and the number of moneyers each might have: seven at Canterbury (one the abbot's, two the archbishop's, and four the king's); three at Rochester (one the abbot's, two the king's); eight at London; six at Winchester; two each at Lewes, Southampton, Wareham, Exeter and Shaftesbury; one each at Hastings, Chichester, Dorchester and all the fortified burghs. In his turn Edgar too pressed for a stable and standard coinage ("Let one measure and one weight be used, such as is observed in London and Winchester"). Ethelred, harassed by the Danes, made a frantic effort to control the springing up of mints (some apparently in woods and forests), to check counterfeiting, and to stop the merchants from importing false "brass" money and getting the moneyers to change good money for impure light coin; but his efforts were in vain. The number of mints (eight under Alfred, forty under Edgar) jumped to seventy-five under Ethelred, all hastily turning treasure and hoarded metal into coin at the threat of new invasions.

The king's moneyers were appointed by him, the ecclesiastical ones by archbishop or abbot (Dunstan had three, and once shocked his congregation by hanging three counterfeiters on Easter Day); the mints in the lay towns were apparently supervised by citizens of good standing or by the craft fraternities. The fact that Chester, for example, was among Athelstan's mint towns may well pre-suppose that an association of goldsmiths was established there in the tenth century. The presence of goldsmiths is recorded in Lincoln in 1155, in Newcastle in 1248, in Norwich in 1285, in York in 1313, in Exeter in 1327; it seems very likely that they had formed their own guilds for self-protection.

The Norman kings made intermittent efforts to establish a stricter control of the coinage, and in 1248, when a trial of old and new coin was staged in London in the presence of the Barons of the Exchequer, a sworn jury of twelve elected citizens, and a dozen goldsmiths of standing, the authorities of a number of towns were each ordered to elect openly and publicly four minters, four die-keepers, two goldsmiths "of unblemished fidelity and knowledge" to be assayers, and one clerk. The assayers were supplied with standard pieces of silver, and ordered to conduct public assays of finished coin. (The towns, London apart, whose coins were assayed, were Canterbury, Bury St. Edmunds, Bristol, Carlisle, Winchester, York, Exeter, Gloucester, Hereford, Ilchester, Lincoln, Newcastle, Northampton, Norwich, Oxford, Shrewsbury, Wallingford and Wilton.)

Some time between 1248 and 1280, when the first known writ for a trial was issued, the ceremony now known as the Trial of the Pyx was instituted. The Goldsmiths Company appears to have been long associated with this testing of the weight and quality of the coinage, and has actual records of the proceedings from 1604 onwards.

The Trial of the Pyx

The pyx was the chest in which coins lay awaiting trial, kept in the Chapel of the Pyx at Westminster Abbey which for centuries was used as the Treasury of the Exchequer; there the assay took place in the presence of the Privy Council, presided over by the Lord Chancellor (the monarch occasionally attended too). This room, empty and silent now, is open to the public on certain days. An illustration of it was included among the many exhibits at the splendid 1971 exhibition, *The Trial of the Pyx*, mounted at Goldsmiths Hall, unfortunately for four days only. The earliest exhibit was the standard silver ingot-shaped plate of 1279, together with an Edward I silver penny of the same year; it is, however, generally agreed that examination of the justness of the coinage by assay and comparison with trial plates was practised as early as Saxon times, possibly even under the Roman Empire. (The exhibition also showed that decimalization was advocated as early as 1682, and favoured by Sir Christopher Wren in the sixteen-nineties, and that experimental decimal coins were actually made in 1857 and 1859; but the idea was dropped because the Royal Commission concluded that it was not desirable "to disturb the established habits of the people".)

The Coinage Act of 1870 and the passing of the Order in Council of 1871 resulted in the changing of several features of the trial: it was to be held in Goldsmiths Hall, it was now to be strictly an annual event (this had not been considered necessary before) and it had to be conducted by the Queen's Remembrancer. The Chancellor of the Exchequer was to be master, worker and warden of the Royal Mint, and therefore personally reponsible for the quality of the coin of the realm.

During the last few decades, the number of real silver or gold coins to be tested has grown fewer and fewer. Apart from the Maundy money (presented by the monarch to chosen pensioners at an annual ceremony on Maundy Thursday), no silver coin is now minted in Britain; and the last gold coin was seen at the trial in 1969. However, the Goldsmiths are still asked to test "the coin of the realm", not only its weight and composition, but also now the accuracy of its measurements, because of the growing number of slot machines in use in daily life.

ASSAYING AND HALLMARKING

Most people in Britain are not really aware of the fact that they still rely on the Goldsmiths Company to keep up standards. The fact is not brought home to us until we travel abroad. An Englishman abroad decides, perhaps, to buy some silver or gilded article in a shop there. How, he wonders, can he be certain that the silver is up to standard? How can he be sure that the gold charm he is buying is really gold? Where are the hallmarks, the maker's mark, the quality figures? To whom can he appeal if he has been swindled? In Britain, however, he knows that a hallmarked article is guaranteed genuine—and if he is in any doubt, the Goldsmiths will check for him. For six and a half centuries the Goldsmiths have had an unbroken record of looking after the public, and they continue to do it today. There is not another country in the world with this reputation. Elsewhere frontiers have shifted, guilds been disbanded, records been lost; but the Company still maintains its standards, and in its Hall lies a voluminous library on which one may completely rely.

The "Touch" and the First Hallmarks

In 1238 Henry III decreed that six goldsmiths of London should be appointed to superintend the testing of silver to check its quality. Actual hallmarking did not follow for two generations more, being introduced in 1300. The ancient method of testing was known as "the touch" because the metal article was rubbed on a touchstone (this was a black siliceous stone or an earthenware block). The streak thus made was compared with the streak made by gold or silver of a known standard; and the method was remarkably accurate. On the Continent it is still used fairly universally for assaying, but in Great Britain the "cupulation" method (for gold) and the "titration" method (for silver) are now used; these methods, which are reported to be accurate to the nearest 0·01 per cent, are described on page 51.

Henry III's decree meant that all silver had now to be brought to Goldsmiths Hall in London for testing, even if the article concerned had been made hundreds of miles away across the country. For almost two hundred years unfortunate provincial goldsmiths ran the gauntlet of robbers and murderers as they brought their goods to London to be tested; then, in 1423, seven provincial towns were set up as alternative controls. These were Newcastle-upon-Tyne, York, Coventry, Lincoln, Norwich, Bristol and Salisbury.

The leopard's head punchmark, guaranteeing that the metal had been tested and found to be of true quality, was first applied in 1300. Other marks were gradually introduced. The "lion passant" mark, for example, was first applied to silver in 1544, to guarantee that it was of "sterling standard" (since it is too soft to withstand commercial use, silver is commonly alloyed with copper; the sterling silver standard is 92·5 per cent silver to 7·5 per cent copper). Various derivations for the name "sterling" have been suggested, among them that the name came from the Easterlings—the German metalworkers who were brought over to England by Henry II, and who had a great influence on British silver. The Britannia mark was compulsory from 1697 to 1720, during which period the standard for plate had to be raised to 95·8 per cent pure silver. There was such a scarcity of silver in the country at that time that people had been melting down silver coins or chipping pieces off their sides. To this day anyone who wishes may have silver made to this higher quality and marked with a figure of Britannia.

Assaying Today

The present-day Assay Office in Goldsmiths Hall is like a complicated laboratory, where quite the most modern and efficient methods are used to test the metals.

About four million articles are sent to Goldsmiths Hall in London for assaying and marking each year (every article must be complete). Most are sent before they have their final polishing, so it is inaccurate to visualize Goldsmiths Hall filled with brightly polished silver goblets and shimmering golden jewellery; they look dull and rather disappointing on the whole.

The first operation is to weigh each article. This is most important because a minute amount will be taken from it for testing, and this must be duly returned to the owner at the end.

Once weighed, the article goes to the drawing department. The name has nothing to do with members of staff taking quick sketches of the item; instead minute scrapings are drawn off every moveable or jointed section (Fig. 3). A plain gold wedding ring is made in one piece, and would only have one tiny scraping taken from it, but a gold bracelet might have twenty links and each link must be tested in turn. Taking these samples is a highly skilled operation, for it is imperative that the metalwork is not damaged.

The weighing machines are again brought into play, for the samples must also be accurately weighed. Then they are tested (Fig. 11).

If the article being tested is **gold**, the assaying method differs very little from that

Fig. 3 and Fig. 4: the Worshipful Company of Goldsmiths was incorporated in A.D. 1327, though the craft had been practised in Britain for many centuries before that and it seems likely that the goldsmiths of Saxon towns and medieval cities had banded together for mutual protection long before the actual date of incorporation. The Company has long been associated with the maintaining of high standards of workmanship, and it is a measure of the high esteem in which the Goldsmiths were, and are, held that they came to be appointed to check the coin of the realm, and to test and approve with special hallmarks the standard of the metal used in almost every gold or silver artefact offered for sale in Britain, thus protecting both craft and patron. In the upper illustration a minute scraping is being taken from a small gold cross (this has already been weighed); it is skilled work, for the article must not be damaged. The scraping is also weighed (the exact amount must eventually be returned to the owner), and then tested to see if the metal is up to standard. If it is not, the article is broken up and returned to the maker. If it is, the article is hall-marked (as in the lower illustration) with the current date-letter, the town mark, the maker's mark, and the quality mark. Great care is taken to ensure that the article is not damaged in the process. With very few exceptions, every gold or silver article offered for sale in Britain must by law be tested and approved by the Company.

By courtesy of the Worshipful Company of Goldsmiths

his is the booke that Euax the kynge of Arabye
sente to Tiberie the Emperour. of rome of all ma
ner of precious stones. aswell of theire names and
vertuous. as of theire coloures and of the cuntreyes that they
ben founden m. And how ye shall knowe them by prouyng &
assayeng & And also he sayeth. that no man shoulde be m doub
te of. that god hath sett and put great vertu m. As m worde
stone and herbe. by the whiche yf yt so were that men wer not
m mysbileue. and also owte of fowle synnes that many and won
derfull maruaylles myght be wrought thurgh there vertuous
and so men shoulde take these stones for a precious treasure and

described by Samuel Pepys in his diary on May 19, 1669. The scrapings are wrapped in small sheets of lead with pieces of fine silver, and placed in cupels—cup-shaped depressions in a refractory block. This is then fired to a temperature of 1,100 degrees Centigrade. The lead and any base metals are oxidized and leave behind a bead of pure gold and silver. This bead is flattened and rolled. The silver is dissolved by boiling the bead in nitric acid, the gold is weighed, and the gold content of the sample is calculated.

If the article being tested is **silver**, the titration technique is used. Basically, the silver is dissolved in nitric acid, and an iron nitrate indicator is then added. An exact quantity of ammonium thiocynate is titrated. This results in the formation of a silver salt, silver thiocynate, which sinks to the bottom of the test jar. A known quantity of ammonium thiocynate will combine with a known quantity of silver. Thus it is possible to compare the solution with a standard sample, to discover if there is either too much or too little silver for the ammonium thiocynate. In this way one can calculate the exact percentage of silver in the article.

If an article is not up to standard (and no tolerance at all is permitted), it is broken up before being returned to the maker. Exceptions are made in the case of imported

A lapidary dating from A.D. 1513: one of the 32 still extant in Great Britain, the property of the Worshipful Company of Goldsmiths. The principal source of this lapidary is believed to be the famous medieval manuscript of Marbode, Bishop of Rennes (A.D. 1067–1081), which in turn is derived from the Hellenistic lapidary of Damigeron— although the Goldsmiths manuscript, following Damigeron, names Tiberius, whereas the Marbode manuscript names Nero. The lapidary describes the medical and magical properties of sixty gemstones, and is a fascinating source of examples of the belief, which persisted through thousands of years, that gemstones have intrinsic powers. Medieval jewellery, like much of the work of earlier centuries and cultures, was profoundly influenced by this belief, the gemstone being valued as a curative or talisman rather than for its beauty or richness; its monetary value was very much a secondary consideration. As the manuscript says: "No man should be in doubt of that God hath set and put great virtue" in gemstones and that were it not for the foul sin- fulness of man "many and wonderful marvels might be wrought through their virtues". Men should thus regard gemstones as "a precious treasure". The lapidary is said to have been sent to Tiberius, Emperor of Rome, by Evax, King of Araby, and to describe "all manner of precious stones, as well of their names and virtues as of their colours and of the countries that they are found in. And how you shall know them by proving and assaying—" Such beliefs were to persist into the seventeenth century A.D.—the number of lapidaries actually increased in the sixteenth century for they were so closely derived from classical sources that they were not radically affected by the Renaissance advances in scholarship.

By courtesy of the Worshipful Company of Goldsmiths

articles which are to be returned abroad, or in the case of foreign gold or silver which is more than one hundred years old. Over four million items are assayed each year in London alone, and even today quite a few pieces are smashed and returned to their maker as being below standard.

Hallmarking Today

Once passed, an article is hallmarked (Fig. 4). The hallmark is the proof that the article is genuine, that it has been tested by the Assay Office and found to comply with all the laws and regulations. The penalties for offences against the law are very strict, and forging a hallmark still carries a maximum penalty of fourteen years in prison. It must be conceded that it is some time since the wardens of Goldsmiths Hall have deported or imprisoned anyone, or even sliced off both their ears and put them in a pillory—but they still have their powers.

Most jewellery made in England, from 1300 to the present day, was and is obliged by law to carry a hallmark which guarantees the metal's quality. The laws are rather confusing, and in some cases complicated, but one fact stands out as being of prime importance—owning unmarked jewellery is not an offence against the law, but selling it is (or even offering it for sale). Should an owner wish to sell an unmarked piece, he should have it hallmarked at once. Hallmarks need *not* be applied at the moment of making, but *must* be applied before the moment of selling. Naturally in such a case the hallmark would give a contemporary date, not the date of actual manufacture, for each date-letter punch is destroyed at the end of its yearly period to prevent any suggestion of forgery. If the piece were an antique, its value would be considerably reduced by the modern date-letter, but at least it would now have a mark and be saleable.

Should the owner of a piece of jewellery be concerned by its lack of marks, he or she could easily have it assayed and marked at Goldsmiths Hall. The cost is ridiculously low, well under £1 for each article and often merely a few pence.

There are, however, **exemptions**, and certain articles may be offered for sale even though they are not hallmarked. Some chains are exempt—watch-chains, Alberts, dress-chains, key and fob chains; but almost all other chains—bracelet chains, for example, or necklace chains, or chains of office—have to be marked. A charm bracelet would have to be assayed and marked, and so would every charm attached to it. On the whole, anything made of silver or gold which weighs less than 10 dwt (10 pennyweight) and which is extremely small and thin is exempt—but *both* conditions must be fulfilled for the exemption to be granted. Jointed sleeper earrings are a case in point, and so are certain finger rings (all wedding rings, however, have to be marked). Leniency is also shown to any gold article "so richly engraved, carved or chased or set with jewels or other stones as not to admit of an assay to be taken or a mark to be struck thereon without damaging, prejudicing or defacing the article".

Generally speaking, however, an article which has been assayed and passed is now marked with the date-letter of the current year, the town mark, the maker's mark and the quality mark. These marks are made by punches which are struck with a hammer to impress the mark into the metal. In the past hallmarking was a rather hit and miss procedure, but nowadays there is an infinite variety of shaped beds (some made of plastics) on which individual articles can be placed so that they will not be damaged when marked.

In Great Britain there are four legal standards for gold: 22 carat, 18 carat, 14 carat and 9 carat. The carat system is merely a method of expressing the proportion of gold to other metals used in the particular alloy of which the article is made. Pure gold is 24 carat; thus 22 carat gold is made up of 22 parts gold mixed with 2 parts alloying metal; and so on. There is nothing in the law to prevent a jeweller from selling 13 carat gold, for instance, but since such an alloy does not quite reach the standard of 14 carat gold, it will be marked down to 9 carat. The law does, however, make it illegal to sell gold articles in Britain if the standard is below 9 carat.

Silver apart, a variety of metals can be used to alloy gold; copper, for instance, nickel, zinc, cadmium, iron and aluminium. Each of them gives a slightly different colour to the resulting metal, and slightly different wearing qualities. Red gold is alloyed with copper, green gold with silver and cadmium, white gold with nickel or palladium, blue gold with iron, purple gold with aluminium, and lilac gold with zinc. Copper is added to strengthen the metal, so that pins or snaps, for instance, which are constantly in use might well be made of red gold; whereas silver is softer, and an alloy of gold and silver would be preferable if one wanted the resulting metal to have sculptural qualities and general malleability.

Every part of the article must pass the testing by the Goldsmiths—from the gold sheet and gold wires to the solders which join them together. Once this has been done, the carat mark and the other marks can be applied.

The **quality marks on gold** are a little complicated. If the article being marked is made from gold of the highest commercial standard—22 carat—it is marked with the number 22 in a shield, and with a second separate mark showing a crown in a shield. If the article is made from 18 carat gold, it is marked with an 18 in a shield, and with the crown in a shield as before. If it is made from 14 carat gold or 9 carat gold, it again carries two marks, the first being the carat number in a shield, and the second a number which shows the percentage of gold in the alloy. So an article made from 14 carat gold would have two shield marks, the first containing the number 14 and the second the figures ·585.

In years gone by, different regulations were in force, and different standards of gold. From 1477–1576 the minimum legal standard was 18 carat; from 1576–1798 it was 22 carat; and from 1798–1854 it was back to 18 carat again. In 1854 additional standards were introduced—9 carat, 12 carat and 15 carat. This lasted until 1932 when the present-day regulations of 9, 14, 18 and 22 carats were brought into force.

There are two legal standards of silver which are indicated by the quality mark. **Sterling silver**, already mentioned, is the minimum standard allowed by law, and is 925 parts pure silver to 75 parts other metal, the alloying metal generally being copper. The higher standard occasionally used since 1697 (and compulsory during the years 1697–1720) is **Britannia standard silver**, which is 958 parts pure and is carefully marked with an extra mark. Continental standards vary considerably, and the quality may be very much lower. If less than 5 dwt (5 pennyweight) of silver is used in a piece of jewellery, it need not be hallmarked, but it must still be of sterling quality.

Unlike gold, which does not tarnish, silver often turns black on the surface as a result of sulphur dioxide in the atmosphere. To prevent this silver used often to be plated with gold. Nowadays it can be protected with a coat of modern transparent lacquer (as long as it is not subject to wear or heat) or silicone, or it could even be plated with a rhodium-based alloy.

The **town mark** on silver or gold indicates the place where it was assayed. In the past there have been quite a few towns other than London which have had assay offices, but nowadays there are only three: Birmingham, Sheffield and Edinburgh.

The **date-letter** changes annually, though the date of the actual change varies from one assay office to another; at Goldsmiths Hall in London, it changes each May, the old punches being destroyed to prevent any possibility of fraud. It consists of a single letter of the alphabet—a variety of forms is used—enclosed in a shield (different shapes of shield are also employed). With few exceptions, the letters follow in sequence through the alphabet year by year, the type of letter and the shape of the shield remaining the same until a new alphabet is begun.

By 1363 every master goldsmith was required to have his own distinguishing **maker's mark**. In early days this could be a simple motif—a flower, an animal, a cross—or a series of symbols which punned on the maker's name: Mr. Fishman, for instance, would use a fish-and-man mark. By 1720, however, a new Act had been passed decreeing that all former marks be destroyed and that a maker's mark should consist of the initial letter of his given name and the initial letter of his surname—this Act is still in force.

One may encounter a number of other marks (such as the duty mark which had to be marked on silver between 1784–1890, to give a single example), and these may be checked against one of the excellent books now in print.

Substitutes for Gold and Silver

Christopher Pinchbeck, who lived from 1670 to 1732, was a watchmaker from Fleet Street who gave his name to a substitute for gold. He experimented with metals in order to produce an expensive-looking watchcase which could be marketed cheaply, and evolved an alloy which looked like gold but had no gold in it at all, being composed of 83 parts copper to 17 parts zinc. **Pinchbeck**, as it was called, was much lighter in weight than gold, but appeared just as durable. It was immediately used for making watchcases, but was taken up more enthusiastically by the makers of jewellery.

Pinchbeck was not, however, much used after 1817, the year in which **rolled gold** was invented. It was made in exactly the same way as Sheffield Plate, which is described in the next section. The base metal was sandwiched between two slices of gold; and the sandwich was worked under great heat until the three layers became fused together; the fused material was then rolled under great pressure—hence its name—until the sheet was exceptionally thin. As rolled gold is not pure, it cannot be hallmarked, but it *can* reach a recognized standard; 9, 10, 12 and 14 carat rolled gold are "the more usual qualities" according to Johnson Matthey, the largest bullion firm in England. It is also offered by them in three slightly differing colours: red gold, yellow gold, and white gold.

In the past, the quality of rolled gold was not controlled, and some articles were made which were of such exceptionally poor quality that the gold surface was polished off almost at once. But in 1960 a British standard was agreed, and it was suggested that marks should be applied to rolled gold articles also, to show the quality and quantity of the gold used in their manufacture. It is to be hoped that the trade will eventually agree universally to these conditions.

The techniques of **gilding**, **electro-gilding** and **hard gold-plating** are used in the manufacture of present-day watches and costume jewellery, but will not be dealt with in this book.

During the eighteenth century one of the substitutes used for silver in the making of jewellery and ornaments—especially buttons—was **Sheffield Plate**. In 1743, entirely by accident, Thomas Boulsover invented it and hardly realized he had done so—and certainly never took commercial advantage of it. He happened to be a cutler by trade and was repairing a knife which was made of both copper and silver. By some extraordinary mischance he fused the metals together—and immediately realized how simple it was to do so (metals usually react in completely different ways to heat, and it was a total surprise to discover that silver and copper reacted in so similar a way that they could be bonded together). Until this time silver had been an expensive luxury, reserved for the wealthier class of person; now it seemed as though it might be possible to produce a silver substitute at a lower price. The technique used involved sandwiching copper between two sheets of silver (the first experiments were made with only one sheet of each metal), fusing them together in intense heat, and then rolling them out to the required thickness. In 1830 Sheffield Plate was superseded by George Elkington's developments in the use of **electro-plating**—which, however, was not used for precious jewellery.

Platinum

Platinum is one of a group of six associated metals. The "heavy platinum metals" are platinum itself, osmium and iridium; the "light platinum metals" are ruthenium, rhodium and palladium.

Platinum is extremely heavy for jewellers' uses, and so is mainly employed in rings. It is exceptionally strong, it does not tarnish, and it is remarkably malleable and ductile. It was not used generally until after the middle of the nineteenth century because of its very high melting point. (Throughout metallurgical history, a metal's melting point has been crucial to its development.)

Unlike silver, which is easily worked, platinum when first discovered proved to be an enigma—almost a nuisance. The first discoveries were made in South America where the metal was christened *platina*, the diminutive of the Spanish word for silver, since although it would not behave like silver, it was the same colour. It was first written about in 1731. Ten years later some was sent to England for scientific investigation. The metal was then known only in the form of small grains, and it took some time before the workers discovered how to consolidate them. In 1789 platinum is for the first time recorded as being used for a ceremonial vessel; the first platinum chalice was given to Pope Pius VI. Luckily in 1847 an American scientist called Robert Hare invented the oxy-hydrogen blowpipe, which meant that platinum could now be worked with relative ease, because of the higher temperatures which could be achieved.

From the time of its discovery until 1916, the principal sources of platinum were in South America (mainly in Columbia). Since 1832 it has been known to exist in the Urals. The main present-day sources are Canada and South Africa.

Palladium was first isolated in 1802. It is not very popular with jewellers, in spite of the fact that it is both lighter and cheaper than platinum, and is mainly used for the settings of diamond rings.

Rhodium is harder and whiter than platinum, and is the most reflective of all the platinum metals. Jewellery made from platinum or from white gold is often plated with rhodium as it is so hard.

A campaign to ensure that platinum articles should be hallmarked to guarantee that the quality of the metal had been tested and approved was initiated in the early nineteen-seventies, and this seems likely to be enforced. The suggested mark is an orb surmounted by a cross.

Craftsmanship: the Middle Ages to the Present Day

It is a measure of the great repute in which the Goldsmiths were held that they came to be appointed to check the coin of the realm, to assay gold and silver and guarantee its quality, to hallmark artefacts as a proof that the metals used in their making had reached the standards required by law. But they had and have other activities and other duties—the activities and duties, in fact, that were common to the medieval craft guilds: to oversee the training of those who wished to practise the craft, to keep records, to care for their members in time of trouble, to keep up a spirit of charitable and educational enterprise, to promote trade, to maintain proper standards of craftsmanship.

During the Middle Ages, most of the arts were exquisitely refined because the craft guilds established, and rigidly maintained, such high standards. Naturally the goldsmiths, whose art held the premier place at that time, had to ensure that an apprentice underwent a training which produced an experienced and highly skilled worker, and which ensured that the craft would not be brought into disrepute. Apprentices were bound to their masters at Goldsmiths Hall and their names entered in a register (the earliest dates from 1444). It was by no means easy to secure an apprenticeship. The company took an interest in the apprentices during their seven years' service. When they had served their full term and produced an approved "master's piece" they became freemen, being given the Freedom of the Goldsmiths Company and the Freedom of the City of London. Five and a half centuries have passed since the heyday of the craft guild, but the standards and the general system of apprenticeship to the company are unchanged, though the period of apprenticeship has been cut to five years, minor rules and regulations alter with contemporary conditions, and the introduction of machines has cut down the endless time that the medieval apprentice spent on chores.

There was indeed a period when it seemed as though the introduction of machinery would permanently change the character of the craft. Until the nineteenth century all jewellery was basically made by hand, although at times some mechanical processes were involved. But the advent of the Industrial Revolution meant that machines, still very much in their infancy, were introduced to the jewellery trade, and stamped metal components produced in their thousands. This upset the purist for two reasons: first, it meant that a piece of jewellery was no longer individually created for a particular patron or customer, and secondly, the limitations of machine production imposed rather crude designs and finishes.

But this was changed by the great international upheavals of the two world wars, which undoubtedly altered completely the concept of using machines in the production of jewellery. The switch to wartime needs meant that workers got, for the first time, a thorough engineering training; and when peace came they carried on experimenting with basic engineering concepts and developed such techniques as centrifugal casting, which had not been much used before in the trade. The balance was redressed: the craftsman made use of the machine, rather than the machine dictating to the worker; jeweller and machine worked in harmony.

For the jeweller's role too has changed—or rather, has come full circle. The medieval craft guilds saw to it that the members of their craft were skilled and experienced in execution; the Renaissance was to bring that craftsmanship to a supremely beautiful flowering. It is impossible to give any accurate date for this magnificent period; one cannot say "It began in the year X and finished in the year Y"; but in the fifteenth and sixteenth centuries of the second millennium A.D. there occurred a shift in ways of thinking and acting and experiencing that was to affect every climate of opinion—social, religious, political. A new commercial prosperity, a new sense of independence and freedom, a new enterprise thrusting men out to explore and discover, a new feeling for the importance of classical scholarship, a new interest in learning, a new delight in the antique, new influences shaping the arts: all these were facets of what men came to call the Renaissance—the Rebirth.

The Renaissance raised the position of the artist to a level never known before—and he was not only an artist, he was also a craftsman. And prime among artists and craftsmen was the goldsmith. Renaissance artists were often trained as goldsmiths first, artists second—Lorenzo Ghiberti (1378–1455), the great Florentine artist, sculptor and goldsmith, is a good example. The jewellery of the Renaissance period is immensely satisfying because this was a time when the artist was a trained craftsman who really understood the metals and gemstones he was using; and equally the goldsmith was an artist who could appreciate and correctly interpret every line or colour in a design. The artist was, moreover, expected to be an educated man. His designs for jewels became witty, elegant, thought-provoking, personal. Many of the supreme artists created beautiful works of art in gold, which were later melted down by wealthy patrons, and they turned in fury from goldsmithery to painting on canvas, a virtually worthless medium, commercially speaking, which therefore stood a better chance of survival.

Ever since the Renaissance the design of a piece of jewellery has been of paramount importance. But as the splendour of the Rebirth faded, this emphasis on design led to a split between the artists who designed jewellery but who were not necessarily craftsmen, and the craftsmen who made jewellery from those designs but who were not necessarily educated men or artists. Broadly speaking, this was the position during the seventeenth and eighteenth centuries, before the advent of the machine. That is why in fifteenth- and sixteenth-century jewellery one sees the nucleus of all that was really worthwhile.

Yet now the Renaissance condition happily again prevails. Since the Second World

War, a jeweller has been trained to be both artist and craftsman, as well as being an educated man. When a modern jeweller sets out to make a piece of jewellery, the design is of the first importance. There is always a concrete reason behind each design: it may be a personal design made for a patron, influenced by his or her interests, personality, and ideas on colour and size; or it may have to incorporate some given stone which has to be suitably set; or it may be for a certain market or even a certain price range. Whichever the reason, the design has to conform to it—even if the brief is for some wildly extravagant eccentricity. Very often several designs are submitted from which the patron makes a choice, and equally often the chosen design is then made up with the stones embedded in wax to give a correct three-dimensional appearance, so that the cost of the piece can be worked out and agreed upon.

The craftsman at the bench then studies the design and collects, or is issued with, the raw materials for the piece. In the past everything had to be done by hand, from the hammering and annealing of the gold to the making of the catches. Nowadays the jeweller can easily buy sheet metal from the bullion dealers, together with solders, fasteners and so on, and adjust any inconsistencies with his hand tools. The basic tools have been unchanged for centuries—one can see them illustrated in the woodcuts and paintings of the past ages: the craftsman seated at his cup-shaped bench, surrounded by the hammers and drills, the saws and files, that are still in use today, with the sheepskin hanging below his work to catch anything he might drop. Some power tools have now, however, been added.

Almost no article of jewellery is ever made in a single piece. If one looks at it very carefully, one sees the separate sections which have been made and then soldered together. One of the most painstaking of hand-made items is a wide-meshed gold bracelet of the kind known as Milanese work—especially an enamelled Victorian one. Each tiny link is made by hand, enamelled and assembled; it may even be given a final textural finish with an added pattern of punch-marks. After all this, it is polished in several stages with jeweller's rouge, and then finally cleaned.

Once the metalwork has been assembled, the stones are put into their settings (no easy task this, for each type of stone reacts differently to being held) which are chosen to show them off to their best advantage, as well as to hold them securely. Finally, the jewel is housed in a leather case lined with velvet and stamped in gold with the maker's name. It is unwise to abandon the case, which is designed to keep the jewel clean, static and secure. The value of antique jewellery rises considerably if it is offered for sale in its original case, for though the case itself is worthless, its existence means the jewel has been properly cared for all these years.

CHAPTER FOUR

Medieval England

Norman and Plantagenet—The Gothic—A Line of Kings—Fourteenth and Fifteenth-Century Fashion: Gothic Enamelling, *En Ronde Bosse*—The Visual Impact—Orders of Chivalry—Sumptuary Laws—Medieval Jewels: *Enseignes*; Secular Badges; Necklaces; Brooches and Clasps; Rosaries; Posy Rings

Norman and Plantagenet

In 1066 the last successful invasion of England took place, and Normans and English clashed near Hastings. "In the English ranks the only movement was the dropping of the dead," wrote the chronicler; but they lost the day, and on Christmas morning their new lord, William the Norman, was crowned at Westminster.

William and his Normans were descended from the Vikings who in the tenth century, driven back from Alfred's England, had seized a stretch of Francia and settled there, absorbing the Frankish-Gaulish tribes whose land they had rapt away—and absorbing also any fighting men willing to enrol in their mighty and disciplined force. There too they adopted the Christian faith, building great monasteries and solid Romanesque churches: a style of building that they brought with them into England. Efficient, energetic, ruthless: once William had England he set about securing her, distributing almost all her lands to his own followers, on clearly stated terms. The lords and the great churchmen bound themselves to render feudal service to the Crown, swearing to pay fixed dues to the king and to keep ready, against his summons, a fixed number of fighting men; and then in turn divided their lands among vassals who were bound both to their immediate feudal lord and—so that the lords could not call out their vassals against the Crown—above and beyond him, to the king himself. The peasants too were bound into this rigorous pattern, it being their part to render specified services, in act or in kind, to their lords. William went so far as to have a survey made of every manor and every village in his realm, every feudal holding he could tax, every wood, every mill, every man. The English called it the Domesday Book because it was like the great Day of Judgment (*dom* being the Anglo-Saxon word for "judgment")—there was no appeal against it. By the time of his death in 1087 William had made England a strong, disciplined and feudal land. Her borders were secure—Norman castles planted all through Wales, and Welsh rebels driven back into the hills, the Scots and the Norsemen thrust back beyond Northumbria, the Danes thrust back from the eastern coast—and she herself was linked firmly to the European mainland, and to the western European civilization.

After William came his two sons, William Rufus and Henry I; and then the agony of civil war ("Men said that Christ and His saints slept") in the long battling between Henry's daughter, Matilda, and his nephew, Stephen, until a compromise was reached, and Matilda's son, Henry Plantagenet, named as Stephen's successor, was crowned king amid great rejoicing in 1154. The founder of the Plantagenet House, which was to rule in England for over three hundred years, he held all England and half France and was the richest king in Europe.

From Henry the crown passed first to his Crusader son Richard I, then to Richard's younger brother John. When John died in 1216, a year after the sealing of Magna Carta, the country was again ravaged by invading armies, and his son, the nine-year-old Henry III, was crowned in haste at Gloucester Abbey with a golden bracelet of his mother's. The reign thus precariously begun was to last fifty-six years and to see the finest flowering of the Gothic Age in England.

The Gothic

By the twelfth century A.D., after centuries of restlessness—migrations, raiding, plundering, shifting boundaries, shifting peoples—Europe was settling into a pattern of frontiers. People began to build: not simply defensive castles and great abbeys, but cities—trading cities, whose craftsmen banded together in guilds. The middle classes were emerging. In spite of the long periods of civil struggle, in spite of the everlasting foreign wars, in spite of the monetary drain of the Crusades as the lords and the devout went crusading to free Jerusalem (the first crusade set out in 1096, the seventh in 1270), trade took root. Very gradually a new class of person was coming to the fore: the merchant with a little money to spare. Throughout the Plantagenet period, from the twelfth century clear through to the sixteenth, the king and his court were of supreme importance as patrons of the crafts and arbiters of fashion; throughout this period too, the influence of the Church was immense; but none the less, at least *some* pieces of jewellery came to be made for "ordinary" people, the commercial class, rather than the nobles and the ecclesiastics.

With this gradual change in the patterns of life there had come, in the thirteenth century, the gradual emergence of a new art style: the Gothic. Its heyday in England was the reign of Henry III (1216–72), and undoubtedly the king's character was of great importance in this flowering. Though unquestionably foolish and spendthrift, he was also a devout and artistic man, a great church-builder, a garnerer of treasures, who did much to enrich his realm. His cousin, Louis IX of France, had built an exquisite Gothic masterpiece in Paris, Sainte Chapelle, which Henry admired so greatly that men said he wanted to put it in a cart and trundle it off to England; instead he began rebuilding Westminster Abbey, with a wonderful jewelled shrine where the Confessor's bones might lie.

The Gothic period was characterized by an upsurge of absolute joy in the arts, a plunging in, heart and soul, to enrich and glorify; but dominant above all the other arts at this period was undoubtedly that of the architect. This was the time when the great new cathedrals were being built all over Europe in an intoxicating burst of religious fervour, reaching forever upwards to heaven. Attempts were made to build the New Jerusalem, the "Heavenly City" of the Book of Revelation, jewelled, translucent, crystalline, in earthly terms. Stone and wood soared aloft into the echoing air, light streamed through richly stained glass bathing the fervent worshipper in an ever-changing glow, beeswax candles twinkled on the High Altar and in the smaller private chapels, their flames reflected in the gold and silver vessels and the jewelled reliquaries. (In the thirteenth century, Durandus actually promulgated theological reasons against the use of common materials—wood, horn, glass, brass—in the adoration of the Blessed Sacrament.) A man kneeling in worship at one of the great shrines was transported into another world, heady with incense, crammed with appeals that were calculated to delight his senses. These hypnotic effects must have made a lasting impression on him, teaching him that everything worthy stemmed from the Church with her great houses of worship and beyond her, from God in His heaven.

The English have always had an intense love of linear decoration, and in the full glory of the Gothic Age her architects and builders clustered their columns, filigreed their wooden screens, spread fan-vaults above their heads. They spent less time sculpting the outsides of their cathedrals than they did on enriching the interiors (the French being the other way about), carving and painting, gilding and embroidering—their church vestments were the finest in the known world.

With such a magnificent setting, it is understandable that the ecclesiastical jewels were equally splendid. The bishops' cope-clasps were among the most dramatic and decorative pieces ever made, and one of the loveliest is the **Founder's Jewel**, bequeathed to New College, Oxford, in 1404, by the college's founder, William of Wykeham, Bishop of Winchester.

The Founder's Jewel, a poem of mannered elegance, is a gilded and enamelled monogram, the letter M—for Mary—in Lombardic script. It looks like a church portal in miniature. The outer strokes of the letter are divided into compartments and set with *en cabochon* emeralds and rubies; the centre stroke is designed in the form of a vase of lilies (the flowers which are symbolic of purity, and which the Archangel Gabriel carries in medieval portrayals of the Annunciation); more lilies and pearls crown the letter. But the outstanding feature of the jewel is the way in which the two spaces between the strokes of the letter have been turned into tiny architectural niches with pierced tracery at the top. In these, facing one another, are two miniature yet beautifully modelled enamelled statues: on the right Mary herself, the Madonna, and on the left Gabriel, the Angel of the Annunciation.

A cope-clasp like the Founder's Jewel must have been seen by many awed worshippers. No doubt it influenced the more modest designs that simpler people purchased for their own adornment. The same "modelled" effect, like sculpture in miniature, can be seen on rings and brooches of the period. A raised gemstone might, for instance, have a setting of modelled beasts, like armorial supporters. The buckles men and women wore on their belts were intricately wrought, echoing the tracery in the stained glass windows.

It was during the Gothic period that the word "jewel" developed its present-day meaning. It came to us originally from the French *joyau* which was in turn derived from

61

the Latin *gaudiam*, both meaning "joy". Until the late fourteenth century the word was used in France for the royal table silver and the elaborate centre-pieces set on the king's board, but at about this time there was evidently a shift in its meaning, and it came to be applied instead, both in French and English inventories, to jewels which were worn on the person. The shift in meaning was a significant one, for the idea that a jewel is simply an adornment worn "on the person" completely does away with any need for a strong sustaining structure. Jewels alight like butterflies on a flower, and like butterflies, can be perfectly beautiful but wonderfully fragile. One does not expect to sit on a jewel as one sits on a chair; equally, of course, one does not expect it to crumple if touched—it should withstand wearing, but nothing more. Its strength and structure are relative to its function, which is simply to adorn, and this can be turned to good account by the designer, creating something as bright and delicate as a butterfly and, at its best, exemplifying the same perfection of craftsmanship.

A Line of Kings

Henry III's reign was also marked by the development of parliamentary power: it took civil rebellion to bring it about, but the principle that De Montfort and his rebel party groped towards, that the monarch should take counsel with the freemen of his realm, through their representatives in Parliament, was acknowledged by the king's own heir, the young Prince Edward: "That which touches all should be approved by all." It was a new indication of the gradual consolidation of the middle classes. In 1272 Edward succeeded his father; after him came his son, Edward II, and then his grandson, Edward III, whose love of the principles and ceremonies of chivalry exposed at once the generosity and gallantry of his character and its reverse, extravagance and self-indulgence. When Edward III died in 1377 the reign of chivalry seemed assured, for the crown passed to his ten-year-old grandson, Richard II, son of that paragon of knights, the Black Prince. But Richard grew into a devious and mercurial man, whose real ability and statecraft were counter-balanced by astounding recklessness, and in 1399 he was deposed by his cousin, Henry of Lancaster. The Lancastrians were to rule England for seventy years, through three reigns—Henry IV, Henry V, and the most saintly and honest of kings, gentle Henry VI, under whom the country plunged again into civil war with the long and bloody struggle of the Wars of the Roses. Edward IV, first of the Yorkist kings, the "Sun in Splendour", brought England a brief resurgence of ceremony and tournament, richness and pleasure; but his death in 1483 reopened the power struggle; his young sons vanished into the Tower; and his brother, Richard III, held the realm for two years only. In the summer of 1485 the Lancastrian claimant, Henry of Richmond, landed in England with an army at his back, and defeated Richard's forces at Bosworth Field. They found the crown of England in a hawthorn bush and set it on the victor's head, and a new royal house was founded, with a strange Welsh name: Tudor.

Fourteenth- and Fifteenth-Century Fashion

It was during the fourteenth and early fifteenth centuries that jewels came into their own as adornments: a time when the European courts were at their most extravagant.

The ceremonials and festivals were lavish, opulent, elaborate; and inventories and contemporary accounts make it clear that for the rich and privileged, luxury reached an almost unbelievable peak.

The fashions, fantastic and, in their silken brightness, almost lyrical, highlighted the extremity of refinement achieved by the High Gothic period, as well as the formal rigidity of court life. In the closing decades of the fourteenth century and the opening decades of the fifteenth, men and women alike wore garments which were extraordinarily exaggerated: ladies in high-waisted dresses with tight bodices and dangerously low necklines, their wide flowing sleeves and scalloped trains counter-balanced by elaborately tall conical head-dresses; men like preening peacocks in slender belted *houppelardes* padded across the shoulders and ballooning into leg-o'-mutton sleeves, parti-coloured hose fitting sleekly from thigh to ankle, long narrow shoes with thin points curling upwards from the toe—these were sometimes so long that they had to be looped up on chains which fastened neatly about the wearer's leg—and a variety of draped and elaborate headgear, amongst it the flapping cock's-comb hood. These garments were slit and puffed and embroidered for further garnishing (a hundred and fifty years later, in the Tudor period, people were even sewing gems on to their clothes to bedeck them yet further). Not only were the fashions outrageous and amusing, clearly signifying that their wearers were too rich and too well-born to engage in manual work; they were also in brilliant contrasting colours—vermilion, white, burgundy, violet, rose-scarlet—and made up in contrasting fabrics, so that glowing silks and brocades were juxtaposed with luxurious furs.

Yet however exciting the fashions, and however glittering the jewels, the two were not usually designed to complement one another; nor were the jewels necessarily designed for wear by one specific sex or with one specific garment. Men and women alike wore chains and rings and rosaries and gay jewelled girdles. A woman wore her girdle to gather in the loose folds of her gown and shape it to her figure, a man to emphasize his elegance—he did not necessarily wear it about his waist, either; in 1370, for instance, men were wearing their girdles so low about their hips that a series of small hooks had to be provided to keep the whole thing from falling off. Even if one could not afford an enamelled girdle set with gems, one might purchase a jewelled buckle to sew on a fabric belt: there is a most elaborate buckle-and-mordant in the Victoria and Albert Museum, exquisitely made in gold, with a Gothic foliaged design— the "naturalistic" Gothic style set leaf-and-flower motifs wreathing everywhere— incorporating a coat-of-arms, which is again characteristic of the time's passion for the heraldic. From a purely practical point of view, fashion did affect the types of jewellery that were in use: there was, for instance, no call for earrings when a lady's hair, shaved back to give her the desired high forehead, was tucked away out of sight in an elaborate head-dress; conversely, a wealthy court lady might wear a coif delicately wrought from gold netting caught up at each intersection with pearls (a Henry III fashion). In this atmosphere of supreme refinement of dress and decoration, splendid jewellery became a mark of prestige, and every conceivable accessory, from the coif to the toothpick, was enriched with gold and precious stones; fashion was an affair of highlights, dominated, like all decorative Gothic art, by colour and luminosity. Gemstones were still not faceted, but were so set that they would catch whatever light there was, in metalwork of such refinement that it too scintillated with light; and enamels, increasingly rich and luminous, heightened the whole effect.

GOTHIC ENAMELLING: EN RONDE BOSSE

With this access of court refinement and colour, fashions began to change rather more quickly, and craftsmen experimented with new adaptations of their old traditional techniques. In the last years of the fourteenth century, a new enamelling technique was to flower from one of these lines of experiment: *en ronde bosse*. This consisted of covering a gold core, which was worked in high relief, with layer upon layer of differently coloured opaque enamels. One can see this technique in some of the beautiful reliquary pendants that are still extant, adorned with tiny sepulchral scenes. There is also a set of early fifteenth-century brooches, now in the British Museum though believed to be of Germanic origin. These incorporate a number of motifs in the Gothic style, with its sophisticated and animated naturalism crystallizing into formal fantasies reminiscent of the heraldic emblems: an eagle, a small sculptured figure, two harts, a wreath of flowers, a star—all small, basically circular, exquisitely worked in gold with *en ronde bosse* enamelling, and framed in luminous pearls.

The Visual Impact

All forms of sculpture and carving were painted in the full brightness of the medieval period: everything was coloured and gilded, from a tiny ivory diptych to a great stone screen. Westminster Abbey, for example, cool and serene today, once rioted with colour; only a few traces still remain—gleams of alternate green and red on an archway; the wall paintings in St. Faith's Chapel, showing a gigantic St. Christopher mantled in lake colour against a ground of deep green sprinkled with roses, and St. Thomas, in yellow tunic and green mantle, thrusting his hand into the side of a blue-mantled Christ, all against a background of vermilion scattered with fleurs-de-lis; traces of paint on the altar screen (completed in 1440–41), more on the thirteenth-century Censing Angels high under the South Rose, more on the tombs. The place must once have been a bonfire of bright primary colour. The purpose of the visual arts was to decorate life, to adorn it, to heighten its splendour to the glory of God or man; it was not then viewed as something whose existence was its own justification. One collected art, as it were, for one's own self-aggrandizement—one did not contemplate it. Medieval art is extremely practical in its motives, and correspondingly sophisticated in its workmanship. Accordingly, there was as yet no distinction between the artist and the craftsman: a man was not one or the other, he was both. Accordingly, too, beauty was incidental to magnificence; decoration ran riot, becoming, at its finest, exquisite, and at its worst, finicky. Yet out of the extraordinary lavishness of the Burgundian court *fêtes*, with their parades of huge gilded and painted set-pieces, there came the serene work of Jan van Eyck (*circa* 1389–1441) who moved and worked in these court circles with their elaborate and luxurious trappings. Towards the end of the fourteenth century, pictorial art, once very stiff and formal, gradually developed a more representative and narrative style. Portraiture began: the painting of Richard II, which hangs now in Westminster Abbey, is the earliest known portrait of an English king. The king is also shown in the Wilton Diptych, which is now at the National Gallery in London, kneeling before the Virgin and Child. He is richly attired in a gown of brocade interwoven with gleaming gold, and wears a gem-studded golden crown, a heavy collar of gold and gemstones around his neck, and a jewelled badge showing the white hart, his own personal emblem, on his shoulder. An even greater interest in painting was to develop throughout the fifteenth century, when the court painters of Burgundy and the Netherlands—linked by commercial and political ties to England—were portraying in meticulous and supremely visual detail the life that was vibrating around them. This was not painting in the style of the Early Renaissance Italian masters, with their striving to show "the things beyond the eye and in the soul"; this was North European accuracy at its most scrupulous, in which the Archangel Gabriel is robed in brocades fit for any Burgundian duke and decked with a lavish display of jewels. The true freshness of van Eyck seems to the contemporary eye to derive from the landscapes and street scenes, charmingly intimate, which back the divine figures; but these are an incidental bounty—a detail added by the artist to the patron's general brief.

This new interest in pictorial art affected the jewels of the period, with their amazing refinement of detail, but also, above and beyond this, the enamelling techniques, for the craftsmen began to apply their glowing enamels like paint, using an artist's brush and developing the design with exquisitely careful strokes.

Orders of Chivalry

The fourteenth and fifteenth centuries also witnessed the emergence of innumerable Orders of chivalry and knighthood, the direct result of the medieval conception of chivalry—the ideal life of the man of honour, its rules governing his conduct both in love and in war, and shaping him in the image of the antique hero; the whole ideal centring on the Christian virtues of self-sacrifice, compassion, faithfulness, and so on. Towards the end of the fourteenth century and in the opening decades of the fifteenth the military significance of knighthood was gradually lessening as diplomacy was elevated into an art of its own; the various rulers tried to keep alive their personal prestige and the splendour of their courts by founding new Orders and Societies, all very splendid and dramatic—far more so than the actual deeds of the recipients. (Some knights travelled happily from court to court acquiring extra Orders on the strength of their past reputations.) A complete list of all the European Orders would fill several volumes (but who would read them?), most being long forgotten. They filled a need at the time, however, keeping alive the chivalric ideal and the stories of knighthood which continued to inspire men for many hundreds of years. Even today one may see the pride with which a regiment will buy back a cherished Victoria Cross some retired soldier has been forced to sell. People still go, even now, to admire the Chapel of the Order of the Garter at Windsor Castle, where hang the banners of the Garter Knights, the present members of that great company first founded by Edward III in 1348; and the Henry VII Chapel in Westminster Abbey, hung with the banners of the Knights of the Most Honourable Order of the Bath, founded by George I in 1725 but originating in the reign of Richard II. The brilliant banners, the heraldic supporters, the enshrining beauty of glass and stone, the atmosphere of religious and monarchial awe, can still stir the imagination; how much more forcible must it have been for the people of the Middle Ages, its images drawn from the actual life they saw about them—the tournaments, the ladies tossing favours, the king and his army riding out to war—just as they visualized God's angels decked in brocades and jewels, and the Archangel Michael as the first of knights, God's Champion downing the Devil. Exaggerated and elaborate as they became, the Orders kept up for many decades an ideal standard of manners and behaviour, and life would have been yet more brutal, and certainly far less colourful, without them.

Sumptuary Laws

In fourteenth- and fifteenth-century England each man had his place in the social scale, and his duties to those above him and, according to the chivalric and feudal ideal, those below him as well. Society was strictly layered: at the head, the king and his queen and his family, below him the nobles and the lords of the Church, many of them in frequent attendance at his court, below them the knights and the lesser churchmen, and below that again the freemen, in descending order of wealth and status; the peasants and serfs were at the bottom. In so far as they could do so, the freemen, especially the self-confident merchant class, aped the fashions of the king, his court and his lords, mirroring as best they could in their own lives his behaviour, his sports, his style of dress, his furnishings, his jewels. In some cases they did this so skilfully that there was a danger, slight but alarming, that they might outshine the king himself, and sumptuary laws were introduced to counteract this and to protect the organized system of society; a man had his place and he must not only be in it, he must be *seen* to be in it. These laws were stricter in France than in England, but in both countries were imposed to ensure, among other things, that the jewels a man or woman wore were suited to his or her rank. The Edward III Statute *De victu et vestitute*, introduced in 1363, laid down that merchants who owned goods to the value of £500 might wear clothes which were "reasonably" garnished with silver, and that their wives might wear head-dresses garnished with stones; this same rule applied to esquires worth in land or in rents 200 marks a year. Knights were not permitted to wear rings or brooches made of gold or jewelled with precious stones; handicraftsmen, yeomen and their families were allowed almost nothing that was precious. The royalty and nobility, on the other hand, owned more and richer jewels than ever, bringing them out on State occasions when they appeared in all their glory, *enseignes* in their hats, great chains spread from shoulder to shoulder, brooches, girdles and clasps, rosaries dangling from the hand, pendants swinging round the neck and rings blazing on the fingers.

Tomb sculptures are often splendidly illustrative of the fashion and jewels of the time, particularly towards the end of the period. There is, for example, the carved alabaster figure of Sir William de la Pole, Mayor of Hull and Baron of the Exchequer, who lies in Holy Trinity, Hull. Sir William, who died in 1367, seems to have won Edward III's favour by raising money for him—£76,180 by Midsummer 1339—and was rewarded with manors and the promise of wealthy husbands for his daughters. He looks like a Scandinavian, bearded, moustachioed, with thick hair almost to his

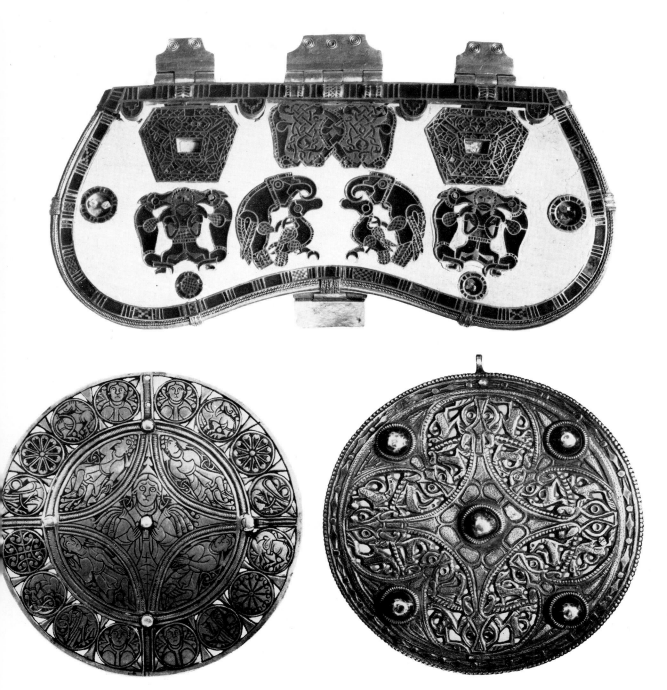

Three Saxon treasures from the British Museum: *Fig. 5*, a purse lid from the Sutton Hoo ship burial hoard, with characteristic Celtic zoomorphic motifs and intricate rhythmic patterning; *Fig. 6* (left), the Fuller Brooch, a *fibula* whose complex design plays on the numeral four, left and right being almost mirror images of one another, linked by a central figure, Sight, which is reminiscent of the Alfred Jewel; *Fig. 7* (right), the Strickland Brooch, sculptural interlaced design following the lines of Mediterranean tracery alternating with bezels for gemstones, the four-lobed central section resonant with movement and vitality disciplined by the external frame.

Fig. 8: A medieval rosary, now in the
Victoria & Albert Museum. The enamelled
gold beads are decorated with saints and
religious symbols, and inscribed round the
sides. Each decade consists of ten *ave* ("Hail
Mary") beads; the lozenge-shaped beads
represent the *paternoster* ("Our Father")
which opens a decade and the *gloria* ("Glory
Be") which closes it. Notice the big chunky
knop. *Fig. 9:* Magical rings from the Victoria
& Albert Museum, once so treasured that
they held inestimable psychological power.
The silver ring set with bone (lower right)
is 18th century; the others all date from the
15th and 16th centuries, the top two being of
horn mounted in silver and set with toad-
stones, the central one being horn mounted
with copper wire and having an engraved
silver bezel, the one to lower left being iron
set with a fossil tooth.

Fig. 10: A gilded statue of St. Dunstan, the 10th century goldsmith and archbishop who became patron of the craft, made in about 1680 for the Worshipful Company's Barge, and now in Goldsmiths Hall.

Fig. 11: Almost without exception, any gold or silver article offered for sale in Great Britain must first be tested at Goldsmiths Hall to ensure that the metal used is up to the approved standards.

Fig. 12: One of the touring exhibitions staged by the Worshipful Company of Goldsmiths to display world-wide the vitality and supremely high standards of the contemporary jeweller's craft.

Fig. 13: The badge of the Prime Warden of the Worshipful Company of Goldsmiths, in gold and enamel, set with diamonds, emeralds, rubies and sapphires, designed by Donald Abbott in 1954.

Fig. 14: St. Thomas More's reliquary pendant, dating from the early 16th century, and now at Stonyhurst, is approximately 2⅜″ in diameter, enamelled with a figure of St. George on one side, and Christ, His Cross and some of the Emblems of the Passion on the other. *Fig. 15:* The signs of the Zodiac, portrayed on talismanic jewels for thousands of years, here seen on the Great Clock at Hampton Court (here dismantled for cleaning).

Fig. 16: The Eworth portrait of Mary I, in 1554, with jewelled headdress and girdle, richly worked rings, a crucifix to emphasize her devotion to the Catholic cause, and the huge pearl, *La Pellegrina*, given to her by Philip of Spain (National Portrait Gallery).

Fig. 17: Elizabeth I portrayed by Hilliard, *circa* 1575–80, in a costume so stiff with gems that she looks like an icon and the enamelled Phoenix Jewel, pendant at her breast, is lost in a glitter of gold and pearls as thick as raindrops (National Portrait Gallery).

Two contrasting late Tudor jewels from the Victoria and Albert Museum both just over 3″ long: *Fig. 18*, the Pasfield Jewel, a sophisticated conceit in enamelled gold set with emeralds, containing toilet implements; and *Fig. 19*, the Tor Abbey Jewel, *circa* 1600, a *memento mori* pendant jewel, its cover painstakingly *champlevé* enamelled in spider-fine black lines, and an inscription round the sides reading "Through the Resurrection of Christe we be all sanctified."

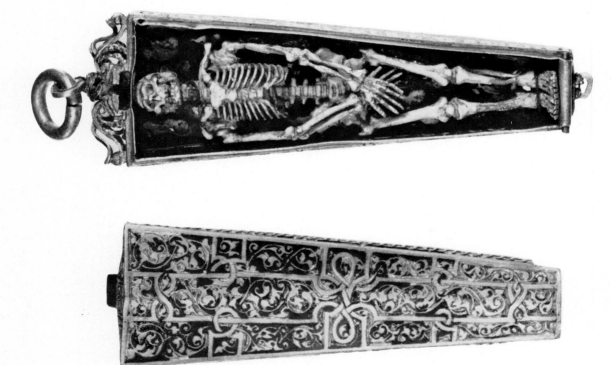

Fig. 20: An English 17th century agate showstone with engraved silver mounts. Such stones have been found in Merovingian and Dark Age graves, and were much prized as talismans and luck pieces.

Fig. 21: A gold pomander, dated 1679, and shaped like a skull, opening to reveal compartments for spices with a dividing plate inscribed "Man proposes but God disposes"; a *memento mori* conceit.

Two English jewels, late 16th century: *Fig. 22*, a *memento mori* gold coffin with Adam, Eve and the Serpent enamelled on the lid; and *Fig. 23*, a reliquary crucifix, traditionally owned by Mary, Queen of Scots, engraved with the Emblems of the Passion, and inscribed round the sides "Behold who suffere what and for whom he suffered."

Fig. 24: Miniature cases now in the Fitzwilliam, Cambridge, dating from the early 17th century (the upper one bears Anne of Denmark's monogram), exemplify the British love of linear decoration. Colourful enamelling and glowing gems are here equal in importance.

Fig. 25: In the early 17th century, Anne of Denmark, wife of James VI of Scotland, who became James I of England in 1603, popularized the wearing of *aigrettes* in the hair. Although the stiff, elaborate Jacobean fashions were to yield to the simpler, more dignified styles favoured by Charles I and Henrietta Maria, the fashion for *aigrettes* was later revived in the glittering diamond Court *toilettes* of the Hanoverians. Arnold Lulls, Anne of Denmark's Dutch Court jeweller, drew up many *aigrette* designs like the rather coarse flourishing one shown above left.

Fig. 26: A wax effigy from Westminster Abbey, showing Frances, Duchess of Richmond, one of the beauties of Charles II's Court, as she was at the end of her life, in the Court fashions of the turn of the century. She is portrayed wearing the robes and jewels in which she attended Anne I's Coronation in 1702, with a paste *demi-parure*: a three-loop necklace, drop earrings, sleeve-clasps, and a scrolled brooch ornament.

18th century jewels from Blooms: *Fig. 27*, rings, including a *marquise* ring—*post* 1760—upper right, and a bow ring (this, with the flower and star, was among favourite Georgian motifs) showing how designs gradually opened up and mounts became lighter; *Fig. 28*, earrings and pendants, exemplifying the Georgian love of diamond glitter; and *Fig. 29*, gold and diamond brooch and earrings from 1720, featuring a surprisingly early use of porcelain.

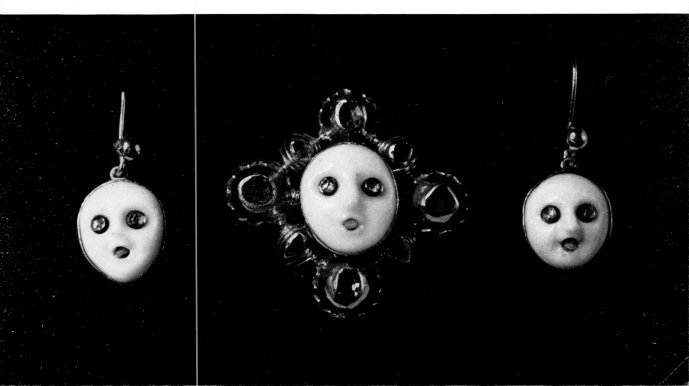

Échelles were sets of matching brooches exclusive to the Georgian era. They demonstrated the characteristic Georgian practicality as well as the equally characteristic love of a dramatic display of diamonds: a set might be worn round the hem of the gown for one ball, massed on the bodice for the next, stitched to the skirt panels for a third; then, when one tired of it, sent back to the jeweller, so that the metalwork could be melted down and the gems re-set to a new design. The three shown above left, in *Fig. 30*, are now in the Victoria and Albert Museum. Metal loops are incorporated at the back of each *échelle*, so that it could be sewn into place. The diamond bow was a popular Georgian motif: these three are very formal, and no attempt is made to represent a "natural" bow with inequal loops and trailing ends; none the less, they have a curving, three-dimensional look. In *Fig. 31*, the National Portrait Gallery's portrait of Caroline of Anspach, wife of George II, painted in about 1727 and assigned to the Studio of Charles Jervas, the Queen is wearing a most impressive set of diamond *échelles*. In addition, she is decked with pearls in the true Georgian style: tasselled strings of them looped round her waist, round her sleeves, and on her shoulders.

shoulders, a simple cloak, a jewelled sword belt. Beside him lies his patient wife, Catherine, her delicate face almost obscured by her elaborate head-dress.

Sir Edmund and Lady de Thorpe of Ashwellthorpe in Norfolk are richly dressed in the contemporary costumes of their period, some fifty years later than the hard-working Mayor of Hull (Sir Edmund died in 1417). Both are wearing the SS Collar of Lancaster, apparently worn by the most distinguished adherents of the Lancastrian cause after Henry IV seized the throne in 1399 (in earlier usage, it seems to have been a simpler affair of gilded latten Ss attached to a band of green leather, or some similar material, worn by members of the household of John of Gaunt, Duke of Lancaster, Henry's father); the Yorkists wore collars of suns and roses. The origin of the SS symbol is not known, though it may refer to the triple repetition of *SANCTUS SANCTUS SANCTUS* ("HOLY HOLY HOLY"), from the Mass (church vestments were not infrequently powdered with Ss), or from *SALVATOR* or even *SOVERAYNE*, which Henry IV used as his motto. The de Thorpe tomb sculpture shows that symbols of rank and allegiance were at this period far more important than personal and intimate jewels—for general display, at least—and illustrates the unisex nature of much medieval jewellery.

The tomb of Lady Benedicta Vernon in Tong, Shropshire, dating from 1451, shows her wearing a horned head-dress of extravagant proportions, its fabric held together with gold and jewels, a great many rings on the knuckle-joints of both hands, chains, an elaborate necklace, and decorative cloak-clasps; she evidently wanted the sculptor to portray her in full fig, awaiting the Resurrection as befitted her rank and station.

Medieval Jewels

ENSEIGNES

Enseignes were badges worn customarily in the hat or cap, and bought by pilgrims at the shrines to which they made pilgrimage. (Surviving examples are often mistaken for brooches.) They usually incorporated the emblem of the saint at whose shrine they were sold: the cockle shells of St. James (Santiago) of Compostela in northern Spain, St. Catherine's wheel, St. Victor's foot, St. Hubert's horn (he was one of the patrons of the hunt), St. Blaise's comb, St. Thomas of Canterbury's mitre. Canterbury was one of the great pilgrim shrines of medieval England and pilgrims who travelled there bought Canterbury *enseignes* of lead or pewter or brass, little memento bells, and tiny ampullas to fill with water from the holy well that was said to have been coloured with Becket's blood. Another great shrine was the priory of Walsingham in Norfolk, where a phial of the Madonna's milk was treasured (the shrine was destroyed at the Reformation). A forge for the working of metals existed there, and traces of this have been found; one can also see, at the British Museum and the Guildhall Museum in London, examples of *enseigne* moulds. The fashion persisted even after the Reformation, though now simply as a secular means of adorning the fashions of the nobility: there is, for example, a head-and-shoulders painting of Henry, Prince of Wales, dating from about 1604 and associated with Robert Peake, now in the Royal Collection at Windsor; it shows the prince in Garter robes, with three very elaborate openwork jewelled *enseignes* in the plumed hat of the Order.

F

SECULAR BADGES

Livery badges were worn by the members of any great medieval household, a sign of allegiance to the head of the house. He himself wore a magnificent jewelled affair, his wife and children rather smaller ones, and so on, down to the less important members of the household who wore inexpensive badges in base metal. The motifs featured in the design were taken from the lord's coat of arms and were as readily recognizable as his personal embroidered standard.

NECKLACES

The necklaces worn at this time fell into two general categories. The first were simple chains from which depended a pendant jewel, either religious in design, in which case it could be displayed over the clothes, or talismanic and tucked away out of sight. Contemporary inventories sometimes add the words *ad pendendum circa collum* beside the description of such jewels, indicating that they were worn about the neck, next to the skin where their magical powers might best benefit the wearer, instead of spread dramatically from shoulder to shoulder, curving steeply in between, like the jewels of the second category, the great chains of the Orders, with their pendant devices; one may get the effect from many of the Holbein portraits of Henry VIII.

BROOCHES AND CLASPS

Brooches were generally circular or wheel-shaped, sometimes with lobes. A familiar late medieval motif was that of clasped hands or hands folded in prayer. Many had engraved inscriptions carried out in *niello* enamelling; others were studded with stones *en cabochon*.

Belt buckles have already been mentioned. Cloak clasps were also worn, brilliantly colourful but heavy, as befitted practical contemporary jewellery.

ROSARIES

The use of the rosary dates back to the old practice of counting, or "telling" one's prayers with the help of a string of beads, the word "bead" itself coming from the Old English word for "prayer". We do not know exactly when the rosary devotion took its present definite shape, with its fifteen decades each dedicated to one of the fifteen Mysteries of the Virgin—five Joyful, five Sorrowful, and five Glorious—and each consisting of one *paternoster* (the Our Father), ten *aves* (Hail Maries) and one *gloria* (Glory Be); but a string of medieval rosary beads was usually made up of one larger bead followed by ten smaller ones, the bigger bead serving both as the *paternoster* to open each decade and the *gloria* to close the preceding one. Rosary beads were in use in England in the late fourteenth and throughout the fifteenth centuries. Chaucer's Prioress (*post* 1387) had a very gay set:

> "*Of smal coral aboute hir arm she bar*
> *A peire of bedes, gauded al with grene,*
> *And ther-on heng a broche of golde ful shene*
> *On which ther was first write a crowned A,*
> *And after,* Amor vincit omnia"

(Prologue to *The Canterbury Tales*)

68

Many more are listed in inventories and lists of property. The list of property of the Guild of Corpus Christi at York in 1465, for instance, mentions a great many carved coral rosaries, and the Scottish Royal Inventories of 1488 include a description of a gold one with 122 beads and a knop (the tassel, or stud, or short string of beads, often with a crucifix attached, dangling from the linked beads), which was inherited by the King of Scotland.

Luckily a magnificent example of a gold rosary (Fig. 8) does still survive—many were melted down or destroyed at the Reformation—and is now in the Victoria and Albert Museum. This belonged originally to the old Yorkshire Catholic family of Langdale, and was discovered in an old chest at Houghton Hall. It is made up of fifty *ave* beads of enamelled gold interspersed with six lozenge-shaped *paternoster* beads (these were also known as "gauds"), and a chunky rounded knop. Each bead is hollow, and is decorated on both sides with a figure or scene (St. Andrew, for example), together with an explanatory inscription in black letter, making the owner's devotions most varied and entertaining.

During the latter half of the fifteenth century the English seem to have begun to wear their rosaries about the neck, like a necklace; and gradually the word "bead" lost its prayer meaning, and the names for the individual beads, such as "gaud", became applied to the beads of an ordinary secular necklace.

According to Riley, whose *Memorials of London and London Life* were published in 1868, the names of Paternoster Row and Ave Maria Lane in the City of London indicate that the rosary-makers had their shops there in medieval times, though these have all been sadly swept away by time and the ravages of war. Among these rosary-makers there was, in 1381, a jeweller named Adam Ledyard, whose stock included *paternoster* beads of white and yellow ambers, coral, jet and silver-gilt, and *ave* beads of jet and blue glass, as well as cheaper sets in maplewood (this was the wood of which turned mazer bowls were made) and white bone for children. As has already been seen, costly rosaries were also made of gold, enamelled and *niello*ed.

POSY RINGS

A ring is probably the most significant of all jewels. One may consider, for instance, the papal rings, a bishop's ring, the coronation ring and the rings of investiture: symbols of tremendous authority. Consider too the simpler rings which are none the less invested with great private and personal significance: an ordinary wedding ring blessed in church, a nun's ring, or an engagement ring given by a man to a woman as a symbol of love and a promise of marriage—the fashion for these may be traced back to the ancient betrothal ring. Consider the signet ring's position in law. Consider the talismanic rings with their cabalistic inscriptions (Fig. 9) or the rings blessed by the medieval kings and worn by their subjects as a hopeful defence against cramp.

During the Middle Ages, and this must be quite clear, love had nothing whatsoever to do with marriage, which was a legal contract bound up with the proper distribution of family property. Courtly love was formalized, ennobled, made honourable. No gift between lovers was complete without an accompanying verse or motto, and perhaps a small bunch of flowers as well. The *motto* was called the "posy" (from the French *poésie* or "poetry"), and this name we now apply to the flowers—originally a "nosegay";

quite rightly, these charming bunches are still carried by bridesmaids at a wedding, though the old ritual is long forgotten. Many of those early gifts were intimate little jewels, on which were inscribed mottoes, or "posies", which spoke of love or the lover's qualities. There are still a good many posy rings in the museums of Britain; especially noteworthy ones are in the British Museum and the Victoria and Albert Museum. In the thirteenth and fourteenth centuries the inscriptions were generally in French—just occasionally in Latin—and were inscribed on the outside of the ring shank; if the outer surface was decorated, however, the inscription was engraved on the inside; and by the sixteenth century it customarily appeared there, whether the outer surface were decorated or not. During the fifteenth century a great many posy rings, bearing messages of love, seem to have been made in England, and examples can be seen in a good many European museums. They were originally in black letter—the elaborate Gothic-style script—but clear Roman capitals were later adopted, when the influence of the Renaissance reached England.

One fourteenth-century example at the Victoria and Albert Museum (Catalogue No. 624) is a silver parcel-gilt hollow hoop with six lobes, the letters of its motto

JE LE DE SIR

alternating with crowns. Another in the same collection (No. 658) was made in England in the sixteenth century and is a gold hoop inscribed on the outside

✠ MY WORDELY IOYE ✠ ALLE MY TRVST

and on the inside

✠ HERT THOUGHT LYFE AND LUST

The fashion continued throughout the seventeenth century, and amongst many other examples at the Victoria and Albert Museum is one (No. 674) inscribed

AS TRUE TO THEE AS DEATH TO ME

Sadly, by the end of the eighteenth century posy rings had died out of fashion completely. Just a few are recorded during the nineteenth century, but in general the inscribed rings of the Victorian period were mourning rings.

Perhaps the most famous reference of all appears in *The Merchant of Venice*:

> "*A hoop of gold, a paltry ring*
> *That she did give to me; whose posy was*
> *For all the world like cutler's poetry*
> *Upon a knife, 'Love me, and leave me not.'*"

CHAPTER FIVE

The House of Tudor

Introduction—Henry VII: The Age of Discovery; Treaties and Alliances
—Henry VIII: A Prince of Promise; Hans Holbein; Developments in
Design; Monogram Jewels; Diplomatic Interlude; The Reformation;
The King's Appearance; The New Use of Gemstones; Engraved Pattern
Books; Court Fashions in Jewellery; Tudor Portraiture; King Supreme—
Edward VI—Mary I—Elizabeth I: Gloriana; Treasures from West and
East; The Use of Diamonds; New Textiles, New Fashions; The Ropes of
Catharine; Pendants; Nicholas Hilliard; The Armada Jewel; An Amulet,
The Danny Jewel; Elizabeth's Rings—Mary, Queen of Scots

Introduction

The Tudor Age saw the monarch and people of England faced with two main problems,
both of which were to be solved through brute force and determination. The Tudor
monarchs had a very shaky claim to the throne and spent a hundred years consolidating
it; and the country as a whole fought hard to be recognized as an equal among the other
powers of Europe. It was a time of division and change; and these divisions, these
radical changes, were to have an immense effect on the course of jewellery's
development.

There was a religious division: the split between the Catholics, acknowledging the
ultimate religious authority of Rome, and the Protestant Reformers. The Reformation
in England was to sweep away the old Church patronage of the arts, generous if
conservative and authoritative, and with it the market for rosaries, reliquaries and other
religious jewels—for the great, for the merchant class, for the yeomen and even the
poor; it was also to result in the terrible destruction of much of the earlier work.

There was a sexual division, created by the fact that for the first half of this period
England was to be ruled by male monarchs, for the second half by a woman—equally
powerful, equally dominant, turning the face of fashion away from the male to the
female.

There was a stylistic division, created by the discoveries of new trading routes to Asia
and of a vast new continent, America, the New World. The finding of abundant supplies
of gemstones meant that the accent slowly changed from the creation of jewels like
enamelled gold sculpture in miniature to deeply glowing gems held in gold and silver.

Last, but by no means least, there was the development of printing, which made it possible for books of engraved patterns to be circulated all round Europe. This was to change the role of the goldsmith radically: originally the designer and creator of jewellery, he now began to work from other men's designs, adapting them to suit a patron's preference. His part was to diminish gradually in importance as the split between designer and craftsman widened further and further.

Here are turning points indeed.

During the Tudor Age, which covered the whole of the swashbuckling sixteenth century and overlapped at either end—from Henry VII's accession in 1485 to Elizabeth's death in 1603—jewels in England were large, important, dominant and dramatic. When the age began, they were unisex in content, as easily worn by a woman as a man, and often religious in design, feeling and purpose. Secular jewellery, in particular, showed the inspiration of the work being carried out in the Italian States, which had become centres for the Renaissance study of classical antiquity. The revival of classical scholarship dates back a long way before the opening of the sixteenth century—as a boy, the Italian Petrarch (A.D. 1304–74) had burned his medieval texts and studied instead Roman history and Virgil—but the siege of Constantinople which fell to the Turks in 1453 was to give the European revival of classical scholarship a particularly powerful thrust forward, for the philosophers and scholars of the city, seeing the steadily increasing threat of Muslim seizure, fled with their manuscripts to Europe, and found especial sanctuary in the courts of Italy's merchant princes.

The jewels of the early sixteenth century are still sculptural designs created in wrought gold and decorated with enamelled scenes. These were slowly to yield place to architecturally based patterns incorporating gemstones; and by the time Elizabeth died, these too had been replaced, by an extravagant profusion of scattered gems.

Extravagance, indeed, is one of the keynotes of the century. The very richness of the jewels worn by the men and women of the Tudor courts and the well-to-do merchant class was part of the deliberate statement made by monarch and nation, matching the splendour of their clothes and often contrasting completely with the depleted state of their personal finances. Everyone of any standing in Tudor England seemed to live according to the theme of the modern advertising executive: "It is essential to keep your name before the public." Whether there was money in reserve or not, the Tudor monarchs and their courtiers presented a brave front.

Henry VII

Henry VII took the crown of England by right of conquest in 1485, when he and his army defeated at Bosworth the forces of the last Plantagenet and Yorkist king, Richard III. Henry's "legal" claims to the throne were shaky in the extreme and he immediately set about reinforcing his position. He first secured a declaration from Parliament that the crown should "be, rest and abide in" him and his heirs, and then, only then, graciously consented to their petition that he marry Elizabeth, eldest daughter of Edward IV, the heiress of the House of York. Their marriage, uniting the two houses, closed at last the long and bloody struggles of the Wars of the Roses, and introduced into England the famous emblem of the Tudor Rose, red and white in the one bloom; however, Henry could not feel really secure until he had a son—luckily Elizabeth gave him two, Arthur and Henry—and even so the first decade of his reign was threatened by conspiracy, uprisings, and invasion. To keep his hold on the country, he needed to achieve her financial stability and to strengthen her administration. In the years to come the Tudor grip on the Crown tightened more and more; until Henry's son, Henry VIII, was able to dispose with increasing ruthlessness of any rival claimants and any rebellion against the royal authority.

At the time of Henry VII's accession, however, England's financial resources were very small. He took the country's finances under his direct control, and is said to have audited the treasurer's books himself. ("He spends all the time he is not in public or in his Council in writing the accounts of his expenses with his own hand," the Spanish Ambassador reported in 1498.) Some of his methods of gathering in money were shameless, but he managed in general to keep the goodwill of the middle classes who were only too pleased to see the power of the great lords curbed by the king. Within a few years of his accession, Henry was solvent, a rare achievement for a king of England; and by the time of his death in 1509, had invested between £200,000 and £300,000 in jewels—some no doubt for gifts to ambassadors and men of standing, some for the personal use of himself or his family, but the balance a useful investment his son was to inherit and thoroughly enjoy.

THE AGE OF DISCOVERY

The plums of the Age of Discovery were to go to the Spaniards and the Portuguese, not to the English. In 1487 a Portuguese seaman named Bartolomeo Diaz came sailing home from a long voyage down the coast of Africa in the course of which he had rounded the Cape. Five years later Columbus set sail on his first voyage, sponsored by Ferdinand of Aragon and his wife Isabella of Castile (the queen pawned her jewels to equip the expedition), and found the Caribbean Islands, where he saw natives decked in pure gold; to the end of his days he believed he had landed in Asia. In 1497 another Portuguese, Vasco da Gama, set sail for India, rounding Africa as Diaz had done before him and sailing on across the Indian Ocean, to return two years later with a cargo of ginger, pepper, cinnamon and gems. In the year of that triumphant return, Amerigo Vespucci explored the south-eastern coast of the continent which was to bear his name. A generation later, Balboa sighted the Pacific from a South American peak: could it be possible they were not, after all, in Asia? And now the Spanish were in full cry after the riches of the New World: Cortés conquered Mexico, Pizarro raped Peru, the *conquistadores* looted millions of pounds of treasure. (The Peruvians paid £8,000,000 in gold to ransom one captured Inca; they were assured that not a drop of his blood should be spilt—the Spaniards took the gold, shipped it home, and kept their word by strangling the hostage.) And in 1520, Magellan found the straits that still bear his name and sailed out across the Pacific Ocean towards Asia; in 1522, three years after they had set out from Spain, eighteen of his men reached home again, having completed the first-ever voyage round the world; Magellan himself and most of their shipmates had died on the way.

India, Asia, the Spice Islands, the treasures of the New World and the slaves of Africa, all were now within the reach of the European looters.

TREATIES AND ALLIANCES

Henry did not live to see these manifold discoveries, and English seamen played no real part in them; he managed none the less to use such resources as he had with great skill—too canny to waste his revenues on foreign war, too shrewd to leave England isolated among hostile powers. In 1489 he made an alliance with Spain (which was then ruled jointly by Ferdinand and Isabella) and betrothed his elder son Arthur to their daughter Catharine. The marriage took place in 1501, but the groom died a few months later, and an undignified monetary wrangle flared between the two fathers; Catharine struggled on in England, lonely, friendless, virtually penniless, for seven years, until her marriage to Arthur's younger brother, Henry, was at last concluded in 1509, a few months after Henry VII's death; she thought, poor girl, that all her troubles were over at last.

Peace with Scotland had been made in 1499, and this too was cemented by a marriage—greatly to the alarm of the English, who put no trust in the Scots at all—Henry VII's elder daughter Margaret becoming the wife of James IV.

Henry had brought the country peace and a measure of stability. Although he invested a considerable sum of money in jewels, and seems to have enjoyed a certain amount of pageantry and display, it is impossible to imagine him decked in the wealth of jewellery worn by his son and successor Henry VIII. Very seldom does one see portraits of him wearing a crown, he seems to have preferred the velvet cap and mantle of the merchant. There is a bust of him in the Victoria and Albert Museum which is a splendid example of the image he evidently wished to promote. It shows a merchant rather than a king, with a fur-lined cloak—remarkably sober for a monarch—and a winged hat set on shoulder-length hair. The features closely resemble those of the effigy of Henry VII by Pietro Torrigiani which is now in Westminster Abbey; the portrait-bust, which is life-size and made of painted and gilded terracotta, is by the same sculptor.

Henry VIII

A PRINCE OF PROMISE

When the young King Henry ascended the throne in 1509, the scholars thought that a new age of English culture was about to begin. Among those who came to watch its dawning was the gentle and scholarly Erasmus (A.D. 1466–1536), who came from Italy to re-visit his dear English friends and wrote the famous Renaissance satire *In Praise of Folly* while staying with Sir Thomas More at Chelsea. The reign was off to a fine start, and at first all went merrily. The young king, then aged eighteen, was highly accomplished: a scholar, a linguist, a fine athlete, a musician and composer, devout, healthy, patently handsome, and set to found a dynasty. His marriage to Catharine of Aragon allied him to the power of Spain; his elder sister Margaret was married to the King of Scots, which, theoretically at least, should ensure Border peace; his younger sister Mary was beautiful, charming, and of marriageable age, a useful asset. Catharine's first child, a son, was born on New Year's Day 1511; there was a tremendous outburst of rejoicing, in the middle of which the baby caught cold and died—but they were young, there was plenty of time.

Following in his father's footsteps, the young king sought to carry out the Tudor ideal of raising the country to true economic, diplomatic and cultural equality with the European powers.

Trading brought sumptuous luxuries into the country: shimmering tapestries from Brussels, glowing brocade and velvet from Genoa, fantasies in glass from Venice, jewels and leather from Florence, and carpets from the Levant.

Diplomacy meant winning recognition from the European men of power and their courts, and consequent valuable exchanges of ideas, affecting government, commerce, and the arts.

Conscious of the great strides taken during the Renaissance, whose princes were patrons of art and scholarship, Henry and his father wanted to gather in the finest artists of the Continent, until England's name was as great as that of any of the creative courts of Europe. It was obvious to them both that contemporary English artists did not compare with those flourishing overseas, so they set to work to import suitable men, together with sophisticated craftsmen. Several did come, but found the English climate too wet and cold after the glorious Mediterranean weather—for naturally the Tudor kings looked first to Italy.

One Italian who came was Pietro Torrigiani, a fellow pupil of Michelangelo at the Medici Academy (they got into a fight, and Torrigiani broke Michelangelo's nose and had to leave in haste). While in London he created the tombs of Henry VII, his wife, Elizabeth of York, and his mother, Margaret Beaufort, in Westminster Abbey; they are the earliest important examples of Italian Renaissance art in the country. In June 1519, however, Torrigiani departed abruptly for the Mediterranean, without fulfilling his contracts, without getting the king's permission, and without any intention of returning; Englishmen, he said, were beasts.

Others came: among them Benedetto de Maiano (1442–97) who did some sculpting for Henry VII; and Antonio Toto del Nunziata, the architect and artist, who became Sergeant Painter to Henry VIII; some of his paintings may still be seen at Loseley House and Sutton Place in Surrey, and he also created the wall paintings in the Wolsey Closet at Hampton Court Palace, and may have worked on Henry VIII's darling project, Nonesuch Palace; but he too left for home again. But one great artist did spend a number of years working in England, dying there in 1543. This was a northerner, the German artist, Hans Holbein (1497–1543).

HANS HOLBEIN

Hans Holbein, an artist's son, was born in 1497 in Augsburg, one of the principal metalworking centres of Europe, which was situated in Bavaria—splendidly positioned, a focal point of trade between Italy and northern Europe. When he was eighteen, Holbein moved to Basle, one of the leading trading cities of Europe and a stronghold of the Reformation—Basle's wealthy burghers had kicked out their bishop-ruler and joined the Swiss Confederation in 1501. A Bavarian printer named Johannes Froben had settled there and established a printing press, always useful for any reforming movement. Froben was Erasmus's publisher, and in 1515 was considering a new edition of *In Praise of Folly*. He thought some illustrations might help, and he commissioned Holbein as the artist.

Holbein is believed to have made his first visit to England in about 1526. He made many friends there, among them More and his fellow humanists, to whom he brought letters of introduction from Erasmus (in 1515, when it became clear that the young Henry VIII was hoping to carve out a career of military and diplomatic glory, Erasmus had left England and had eventually settled in Basle, where he moved in with his publisher; Froben's house became his sanctuary from the religious struggle convulsing Europe). He returned to Europe for a couple of years—taking along a drawing of Thomas More for Erasmus—but was back in England in 1530, doing a good deal of work for the German merchants there.

It is believed that Holbein entered the service of the king in 1533 after having painted *The Ambassadors*, which is now in the National Gallery in London, and worked for him untiringly until he died of the plague in 1543. Fortunately there are still many penetrating portraits by Holbein to be seen in England, as well as a great many of his designs for jewellery and personal adornments preserved in the British Museum. The 1593 copy by Rowland Lockey of his famous painting of Sir Thomas More and his family (*circa* 1526–8) is now in the National Portrait Gallery.

Among the loveliest of Holbein's work is undoubtedly the Holbein Cup, which is one of the most beautifully compact works of art of the sixteenth century, a perfect example of the Renaissance interest in the antique and of its delight in sheer perfection of craftsmanship. Henry VIII had been presented with an antique rock crystal bowl with the most graceful turned fluting (it was probably carved by Venetian lapidaries in the early fourteenth century) and commissioned Holbein to design a fitting setting for it. The bowl is understood to have been mounted to Holbein's design in about 1540, with a most elaborately bejewelled gold cover and an equally ornate gold foot. There is a lateral handle which shows it was used for drinking—the justification for calling it a "cup"—and, rather amusingly, inscriptions on the lid which glorify the virtues of sobriety and further inscriptions on the foot which glorify the pleasures of drinking but warn of the dangers of excess. While Henry VIII lived, the cup seems to have been kept in Westminster; it was later transferred to the Jewel House in the Tower of London, and finally offered for sale during the Commonwealth period. It appears there were no immediate buyers, so Wilhelm Kalf was commissioned to paint it, as a kind of advertisement. There are two paintings extant, one in Copenhagen and one in Weimar. The cup was at last bought by the Elector of the Palatinate, and is now displayed amongst the other magnificent jewelled works of art in the Schatzkammer in Munich, where it most certainly holds its own.

Holbein's diverse works show that he not only had a great feeling for, and a great understanding of, Renaissance thinking and experience, but also a Germanic linear precision which was much appreciated by the English. He was not a craftsman-jeweller, although he understood the craft (he had grown up among the workshops of Augsburg, and both his legitimate sons became goldsmiths), but an artist and a designer. If commissioned to create a dagger sheath, for instance, he drew his design and, when this had been approved, handed it over to one of the multitude of other foreign craftsmen who worked for the king—men such as Hans of Antwerp (also known as John Anwarpe), Robert Amadas, John Cryspyn, Nicholas Oursian the clock-maker, Cornelius Hays, John Cavalcant, Guillim Honyson, John of Utrecht, Allart Ploumyer, Jehan Lange, Baptist Leman, John Baptista de Consolavera, and Alexander of

Brussels. The king's geometrician was a German, Nikolaus Kratzer, who lived and worked in London for over thirty years and never found any necessity to learn a word of English.

DEVELOPMENTS IN DESIGN

It is obvious that this division between the designer and the craftsman (influenced by the developments in printing and engraving which are described more fully on page 83) had a great effect on sixteenth-century English jewellery. First, the designer was now of greater initial importance than the craftsman; secondly, it becomes exceptionally difficult to fix a jewel's "nationality".

Designers in Italy, France, Germany and England were using very similar motifs, taken from classical mythology. Sea-creatures abound—mermen, mermaids, dolphins and hippocamps; so too do the decorative emblems from the classical temples—garlands of fruit and flowers, animal masks, acanthus leaves, caryatids and amorini. Some of the jewels exhibited in the Hofburg, in Vienna, and the Louvre in Paris show this very well; and the plasterwork in the ballroom of Knole House, near Sevenoaks in Kent, riots with classical images.

The accent too was the same, no matter what the nationality of designer or wearer: it was constantly laid on the personal and the individual, with a feeling for the unusual which is exemplified by the use of baroque pearls. The name "baroque" comes from the Portuguese word *barroco*, which means "irregular", and these pearls, which are curiously formed, became extremely popular. Holbein used them, according to the fashion of his time, but he did so in his own way. He designed jewels with Germanic thoroughness, using the pearls as pendant drops, rather than taking the completely misshapen ones used by the Florentines, Milanese and Venetians, and centring a complete design round them. In the British Museum there is a Holbein design for a monogram jewel for Henry VIII—*E R* for *Enricus Rex*, the letters embroidered with acanthus leaves, four gemstones, and three pendant pearls; this may be compared with the supreme individuality of the Canning Jewel, a masterpiece of Italian jewellery dating from the late sixteenth century, which is described on page 82.

Monogram Jewels

The cult of monogrammatic jewellery is one that reflects vividly the Renaissance emphasis on the importance of the individual. Henry VIII had a particular liking for monogram jewels; no doubt they suited his strong and assertive personality. Some, like the Holbein *E R*, displayed his own initials, others entwined the king's initial with that of a current wife—there is, for instance, a design which incorporates *H* for Henry and *I* for Jane Seymour. The portrait of Anne Boleyn, painted by an unknown artist, and now in the National Portrait Gallery of London, shows her wearing about her throat a gold monogram *B* with pendant pearls. There is a painting at Hampton Court Palace, dating from about 1545, which shows the king with his son Edward and one of his wives (the lady is thought to have been painted in later, and identifications vary as to which wife it is), and his two daughters, Mary and Elizabeth, both richly dressed; Mary wears a heavy cross pendant among her jewels, Elizabeth a monogram pendant jewel in the shape of an *A*—perhaps this too was Anne Boleyn's. The 1530 inventory of the king's jewels mentions others: "A diamond *Y* with a hanging pearl, a diamond *M*, standing in a flower; and an *E* enamelled red." In 1515 the king gave his sister Mary a double *A* monogram jewel, set with a diamond, a ruby and a pearl; Joan Evans suggests that it may have belonged originally to his brother Arthur. The gift marked the period when Henry was setting out on a hopeful and promising career in search of military and diplomatic glory.

DIPLOMATIC INTERLUDE

Early in Henry's reign his father-in-law, Ferdinand of Aragon, allied himself with the Pope and the city of Venice, in a misnamed Holy League whose blessed purpose was to drive the rampaging French out of Italy for good. The Holy Roman Emperor, Maximilian, joined them, and so did Henry, only too pleased to show that he stood at the head of a powerful nation. In 1513, like many English kings before him, he invaded France, and had the great delight of winning his first battle. (The King of Scots, following the example of his own predecessors, invaded his brother-in-law's kingdom while Henry was occupied across the Channel, but suffered a terrible defeat at Flodden Field, where he and the flower of his people were mown down together.)

The French were duly driven back from Italy and Henry's allies, satisfied, saw no reason to pursue the war just so that he could prove himself another Henry V; he accordingly came to terms with the ageing French king, Louis XII, and sealed the peace by giving him his young sister Mary in marriage (it is said that she only agreed on condition that next time she could choose a husband for herself). Within a few weeks Louis was dead—the gossips said maliciously that his young wife had worn him out; she, rightly putting little faith in her brother's promises, hastily and secretly married the Duke of Suffolk, greatly to Henry's fury since he had been considering marrying her off to the new French king, Francis I.

Francis was to prove himself a great patron of the arts—men said of him that he looted the Renaissance from Italy and carried it off bodily to his own kingdom. His greatest achievement in a wholesale garnering of artists and craftsmen was the snaring of Leonardo da Vinci, whom he regarded with such reverence that a whole castle was set aside for the master painter.

In 1519 the Holy Roman Emperor died, and the electors prepared to make their new choice. Henry VIII offered himself as a candidate, a gesture to show that his was a nation to be reckoned with, but it was clear that the true contest lay between Francis I and the old emperor's grandson, Charles V of Spain. A tremendous amount of bribery now went on (it had begun even before the old emperor died; he had spent half a million gold florins to buy votes for his grandson and sent the bill to Charles in Spain, tucking in an extra fifty thousand for expenses). After a complicated see-sawing of threats, negotiation and bribery, Charles was elected, and a lifelong rivalry inaugurated between him and Francis.

It was clear that fresh wars were inevitable, and Henry, secure in his own island, was in the pleasant position of being courted by both sides. The ambassadors wrote their reports home, describing him in his jewelled prime, dressed in the height of European fashion: slashed and striped and puffed velvets and satins, damasks and taffetas, hung with diamonds and girded with gold. (The absolute nature of Henry's control over who wore what is indicated by the fact that all jewels and plate imported under licence during his reign had to be submitted to him before they could be sold; if he fancied anything, he bought it, and the rest was then handed back to the jeweller or goldsmith for sale.) There is one famous report from the Venetian envoys written when Henry was about twenty-nine. He is "as handsome as nature could form him—handsomer by far than the King of France" (it seems quite likely that spies checked on outgoing papers, and such a remark could hardly fail to please), "exceedingly fair . . . an excellent musician and composer, an admirable horseman and wrestler . . . very devout . . . affable and benign, he offends no one. He has often said he wished that everyone was content with his condition, adding 'We are content with our islands.' "

THE REFORMATION

In spite of his fair words, however, Henry was not content. Above all else he needed a legitimate son, and Catharine had only given him one surviving child, a daughter, Mary. By 1527 Henry appears to have been set on his purpose: he would divorce Catharine (unquestionably virtuous, steadfast and devout, she absolutely refused to retire into a convent or to deny that she was Henry's true wife—he had developed religious scruples because of her brief long-ago marriage to his brother—and their daughter Mary his true and only heir); and he would take another wife, Anne Boleyn. Catharine, however, had allies of her own, notably her nephew, the Emperor Charles, who could bring pressure to bear in Rome on her behalf. After three years of difficult and inconclusive negotiation, Henry resolved to authorize the divorce himself. In 1531 the clergy were compelled to accept him as Supreme Head of the Church in England, and two years later he married Anne Boleyn; she was pregnant with Elizabeth when she came to her coronation. In 1534 the passing of the Act of Supremacy gave the king absolute power over the Church in his kingdom. He authorized the English Bible and allowed some approach towards the Protestant Reformers' doctrines in the Ten Articles of 1536; and in the same year, and for two years afterwards, the great monasteries and abbeys and convents of the realm were first inspected and then finally suppressed. At the end of this time, however, Henry checked the Reformers, taking his stand on traditional Catholic doctrine in the Six Articles of 1539, which, among other matters, declared for the practice of auricular Confession and insisted on the celibacy of the clergy.

Hardly any religious jewellery now survives from that pre-Reformation period. We know of it only through descriptions in inventories, wills and accounts. The Reformation, and the subsequent religious purges of Edward VI and the Commonwealth, saw the destruction of much early religious jewellery. Back it all went into the melting pot. The everyday trinkets went—the cheap pilgrim badges, the rosaries, the holy medals from the great shrines of England. The private altars went, the silver statues, the reliquaries, the religious pendants, the *enseignes* incorporating religious designs—in the king's inventories for 1526 are descriptions of *enseignes* showing St. Michael between red and white roses, and St. George, and among the Holbein designs are two for religious *enseignes*, one centring on a portrayal of the Annunciation and another showing the three beings of the Trinity set in a charming border of Tudor roses with the motto

Trinitas gloria satiabimur

It did not, of course, happen at once; indeed, the effects were to spread out steadily through the succeeding decades, each with their own religious upheavals; but what did happen almost at once, and what was especially terrible, was the total breaking up of ecclesiastical jewels and the seizing and melting down of accumulated treasures from medieval times. Once the total suppression of the great religious houses and shrines had been decided upon, orders were given to seize the golden reliquaries, toss out the relics—there were some shocking cases of fraudulent "miracles" and miracle-working relics created to gull the pilgrims—and melt down the metalwork. From the Canterbury shrine of Thomas à Becket alone came two huge chests which half a dozen men could hardly lift. All the contents went to the king, including a great diamond which had been presented to the shrine in 1179 by Louis VII of France. This was promptly re-set for Henry.

Dunstan's Glastonbury went the way of all the others. "We have in money £300 and above," wrote Cromwell's servants, at a new Visitation in 1539, "a fair chalice of gold and divers other parcels of plate which the abbot had hid secretly"—but not, it seems, secretly enough. The shrine of Edward the Confessor in Westminster Abbey was the only one to escape, and even here the solid gold top was stripped off and seized. (Henry probably spared the Confessor because he was a king as well as a saint—monarchs had to be defended; Thomas à Becket, on the other hand, was a churchman who had defied his king; there was no reprieve for him.)

Most of the medieval gold work was melted down and refashioned, often into great golden chains. These chains did not hang quietly round the neck, half-lost in the clothes, but were boldly displayed in a great curve across the chest, stretching from shoulder to shoulder. They were made up of repeated and clearly recognizable symbols, like the linked Ss in the historic SS collar of Lancaster which Sir Thomas More is wearing in one of the Holbein portraits, now in the Frick Collection in New York (there is a contemporary half-length copy by the School of Holbein, now at the National Portrait Gallery in London). They were not only strikingly dramatic to wear, but gave a comfortable impression of plenty of reserve currency. Henry had a good many of them, and the fashion was to persist throughout the century—his daughter Elizabeth once received a golden chain weighing 161 ounces among her manifold New Year gifts, and her cousin Mary, Queen of Scots, wore an ornamental chain of gold coins formed by the linking together of all the golden angels she had herself received one New Year.

Luckily, however, one of those early sixteenth-century jewels has survived, and is now at Stonyhurst College, near Blackburn in Lancashire. This is the reliquary pendant which belonged to Sir Thomas More, martyred during the Reformation and subsequently canonized. It was given to Stonyhurst by one of his descendants, a Jesuit priest, in 1773.

The **More Reliquary** is illustrated in Fig. 15. It is 2⅜ inches (60 mm) in diameter, and just over ½ inch (12·5 mm) deep. On one side is an enamelled St. George smiting a dragon with plenty of verve, and on the other the figure of Christ by the open sepulchre, with some of the emblems of the Passion, notably the ladder and the spear (these emblems, as portrayed in medieval and early Tudor art, were the two swords of the Apostles, St. Peter's sword, the pillar, the cord, the scourge, the crown of thorns, the dice with which the Romans cast lots for the garment Christ wore, the seamless garment itself, the spear with which Christ's side was pierced, the sponge, the nails, the cross, the thirty pieces of silver paid to Judas, the hammer and pincers, the ladder, the lantern, the boxes of spices, the purse and the cock—more of them appear in Fig. 23). The scene contrasts starkly with the charming continuous border of enamelled pansies round the frame—pansies being emblematic of thought (from the French *pensée*), of heart's-ease, and of the Trinity (three petals forming the one bloom). The arrangement of the scene by the sepulchre is particularly interesting because of the curious geometric patterning of the various items portrayed.

Inside the reliquary there is now a faded portrait of Sir Thomas More in water-colours. George Vertue, the engraver, apparently inspected the reliquary in the early eighteenth century, for in his diary for 1728 he wrote that it contained "in small by holben the picture of Sr. Tho. More in water-colours, faded". According to the Stonyhurst authorities, it is difficult to know what evidence Vertue had for ascribing the portrait to Holbein, other than the known fact that Holbein had painted other portraits of More.

THE KING'S APPEARANCE

The flavour of the clothes in Henry VIII's reign was richly masculine. Breadth was forced from top to toe; the width of the velvet hats was enhanced by swirling plumes and feathers, the shoulders of gold-sewn velvet jackets were puffed out inches beyond any possible flesh and bone, even the toes of the shoes were squared off and padded.

When Henry was young, the athlete look was promoted: alert and springy, gay and colourful, like the young king himself. He surrounded himself with gaudy and dashing companions, his exploits in the chase were ostentatiously spectacular, his exploits in every other field a glittering triumph. He lived for the moment, he wore the latest fashions, and his jewels were as magnificent as any peacock's. To subsidize his wardrobe he evidently dug deep into his father's coffers, leaving them much depleted.

Portraits of the king always show him wearing jewellery. There is one after Holbein, in the Walker Art Gallery in Liverpool, which exemplifies his swank and swagger. He is shown wearing velvets and silk-brocades, slashed so that puffs of fine silk can be pulled through the slits, the contrasting textures enhancing the effect of richness. His large flat velvet hat, with its curling plume, is sewn with *enseignes* and pearls. He wears a great golden chain punctuated with balas rubies; it is slung from shoulder-tip to shoulder-tip, the solid weight of it causing it to dip down across his chest. A second, more slender golden chain hangs around his neck, with a circular pendant locket almost reaching to his waist. Gold and ruby matching brooches march in pairs down his barrel chest and along his sleeves to the wrist, emphasizing the slashing of the imported silk-brocade. On his fingers he wears large rings. Beneath his knee is the jewelled Garter. His gold-enriched dagger and its sheath were designed by Holbein.

In spite of all this finery and show, there is absolutely no question at all about the king's masculinity. He stands balanced on the balls of his feet, confident and solemn, yet with an air of excited anticipation. His very squareness is the opposite of effeminate —yet he is loaded with jewellery. The carpet on which he stands is soft and luxurious. The curtain which hangs beside him shimmers with the same gold as the embroidery on his own velvet. He is the epitome of the hopes his people felt during the Tudor prime:

81

a man of his own time, supremely individual, yet with a certain regularity about his stance and appearance.

As time went on, this youthful jauntiness was replaced with stately and majestic formality. The clothes became more voluptuous, often reaching full-length. The jewels grew larger to dazzle at still greater distances. They were the outward sign of monarchy and confidence, and always made in the newest continental fashion.

In 1546 Henry's agent in Antwerp, Vaughn, wrote to Paget in London to inform him of a magnificent jewel which one John Carolo of Antwerp wished to sell. He described it in detail, and accompanied his description with a scale drawing, which shows a pendant of a large table-cut diamond centrally set in a gold framework of scrolls and masks, a satyr and a nymph, with a spherical pendant pearl below. In his letter to Paget (now in the Public Records Office), Vaughn says that he had promised to send the pattern to the king, but is not doing so because "the time is unmeet to pester the King with jewels, who already hath more than most of the Princes of Christendom". Henry, it seems, always dressed the part.

THE NEW USE OF GEMSTONES

The increasing supplies of gemstones meant that the old fashion of wrought gold jewellery was gradually yielding place to a new style. The discovery of the New World, and the opening up of routes to India and Asia, had resulted in the arrival of new gems. South America was a great new source of supply, especially for the emeralds which the Spaniards loved. Rubies and sapphires were brought overland from the East. Diamonds came from Golconda in mid-India.

Pearls were still valued, especially pearls of fantastical shape; the larger they were, the rarer, the more expensive—and the more they tested the ability of the jeweller. It was fairly easy to create patterns for the usual types of jewels: golden chains, for instance, or engraved or *niello* work; but a strange and irregular pearl was a challenge, demanding the creation of a strange and fantastic jewel. These baroque pearls always now formed the central part of the jewel. They were set in gold, which was often textured, with other smaller gems set individually in the enamelled metal. Such jewels are shaped like humans, or birds, or insects, with the pearl forming the body. The most diverse jewels of this type were created in Germany and Italy. A splendid example, though rather later in period, is the **Canning Jewel**, which shows a merman brandishing a sword over his head and holding a shield in the other hand. A great baroque pearl forms his torso, tapering from the broad shoulders to the waist. This is mounted in enamelled gold, and set with rubies, diamonds and other pearls. A jester's cap crowns the tail. The jewel combines the literary symbolism of the Hebraic and Hellenic cultures, for the sword is not merely a sword, it is also the jawbone of an ass in allusion to Samson's killing of the Philistines, and the shield is not merely a shield, it is also Medusa's snaky-locked head. Set in the tail is a carved ruby; this has led to the associating of the jewel with Piero de Medici, who was instrumental in reviving the antique art of carving gemstones; it may, however, have been added later. The back of the jewel is as lovely as the front, being superbly enamelled. The jewel, created in Italy, was later given to an eastern Mogul, being brought back to Europe by Lord Canning. It is now in the Victoria and Albert Museum.

A sister jewel to the Canning Jewel was sold at Sotheby's in London in November 1970, at the sale of the effects of the late Arturo Lopez Wilshaw, for a huge price, being bought for a private collection in America so that it cannot, unhappily, be hung by its twin. This is the **Siren Jewel**, which is so similar in workmanship that it is generally agreed to have been made by the same great craftsman. It is a pendant centring on an enormous baroque pearl—a lustrous mermaid, rather than a merman, who is studying a looking-glass as she combs her hair with a golden comb, the "glass" (held with the handle upward) being a large diamond. A pearl drop is unfortunately missing from the final fin of her enamelled tail, and though the jewel is very colourful and beautifully made, it is a little less balanced than the Canning Jewel—the head for instance is proportionately too small. There is, however, an enamelled inscription on the reverse of the tail, which may be translated:

"Not only the song but the appearance of the Siren deceives"

Added to this are the initials *V.D.*, something unique in sixteenth-century jewels which were never normally signed. What is so annoying is that the maker has not yet been identified, although it seems almost certain that he was an Italian.

At about this period, the use of *cabochon* stones began to die out. They were replaced by the chiselled facets of sharp square cuts. The lapidary had begun to come into his own, and was to grow increasingly more confident as changing fashion demanded faceted gems. Experiments were also being made in the cutting and setting of diamonds, although on the whole they were still simply embedded in the metal, often with an irregular cut or a "writing" point in which the diamond was ground into a kind of pyramid. Other stones were held in the old-style box or collet settings.

In order to maintain the effect of great richness, jewellers used enamelling to introduce voluptuous colours. The materials worn in the first half of the sixteenth century were often sombre, dark and rich: splendid black velvets, woven burgundy red brocades with huge repeated patterns. Against these white enamels (these were of German rather than Italian origin) stood out dramatically, especially with the flicks of light sparkling from the faceted stones they framed.

ENGRAVED PATTERN BOOKS

The spread of designs across sixteenth-century Europe depended initially on the development of printing. Johann Gutenberg (*circa* A.D. 1398–1468) is credited with the building of the first operative printing press in the mid-fifteenth century. Ink and paper were already in adequate supply, and so too were presses of various kinds, ultimately deriving, it is thought, from the simple wine presses of classical times, and blocks, which were used for the printing of textiles and playing cards. What was needed was type, and it was this which Gutenberg is thought to have developed, after experimenting with a special alloy of lead, tin and antimony. The printing of texts was under way at last, and by 1500 there was a printing press in every country of Europe except Russia.

The introduction of pattern books depended on the development of engraving. This art is believed to have derived from etching, a chemical process used for the decoration of armour, which may have begun in the armourers' workshops of Augsburg, as is sometimes suggested, or alternatively in the great arms factories of Italy. Engraving is very similar to etching, but the lines are incised by hand with a tool called a graver. The art is thought to have been developed in the goldsmiths' workshops in northern Europe. The earliest known engravings, which date from about 1420, are believed to be by a goldsmith, and are surprisingly sophisticated in technique. This anonymous "Master of the Playing Card" was succeeded by a new anonymous master, known simply as E.S., who was working in Germany in about 1466; Martin Schongauer may have been his pupil. Schongauer, a painter from Augsburg and a goldsmith's son, took up this new and essentially Germanic art, and developed a most precise and delicate technique of his own, drawing on a soft metal with a dry point needle.

Type, like woodcuts, was printed by a relief process, each letter standing proud of the surface—but why not print also by the contrasting intaglio process, thus reproducing an engraved design which had been incised on a copper plate? By so doing, one could reproduce a single drawing a hundredfold.

Hence the pattern books which were to circulate round the courts of Europe. Holbein's designs for the king and his court are preserved at the British Museum, but fall into a different category, since they were original work; but the first known collection of engraved ornament designs, which any artist could purchase and copy, was published in England some years after his death. This was by Virgil Solis (1514–62) and was entitled *Moryse and Damashin renewed and increased, very profitable for Goldsmyths and Embroderars, by Thomas Geminus at London Anno 1548.*

Among the other important designers whose work was to circulate round Europe were three influential men: Etienne Delaune (born in Orleans in 1520, and still working in 1590), Theodore de Bry (1528–98) and Hans Collaert (1540–1622).

The experienced professional can pick out at a glance a design by one of these early artists, glimpsed in a present-day museum: an ivory knife-case, for instance, a *nielloed* belt-harness, a jewelled pendant, a silver watch. Their influence on the jewels of the later sixteenth century was enormous.

COURT FASHIONS IN JEWELLERY

During the sixteenth century, almost every type of jewel was worn by the rich and famous. Jewels were worn on the clothes, over the clothes and under the clothes. They were sewn to sleeves, they were used to clip together folds of fabric, they were embroidered like confetti on a doublet and stitched to a velvet shoe to emphasize its lines. Private and personal jewels, often believed to have magical or medicinal powers (or, in the early part of the century, religious meaning) were hidden away under a shirt—concealed, but easy to clutch in times of stress. As for jewels worn *over* the clothes, these were legion. Hats could be pinned through with personal *enseignes* or badges; a *carcanet* worn around the throat, either as a short necklace or as a jewelled collar; and a *cotière*—a longer necklace, generally with a pendant attached—worn over that. A man might wear an earring, or even two (they were not much worn by ladies in the early sixteenth century, as a woman's head was still primly covered and her ears hidden); such earrings were pendant, and made of gold. (This fashion persisted through the Elizabethan period, and William Harrison, raging against "the fantastical folly" of his countrymen, from courtier to carter, included it in his invective: "Some lusty courtiers also and gentlemen of courage do wear rings of gold, stones or pearl in their ears, whereby they do imagine the workmanship of God to be not a little amended. But herein they rather disgrace than adorn their persons." Harrison particularly loathed any kind of unisex or flamboyance in fashion, feeling that men should be masculine, sober and saving, and women feminine, decorous and docile.)

Both sexes, however, wore necklaces, men as well as women, and both sexes wore pendants, which were not necessarily attached to a necklace—they could be fastened to a padded and embroidered sleeve instead, thus enabling the owner to display several at one time. Pendants worn in this fashion can be seen in several Tudor portraits, among them, for example, the Marcus Gheeraerts family portrait of Barbara, wife of Sir Robert Sidney (Sir Philip's brother) and six of their children, at Penshurst Place in Kent.

Brooches were used to fasten folds or seams together, to hold a long and swinging chain in place, or—a special use, this—to emphasize a particular fashion point.

Chains were worn in great loops and curves. Huge chains of office were spread across the shoulders; smaller ones hung in profusion around the neck—contemporary paintings show how many the Tudors managed to don at one and the same time. There is a famous miniature by Holbein showing Anne of Cleves, which is now on display at the Victoria and Albert Museum. This delicate portrait, dating from 1540 and set in a box whose lid is a carved ivory rose, was made for Henry VIII so that he could judge the beauty of the prospective bride; he found the reality a sad disappointment. In Holbein's miniature Anne is wearing a wrought gold collar, set with white enamelled flowers with gemstone centres, and with a pendant cross, and two plain gold chains (this may be one long chain wound twice about the neck); the neckline of her gown is studded with eleven matching enamel-and-gemstone flowers, and her head-dress is crusted with gems.

Another chain could be worn as a colourful and decorative belt, fitting snugly around the waist and then dangling in a long jewelled fall to the ground. Such a belt often terminated in some precious object: perhaps a book of devotions with a jewelled cover, or a pierced gold pomander full of spices (Fig. 21), or a small *châtelaine* with a toothpick and nail-cleaner attached, or even the newest conceit of all, a jewelled watch. One such *châtelaine*, the **Pasfield Jewel** (Fig. 18) is now at the Victoria and Albert Museum. It is shaped like a tiny wheel-lock pistol, about 3 inches long (75 mm) and very slender, and is of enamelled gold; it incorporates a whistle (to summon a servant, a hound, a hawk?) and three toilet implements which fan out rather like the blades of a penknife—an earpick, a toothpick and a nail-cleaner. (Henry VIII's inventory for 1519 mentions another such jewelled whistle, hanging from a ring and set with a ruby and seven diamonds.'

People of both sexes wore rings in profusion on every finger of each hand, and both thumbs as well, and then sighed that they had "finger fatigue".

TUDOR PORTRAITURE

The tremendous rise in the importance of portrait-painting during the Renaissance is attributable in part to the passion of the time for individual glory and natural portraiture; but it was also owed in large measure to the experiments and discoveries of the Flemish brothers, Hubert van Eyck (1366–1426) and his younger brother Jan, bred up in the medieval tradition of manuscript illumination, who discovered a method of mixing paint with linseed oil rather than egg; this cut out the long complex preparation of the backing material which had been necessary before, and made it possible to scrape off the paint and start again if need be—a great asset in portraiture. Oil painting had begun. The new art spread across Flanders and the Low Countries—whose artists included van der Weyden, van der Goes, Gerard David and Hans Memling; and thus across Germany and northern Europe and down into Italy, where it later reached fresh and glorious heights in the work of Titian, da Vinci, Raphael, and Michelangelo.

Fortunately for us, the Tudors had a passion for portraiture. We can see their jewels blazing in profusion from sixteenth-century portraits. This does not necessarily mean that the country gentlemen and their wives always decked themselves so lavishly. Pendants, for instance, were the kind of jewels which were generally kept in a small jewel cabinet or *wrangelschrank*. One might perhaps take a treasured pendant out on occasion to show a personal friend. Such a jewel was, in all senses, a lovely work of art, beautifully finished inside as well as out, rarely worn; it would open up to show the concealed portrait of a sweetheart, child or husband; it was completely personal, often secret. The friend would share it with you, examine all its points, admire its craftsmanship; then it would be lovingly put to rest again in its velvet-lined box.

But for people of the "ordinary" classes a family portrait was a once-in-a-lifetime event. Every single jewelled object would be worn on such an occasion, and the artist would be given strict instructions to portray each jewel most faithfully. It is from these family portraits that many jewels have been recognized (in some cases, we have even recognized the owner from the jewel) and they are a fascinating source of information about styles and fashions.

Examples of these family portraits may be seen in many of the old stately homes and manor houses of England, among them Knole in Kent, Hatfield House in Hertfordshire, or Wilton House in Wiltshire. One interesting painting is at Audley End in Essex, and shows Margaret, daughter of Lord Audley, who married the Duke of Norfolk, with magnificent jewels and an embroidered coat of arms; the whole composition exhibiting the *horror vacui* felt by the men and women of sixteenth-century England.

KING SUPREME

By the time of his death in 1547 Henry had amassed a vast collection of jewels, plate and personal ornaments. Did the impulse to collect and display jewels spring from his own character, or out of his ceaseless need to compete with the other rulers of Europe? We do not know. As he had such an artistic eye and ear, however, it is probable that he took a true voluptuous delight in jewellery for its own sake.

In his time Henry had married six consort queens and taken at least two mistresses. Jewellery and plate was bestowed on each queen in turn; their personal jewels were generally treated as private property (this depended somewhat on the terms of their parting from the king), but the bulk of their jewellery was Crown property and reverted to him. Catharine of Aragon, for instance, had a number of jewels linking her monogram with the king's and dating from the happy early years of their marriage, as well as a quantity of jewels which were religious in inspiration; these were eventually handed over to her daughter, Mary, and are listed in the 1542 inventory. Anne Boleyn, her successor, was in turn supplanted by Jane Seymour, Henry's third queen, who died a few days after the birth of their son. After her came Anne of Cleves, then Katharine Howard, and then the gentle Katharine Parr, who was still, precariously, queen at the king's death. A contemporary description of a miniature of her runs:

> "She wears a round crimson velvet hood or cap of state, edged with pearls, and surmounted with a jewelled frontlet of goldsmith's work set with rubies and pearls . . . the bodice edged with a row of pearls between pipes of black and crimson velvet. She wears a double row of large pearls about her neck, from which depends a ruby cross, finished with a fair pendant pearl."

After the king's death Katharine married her sweetheart, Thomas Seymour, the Lord High Admiral, and was deprived of these jewels on the grounds that they belonged to the Crown.

In his attempts to secure the succession, Henry bastardized both his daughters—first Mary, Catharine of Aragon's daughter, then Elizabeth, Anne Boleyn's child; there was, indeed, a point at which it seemed he might even legitimize his bastard son Henry Fitzroy (no marriage ceremonies at all in this instance, no divorce, just a pleasant liaison)—if all his children were illegitimate, why not at least pick the boy?—but Fitzroy died in his teens, and Edward VI was born, triumphantly legitimate. (It is perhaps worthy of remark that when Mary succeeded to the throne she annulled all the enactments illegitimizing her; Elizabeth never bothered.) But he was not deliberately cruel to them, illegitimate or not, provided they were willing to submit to his authority, and the royal inventories show that he was not fettered in his treatment of their material needs by any of his own pronouncements; their households, like Edward's, were supplied with royal plate from time to time. He was never indulgent, but on the other hand they never went without.

It was the king who was the focus of all eyes. Far less concern was shown about the jewels worn by the queens and their ladies, or by the royal children; it was to the king that England, and beyond her, Europe, looked.

The second half of the century was to see this emphasis abruptly changed. The short reigns of Edward VI and Mary I had little lasting effect on fashions in clothes and jewels, but Elizabeth I was to show herself a true daughter of her flamboyant father.

Edward VI

Edward VI, Henry VIII's only son, succeeded to the throne in 1547 at the age of nine. There is a portrait of him at Hampton Court Palace which is believed to have been painted and sent to the court of France in 1550 when a match was being considered between him and the French king's daughter; to everyone's surprise, the French returned it after the boy's death. It is attributed to William Scrots (*fl.* 1537–54) who had succeeded Holbein as King's Painter. Edward, then aged twelve, is wearing a black doublet and cloak richly and elegantly embroidered in gold thread. There are *enseignes* in his hat, and a splendid jewelled sword about his waist. He has a calm, set, rather secretive oval face, and though he is dressed with propriety and dignity there is no trace of his father's swagger—though the pose is based on that of the Henry VIII

Holbein frescoes for Whitehall Palace (these are no longer extant, but a Charles II copy survives at Hampton Court Palace and the cartoon for this is at the National Portrait Gallery).

Edward's reign was principally remarkable for the zeal with which the Reformed and Protestant religion was enforced. In 1548 his council ordered a thorough purging and cleansing of the parish churches; any wall paintings were to be defaced, any statues hacked down, any carved and idolatrous screens chopped up, any reliquaries and other superstitious metalwork melted down, in a wholesale destruction of the smaller scale medieval art which had adorned the parish churches, rather than the great pilgrim shrines which had already been dealt with; we are fortunate that so much escaped.

A Protestant heir was essential. Edward's elder half-sister, Mary, held tenaciously to the Catholic faith; the younger, Elizabeth, kept her own counsel to such an extent that the zealots mistrusted her. Failing them, there were two possible lines of claimants. The first was the Scottish: Henry VII's daughter Margaret had had a son, James V, King of Scots, by her first marriage, and a daughter, Margaret Douglas, by her second (Margaret Douglas was to marry the Earl of Lennox and bear two sons, the elder being Henry Lord Darnley). James V was dead, but he had left an infant daughter Mary, Queen of Scots, now being educated at the French court. The second possibility was the Suffolk line, descended from that Mary Tudor, widow of the French king, who had infuriated her brother by her marriage to the Duke of Suffolk; the claim here rested in her two daughters, and in the elder daughter's three girls, the Ladies Jane and Katherine and Mary Grey, all English, and all Protestant. When it became evident that Edward VI would not live to manhood, he was persuaded to override his father's will, which had been approved by Parliament, and to name as successor the Lady Jane, wife of Guildford Dudley whose father was now the power behind the throne. Jane reigned barely a week. Catholic or not, Mary was true Tudor; within days she had gathered a great army of men, the rebels scattered and fled, and Mary came in triumph as queen into London, while poor Jane Grey was taken to the Tower where she was to die a few months later.

Mary I

Mary was thirty-eight when she became Queen. It was the dearest wish of her heart to restore the Roman Catholic Church within her realm; she needed a Catholic heir—and there was no trusting her sister Elizabeth. She must marry, and if God was good to her, which He would surely be, there was still time to bear a son. In July 1554 she married Philip of Spain ("Madam, he is the very paragon of the world") and soon she thought she was with child; her cousin the Papal Legate greeted her with the words once used to the mother of her Saviour: "*Ave Maria, gratia plena, Dominus tecum—*" But it was only sickness and delusion. Convinced that Heaven was punishing her, she tried to burn out heresy from the land; crazed with suffering she died at last, in November 1558.

All the known portraits of Mary as queen derive from two sittings in 1554, the first to Sir Antonio Mor and the second to Hans Eworth, which resulted in two basic portrait-types; several superb examples survive, notably at the Fitzwilliam Museum in Cambridge, Hever Castle in Kent (ironically, since it was Anne Boleyn's home), the Society of Antiquaries and the National Portrait Gallery in London. The Eworth portrait (Fig. 16) shows her in a burgundy brown velvet gown, against a dark green velvet background. She is wearing the huge pearl—*La Pellegrina*—which Philip sent to her in the June of 1554, a month before they were married. It is suspended from a gold and emerald double-jewel, and marks the apex of a jewelled triangle, its other points being the jewels on her hands. The whole painting is a series of triangles and squares, and nothing is squarer than the steady look Mary gives the world. Confident in her position as the rightful and Catholic queen, she wears too a large gold and emerald crucifix.

Much of Mary's jewellery was religious; indeed, it seems from her inventories that almost every jewel she had was either religious or foreign. She wore rosaries—agate, garnets, gold enamelled with black, "lapis lazell gauded with gold"—and pictorial jewels made to a religious design—in 1542, for instance, she had four brooches made showing Old Testament themes, in 1543 a further six including "Noyes floode" and "thistory of Jacob being a Slepe"; and she carried books of devotion with jewelled ornamental bindings—amongst others, one of gold "wt the Kings face and his graces mothers" (Elizabeth was to wear a rather similar one which is now in the British Museum, and which shows the Worshipping of the Serpent in the Wilderness and the Judgement of Solomon). Only one pictorial jewel with a secular theme is recorded among her jewellery: a locket showing "thistory of Piramys and Tysbe". The introduction of the old religious practices led to a certain revival of Catholic jewels of this kind, though it was not long-lived; one of her lords, on hearing she was considering whether she could force the nobles and gentlemen to hand back the lands they had acquired at the Dissolution of the Monasteries, was so furious that he threw his rosary into the fire; trinkets, yes; acres, no.

The foreign influence was evident in the introduction of jewels of engraved mother-of-pearl, then fashionable on the Continent, and the wearing of earrings, a Spanish custom (the close head-dresses of earlier reigns had made this impossible). There is, for example, a portrait by Johannes Corvus which shows Mary wearing long earrings of pear-shaped ruby drops threaded on gold wire.

When that longed-for, hopeful marriage to Philip took place at Winchester, Mary chose, touchingly, to be married with a plain gold ring "like any other maiden"; this apart, however, well-schooled by her father, she fulfilled her duty by wearing splendid jewellery that would maintain and enhance the glamour of the throne. Holinshed described her on progress early in her reign, when the world was still a place of promise:

> "She had on her head a Kall of cloth of tinsell beset with pearls and stones, and above the same upon her head a round circle of gold beset so richly with precious stones that the value thereof was inestimable; the same Kall and circle being so massive and ponderous that she was faine to bear up her head with her hand."

Elizabeth I

GLORIANA

Elizabeth I's role as sole monarch lasted for almost half a century. She succeeded to the Crown in 1558 at the age of twenty-five; she died forty-four years later, "a lady whom

Time hath surprised", sixty-nine but still indomitable, in 1603, at the start of the new century. Her long reign was to alter completely the social position of the sexes in England, making female fashion every bit as important as male.

The Elizabethan era saw the beginning of the use of jewellery as an integral part of costume, making it, as a result, dependant upon changing fashions in dress. The queen herself exhibited one of the most striking realizations possible of the way in which jewels could play their part in fashion, and above and beyond this, could display the country's prosperity and stability. She shared her father's emotional need for gems, and all the contemporary portraits of her show her wearing an almost incredible load of jewels. Perhaps more than any other woman in past or present history, she made the changing fashions of the day serve the purpose of providing a fitting setting for her jewellery, and emphasizing her own position, both as supreme ruler of England and Wales, and as a monarch standing on equal terms with the other rulers of Europe. There was sound strategy behind this. Brilliant and intellectual, she was shrewd enough to know that her jewels would be appraised by the foreign ambassadors, envoys and observers who sent home their reports to foreign courts. Many of those foreign rulers hoped, in her early days especially, to conclude marriage contracts with the English queen; many of them (often the same ones) were considering the chances of war against her. Her jewels were a visible image of wealth and power.

In 1598, when the darkness that was to lead to the Essex storm was beginning to gather about her, and her government was struggling to raise money with which to pursue the costly campaigns to subdue Ireland, a foreign visitor named Hentzner wrote a long and lucid description of the ageing queen:

> "She had in her ears two pearls with very rich drops; she wore false hair and that red; upon her head she had a small crown reported to be made of some of the gold of the celebrated Luneberg table; her bosom was uncovered as all the English ladies have it till they marry, and she had on a necklace of exceeding fine jewels . . . She was dressed in white silk, bordered with pearls the size of beans, and over it a mantle of black silk shot with silver threads; her train was very long . . . instead of a chain she had an oblong collar of gold and jewels."

The effect of black and white worn with her false red hair and sparkling jewels was very deliberate and dramatic. It matched her era: a time of extravagance, of eloquent sentiment, of emblems and allegories and symbols (the first printed emblem book was published in Italy in 1531, and by the middle of the Elizabethan Age they were enormously popular), of classical scholarship, of splendid language, of discovery and exploration, of theatre, masque and drama. The elaboration in dress and jewels echoed the vigorous uprush of life in music, poetry and the drama; the whole country mirrored the radiance of Gloriana.

Elizabeth's deliberate and regal splendour of dress was forced, like a psychological thrust, on the consciousness of all who saw her. However they viewed the queen, whether at court or on progress, in person or in paint, there was no room left to doubt her power. Her personality and her wealth were driven home. Every one of her gowns, and in her time she had thousands, was embroidered or clasped with gems: these were not small and inexpensive trifles either, but large and of great intrinsic worth.

The queen made a feature of expecting a New Year gift from members of her court (a habit which was quickly and naturally extended to all who expected and hoped for her favour). Gladys Scott Thomson points out that custom and status strictly regulated what was given; an earl was expected to give twenty pounds in gold—more if he wished, but not less. The donor received a gift in return, often chosen from among the stock of other presents the monarch had received, and this too—except for the especially favoured—was regulated; in the Stuart era, the king usually gave the earls a piece of gold plate each; and if that plate weighed more than thirty ounces, Miss Scott Thomson has remarked, the earl in question had to pay over the difference to the Lord Chamberlain.

Until the Commonwealth period, the New Year gifts were duly entered on special Gift Rolls which were kept in the Jewel House at the Tower. Each gift was described, whether rich or modest, together with the name and rank of the donor, and the name of the person into whose custody it was given (this was most important, as there were strict controls over what happened to the various jewels and plate). On the reverse of the Rolls was a list of the gifts presented by the sovereign, together with their value.

Henry VIII's New Year Gift Rolls were written on paper, and there were just four of them representing a reign of thirty-eight years. Elizabeth I's Rolls were very much more numerous and written on vellum, measuring from ten to twenty feet in length. They can still be seen at the British Museum, most of them duly signed by her. The descriptions of the more personal jewels she was given evoke the age: from Edward de Vere, Earl of Oxford, "a fair juell of golde being a shippe garnished fully with dyamondes and a mean pearle pendant"; from the Earl of Warwick, a jewel formed like a branch of bay-leaves with seven gold roses on it, one enamelled white, the other six red, together with a spider and a bee (1572); a pictorial jewel showing the story of Neptune with verses on the back which made up an acrostic of ELIZABETH: from the Countess of Bath "a fanne of swannes downe, with a maze of gilene velvet, ymbroidered with seed pearles and a very small chayne of silver gilte, and in the middst a border on both sides of seed pearles, sparkes of rubyes and emerods, and thereon a monster of gold, the head and breast mother of pearles" (1588-9); and in 1574, from her dear Leicester, another fan of white feathers set in a handle of gold, garnished on one side with diamonds and rubies and two "very fair" emeralds, and on the other with more rubies and more diamonds, with a white bear (his cognizance) on each side, two pendant pearls, and, emblematic of his being bound to the queen, "a lion ramping with a white muzzled bear at his foot".

Gifts like these, and all the other less personal ones, were accepted not merely as simple presents, but as a measure of loyalty to the Crown and the country, thus elevating basic bribery to a much higher level. (They also helped Elizabeth to achieve solvency; it took her fifteen years to pay off the debts her father and brother owed to the City of London, but she managed it at last. Her London merchants had solid financial grounds for their adoration.)

The portraits of Gloriana—fortunately many survive—show a gradual change from a young girl, discreetly dressed and perfectly assured, to a bare-breasted and terrifying harridan; the court artists who painted her in her early years could create pure and simple portraiture, but as time passed, the style seemed to grow stiffer and richer and more distant, until they were painting an icon rather than a woman—face and hands set in a rich crust of embroidery and lace and jewels. In Warwick Castle there is a painting by an unknown artist, *circa* 1559, which records Elizabeth in her coronation robes: "One mantle of clothe of golde, tissued with golde and silver, furred with powdered armyons [ermines], with a mantle lace of silke and golde, with buttons and tassels to the same." Her face is small and pale but determined, a close ruff lapping up about it so high that it conceals her ears; her breast is covered by the high-necked bodice—indeed, apart from the pale oval of face, the only flesh left bare is that of her slender hands, grasping the sceptre and the orb. On the limp red-gold hair that ripples across the mantle she balances the crown, and curving from shoulder to shoulder is a huge jewelled chain.

At the National Portrait Gallery in London is a portrait of Elizabeth, painted by an unknown artist in about 1575, when she was about forty years old, which is called the Cobham Portrait. It is supposed to be the best life-scale portrait ever painted of her. Her face is, as it were, stiffening into the blanched mask of her later years, as if she were retreating behind it. She is still a human being, but remote now, and impenetrable. Her dress is gay with golden flowers and leaves, frogged down the front of the bodice, and with a high ruff. In her hand she holds a feather fan (these were just beginning to come into fashion) with a jewelled handle, another jewel is attached to her waist, there are pearls sewn to the fabric of her dress and two huge ropes of pearls looped across the bodice. For all the trappings of crown and sceptre lying half-hidden by her side, she is dressed in a form-fitting gown which looks natural and comfortable, and her flesh is not over-exposed.

In the Victoria and Albert Museum there is a series of miniatures of the queen as she was in her old age. Her humanity is here completely suppressed, she is a formal icon, her face and bosom covered with cosmetics, her breast uncovered, her dress thick with embroidery, so stiff it would surely stand alone, framed in elaborate lace, heaped with jewels. It is as though Hilliard made a supreme effort to idealize the queen; the results are a sophisticated caricature of sheer horror.

TREASURES FROM WEST AND EAST

Elizabeth inspired a personal devotion in many of her subjects which amounted almost to a religion. This devotion was especially strong among her men of action, her pirate sailors. She wanted luxuries for herself and her people, and since the country lacked resources of its own, these could only be brought from abroad. Of especial significance were the loads of gold and silver which the Spanish *conquistadores* were looting from the New World and carrying home across the high seas. The buccaneer English sailors of the time treated the ocean as a Tom Tiddler's Ground, gleefully searching out the Spanish galleons with their cargoes of precious metals, spices and silks. Elizabeth closed her eyes to the illegality of these high sea robberies whenever possible and graciously accepted the stolen booty, generally protesting to Spain that she was completely innocent and would deal stringently with the offenders. Foremost among these pirate seamen was Sir Francis Drake (*circa* 1543–96), who in December 1577 set sail from England to encompass the world in his *Pelican* (later re-named *Golden Hind*), returning triumphantly in 1580 with a looted cargo of over thirty tons of precious metals. "As we sailed along," wrote one of his men, according to *The World Encompassed*, "continually searching for fresh water, we came to a place called Tarapaca, and landing there we lighted on a Spaniard who lay asleep, and had lying by him 13 bars of silver, weighing in all about 4000 Spanish ducats; we would not (could we have chosen) have awakened him of his nap: but seeing we, against our wills, did him that injury, we freed him of his charge which otherwise perhaps would have kept him waking. . . ." They sailed on to a town called Arica, and there found two ships containing "some forty and odd bars of silver (of the bigness and fashion of a brick bat, and in weight each of them about 20 pounds), of which we took the burden on ourselves to ease them" and a few days later encountered "another bark laden with linen, some of which we thought might stand us in some stead and therefore took it with us". The linen came in useful when they "took" another ship which was carrying a cargo of fruit, conserves, sugar, meal and other foodstuffs, and "(that which was the especiallest cause of her heavy and slow sailing) a certain quantity of jewels and precious stones, 13 chests of rials of plate, 80 pound weight in gold, 26 tons of uncoined silver, two very fair gilt silver drinking bowls" and, as he grandly said, "the like trifles"; they tossed the unfortunate master a little linen as a consolation prize.

The profits of the voyage are said to have exceeded £500,000. With his share Drake bought Buckland Abbey in Devon. He had some of the gems made into a crown set with diamonds and emeralds, which Elizabeth was graciously pleased to accept. In 1587, when the Spanish Armada was preparing to sail against England, it was reported from Antwerp that the pirate Drake had brought into Plymouth a great carrack, the *San Felipe*, belonging to Philip of Spain himself, laden with 400,000 ducats in gold (about £100,000).

Together with these lucky windfalls (and there were many more), were the more regularized imports of gemstones from the East.

> "*Give me the merchants of the India mines,*
> *That trade in metals of the purest mould;*
> *The wealthy Moor that in the Eastern rocks*
> *Without control can pick his riches up,*
> *And in his house, heap pearls like pebblestones,*
> *Receive them free—and sell them by the weight.*
>
> *Bags of fiery opals, sapphires, amethysts,*
> *Jacinth, hard topaz, grass-green emeralds,*
> *Beauteous rubies, sparkling diamonds,*
> *And seld-seen costly stones—*

(Marlowe, *The Jew of Malta*, I, i; *circa* 1589)

With all this wealth of materials for the creation of jewellery, the designer found endless scope for his talents and his fantasies. Yet, in a curious way, this bounty almost proved to be a drawback. During the earlier centuries, when there had been a great scarcity of metals and gems, the designer had had to rely on his sense of form and his imagination, and had made beautifully sculptural works of art. Once he had all these new materials in abundance, however, the jeweller seems to have worked more quickly, hurling coloured stones in together to give a massed effect of flashing lights, reflecting the patron's wealth rather than any artistic inspiration. This resulted in a loss of form. Few works of art in gold and enamels were created. Quite a proportion of the English jewels of the later sixteenth century are baldly vulgar. Jewellers also began to take stones from one out-dated piece of jewellery and re-set them in another, to keep up with changes in fashion or with the owner's desire for something new.

The ever-increasing importance of trade had naturally resulted in a similar growth of importance for the wealthy merchant class. Elizabeth was to give many of them positions at her court. There was, for instance, Sir Thomas Gresham, whose father and uncle were both mercers, each of them serving as Lord Mayor of London. Sir Thomas built London's Royal Exchange at his own expense (but got the investment back by renting out shops in the upper parts of the building), and in 1571 Elizabeth came to open it, first dining in the city with her trusted and faithful servant. Men like Sir Thomas were hard-working, industrious and enterprising; "in trade" and proud of it. The merchant class was flourishing all over England, and its members no doubt enjoyed dressing the part.

Some of the simple enamelled chains sold in Cheapside or in those prosperous Royal Exchange shops were perfectly charming; and although many of the big lavish pieces, displaying a handful of gems from the New World, lacked discipline and style, one must add that others were clever and amusing, and some quite lovely and wrought with great technical skill.

The Use of Diamonds

The more general use of the diamond was another pivotal point in the history of jewellery, and came during the Elizabethan era.

In most of the early Elizabethan jewels there are almost no diamonds at all; and even when they are set in a jewel, they are certainly never the focal point. During her reign they came gradually to be used as quiet contrast, placed like pale punctuation points to separate the other coloured gemstones and enamels (the Barbor Jewel is one example). They were still not cut in a truly geometric way, and their fire was still not properly released (the back of a diamond was usually touched with a spot of black paint to minimize the shimmer) but the lapidary's skill was increasing. The growing fashion for diamonds was no doubt due in part to this, but was also influenced in England by the Elizabethans' passion for light as well as colour. During the early decades of the sixteenth century English men and women generally lived out their lives in dark-panelled rooms lit by small rushlights; during the second half of the century, however, the English glassworkers were manufacturing window glass—and the Elizabethans enthusiastically let the light into their new brick manor houses through huge glass windows, "Hardwicke Hall, more glass than wall" is a case in point; brilliant Bess of Hardwicke (1518–1608), said to be the wealthiest woman in England by the time she contracted her fourth marriage, which made her the Countess of Shrewsbury, reigned there almost as proudly as the queen herself (at one time, indeed, thinking her far too ambitious, Elizabeth slapped her in the Tower). She was one of the greatest builders of her time; people said, in fact, that she would never die so long as she had some building project in progress, and it took severe February frosts to stop her and send her to the

Derby tomb she had had built and inscribed to her own specifications. Hardwicke Hall still stands in Derbyshire, glittering with its glass, and is one of the finest of the late Elizabethan buildings.

NEW TEXTILES, NEW FASHIONS

The silk industry is believed to have originated in prehistoric China. Silk was among the costliest Eastern products imported and prized by the Romans. The Emperor Justinian set up silk looms within the imperial palace of Byzantium; and in about the year A.D. 550 the first silkworms were smuggled out of China by a pair of Persian monks, hidden in their hollow staffs, and presented to the emperor. Luckily they flourished, duly producing a breed of worm from which were descended all those varieties used in Europe for the next thousand years and more. From Byzantium the Saracens carried the silk trade out into Asia Minor and eventually to Sicily (where the weavers also wove with bullion). From here the cultivation of silkworms and the manufacture of silk travelled north into the great medieval trading cities of Italy—Florence, Genoa, Venice and Milan. (Francis I is said to have obtained a supply of silkworm eggs from Milan, for rearing in France.) By the mid-sixteenth century the weaving of textiles was an important and valuable trade. The weavers of Genoa were especially famous for their fine silken velvets, the weavers of Venice for their smooth silvery watery damasks—a beautiful patterned fabric of Asian origin, introduced into Europe by the Crusaders; much depended on the kind of water available in each city.

The Elizabethan era saw the growth of a new feeling for lighter fabrics, paler shades, greater varieties. The Florentine weavers, for example, were particularly skilled at bleaching, and fine white Florentine textiles were carried along the trading routes. Some textiles were designed for furnishing, others to be worn; one no longer made doublet and curtain of the same rich silk velvet with huge dramatic patterns and heavy folds. Patterns were produced which were slightly smaller in scale, and thus more suitable for wearing on the human body. Fabrics became rather more supple and sympathetic, designed to be displayed against the exposed flesh—for now women were beginning to bare both head and breast. Supple silk could be used for more intimate female garments as well: Elizabeth had her own silk woman (the manufacture of silk had been introduced into England by Henry VI, but was not to flourish until the arrival of Protestant Flemish weavers seeking sanctuary from the religious wars; the first wave of these arrived from the Low Countries in 1585) and it was this Mrs. Montagu who, early in the queen's reign, presented a New Year gift of her own, a pair of silk stockings. This gift was a tremendous success, more so, perhaps, than some of the courtiers' dutiful jewelled conceits; "They are pleasant, fine and delicate. I will wear no more cloth," Elizabeth at once declared.

The Renaissance had reduced to some degree the stern universal rule of the Church, and its stress on individuality and personality was bringing women to the fore. Henry's queens had covered their heads; Elizabeth, proud of her virgin status, often chose to display her auburn hair. It had always been thought unclean for a married woman to show her hair—this was an especial prejudice in Italy—but now the ladies of the European courts began to leave their heads uncovered, and even emphasized the fact by wearing jewels twisted and looped through their curls. As the head was uncovered, so the neck was bared; the bosoms of unmarried ladies were once again on view, a splendid focus for the huge ruffs, frills and wire-stiffened lace collars displayed in the portraits of the Elizabethan era.

As a result, a new fashion came into play: ladies began to wear hair ornaments and earrings. Elizabeth was particularly fond of pearls, and in almost every portrait ever painted of her she has chosen to wear pearl earrings. These elaborate and costly fashions did not meet with universal approval. Thomas Nashe wrote furiously in *Christ's Teares over Jerusalem* (1593) about the folly and vanity of women who beset their foreheads "with glorious borrowed gleamy bushes". He thundered on:

> "Their heads, with the top and top-gallant lawn baby-caps and snow-resembled silver curlings, they make a plain puppet stage of. Their breasts they embusk up on high, and their round roseate buds immodestly lay forth to show at their hands there is fruit to be hoped."

William Harrison had preceded him, crying out in his *Description of England* (1587) against the mutability and costliness of fashion; men were transformed from cap to shoe, and even chaste and sober matrons had adopted "staring attire"—doublets with pendant codpieces on the breast, full of jags and cuts, sleeves in sundry colours, "galli-gaskins to bear out their bums", farthingales and coloured nether stocks: he ran out of words to deal with such enormities. Nashe promised the torments of Hell as payment for such vanities. "For thy carcanets of pearl shalt thou have carcanets of spiders." It was not the kind of advice to which Elizabeth was likely to pay any attention; and if she did not, nor would anyone else.

The Ropes of Catharine

Elizabeth's most famous pearls were bought for £3000—a bargain price—from the Regent of Scotland, the Earl of Moray. They can be seen in most of the later portraits of the queen, the most well known being the Ditchley Portrait by Marcus Gheeraerts which is in the National Portrait Gallery in London.

Pope Clement VII had collected together the greatest set of matching pearls ever seen in Europe to give to his niece, Catharine de Medici, on the occasion of her marriage in 1533 to Francis I of France's son, later to be Henri II, King of France. There was little affection behind the present: it was a gesture from one princely ruler to another, diplomatically and politically balanced; the Pope had to pawn the biggest diamond in his tiara in order to pay for the pearls and for the wedding of this fourteen-year-old pawn in the diplomatic game. There were six ropes of these great pearls, each falling well to the waist, and twenty-five teardrops, said to be "the biggest and finest ever seen".

Catharine eventually gave these pearls to her daughter-in-law, Mary, Queen of Scots, wife of the young Dauphin, Francis. The boy died in 1560, and Mary sailed sadly back to Scotland, taking the pearls with her ("*Adieu donc, ma chère France*"); it had been suggested that she should leave her jewels in France, rather than risk them on the dangerous voyage to Scotland, but Mary decided that where she went, the jewels went too. Six years later, after a rash and tragic reign, she had been forced to abdicate; Moray, her own half-brother, seized her jewels and, hoping to get Elizabeth on the rebels' side, sent the pearls to London. Catharine de Medici wanted to buy them back; but there was no hope of this, Elizabeth had inspected the pearls, with Leicester to help her, and was delighted with them. She bought them as her right (Moray is said to have let her have them for a third of their actual value), wore them endlessly, and was no doubt bitterly reluctant at having to leave them to her successor.

On Elizabeth's death, the crown of England passed to James of Scotland, whose wife, Anne, wore the pearls with the greatest of pleasure. When their daughter, Elizabeth, married Frederick the Count Palatine—later, and briefly, King of Bohemia —in 1613, they gave the pearls to her. Elizabeth, doubly nicknamed the "Winter Queen" (because her husband's reign proved so short) and the "Queen of Hearts" (a name which speaks for itself), had thirteen children. In time she gave the pearls to her youngest daughter, Sophia, who married the Elector of Hanover in 1658. The direct line of the Stuarts in England came to an end with Queen Anne, who died childless in 1714; the Electress Sophia was the next heir, and hung on grimly to life in the hope that the words *Queen of England* might yet be inscribed on her coffin, but lost the race by six days. Her eldest son became George I of Great Britain, and the Ropes of Catharine (now called the Hanoverian Pearls) returned to England. His daughter-in-law, Queen Caroline, wore them, so did George III's wife, Queen Charlotte; eventually they came to Queen Victoria. But in 1837 her uncle, Ernest Augustus, King of Hanover, appealed to Victoria to hand them back, maintaining that now that the monarchies of Hanover and Britain were independent of one another, the jewels should be returned to the Hanoverian side of the family ("I hear the little queen is loaded with my diamonds"). Twenty-one years later—years of pure legal prevarication—the Hanoverian family was sent a fine string of pearls. (By this time old King Ernest was dead.) Were those pearls the original Ropes of Catharine? It seems we can never now know.

Pendants

Her pearls apart, Elizabeth had many jewels: crowns, chains, necklaces, jewelled fans, finger rings, brooches, pendants. Lockets embodying portraits, emblems and symbols abounded towards the end of her reign—portrait lockets, indeed, were worn more at this period than ever before or since.

A symbol often worn by the queen was that of the Phoenix: that legendary and unique bird which was said to live five hundred years, then burn itself on a funeral pyre and rise anew from its own ashes; it was the emblem of immortality. In the hands of the Elizabethan poets and courtiers the image underwent a subtle change, symbolizing the virginity and "one-ness" of their virgin queen. Old Lord Norreys, whose dear wife was nicknamed "Crow" by Elizabeth, greeted her with a charming compliment when she came to visit him: "Nothing can be more unfit to lodge Your Majesty than a Crow's nest, yet shall it be most happy to us that it is by Your Highness made a phoenix nest." Her **Phoenix Jewel**, which she is known to have enjoyed wearing, can be seen in several portraits of her, among them the Hilliard portrait, dating from about 1575 (Fig. 17), which is now in the National Portrait Gallery in London (though on occasional loan to the Tate). She wears the jewel on her bodice, pendant from a golden Tudor rose; it is almost lost amongst the colours of the textiles, the gold embroidery, the sewn gemstones and pearls, the puffs of silk and the sumptuous jewellery. Made of enamelled gold, it shows a sculptural model of the Phoenix with outstretched wings trying to lift itself out of the flames which lick about its feet; the enamelling is particularly realistic. The jewel is now in the British Museum, having been presented in 1753 by Sir Hans Sloane.

A supreme example of an emblematic jewel is the **Lennox Jewel** (also known as the **Darnley Jewel**), another pendant. The Countess of Lennox may have commissioned this jewel in 1571, in memory of her husband, who was murdered while acting as Regent of Scotland. She was a most devious woman, constantly intriguing—first, in favour of her son Darnley; then against his wife, Mary, Queen of Scots, who was, she believed (so did almost everyone else), implicated in Darnley's murder; then, thinking Elizabeth might die and Mary succeed her, becoming reconciled, formally at least, to Mary again. The jewel is a heart-shaped pendant locket, and is probably the most complicated jewel ever made in that century. It is no more than 2½ inches (about 65 mm) long, yet it incorporates six mottoes and no fewer than twenty-eight symbols and emblems. These emblems plainly had great significance for Lady Lennox, and may symbolize events in her unhappy life or carry some concealed message. Perhaps so devious a mind, accustomed to the need for constant watchfulness and secrecy, naturally expressed itself in symbols. The jewel is as complex as some of the poems of the era, as enigmatic as some of the riddles. The innermost portrait is now missing. Presumably, as Joan Evans suggests, this showed the Regent Lennox.

The jewel seems to have suffered from much handling; perhaps in its early career it was displayed to friends, handed around, discussed, admired, even dropped. It was exhibited in 1959, and has sometimes been on display at Windsor Castle; it is in the possession of Her Majesty the Queen.

Elizabeth's own portrait was often incorporated into contemporary jewels, in much the same complimentary fashion as the skilled Flemish weavers of an earlier era had portrayed their patrons, the Dukes of Burgundy, in tapestries telling some heroic tale—the Life of Alexander, for example. One of the most famous of these portrait pendants is the **Barbor Jewel**.

There is a charming legend about the Barbor Jewel which is best related colloquially, to give it a contemporary flavour.

There was once a man named Sir William Barbor who worked in the service of the king, Henry VIII. When the time came for the English to renounce their allegiance to the Pope in Rome and to follow the new religious teachings, Sir William Barbor felt he could not change. "Well, Sir William," said the king, "should you not think again? You know what might happen if you went against my wishes." So Sir William went away for a few days and carefully considered the position, returning to the court and renouncing the Romish allegiance.

All went well through the reign of the Protestant king, Edward VI, but once the Catholic queen, Mary I, came to the throne, there was strife again. "Change back to Catholicism," she said, "and renounce the Protestant faith."

"I cannot," said Sir William. "I changed before, and it was almost too painful for my conscience."

"Well, Sir William," said the queen, "you know what might happen should you go against my wishes."

The Armada Jewel: this richly decorated pendant is said to have been presented by Elizabeth I to Sir Thomas Heneage after the defeat of the Armada in 1588. It has been attributed to Nicholas Hilliard. It is small—2¾ inches (70 mm) deep by 2 inches (50 mm) wide—and elegant, as splendidly decorated on the reverse, with its delightful enamelled Noah's Ark and its clear-cut motto ("Calm through the savage waves"), as on the front, with its formal gold portrait bust of the Queen against brilliant blue enamel, set in a delicate enamelled frame with small rubies and diamonds. It opens to reveal a portrait of the Queen, and on the inside lid is painted a red rose surrounded by a leafy wreath and a Latin motto. The workmanship is extremely fine, the design balanced and disciplined, and the Jewel itself patently and charmingly personal.

By courtesy of the Trustees of the Victoria and Albert Museum

So Sir William Barbor went away from court again and considered his position, and this time it took him much longer.

When he returned he spoke to the queen and told her he simply could not change back again, it had been hard enough the first time when he was young, now he was too old to go through it all once more; he was prepared to take the consequences.

Sadly the queen watched as he was taken away, tried and condemned to death. He awaited his end patiently in the Tower of London, and said farewell to his family and friends. The day arrived when the sentence was to be carried out, and Sir William was brought to the block, was blindfolded, and knelt down for an agonizing death.

As he did so, a messenger came galloping up, shouting at the top of his voice, "Stop, stop, for God's sake stop. Queen Mary is dead. Long live Elizabeth the Queen."

Thankfully Sir William was helped to his feet and the blindfold removed, for everyone there believed that Elizabeth would prove more sympathetic to the Protestants than her sister had done. And they proved to be perfectly right.

Congratulated by his friends and jailers, Sir William vowed on the spot to have a jewel created as a mark of gratitude to Elizabeth the queen, with a portrait of her on the front. This was to be given to his first grand-daughter (his own daughter was pregnant at the time), and the child was to be christened Elizabeth, as the first-born female child in each generation should be named from thenceforward.

This was done; a charming little pendant jewel was created, with an onyx cameo of the queen in profile on the front, surrounded by small diamonds and rubies set amongst white and blue enamels, with a diamond crown above and a cluster of small pearls below. On the back is enamelled a sturdy oak tree of England.

The Barbor Jewel was handed down from generation to generation, being bestowed in turn on each first-born female child, together with the name Elizabeth, until the twentieth century. Unfortunately the last Elizabeth Barbor did not choose to marry: when she died, she generously left the Barbor Jewel to the nation. It is on view at the Victoria and Albert Museum in London: a commemorative Elizabethan jewel whose elegance and charm are independent of the light and charming legend.

Nicholas Hilliard

Among the loveliest and most craftsmanlike of the Elizabethan jewels are those created by Nicholas Hilliard. In the best traditions of the Renaissance, he was both a goldsmith

Fig. 32 : two views of a *memento mori* jewel, believed to be English seventeenth-century work. It is a small gold coffin-shaped box containing a white enamelled figure of a skeleton. The lid is engraved with crosses and death's heads. Inscribed on the outside at the front are the words *Disce mori*, and at the back an English translation *Lern to dyi*. Such jewels were carried in the sixteenth and seventeenth centuries as a reminder of the transience of earthly life and the inevitable coming of judgment.

From a private collection by courtesy of the owner

and a painter. As a result, his art is generally in miniature and his work as a jeweller exceedingly artistic.

Hilliard was born in about 1537 and died in 1619. He was the grandson of John Wall, a London goldsmith. His father was a goldsmith in Exeter, and he himself eventually became a Freeman of the Worshipful Company of Goldsmiths. He trained, however, as a painter, and entered Elizabeth's household becoming one of her official portraitists. When he presented himself to take his first likeness of her, she told him that the style of painting she most admired was the Italian, in which the face was bathed in clear light; why did painters of other schools use shadow? Hilliard answered that the painters who employed the effects of shadow in their work did so because they were using a "grosser line". His own line was extremely fine and delicate, and he painted her in the Italian style, in full light. The portrait miniature in the National Portrait Gallery, dated 1572, is believed to have resulted from this first sitting, which took place "in the open ally of a goodly garden" in the clear light of day. He painted many other portrait miniatures of her—there are examples in the National Portrait Gallery and in the Victoria and Albert Museum—and in all of them his goldsmith training is made evident by the lightly delicate touches of infinitesimal detail.

At the request of a Mr. Haydocke, Hilliard wrote a treatise called *The Arte of Limning*, a fascinating work which deals with some of the practical aspects of portrait painting (a good north light is desirable, away from the "sulfurous ayr of seacole", "musicke offendeth not" but a wise painter shuts out busybodies and carefully refrains from losing his temper). He goes into detail about jewels (the ruby, for instance, "flickereth and afecteth the eye like burning fyer, especially by the candel light") and describes how the painter can achieve the right faithful effect:

> "You may burnish your goold or siluer here or there as need requireth, as you siluer when you make your diamonds first burnished then drawne vppon with black in squares lyke the diamond cutt. Other stones must be glased vppon the siluer with their proper cullors with some varnish etc; the pearles layed with a whit mixed with a littel black, a littel Yndy blew, and a littel masticot, but very littel in comparison of the white, not the hundred parte. That being dry, give the light of your pearle with siluer somewhat more to the light side then the shadowe side, and as round and as full as you cane, then take good whit delayed with a littel masticot, and vnderneath at the shadowe side give it a compassing stroke which showes the reflection that a pearle hath, then without that a smale shadowe of seacole vndermost of all."

All the bright exact jewelled colour of the age is present in those careful instructions; is it the jeweller speaking, or the miniaturist? It seems they coexisted in him, and that the creations of each were shaped by the other.

The Armada Jewel

One of the most important surviving Elizabethan jewels is attributed to Hilliard. This is the **Armada Jewel**, also known as the **Heneage Jewel**, which was made during the full flowering of Elizabeth's reign. The jewel (facing page 98) was allegedly given by the queen to Sir Thomas Heneage of Copt Hall in Essex, and remained in the possession of the Heneage family until 1902 when it was sold to the Pierpont Morgan Collection;

in 1935 it was bought by Lord Wakefield and presented to the Victoria and Albert Museum, and is now beautifully exhibited in the Jewellery Gallery there.

Sir Thomas Heneage was one of the queen's loyal and trusted favourites; she once amused herself with a flirtation with him, with the happy intention of annoying her "sweet Robin", the Earl of Leicester. He was made one of her gentlemen in 1560, and served her faithfully for the rest of his life, dying as a Privy Councillor and Vice Chamberlain, and leaving a will which called her "most worthy of all my heart's love and reverence". The jewel was a personal recognition of his more than adequate services as Treasurer at War for the armies which were especially recruited during the time of the Armada, 1588.

The Armada Jewel typifies English pendants of the late sixteenth century. Every part of it is beautifully decorated and every part has its meaning; the beauty and significance of the front, for example, are equal in importance with the reverse, each being splendidly decorated. It is small, measuring $2\frac{3}{4}$ inches deep by 2 inches wide (about 70 mm by 50 mm), and colourful, being made of gold and adorned with brilliant enamels; and it opens up to show the surprise that lies within.

The front displays a golden portrait bust of the queen, in profile, copied from the Garter Badge of 1582. This stands out in high relief against a background of translucent blue enamel. It combines the formal treatment of a classical coin with the feeling of a personal portrait, for the framing stands proud of the central section and its delicate gold enamelling and the small rubies and diamonds with which it is set balance the gold portrait bust without overpowering it.

The reverse is smooth and flat with a delightful toy Noah's Ark bouncing about in a rough sea in the pouring rain, enamelled in deep clear colours. Around this scene, framing it, are the words

SAEVAS TRANQUILLA PER UNDAS

("Calm through the savage waves"). The design is the same as that which appeared on the Naval Award Medal of 1588.

The reverse of the jewel forms a locket, and when this is opened up Elizabeth I stares back at you in all her usual finery. The portrait, which is almost full-face, is attributed to Hilliard and has been much restored.

Inside the lid (that is, backing on to the bouncing ark) is painted a red rose surrounded by a leafy wreath and the words

Hei Mihi quod tanto virtus perfusa decore non habet eternus inviolata dies

("Alas that virtue endowed with such beauty should not scatheless enjoy perpetual life"), a fawning motto which had also appeared before, on the reverse of the Phoenix Badge of 1572.

The Armada Jewel is neat, taut, clever and elegant. Technically it is of a very high standard and extremely disciplined. It has, in fact, all the especial attributes one searches for in the best High Renaissance jewellery. Its symmetry shows a definite north European influence, so that it slightly lacks the artistic flair shown in the creations of some of the more sophisticated ducal craftsmen of Italy; none the less, the jewel in its entirety certainly competes on an international level.

An Amulet: the Danny Jewel

Another pendant jewel of the Elizabethan period is of particular interest in illustrating the continuing faith in amulets. This is the **Danny Jewel**, also known as the **Campion Jewel**, which is now in the Victoria and Albert Museum. (The reason for its double name is that it was originally owned by the Campion family of Danny in Sussex.) It is made from a half-section of a narwhal's tusk, set in enamelled gold, and forming a semi-circular pendant. This is 1¼ inches deep by 2⅜ inches wide (about 30 mm by 60 mm), with another 2¼ inches (about 55 mm) of chain. Unhappily nothing reliable is known about its provenance, but it may be stylistically attributed to the late Elizabethan period.

For many hundreds of years, people had believed that the narwhal's tusk was the horn of that most magical of creatures, the fabled unicorn. (Old Sir John Hawkins, one of the great seamen of the age, declared that there were great herds of unicorn in Florida: "A beast with one horne which cometh to drinke, putteth the same into the river before he drinketh. . . .") Naturally such a horn was enormously precious, and anyone lucky enough to get hold of one cut it up into tiny sections and placed them in sumptuous mounts, to be revered as magical amulets or talismans. (Mary, Queen of Scots had a narwhal's tusk.) Jewellers were no doubt delighted to get hold of them:

> *"An angrie Unicorne in full carier*
> *Charg'd with too quicke an eie a Jewller*
> *That watcht him for the Treasure of his browe;*
> *And ere he could get shelter of a tree,*
> *Nail'd him with his rich Antler to the Earth."*

(Chapman, *Bussy d'Ambois*, i; 1607)

People also believed that a unicorn's horn (alias a narwhal's tusk) could be used as a reliable poison detector, for it was supposed to change colour if dipped into poisoned food or drink. (This belief persisted for a surprisingly long time; indeed, at the outbreak of the French Revolution in 1789, the tusk was still being used to test food for the royal table.) A unicorn's horn is listed in the royal inventories for January 1544 (Windsor, No. 1338): "Oone Staffe of Vnicornes horne with a Crosse garnisshid with siluer guilt and a rounde Christall poiz." And in the will of Sir Nathaniel Bacon who died in 1622 there is this thoughtful direction:

> "I give to all my three daughters the jewel of unicorn's horn, according to their mother's direction, that each one may challenge the use thereof when needs require, and my wife may have the use thereof when she needs."

Several complete horns were kept at the Tower of London amongst the Royal Plate and the Crown Jewels. Peter Mundy wrote in 1635 that he saw one there which was "one and a half yards in length and two to two-and-a-half inches diameter at the bigger end", then valued at £2,000 sterling; another in the Lower Jewel House is known to have weighed 40½ pounds. When the limited medical knowledge and trusted herbal potions of the time failed to cure the patient, family and friends would raise heaven and earth to procure some powdered tusk for him; after that, it was agreed, events depended upon "the will of God".

ELIZABETH'S RINGS

When Paul Hentzner visited England in 1598, and there saw the queen in magpie glory of black and white, he recorded that her right hand was "sparkling with rings and jewels" (she had pulled off her glove so that a baron might kiss her hand). Outstanding among the many sentimental and personal jewels made for her during her reign is the ring that she is said to have bestowed on Essex in the last years of her reign, with the promise that "if ever he forfeited her favour, if he sent it back to her, the sight of it would ensure her forgiveness"; it is now in Westminster Abbey. There is nothing especial about the workmanship—it is an emerald engraved with a portrait of her—but the story, related many years later by the Careys (who were kin to both Essex and the queen), has persisted, though modern scholarship casts doubts on it. When Essex lay imprisoned in the Tower, after his rash and crazy rebellion, he is said to have thrown the ring from his window, with a bribe, telling a boy to carry it to Lady Scrope (Philadelphia Carey, one of the queen's ladies). The boy, however, took it by mistake to Kate Carey, Philadelphia's sister, and her husband the Lord High Admiral, one of Essex's greatest enemies, hid it and suppressed the message; and Essex was duly beheaded. That, at least, is the story.

After Essex's beheading, in the February of 1601, the queen sank into a settled melancholy; but she lingered another two years, her spirits still flaring occasionally into their old brilliance. "There is no jewel, be it of never so rich a price, which I set before this jewel: I mean your love," she told a delegation from the House of Commons in one of her incomparable speeches. Many years before she had held up her Coronation Ring and said, "I am already bound unto a husband, which is the Kingdom of England"; now that ring had grown into her finger—they had to file it away. By the Christmastide of 1602/3, it was clear that she was dying; north of the Border, anxiously waiting, was the strongest of the possible claimants to her throne—James VI, King of Scots. When the old queen died in the early hours of March 24, her cousin Robert Carey slipped away to ride frantically north, in the hope of being the first to reach James (the council "caught hold of" him, to check him, but he escaped); with him he took a ring which, according to one story, Philadelphia Carey had thrown from the window of the dead queen's room, as a token to James that the news was true. Carey rode like the devil for two days, and got his deserts when he fell and was struck by the horse's hoof "that made me shed much blood", but he struggled on again to Edinburgh, and there knelt and saluted James as King of England and told him that he "brought him a blue ring from a fair lady, that I hoped would give him assurance of the truth that I had reported". The long rivalry between the two cousins, Elizabeth Tudor and Mary, Queen of Scots, was ended at last by death and the union of their Crowns.

Mary, Queen of Scots

As James V of Scotland lay dying, messengers brought him news that his queen had given birth to a daughter. The baby, born on December 8, 1542, was named Mary; she was Queen of Scots before a week was out. In August 1548 she was taken to France (her mother, Mary of Guise, was French) and there brought up at the court of the Valois, being betrothed to the Dauphin, whom she married in April 1558.

The inventories of her property and the solemn portraits of her reveal that she owned a store of rich and varied jewellery and ornaments, many of them having some religious significance or symbolism in their design. She loved pearls and filigree work and unusual pendants. One little pendant, for example, was shaped like a court jester in enamelled gold, with a Latin inscription meaning "He looks simple but is not". Another was an openwork locket set with bands of seed-pearls, inside which was a painted miniature of herself and her only surviving child, James. Few of the miniatures of her can be authenticated, but there is one, a gold and enamelled pendant, probably made in France, which is now owned by the Duke of Portland, and which is originally said to have been given by Mary to the Duke of Norfolk. In the centre is a cornelian cameo showing a profile portrait bust of the queen; this opens on a hinge, revealing a cavity where a relic could be kept. Another which may be said to be authentic is the **Penicuik Jewel**, given to Barbara Mowbray, one of her ladies. The workmanship is strangely coarse, but there is a miniature of Mary on one side and of James on the other ("a somewhat watery little boy").

Her portraits (in most of which she has a crucifix, emblematic of the claims of the "rightful Catholic Queen") often show her wearing rich chains of the type so popular in the sixteenth century. The Antonio Mor portrait, now in the Fitzwilliam Museum in Cambridge, shows her in a chain of gold, rubies, diamonds and pearls. In the Oudry portrait, painted in 1578 and now in the National Portrait Gallery, she is wearing several: from one, of intricately pierced links, is suspended her precious crucifix, another is looped about her like a girdle, terminating near the hem of her gown, and a *châtelaine* is suspended from a third.

Even as a child, Mary was dressed in accordance with her position in life: her jewels were so numerous that three brass-bound chests would not hold them all. At Candlemas, 1554, when she was eleven, she attended a Mass in Notre Dame, so lovely and so covered with jewels that a woman called out from the crowd, "Are you not an angel?" Before their betrothal, the Dauphin Francis gave her a jewelled pendant in the form of a cupid playing with a mouse (it was mentioned in her will): a fantasy jewel typical of the late Renaissance. Typical too was the splendour of their marriage, at Notre Dame in April 1558; she was crowned with gold and "walled about with diamonds", the whole court melodious with music, luminous with torches, scintillating with jewels.

But this sophisticated life did not last. Francis reigned for only eighteen months (his mother is said to have sent to get the Crown Jewels back again from Mary even more promptly than Mary herself had sent for them when he became king) and the widowed queen sailed home to Scotland, the kingdom she had not seen since she was a child of five. There the first promise, born of her charm which bewitched many of her subjects, soon shredded away; her marriage to Lord Darnley, which took place on July 29, 1565, ended in disaster; her liaison with the Earl of Bothwell ended in a hasty and calamitous marriage; the people rose against her—looting Holyrood Palace of her plate and personal jewels; she was imprisoned and compelled to abdicate in favour of the baby James; escaped, fled across the Border to her "dear sister" Elizabeth, and there entered upon a new captivity that was to last almost twenty years. Her jewels had been sifted through by successive captors, and so few were left to her that when she went to the block in 1587 she wore simply

"A pomander chayne and an Agnus Dei about hir necke, a Crucifix in hir hande,
a payre of beades att hir girdle, with a silver cross att the end of them."

She had once been adorned with rubies, diamonds and pearls, set according to the latest
French fashions; fitting gems for a woman who liked to wear cloth of gold, cloth of
silver, black velvet, crimson velvet and white silk. The inventory of her jewels, taken
in 1562 after her return to Scotland, listed 180 items; in the will she made four years
later, she left the finest of these to the Crown, more to her French relatives, a ring
enamelled in red to Darnley (it was one of the three used at their wedding), a diamond
ring enamelled black and a mermaid in diamonds to Bothwell, a head-dress and collar
and cuffs set with gems to his wife—but most of these were probably seized by the
rebels soon afterwards. Few jewels now survive that can be said to have belonged,
without question, to Mary, Queen of Scots, though a few remain in the royal collection
and in private hands—the Seton family has some, the Howards others. The golden
rosary Mary carried to her death was bequeathed to Anne Howard, Countess of
Arundel, and is still in the family's possession; so too is a necklace of pearls and gold
filigree connected by small links (a style of jewel which could be worn by either sex in
the sixteenth century) said to have been used by Elizabeth after Mary's death, and one
of the oldest still in private hands; rightly these treasures are in the possession of a
leading British Catholic family. But in general, her jewels were dispersed (the English
Government was determined to prevent any hoarding of Mary Stuart relics), sold,
re-set, melted down. For authenticated jewels, one must turn to the inventories (there
are copies at the British Museum and in the Bodleian at Oxford) and to the portraits,
which show her richly endowed with fine jewellery. There are particularly fine portraits at Kelvingrove in Glasgow and at Holyrood House in Edinburgh. Other jewels
survive which are traditionally assigned to her, among them the crucifix shown in
Fig. 23, now in a private collection and reproduced here by kind permission of the
owner. This is an English sixteenth-century piece, which opens up so that relics could
be kept within; a titulus above the corpus is inscribed *INRI*, there is a skull beneath the
feet, and inscribed around the sides are the words:

Behold who suffere what and for whom he suffered

Engraved and enamelled on the back are the instruments of the Passion.

Other jewels from this collection are illustrated in Fig. 32 facing page 99, and in
Figs. 20 to 22. They are fascinating artefacts, essentially private and personal, small
enough to be readily concealed, elegant and religious, with a strong *memento mori* theme—
reminders of the transience of earthly life were popular at this time; Mary, for instance,
had a watch in the shape of a skull. There is a skull among these jewels too, but this is a
gold pomander (Fig. 21), its interior divided into compartments for spices, with a
dividing plate inscribed

Man proposes but God disposes

The date 1679 is engraved on the base. Other pieces include a miniature coffin-shaped
jewel of gold, with the figures of Adam and Eve, enamelled in white, upon the lid and a

serpent enamelled in green, with a Greek inscription around the sides in black enamel, which is late sixteenth-century English work. It once held a skeleton, but unfortunately does so no longer; the small gold *memento mori* coffin in Fig. 32, however, still has its occupant, a white enamelled skeleton; inscribed on the outside is the Latin phrase

✠ *DISCE MORI*

and its translation

✠ *LERN TO DYI*

and on the top and ends are crossed bones and death's heads between the initials *E.W.* This is English, and dates from the seventeenth century. The jewel illustrated in Fig. 20 is an agate "showstone" with silver mounts engraved with a rose and foliage, connected by three straps; again, seventeenth-century English work. Stones such as this have been found in Merovingian and Dark Age graves, and were much prized as talismans and luck stones in the sixteenth and seventeenth centuries.

INTERLUDE

The Cheapside Hoard

Introduction—Chains; Rings; Earrings and Pendants; The Holders;
Enseignes and Bodkins; Buttons; Watches; Pomanders; Other Items;
Summary

Introduction

Our knowledge of the jewellery described in the earlier chapters has been derived from three main sources: descriptions in wills, inventories, and so on; sculptures and portraits; and actual artefacts which have survived either because they were buried in a tomb or grave, or because they were hidden, or, in the later periods, because of their beauty and costliness and high quality workmanship. There are other sources too, of course—trinkets that were lost or mislaid, jewellers' account books, and so on—but those are the chief ones. From this it follows that these jewels belonged to people of worth and standing: an owner important enough to be buried with his treasures about him, wealthy enough for a legal inventory of his goods to survive, high enough in rank to be portrayed in a family or State painting, sufficiently well-to-do to rate a stone effigy in the parish church. But with the Cheapside Hoard we find at last what appears to be the stock-in-trade of the travelling salesman, to be sold to the ordinary man or woman. It is very refreshing.

The hoard was discovered in 1912, when a workman who was digging on the site of Wakefield House, at the corner of Friday Street and Cheapside in the City of London, put his pick through a box which lay beneath a chalk floor. This box was very much decayed because of damp, but on examination it was thought originally to have been fitted with trays. There were about two hundred and thirty separate items inside. Some of the pieces are now in the Victoria and Albert Museum, others in the British Museum and the Guildhall Museum, but the majority are, quite rightly, deposited with the London Museum: a perfectly lovely thing to have there. Some of them are illustrated in the plate which faces page 115.

The individual pieces are light and elegant, feminine but not showy, and far removed from the over-sized baroque pieces being made for the courts of Europe at the same period. They have a charm to which one can relate immediately. They could have been made for oneself or for one's friends. It would be interesting to see whether, four centuries from now, serious historians would view the pieces being made for the man in the street today in the same light as we ourselves view the Cheapside Hoard. Although some of the items are clearly unfinished, one can find no fault with their design, or with the diversity of stones that are used in them. It is, indeed, a revelation to see such a variety of colourful stones, and even more to see the variety of cuts employed.

On general stylistic grounds, it is considered that the Cheapside Hoard was buried in about A.D. 1600. The use of opaque enamels and the great variety of colour seems to point to a date after the sixteenth-century developments in enamelling. The length of the chains, and the fact that many of them are enamelled, indicates a period somewhere between Henry VIII's reign and the gradual dying out of the fashion in James I's. The mass of flower motifs is very English and suits a late Tudor period; but there are also a number of motifs from the animal world—a squirrel, for instance, a lizard, a salamander —which suggests a date before the seventeenth century, when the fashion in jewel motifs shifted and the emphasis fell especially heavily on leaves and flowers. The multiplicity of cheaper precious stones and the number of different cuts used also makes a turn-of-the-century dating attractive.

The majority of the jewellery is made from gold and enamelled so that the gold is rarely allowed to show. The enamels are, as already mentioned, generally opaque, and they are frequently background shades of blue, green, black and amber. The accent on gemstones, and the variety used, is startling. There are emeralds from Colombo, Celanese spinels in varying colours, the blue and brown shades of iolites from Ceylon, chrysoberyls—the chameleon stones—in greens and yellows, the amber-cream of cats' eyes with their curious slit-marking that seems to widen and narrow as one looks, rubies and diamonds brought from India, lapis lazuli and turquoises from Persia, yellowish olivines (peridots) from St. John's Island in the Red Sea. Amethysts, garnets, opals and other stones could be got nearer home, but the topazes and the amazon-stones and the South American emeralds came from as far afield as India and Brazil. And all this was apparently quite normal, and readily accepted by the merchants' wives of Cheapside, Edinburgh and Exeter.

A careful examination of the hoard shows at least eight varieties of fancy cuts. Oval and squared *cabochon* stones were normal enough, and one would expect to find them being used by a sixteenth-century lapidary. So, too, were table cuts and trap or step cuts (facets in long inclined planes cut horizontally around the edge of the stone, and used if colour is important). But the frequent use of rose-cut and star-cut stones was a revelation. Historians used to suppose that the rose cut was first used for Cardinal Mazarin, the French statesman who succeeded the great Cardinal Richelieu in 1642, at the age of forty; however, it is now clear that it had been developed well before this. Indeed, since fashions in stone-cutting took their time to travel in those days, and since the English took their lead from the fashions of the French Court, one would not have expected English provincial jewellers to be using the rose cut for a good many years after its introduction. A rose-cut stone has a flat base and a number of triangular facets above—usually between twelve and twenty-four, though thirty-two may also be found —cut in three rows and meeting in a point. Star-cut stones are cut with a multiplicity of facets.

All in all, the hoard shows the precocious expansion of European commerce at the end of the sixteenth and the beginning of the seventeenth century and the experimenta-tion with new jewellery techniques—rose-cutting, for example, and settings which are open at the back. The craftsmanship is of a very high order, although the pieces themselves are mostly of moderate intrinsic worth. The fashions and tastes of the period are mirrored in this splendid find.

CHAINS

Long chains abound—one of them over four feet in length. There are twenty long chains in addition to this exceptional one, and all are enamelled brightly. Some are composed of petalled flowers, such as roses or daisies, and are essentially English in inspiration. Others are made up of large-petalled, star-shaped flowers, thickly enamelled in green and inlaid with gold; one of the chains made in this style has flower-centres of turquoise. Some, including the turquoise-centred one, are so designed that they may be worn reversed; all are smoothly and neatly finished on the backs. A particularly charming one (No. 14108, London Museum Master Catalogue, 1928) is made up of alternate barrel-shaped and fancy-cut amethysts and fancy-cut crystals, divided by enamelled flowers.

There are also several shorter chains, and no one can now be sure exactly how these were worn. Perhaps like bracelets, draped twice around the wrist? There are no portraits extant which show chains worn in such a way, but it seems possible. Might a pomander or a watch have dangled from them? The whole subject is open to conjecture.

RINGS

Some four dozen gold rings were found in the hoard, the shanks of nearly all of them being enamelled in white. Several are set with seven *cabochon* emeralds—the magic number. Other stones are also used, of course, and in addition there are some intaglios. Only one gem is in a claw setting, the others are box-set.

Two interesting rings from the hoard are a gold one, enamelled and set with one central rose-cut iolite (possibly a water-sapphire) and six star-cut garnets (No. A14233, London Museum Master Catalogue, 1928), and a gold ring enamelled in white at the back and set with nine *cabochon* emeralds, the central stone squared (No. 14214, London Museum Master Catalogue, 1928).

Whereas the men and women of the medieval period had worn a ring on the thumb and perhaps on one finger as well, the Renaissance lords and their ladies liked to wear rings on every finger, on every joint, over the gloves, under the gloves, and with the gloves slashed to let the stones blaze through.

EARRINGS AND PENDANTS

Earrings had again become fashionable for women's wearing during the Elizabethan period; in earlier times women had had to cover their heads—the Holbein drawing of Anne Boleyn for example, now in the Walker Art Gallery in Liverpool, shows her wearing a five-cornered head-dress which completely conceals her famous black hair and hides her ears, emphasizing the lines of the equally famous slender neck—but the Virgin Queen was proud of her Tudor red hair and her maiden status, and during her reign women's fashions gradually revealed the hair and ears. Men had worn earrings since Roman times, depending on the fashion of the moment, and were to continue to do so until the Commonwealth put an end to such vanities. Male fashion was generally for a single earring only. Charles I wore a single pearl earring all his life, until his head rolled on the block.

It is difficult to differentiate between pendants and earrings in the hoard, and the 1928 Catalogue masses them all together. The majority of the earrings are of open-design gemwork, and seem to have been designed to catch the light as much as possible. An especially interesting one is No. 14018 in the Catalogue: a gold earring (or possibly a pendant) enamelled at the back in black and white, and set with crystals with very fine pyramidal cutting, surrounded by very small opals.

Among the pendants, the stones are sometimes much mixed. A good example is No. 14104 in the 1928 Catalogue. This is a three-drop pendant in a gold frame: the first drop being a fancy-cut sapphire with a trap-cut back, the second another sapphire, modified this time with a rose cut, and the third a rough-polished spinel. All the pendants are of enamelled gold, set with clusters of stones, such as rose-cut amethysts or garnets. One or two are in the form of bunches of grapes; these are created from carved amethysts or emeralds. Surprisingly, the hoard also contains three reliquaries or religious pendants.

THE HOLDERS

The most enigmatic pieces of all are the "holders" (some can be seen facing page 115). There are fifteen of these holders in the hoard, all made of enamelled gold and set with gems. They are about two inches to four inches long and very light to hold. Their shape is unusual, but it is clear that they are so constructed that something should be held in the widest section. But what? There are three widely different theories.

It was once thought that they were fan-holders; since, however, the folding fan was then in fashion, rather than the feather fan or even the fixed fan, this seems very doubtful. Moreover, fans were immensely expensive at this period (Marguerite de Valois gave one to Louise of Lorraine which was valued at more than 12,000 crowns). It hardly seems possible that so many fan-holders would form part of an ordinary jeweller's everyday stock-in-trade; nor is it clear exactly how the fan could be fitted into the type of holder discovered in the hoard.

A second possibility is that they were fitted with tufts of feathers and used as hawk lures. Hawking was still a fashionable sport at this time, and the equipment was often very costly. The lure was a decoy, which one swung to tempt the hawk back to the wrist. If, however, these holders were lures, they would have had to be fitted with a wrist chain—and there are no chains in the hoard which are remotely suitable. It seems unlikely that a jeweller would stock the holder without the chain fitment.

A third theory, put forward by an authority at the London Museum, seems the most feasible. This suggests that the holders were indeed designed to hold a tuft of feathers, but for use with cosmetics, not for hawking. Cosmetics were used widely at this time: a glance at any of the portraits of the ageing Elizabeth shows that pastes and powders and rouges were applied to the face, neck and bosom to simulate the brilliant complexion that was admired in Tudor times ("*There is a garden in her face, Where roses and white lilies grow*"). A feather whisk was a cheap and efficient way of applying powders; and soft feathers were readily obtainable.

Descriptions of these little holders show their delightful variety. One, for example

(No. 14160) is catalogued as "holder of white enamelled gold set with *cabochon* garnets, table-cut diamonds, pearls and square-cut *cabochon* emeralds". Another, No. 14118, is "gold, beautifully delicate, enamelled in light and dark green, and made in the form of a lotus flower".

ENSEIGNES AND BODKINS

There are six *enseignes* in the hoard, even though the days of their greatest popularity were now over. One enchanting one is a gold salamander, its back crusted with emeralds and diamonds, its stomach and legs enamelled in white.

There are also two bodkins or jewelled hairpins. One of these (No. 14124) is listed as "a gold bodkin in the form of a shepherd's crook, enamelled, the head set with table-cut rubies and diamonds". The Elizabethan poets had made the idyllic life of shepherd-and-shepherdess a part of popular fancy—Spenser with his *Shepheard's Calendar* (1579); Marlowe with his Passionate Shepherd offering his love a lambswool gown, a cap of flowers, a bed of roses; Sidney with the long elaborate prose romance *Arcadia*—and, as Miss Jenkins has remarked, the elegant pastoral *fêtes champêtres* of these works were echoed by the masques and pageants of court life.

BUTTONS

Jewelled buttons were not employed simply for their utilitarian efficiency, but also— almost, indeed, more—as decorative punctuation points in a spread of rich velvet or lustrous silk. They could also be massed together to create a richer effect. Elizabeth I's wardrobe list for the year 1600 includes "buttons like roses, pierced hearts, lizards, pansies, shells of mother-of-pearl". Arnold Lulls once made a set of two dozen buttons (and a jewel) which James I gave to his wife Anne; he was paid £1550 for them.

There is a charming set of buttons in the hoard. This is No. 14126 in the 1928 Catalogue: "Nineteen gold buttons enamelled in white, blue and green, and set with table-cut rubies and diamonds."

WATCHES

Although watches had been made in Nuremburg and Paris since the beginning of the sixteenth century, they do not seem to have been known in England until about 1540 when Henry VIII gave one to his newest bride, Katherine Howard. This watch was set in a carved emerald. The young queen would have worn it dangling from her belt or girdle on a long chain, and it was most probably highly inaccurate.

There are two watches in the hoard. One of them helps to fix the period of the hoard for it is actually dated. This is No. 14162, "a watch set in a single large emerald of hexagonal shape, perhaps from the famous Muzo mine in Colombia. The loop is also set with small emeralds and with white enamel and the face is enamelled green. Dated 1600." It can be seen in the illustration facing page 115.

The other watch is bulkier, and the Master of the Worshipful Company of Clock-makers has put its date at about 1580. Its enamelled face has four dials in all: one for telling the time, one for counting the seconds, one for calculating the days of the week, and one for calculating the date in the month.

POMANDERS

Pomanders take their name from the French *pomme*, "an apple", because they are shaped like a pierced hollow ball, and *ambre*, "amber", which was often one of the ingredients in the aromatic *compôtes* of herbs, spices, and so on, with which they were filled, to ward off the smells with which houses and streets were so often infested. Pomanders were popular from the fourteenth century right through to the Commonwealth period. They could be hung from a chain around the neck or at the waist, or even delicately suspended from one finger. "*I will have my pomander of most sweet smell*," declared the *Book of Robin Conscience* (*circa* A.D. 1600): "*Also my chains of gold to hang about my neck.*" The perfumes and spices, which were expensive, were sometimes mixed into a ball, which was inserted in a round hollow pomander, or sometimes shared out into tiny compartments within the pomander framework (Fig. 21). The most sophisticated models would open like a flower, releasing an aromatic scent. Elizabeth I had "pomaunder buttons like acorns wt seede perle", according to the 1600 Wardrobe List already cited.

No. 14156 in the 1928 Catalogue is "a pomander of enamelled gold with opaline chalcedony plaques and mounted with table-cut and trap-cut rubies, topazes and diamonds". It evokes the spirit of the age more than almost anything else in the hoard.

OTHER ITEMS

Among the other items in the hoard are a carved squirrel in cornelian and an emerald parrot (Nos. 14272 and 14273), illustrations of the interest people of the period took in the odd and unusual. There are also cameos bearing the queen's head, and, surprisingly, even fossilized fish-teeth (*Lepidotus maximus*) awaiting use.

What, however, is particularly interesting in this modest collection of items is the inclusion of several genuinely classical and Byzantine pieces, which have either been remounted, or are apparently awaiting remounting in a contemporary setting. One, an intaglio stone which is unmounted, is an example of Greek gem-cutting of the Hellenistic era, another is Romano-Egyptian, and still others, such as the ring which is No. 14233 in the Catalogue, are Roman. As they are not top quality pieces, might they have been found on English soil? Two of them even show Christian cameos of the sixth century A.D.

SUMMARY

The hoard was a wonderful discovery, not because of the intrinsic worth or supreme beauty of the pieces, but because of the expert craftsmanship, the multiplicity of designs, the enthusiastic use of new gemstones and new techniques. Jewels were not simply worn at court: the well-to-do and their wives wore them too, the city merchant, the prosperous trader, even the hard-working yeoman farmer—and the pieces they chose were made, it seems, in quite the latest fashions.

CHAPTER SIX

The House of Stuart

Introduction: The Baroque; The Floral Motif; Foreign Influences—
James I: Extravagance and Display; Jacobean Costume; Court Masques;
The Spanish Journey—Charles I: Carolean Fashions; The Royal Sales—
Memorial Jewels—The Restoration: Elizabeth Pepys's Jewels; The
Restoration Court; Dutch Craftsmen—The Last Stuarts

Introduction

THE BAROQUE

The seventeenth century was the age of the baroque: a loosening of formal designs, a feeling for movement and lightness, an exaggerated treatment of light which led to intensity of colour. The movement was born in Italy. It placed considerable emphasis on a heavy accentuation of light and shade, rather than the clear pure suffusion of light which had been seen in earlier painting, and was theatrical and dramatic in its effects. Yet this searching for a new means of expressing substance and reality was itself to become unreal, for its own deliberate exaggeration settled into eventual solidity.

Northern Europe developed her own forms from the Italian-introduced baroque, influenced by the northern feeling for naturalism and exactitude. The seventeenth-century Dutch painters portrayed urbane, domestic scenes. They painted still life: grapes in a china bowl, oysters on a silver plate. Their silverware showed scenes sculpted in the clean shining metal, in low relief with rounded flowing lines. They carved wreaths of acanthus leaves, swags of flowers—above all, flowers, for this was the century when the floral motif reigned supreme in Europe.

The Floral Motif
The floral motif was used over and over again in the decorative arts of the seventeenth century: engraved on a silver watchcase, moulded in marble, carved in wood, portrayed in paint and woven into the beautiful damask silks of the period. Engraved pattern books show an endless variety of flower designs: bloom, leaf and stem looped and linked together, finely executed in beautifully delicate lines. The earlier motifs—mermen, amorini, legendary creatures and beasts and heroes—fell out of favour. Gardens were in vogue. Parkinson's *Paradisus* was first published in 1628, and dedicated to the then Queen of England, Henrietta Maria; and six years later in 1634, the famous tulipomania swept across Europe.

113

FOREIGN INFLUENCES

As Akrigg has pointed out, the literary influence of the Renaissance had reached England rather earlier than the full visual impact. Books, engravings, patterns, fabrics, jewels—these things were fairly easy to transport and appeared on the Tudor scene; but the great masterpieces of Italian visual art did not reach England until the seventeenth century. Imports ran at their peak under Charles I, a connoisseur king who made his purchases out of real love and feeling for art rather than a simple wish to glorify the monarchy, buying tapestries, statues, sculptures and paintings (Titian and Raphael, among others); but the first classical masterpieces arrived in his father's reign.

In 1613 the Earl of Arundel had set off for Italy, taking along with him the craftsman and artist, Inigo Jones, who had studied there in his early years before going off to Denmark, to work for Christian IV, and then returning to England where Christian's sister, Anne of Denmark, was now queen consort. The earl's tour foreshadowed the grand tours of the eighteenth century; like those later Georgian gentlemen he brought back some classical souvenirs, even having the pleasure of doing a little excavating himself. When he and Jones proudly set up the marbles in his English garden, classically formed, gleamy white, Francis Bacon flung up his hands in mock amazement and cried, "The Resurrection!"

But they did not merely bring back artefacts. During his Italian studies Jones had been deeply moved by Palladio's style of architecture, and now, accepting a commission from James I to build a new Banqueting Hall for the warren-palace of Whitehall, he created a masterpiece: a Palladian double-cube building, serenely neo-classical, which was finally completed in 1623. It expressed Jones's own ideal: "masculine, sollid, simpell".

Jones was an Englishman born and bred, who had studied abroad and then returned home to create a masterpiece that was deeply influenced, in conception and design, by all that he had seen and learned there; but many of the craftsmen working in England during this century were foreigners, brought over to work for the Stuart monarchs. They brought with them new ideas, new designs, new modifications of accepted techniques. In her *History of Jewellery*, Joan Evans lists twenty-one foreign craftsmen who were publishing designs in the early seventeenth century—designs which were used all over Europe: among them were Daniel Mignot (working at Augsburg between 1590 and 1616), Jacques Hurtu and Michel le Blon. One foreign craftsman who did a great deal of work in England at this time, and whose designs can still be seen in the Victoria and Albert Museum, was the Dutch jeweller, Arnold Lulls, who worked for Anne of Denmark. His work shows the turning away from the tight disciplined Renaissance look towards lightness and freshness. Fig. 25, for example, shows a Lulls' design for a jewel: the line is free and flowing, simulating a feather.

The painters came, of course. Marcus Gheeraerts, a Flemish exile since childhood, had painted Elizabeth; Anne of Denmark also patronized him. Franz Pourbus became one of the court artists. John de Critz (*circa* 1554–1642), who had come to England as a child from the Low Countries, and whose sisters were to marry the Gheeraerts, father and son, became Sergeant Painter to James I; the painted ceiling in the Double Cube Room at Wilton House (1648) is said to be by him. These were men who married and settled in England; but there were others too—Rubens, Mytens, and, in 1632,

Fig. 33 and Fig. 34: two examples of early seventeenth-century work may here be compared. On the left is the Lyte Jewel, made in England in the early part of the century, probably by George Heriot, and presented by James I to Mr Thomas Lyte of Somerset. The oval "picture" of the King may be by Nicholas Hilliard or Isaac Oliver. The lightness and elegance of the cover, set with diamonds, show the new trend towards the baroque style with its loosening of formal designs and its feeling for movement. The reverse of the Jewel is most beautifully and delicately enamelled in white with thin graceful lines of gold in the long tradition of British linear design. The Naseby Jewel, on the right, is thought to have been made between 1600 and 1615 in Germany. It is a cap badge in enamelled and jewelled gold, with two great rubies. Here too an openwork technique has been used, and this was essential to offset the size, weight and elaboration of the Jewel.

Fig. 33: by courtesy of the Trustees of the British Museum

Fig. 34: by courtesy of the Trustees of the Sir John Soane Museum

at the invitation of Charles I, Van Dyck (1599–1641), who was to become "principalle Paynter in Ordinary to their Majesties". He left in a huff when the sketches he had submitted for painting the walls of the Banqueting House (Rubens had already painted the ceiling) were returned to him because the price he quoted was too high. The Stuarts were already, it seems, desperately short of money.

James I

EXTRAVAGANCE AND DISPLAY

When Elizabeth I lay dying, many of her courtiers opened discreet negotiations with the most likely successor, James VI of Scotland; among them was her godson, John Harington, who, grieving on the one hand over "that evil which we shall get by her death", was with the other sending James a lantern for a New Year's gift, symbolic

The Cheapside Hoard: in 1912 a workman digging on the site of Wakefield House in the City of London found a box containing about 230 items, believed to be the stock-in-trade of a travelling salesman towards the end of the sixteenth century or the beginning of the seventeenth. This was the Cheapside Hoard, a collection of jewels and trinkets for sale to the ordinary man or woman of the time. The majority of the items are now in the London Museum.

The variety, colour and delicacy of the pieces is obvious from these two illustrations. The upper one shows a number of individual items grouped around a central necklace of star-shaped motifs: from left to right, clockwise, beginning at nine o'clock, we have rings, hair-ornaments or perhaps earrings (they could be worn as either) of emeralds and pearls, a charming pomander, a delicate gold chain with faceted amethysts, a little gold and emerald salamander with white enamelled legs, an eye-catching watch set within a chunk of emerald, and a delicate brooch of gold bows.

The lower illustration shows a cornucopia of the delicate pretty work made for the ordinary man and woman in the street, rather than the Court. Amongst the many items are two watches, antique cameos awaiting setting, the enigmatic jewelled holders believed to have held feathers for applying cosmetics (one is by the emerald watch on the far right, two others low left of centre), bowls of unset gemstones, carved amethyst hair-ornaments like bunches of grapes, and over a dozen charming chains with a spattering of tiny enamelled flowers.

The variety of colour, both in gemstones and enamels, is typical of life at the end of the Elizabethan era; the cutting of the gemstones is amazing in its virtuosity (at least eight varieties, including rose cuts and star cuts); and almost everything here can be displayed quite happily on either side—the craftsmen of the period always finished off the back as beautifully as the front.

By courtesy of the Trustees of the London Museum

of one light fading and another being kindled, and inscribed with the words the Penitent Thief spoke to Christ, which were the means of his salvation:

Lord, remember me when thou shalt come into thy kingdom.

Within three months Elizabeth was dead, and James came south into a land full of promise and riches—so many riches, indeed, that he must have felt at first that they were inexhaustible. He had had a most bleak and terrifying childhood, and was in permanent fear of assassination—so much so that he wore a quilted horsehair doublet two inches thick, now in the Victoria and Albert Museum, to fend off the knife; it was amazing that he turned out as well as he did. Welcomed and courted on all sides, he ordered the Privy Council to send off to his wife Anne "such Jewells and other Furnyture which did appertained to the late Queene as you shall thincke to be meet for her estate", and then settled down to enjoy himself. The king and queen were crowned on July 25, 1603, in a city struck by the plague; because of this the usual pomp and ceremony were reduced, the first and last occasion in James's reign on which this was done. James happily handed out cash and gifts to the Scots who had come swarming south— £3,000 to Linlithgow, as a single instance. His brother-in-law, Christian IV of Denmark, came visiting in 1606, and there were great carousals, sightseeing (Christian's tour of London took in St. Paul's, the Royal Exchange, Goldsmiths' Row, and the Tower with its Jewel House and Mint), and exchanges of presents, including, for example, a golden bowl set with diamonds and valued at £5,000. The ambassadors had also to be treated well, of course: each embassy arrived with gifts for the king, often parading through the streets first so that the Londoners could have a good look (in 1619 the Great Mogul sent, among other delights, "certain ombrellaes and such like trinckets"), were entertained with banquets and masques, and ultimately withdrew taking a great many gifts back with them. James was so generous to the plenipotentiaries of the Anglo-Spanish Peace Conference in 1604 that £7,618. 11s. 3d. was needed to replenish the Treasury.

James soon ran short of money, though this did not stop him handing out presents and frantically scraping together enough cash to make a good display. He sold knighthoods for the £30 fee, even knighting a goldsmith who made "a Hole in a great Diamond the King doth wear", melted down plate from the Jewel House, raised gifts of cash from courtiers and judges, and gifts of plate from the bishops (at one such collection they handed over a single piece each), pledged his jewels to the merchants of London (for £100,000 to finance a visit to Scotland), and generally lived from hand to mouth—but none the less, very splendidly. When he married off his daughter to the Elector Palatine in 1613, the bridegroom gave the bride jewels valued at £35,000, including two huge pearls and quantities of diamonds; but the bride's mother appeared at the wedding decked in £400,000 worth, and the bride's father in even more. All in all, the wedding cost James over £90,000, over two-thirds of which was directly chargeable to him. By 1625, when he died, his debts were over the million mark (Akrigg).

Naturally the courtiers followed suit. No one could be arrested for debt within the precincts of the palace, which helped many prodigals to escape their luckless tradesmen; even if the creditors were clever and determined enough to lay hold of a noble debtor outside the palace, they were not sure of getting their money. One goldsmith, banding together with other tradesmen, had a countess arrested for debt; he still did not get a penny. Birth and rank were fast becoming supremely important, and the sums spent on glorifying one's position were incredible. The king had spent £15,000 on adorning the lying-in chamber where his queen gave birth in 1605 to the Princess Mary (who soon died); a few years later one of his nobles spent a similar sum on hanging his wife's chamber with embroidered satin to aggrandize the birth of his heir—it is pleasant to record that he only got a daughter. A Mr. Thomas Lyte, of Lyte's Carey in Somerset, gratified the king by presenting to him a carefully compiled pedigree tracing the royal ancestry back to Brutus, the grandson of Aeneas of Troy (a favourite British tradition of the Middle Ages ascribed the founding of Britain to this descendent of the ancient Trojan kings), and was rewarded with a miniature "in gold set with diamonds, with gracious thanks". This was the **Lyte Jewel** (Fig. 33 facing page 114) which Thomas Lyte wore in the portrait of himself painted in about 1620. It is a superb example of goldsmith's work of the early seventeenth century, and was probably made by George Heriot, the King's Jeweller. The oval portrait of James is perhaps by Nicholas Hilliard, perhaps by Isaac Oliver. The openwork cover and frame are set with twenty-five table-cut diamonds, four rose-cut diamonds, and one pendant pearl. The reverse, which the majority of experts feel is more worthy of remark than the front because of the skilful and delicate white enamelling and thin graceful lines of gold, as lovely as the most accomplished calligraphy, shows the continuing British excellence at linear design, a tradition that may be traced through the centuries from the illuminated manuscripts of the early Middle Ages to the graphics of the twentieth century. The jewel was handed down through the Lyte family, passing eventually to the Monypenys, who sold it to the Duke of Hamilton, and then to Baron Rothschild, who left it to the British Museum in 1898. It is still there: a beautiful example of British workmanship in the early seventeenth century, its fretted openwork cover showing the new trend towards lightness.

The Lyte Jewel may be compared with the **Naseby Jewel** (Fig. 34, facing page 114)—so called because it is said to have been looted from Charles I's baggage after the battle of Naseby in 1645, but thought to have been made between 1600 and 1615, in Germany. It can now be seen at the Sir John Soane Museum in London. This is a large, colourful cap-badge in enamelled and jewelled gold. In spite of the general seventeenth-century trend towards jewellery whose emphasis was on the beauty and flash of faceted gemstones, rather than enamelled gold (a trend that was to widen the goldsmith/jeweller split), Continental jewellers were still developing new enamelling techniques—*émail en resille sur verre*, and variants of the old *champlevé* method. The Naseby Jewel is lavish and typically manneristic: a central bearded figure is seen beneath a crown; he is carrying a sword and a shield, in which is set a large ruby, and is surrounded by an elaborate design of arms and trophies; at his feet lies an acquiescent lion, made in gold, its body formed by another large ruby. The use of the openwork technique offsets the sheer size of the jewel, the weight of which would otherwise be considerable.

JACOBEAN COSTUME

During the first quarter of the seventeenth century, English costume, already stiff and splendid in the last years of Elizabeth's reign, became increasingly elaborate. The old sixteenth-century courtly modes persisted for the first few years—the ruff, the rebato, the farthingale for women, the trunk hose and doublet for men—but were gradually adapted to a yet more lavish and dramatic style. This was particularly so in the case of the men, who, by the middle of James's reign, walked the corridors of Whitehall in huge ruffs, heavy capes, wasp-waisted doublets, vast embroidered breeches reaching to the knee, gold-clocked hose, and rosetted shoes, with broad hats to set on their curled hair; the ladies too dressed their hair in elaborate styles, with silver-and-diamond *aigrettes*, and wore vast farthingales, pointed low-cut bodices with a veiling of transparent gauze, and elaborate ruffs; all, of course, with jewellery to match. At Woburn Abbey in Bedfordshire there is a splendid portrait of Anne of Denmark, attributed to Marcus Gheeraerts. She is wearing a magnificent costume, star-scattered with jewels—pearls in her hair, *aigrettes*, pearl earrings, necklaces, the great "Ropes of Catharine", and a bow brooch from which is suspended a pendant pearl and a monogram *S*, in memory of her mother, Sophia, after whom she named one of her own daughters.

COURT MASQUES

Anne's life with James was not always easy, and was tragically overcast by the death of her favourite son, the dashing military Henry, Prince of Wales (Charles seemed a sad contrast), in spite of the physicians' best efforts to save him—this included a potion of unicorn's horn powdered with pearl and deerbone; but she did manage to have a reasonably pleasant time, particularly enjoying the splendid and costly masques she staged at court, and in which she generally starred. In the early years she employed Ben Jonson as the script-writer and Inigo Jones as the designer, with the court musicians to supply the music, but Jonson and Jones eventually quarrelled over which element should be pre-eminent, script or scene; the designer won, and the dramatist left in a rage.

In his *Annales* of 1615, Edmond Howes set down his recollections of some of the masques that had been staged in honour of the Princess Elizabeth's wedding. These included two stages by the gentlemen of the Inns of Court "without respect of charge and expense". The most "pregnant and active gentlemen" were chosen, and came marching down the Strand to perform: first fifty stately masquers, richly attired, gallantly mounted, each with a footman in attendance; then a "mock-masque of baboons attired like fantastic travellers", mounted on asses, attended by torch-bearers; then a couple of chariots full of musicians, then the chief masquers

> "with great state in white Indian habit or like the great princes of Barbary, richly embroidered with the golden sun, with suitable ornaments in all points; about their necks were ruffs of feathers, spangled and beset with pearl and silver, and upon their heads lofty coronets suitable to the rest. They wore long silk stockings, curiously embroidered with gold to the mid-leg. Their buskins were likewise embroidered, and in their hands, as they rode, they brandished cane darts of the finest gold."

The horses were said to be every bit as splendid, their "caparisons" being chased with gold suns and set with ornamental jewels, with a scarf of silver over all; each attended by two Moors whose heads were wreathed with gold, and by torch-bearers carrying great gilded canes. After this came a last triumphal chariot. It made, Howes said, "a wondrous pleasing show", and they received "royal thanks and commendations".

The Jewel House accounts of 1595–1618 show that Anne of Denmark was apt to borrow the Crown Jewels to give her masques that extra touch of splendour. On one occasion she borrowed her sceptre, and damaged it; on another she used the coronet which had been made for her coronation and which her husband had placed in the Crown Jewels "in perpetuity". Perpetuity turned out to be five years. She removed it in 1608, together with two gold collars set with pearls and gemstones, "to weare at the Maske" (this was the Christmas Masque, an annual affair which usually cost the king about £4,000 for a one-night stand). She seems never to have returned them; they were "saide to remaine with the Quene" (B.M. Add. 12501 ff. 6b–8).

Anne did not, however, set a precedent in this. A hundred years earlier a diadem had been made for the coronation of Henry VIII's first wife, Catharine of Aragon, in June 1509. This was "a Circlet of golde for the Quene set with a fair Emeralde four fair Saphires four rooses of diamontes four balaces all sett in rooses and xiiij perles of one sorte"; it was appropriated by the Protector Somerset in the reign of Edward VI, and never returned. Where is it now? Broken up, no doubt; its gold melted down, its gems re-set.

With such lavishness, it was no wonder that in 1622 an inquiry had to be held to establish why there was not enough silver for the Mint: among the reasons given was the import of Nuremberg plate, the export of bullion and English coinage, the "neglect of the true making of English manufacture", and the fact that the amount of gold and silver used "for spangles and suchlike" was excessive, "it being estimated that the expenditure on such ornaments was more than £100,000 per annum". Theatrical glitter was costing the Treasury dear.

Anne herself had died three years earlier, on March 2, 1619; it took ten weeks to raise enough money to bury her with due pomp and ceremony. Soon after this James sold her jewellery: very little sentimental value seems to have been placed on personal possessions, and this, together with the constant need for money, is one of the reasons why so little early work survives among the royal jewels. His debts apart, James was planning a progress through the Midlands, an expensive pastime. Accordingly he directed that the choicest of Anne's jewellery and ornaments

> "shoulde be sent to our secrett Jewell House in our Tower of London there to be preserved for the Honor and Magnificence of our Crown and State, and some others to be reserved for Presents for Embassadors to save the Expense of our Treasure, and some others to the Custodie and Charge of Sir Henrye (Mildmay) Knight, Mayster and Treasourer of our Jewells and Plate, and some others to be reserved and kepte at Denmark House for Ornaments there or otherwise to be disposed of at our Pleasure."

He named commissioners to sell the rest, "being of smale Worth and Valewe, and not fitt to be preserved for our Use or Service". A valuation of £20,000 had been placed on these jewels ("smale Worth and Valewe"), and Peter van Lore bought them for £18,000 "which, together with some other helps, doth serve to defray the progress". Later on the same commissioners were directed to sell the queen's loose pearls, her worn linen, and some other things: a royal jumble sale to raise the sheer hard cash the king desperately needed.

The king soon needed more "helps" of the same kind, for in 1623 his son Charles set off to woo the Spanish Infanta in person, accompanied by the last of James's favourites, his dearest Steenie, the Duke of Buckingham. They travelled incognito, so cunningly disguised that they nearly got arrested by the English authorities as suspicious persons, before even they reached the Channel coast. Arriving in Paris, under the strikingly original pseudonyms of John and Tom Smith, they went off to the Louvre and being of gentlemanly appearance were admitted to watch the royal ladies rehearsing a masque; among them was the thirteen-year-old princess, Henrietta Maria. (When the secret of the strangers' identity and the reason for their romantic journey leaked out later, Henrietta is said to have remarked that Charles might have had a bride nearer at hand than Spain.)

In order to impress the Infanta, Charles took £80,000 worth of jewels. Among them was an historic jewel famed throughout Europe, the **Three Brethren**. It had once belonged to Charles the Bold of Burgundy. He lost it at the Battle of Grandison in 1476, and it was seized as booty by the Swiss, who sold it to the Fuggers of Augsburg. Henry VIII bought it from them, and it was described in the 1603 inventory of the royal jewels, made on Elizabeth's death:

> "A fayre Flower with 3 great ballaces in the myddest a greate pointed dyamonde, and 3 greate perles fixed, with a fayre great perle pendante."

James sent this to his jeweller, George Heriot, to be re-set; and this too is significant of the way in which jewellery was developing. Now that the accent was shifting to faceted stones and lustrous pearls, rather than metalwork and enamelling, pieces could be broken up and re-set in the newest mode. Perhaps the baroque feeling for drama and theatricality, and the habit of using jewels as stage properties, had some significance; but the major reason seems undoubtedly to have been the increasing skill of the lapidaries, who were learning to facet stones and thus reveal more of their brilliance. Some authorities say, indeed, that the "greate pointed dyamonde" in the Three Brethren was the first stone ever faceted for setting in a jewel.

Heriot had been born in Edinburgh in 1563. He started his own business, as goldsmith and jeweller, in 1586, and was successful enough to be appointed court jeweller to Anne of Denmark in 1597. James awarded him the royal warrant soon after. He followed the newly enriched royal family to London in 1603, and served them both as jeweller and banker. He amassed a considerable fortune—being luckier in this respect than many craftsmen who served the Stuarts—and when he died in 1624 left £23,625 to found a hospital or school in Edinburgh for the sons of poor burgesses (Sir Walter Scott immortalized him as Jingling Geordie in *The Fortunes of Nigel*).

Heriot is said to have sat up night and day to complete the king's commissions, which James then dispatched to his son to further his wooing. He sent him "the Three Brethren that you knowe full well but newlie sette", "the Mirroure of Frawnce, the fellowe of the Portugall Dyamont, quhiche I wolde wishe you to weare alone in your hatte with a litle blakke feather", and half a dozen other hat-jewels (Heriot had been told that these were to be "of £6,000 or £7,000 value, and none under"); it was no wonder that James wrote anxiously to his son "God knowis how my coffers are all-readdie drained", signing himself "youre olde dad".

It was all to no avail. The Infanta's confessor had been urgently pointing out to her that Charles would be an uncomfortable bedfellow; how could she lie quiet knowing that her husband and the father of her children was a heretic, certain to go to hell? The King of Spain refused the English suit, and Charles and Buckingham travelled home rejected; the English, who had loathed the match, were wild with delight. Two years later James was dead, and on May 1, 1625, the new king, Charles I, was married by proxy to the young princess he had seen in the masque at the Louvre.

The first years of their marriage were not happy ones; Henrietta Maria was young, spirited, and Catholic, and undoubtedly resented Buckingham's influence over her husband; it was not until after the duke's murder in 1628 that the young king and queen tentatively fell in love. The domestic happiness which they were to enjoy in the years that followed was unfortunately paralleled by an increasingly bitter lack of sympathy between king and Parliament.

Charles I

CAROLEAN FASHIONS

With the elegant quiet connoisseur king and the pretty stylish French queen at Whitehall, great changes came over court styles and fashions.

In the winter of 1972 a painting by Cornelius Johnson (1593–1661) was offered for sale at Christie's in London. This was the portrait of a woman, "signed and dated 1639, wearing a black dress and white lace collar and cuffs". She had a quiet oval face, dark curling hair simply dressed, with kiss curls on the forehead and a single bow at the back. A double row of pearls was clasped around her throat, above the falling collar of beautiful lace. There were pearl drops in her ears. A delicate pendant dangled at the mid-point of her bodice, below another small bow of ribbon. Before the actual sale took place, the subject was identified: this was not, as had been previously supposed, some anonymous cavalier's lady, but the queen herself.

The clothes and the jewels that the king and queen wore were characterized by dignity, restraint and elegance. Charles himself liked to wear black velvet, a lace collar; a pearl earring in his left ear; hair falling simply to his shoulders; perhaps a pendant on a long satin ribbon about his neck. One characteristic pendant of the period can be seen in the Victoria and Albert Museum, loaned by Lord O'Hagan; this is silver-gilt, with a medal of the king on the obverse and the queen on the reverse, both said to be by Thomas Rawlins (the framing of diamonds was added in the eighteenth century). Henrietta chose fine fabrics—satin and damask, paduasoy and taffeta and lace—in shades which suited her dark hair and French complexion: tawny and russet, blue and amber, oyster-grey and black. To set these off she wore pearls: short necklaces of fine lustrous spherical pearls clasped high around her throat, pearl drops in her ears, a twist of pearl and diamond around the knot of ringlets at the back of her head, perhaps a fine pendant diamond on her bodice. Dresses were no longer stiff, ornate, formal, with tight waists: in the twelve years between the reconciliation and the queen's departure for Holland shortly before the outbreak of civil war, she went through eight pregnancies; it was hardly surprising that she chose to dress in a looser, more comfortable style. Family life became the vogue; Van Dyck painted the royal children in ringlets and lace and little white caps (Charles I is said to have been shocked when one portrait showed them in their pinafores); and Whitehall was transformed into a moral and dignified place.

THE ROYAL SALES

Charles's morality did not, however, extend to financial matters. He was in desperate need of money, and early in his reign decided to raise it by pledging the royal jewels and plate, in spite of the law that held that "ancient jewels of the crowne are heire-loomes, and shall descend to the next successor, and are not devisable by testament". The most wonderful masterpieces were shipped surreptitiously to The Hague. The cargo of gold and silver plate contained the legendary Dream of Paris, the Cup of Jane Seymour, the Morris Dance, ten of the richest jewelled gold vessels owned by Henry VIII and Elizabeth I, and the famous Constable's Cup. With it went some of the historic jewels from the royal collection, including two of those which Charles had worn to court the Infanta: the "Mirrowe of Frawnce", incorporating the great Sancy diamond (this was ultimately purchased by Mazarin, who had a great liking for diamonds, and is now in the Crown Jewels of France), and the Three Brethren, which was valued on arrival at £9,400.

Within three years the debt, and the interest, was so huge that some of the cargo had to be sold to private buyers and more melted down for coin. Between muddle and mismanagement, Charles's agents abroad only managed to raise a trickle of money—£10,000 in place of the £300,000 he had every right to expect. It was evident that he had been cheated, but fraud could not be proved; eventually no one person was punished; instead the nation as a whole paid the penalty.

By 1630 Charles had bargained away most of his personal ornaments; there were sound financial reasons for the simple dignity of his dress. In the summer of that year he even pledged his "coller of esses with a George and a Garter of Diamonds to the number of about eight hundred diamondes" to Thomas Hamond, Lieutenant General of the Artillery, for £500.

Charles also seized the money which the City merchants were accustomed to keep in the Tower Mint, wrongly thinking this a safe place to store their spare cash; thereafter they trusted it to the goldsmiths who, during the war years when both sides were melting down their plate and buying muskets instead, were glad enough to set up as bankers; they found it an extremely profitable occupation, and were soon busily investing the money entrusted to them by merchants and land-owners, and honouring the notes (the first-ever "cheques") sent in by their clients.

In 1641 it was clear that civil war was certain. The Princess Mary, Charles's eldest daughter, was betrothed to the Dutch prince, William of Orange; when she sailed for Holland her mother went with her, taking along a new consignment of her own jewels and the Crown Jewels to pledge or sell at The Hague. She found it difficult: the Dutch were cautious and haggling. The king's set of pearl buttons (398 of them) went at last for £13,000; an Amsterdam merchant advanced 140,000 guilders on her rubies and pearls; Rotterdam and The Hague raised a little more. She wrote to her husband:

"If we put all our jewels in pledge and consume them without doing anything, they would be lost, and we too; for we should have nothing left to help ourselves with, when we should need it. For this reason, lose no time; you have lost enough already . . . And think too that I am risking all we have left in the world to get money, and that, when that money fails, there is no more, and that when it will be needful to pay persons for fighting, there will be no more; wherefore time is precious."

Charles had unfurled his standard at Nottingham, a declaration of war (it fell down in the night, which was ominous); Henrietta sailed for England, bringing with her a mass of trinkets with which to reward Royalists who gave jewels or plate or money to the Cause; they were re-united at last in Oxford, where a mint had been set up in New Inn Hall and the colleges were melting down their plate for the king; it was their last time together.

In March 1642 Charles had lost control of the Jewel House. Parliament, discovering the devastation of historic jewels and plate, was rightly outraged, and printed and circulated notices of the king's secret attempts to raise money with which to make war against his people's Parliament. Defeat and disaster followed; Charles was captured, imprisoned and in January 1649 condemned to death; he stepped on to the scaffold through the window of his cherished Banqueting Hall. Parliament, or its leaders, ruled in England. On August 9, 1649, they gave orders

"that these Gentlemen who were appointed, by this House, to have the Custody of the Regalia, do deliver them over unto the Trustees for Sale of the Goods of the late King, Queen and Prince; who are to cause the same to be totally broken; and that they melt down the Gold and Silver of them; and to sell the Jewels for the best Advantage of the Commonwealth; and to take the like Care of those that are in the Tower."

(Commons Journal, VI, 276)

The original intention, to sell everything the royal family had owned, was modified, and a good deal of the royal plate was converted into coin. Each sale was made public at least a week in advance, but such was the depressed state of the people's morale that the prices fetched were very low (it was at one time suggested that this was due to fraud, but it is now generally agreed that this cannot be supported by the evidence). One portrait went for five shillings. The courts and connoisseurs of Europe bought at cut rates the furniture and tapestries, paintings and jewels that had been Charles's pride.

Memorial Jewels

The fashion for *memento mori* jewellery has already been remarked. The **Tor Abbey Jewel**, now in the Victoria and Albert Museum, is only one example. This pendant (Fig. 19) is made of enamelled gold. It is shaped like a miniature coffin, and opens to reveal a tiny skeleton. The inscription reads

Through the resurrection of Christe we be all sanctified

which is more cheerful than many.

123

Charles I's death gave the fashion an extra impetus: Royalists began to wear mourning jewels in his honour—a tiny skull set in a ring, a portrait of the dead martyr in a pendant, or a wisp of hair concealed in a brooch and plaited to form the letters *C.R.* Naturally a great many of these jewels were so designed that their purpose was concealed. They were worn as an act of faith: precious, secret and sacred. Whereas the earlier seventeenth-century jewellery was pledged, sold or melted down, this was carefully preserved, and a good deal still survives. One such jewel is a small silver locket now in the Victoria and Albert Museum (Catalogue No. M811) which is inscribed

> *Prepared Be to Follow Me C R*

and

> *I live and Dy in Loyalty*

and inside which is another inscription

> *I Morne for Monerchie*

and a medallion of the dead king.

Memorial jewels of this period also feature the Martyr King's successor, Charles II, the exiled king of England. One particularly pleasing jewel commemorates the story of the Boscobel Oak, in which Charles hid when fleeing the country after his defeat at Worcester in 1651. This is a copper-gilt locket from the Victoria and Albert Museum (Catalogue No. 898—1904) which contains a miniature of Major William Carlos. Engraved on the back is a beautiful scene showing Charles II and Carlos hiding in the oak, and engraved on the front are the arms and motto granted to the major in commemoration of the escape. Inscribed inside is a poem:

> *"Renewned Carlos! Thow hast won the day*
> *(Loyalty Lost) by helping Charles away*
> *From Kings-Blood-thirsty-Rebels in a Night,*
> *made black with Rage, of theives, & Hells dispight*
> *Live! King-Loved Sowle they fame by Euer Spoke*
> *By all whilst England Beares a Royall Oake."*

The Restoration

ELIZABETH PEPYS'S JEWELS

In 1660 Charles II was restored to England as her king, and rode into London amid cheering crowds. He had come home in the absolute determination never to go on his travels again; he might, and did, clash with his parliaments, but he would never take up arms against them. They in their turn, soured by their experiences of military government and dictatorship, welcomed him home. Among those who went to Holland to greet him was the great diarist, Samuel Pepys. From his diaries we see something of those first years of the Restoration as they appeared to an eager industrious young official.

In 1660, when Pepys began his diary, he was "worth" £40; by 1667 this had risen to £6,900. It is noticeable that Pepys does not spend his money on jewels to impress his fellows; instead he buys clothes, a new periwig (which he is very diffident about wearing the first time), books, furnishings; these are now the marks of the well-to-do middle-class man. As he rises in importance, people begin to make him gifts, and here again there are very few jewels—instead, candlesticks, oysters, gloves, flagons, gold and silver—though in May 1665 he is given a watch, which delights him (by July it is at the menders, and he has to borrow a larum one instead, which gets him up "betimes"); and in August he bestows on his wife, Elizabeth, a diamond ring worth about £10 given him by a grateful acquaintance "for helping him to be a purser".

Elizabeth's jewels give us some idea of the trinkets worn by a young middle-class matron, pretty and fashionable, with a husband who is proud of her though determined to retain control of his household. In the September of 1660 Elizabeth is "a little impatient" and Samuel, perhaps feeling guilty over one of his flirtations, takes her to buy a necklace of pearls for £4. 10s. (he spent more than this on a dinner party shortly afterward). A year later he records some jealous fretting over Mr. Somersett who "did give her a bracelet of rings which did a little trouble me". In the July of 1664 she lays out twenty-five shillings "upon a paire of pendantes for her eares, which did vex me"; "high and very foule words" pass between them, and he compels her to send the trinkets back to the Royal Exchange; but when she obeys, relents and allows her to keep them. A month later he is examining her household accounts, and she confesses

> "that when she do misse a sum she do add something to other things to make it, and upon my being very angry she do protest she will here lay up something for herself to buy her a necklace with".

In April 1666 he is making inquiries about the cost of pearls, having promised her a necklace "long ago"; the one she buys is a triple row, for £80. Will Hewer, a member of the household, presses her to accept a diamond locket worth £40 as a mark of gratitude—the Pepys have been very good to him—but this Samuel will not allow. Even without this, however, Elizabeth does fairly well, for a few weeks later, on February 23, 1668, she shows him her stock of jewels

> "encreased by the ring she hath made lately as my Valentine's gift this year, a Turkystone set with diamonds; and with this and what she had, she reckons that she hath above £150 worth of jewells of one kind or other; and I am glad of it, for it is fit the wretch should have something to content herself with".

He is, however, careful that what she has is suited to her station, and when that same year his aunt shows him how she has had her wedding ring set with diamonds, for a cost of £12, does not think it suitable "for one of our quality".

THE RESTORATION COURT

Charles II's Court was in some ways as domestic as his father's, though now it was a quarrelsome family of mistresses rather than a decorous group of children: Pepys records seeing Lady Castlemaine's smocks and petticoats spread to dry in the Privy Gardens; dropping in at "my goldsmith's" and there seeing "the King's new medall, where in little there is Mrs Steward's face"; standing in Whitehall to watch the court at dinner, the king in a rich silk vest and Frances Stuart ("Mrs. Steward") in black and white lace with her head and shoulders decked with diamonds.

Everything was growing looser, at least on the high society level: looser morals, big floral-patterned textiles, jewellery made up in big sweeping designs. Strict control and discipline were gone. The baroque scrolls gradually degenerated into florid formalized motifs. Perhaps it is as well that so little now remains. Jewellery became impersonal: whereas the Renaissance patrons had treasured baroque pearls for their very irregularity and their jewellers had created individual fantasy jewels to incorporate them, the ladies of Charles II's Court sat for their Lely portraits in low-cut billowing gowns with necklaces of matching pearls—identical in size, shape and colour—lustrous against the beautiful bare flesh. Diamonds supplanted the brilliant enamels and the glowing gemstones. Louis XIV employed a travelling agent, Jean Tavernier (1605–89), to buy Eastern gemstones for him, especially diamonds; and Charles II had his own man, Jean Chardin, a French Huguenot who travelled to India to buy diamonds in 1663 and spent the next eighteen years shuttling between India, France and Persia—his *Journal du Voyage* gave a great deal of information about the State and customs of Persia at the time of the death of Shah Abbas II and the coronation, amid tremendous intrigues, of Shah Sulaiman; in 1681 he settled in England, where he could practice his religion in peace, anglicized his name to John, was knighted, and became court jeweller to the king.

DUTCH CRAFTSMEN

Much of the work done in this period was, none the less, of great beauty, notably that of the Low Countries craftsmen. Charles II was much beholden to the Dutch during his exile, and once restored to England, showed his gratitude by bringing Dutch craftsmen over to work in his kingdom, much as his father and grandfather had done, encouraging them to enrich the country with their own creative spirit and giving them opportunities to strike out with fresh ideas and techniques.

Supreme among these artists was Grinling Gibbons (1648–1721), whose work shows the style which the North European craftsmen had evolved from their adaptation of the Italian baroque. Gibbons was an expatriate Englishman who was born in Holland where, because of the uncertain political situation in England at that time, he spent the first twenty years of his life. He had learnt about carving in the shipyards of Rotterdam. He was to work for six monarchs of England in turn, carving in wood, sculpting in marble, and also working in bronze. The rich beauty of his wood-carving is exemplified in the swags of fruit and flowers which adorn the Grinling Gibbons room at Petworth House in Sussex, and the carved panels in Wren's Library at Trinity College, Cambridge. The elegance and richness of the natural world, the realism of supreme craftsmanship, a northern accuracy and exactitude of detail, are all magnificently portrayed in Gibbons's work.

Among others who came was the jeweller, Isaac Le Gooch, who arrived in London during the Commonwealth. (A short study of his life was made by Mr. William Wheatley, M.A., assistant master at Latymer Upper School from 1919 to 1953, and published in booklet form by the Hammersmith Local History Group in 1964; and the present brief survey of his career depends to some extent on this.) Le Gooch was born in Antwerp and christened in November 1628. His family came to England during the reign of Charles I, and stayed on through the Civil War, and Isaac eventually decided to join them in London in May 1656. He lived and worked in the City, managing to escape and survive both the Great Plague of 1665 and the Great Fire of 1666; and on December 29 of that year, some ten years after his arrival in England, was sworn in as Principal Jeweller to Charles II, replacing the deceased John and Francis Simpson, who had provided £40,000 worth of "Jewels and other things for the King's use". His salary was £100 per annum. He had the sole authority to make badges of honour and the jewels which the king presented to the ambassadors and other foreign visitors, but his monopoly did not extend to the making of the jewelled George (the decoration worn by Knights of the Order of the Garter) since this was a Jewel House perquisite, obtainable only through the goldsmiths.

The most important type of jewel presented to ambassadors and foreign visitors of note was a miniature of the king—in the early years of his reign this was generally painted by his limner, Samuel Cooper, who died in 1672—suitably mounted in gold and diamonds, at an average cost of £900. In May 1683, for example, the Marquis de Auranches, Ambassador Extraordinary from Portugal, was given a "Jewel of diamonds, with the King's picture", which cost £1,000. Charles also presented rings and other jewels, set with diamonds.

During his fifteen years as king's jeweller, Le Gooch supplied jewels for about sixty envoys or ambassadors at a cost of about £30,000, as well as other more personal jewels for Charles. Details of these political commissions can be seen in the Treasury Books for 1681–85, and in the Letters Patent granted to James Nihill who had to supply the ready cash to settle Le Gooch's account. Getting paid was Le Gooch's greatest difficulty; the king kept on commissioning jewels, but never settled his bills, and at last Le Gooch began to play a waiting game, accepting the commissions but not actually making the jewels until he had been paid at any rate *some* ready money. The major sources from which the cash to pay Le Gooch seems to have been derived were the chimney tax (two shillings—10p—on every chimney), wine licences, Customs and Excise dues, and the hated hearth tax (another two shillings—10p—to the king for every hearth or stove), which was eventually abolished in 1689; the people resented the intrusion on their privacy, and the tax was both troublesome and expensive to collect.

In spite of Charles's dilatoriness, Le Gooch made a great deal of money and became a property-owner. His reputation as a jeweller and diamond-merchant was enviably high. In 1683 he carried out his last public act as the king's jeweller. The king's cousin, Prince Rupert, had died, and his jewels were to be disposed of by lottery. Each lot was to cost £5, and no prize was worth less than £100. The appraisal of the jewels was made by the three most important jewellers in the land: Le Gooch, Christopher Rosse (appointed king's jeweller by Charles's brother and successor, James II) and Richard Beauvoir, who "by her Majesty's command", was to design the crown worn by Mary of Modena, James's queen and second wife (Fig. 36). They valued the jewels at £20,000, the finest piece being a great pearl necklace worth £8,000.

On February 6, 1685, Charles died, and Le Gooch's appointment came to an end. He himself died that August, and in spite of considerable research, no one has yet discovered any jewels which can be authenticated as his. He has no church memorial, but a living memorial of far greater value, for he gave a large sum of money to the Latymer Foundation at Hammersmith, and Latymer Upper School was erected on land he once owned; a tablet commemorating him as chief benefactor is set into the school wall.

The Last Stuarts

James II, who seems to have been absolutely incapable of compromise, lasted only three years as King of England, before he, his wife and their infant son James (the Old Pretender) had to flee into exile. Very few jewels are extant which can be said to have belonged to him, but there is one at the Victoria and Albert Museum: a ring, lavishly set with diamonds and emeralds and engraved with his monogram on the back of the bezel, said to have been given by him to his Catholic chaplain.

The English offered the throne to James's elder daughter Mary and her husband William of Orange (who accepted it) and then settled back thankfully to enjoy a decent Protestant reign, under a king and queen who unquestionably owed their position to the will of the people as expressed in Parliament, and not to any nonsense about Divine Right. It might have been expected that Dutch William, who had been fighting against Louis XIV of France for the greater part of his life (declaring that he would die on the last dyke rather than see the French take Holland), would loathe and outlaw all things French; on the contrary, he had a great liking for French taste, and is said to have read, written and even thought in the French language. With him to England came the French Huguenot Daniel Marot who exemplifies the final division between craftsman and designer. Marot designed anything: furniture, gardens, Delft pottery, dresses and jewels. The formal French style was now all the vogue: women's clothes were becoming more formal and stiffer in style, their hair crowned by the *fontange*, a high lace cap which became modish in the last years of the century, and men were wearing the late Carolean style of long coat, embroidered waistcoat, knee-breeches, cravat, wig and hat, which was to last, with minor adaptations, for about a hundred years.

Mary II died in 1694, leaving William to reign alone until 1702, when he was succeeded by her sister Anne. Among the wax effigies in Westminster Abbey, now kept in the Undercroft though originally they were carried at the funeral and then placed in a case near the grave, are figures of Charles II, wearing his original Garter robes, William III and Mary his wife, and Anne I. A particularly interesting one, however, is that of Frances, Duchess of Richmond, who died in 1702. Frances Theresa Stuart was born in 1647, the grand-daughter of Lord Blantyre, and was eventually appointed maid of honour to Charles II's queen, Catharine of Braganza. She was nicknamed "*La Belle Stuart*", and her beauty and her charms made a great impression on Charles II, though she managed to escape being his mistress, and instead married the Duke of Richmond and Lennox. Pepys thought her "the greatest beauty" he had ever seen, and his description of how she was portrayed on the coinage has already been mentioned on page 125. (She sat for the figure of Britannia, and until decimal coinage was introduced into Britain in 1970, it was the Duchess of Richmond, with her famous "little Roman nose", who adorned the English penny.) Her effigy (Fig. 26) represents her "as well done in wax as can be" in the actual robes she wore for the coronation of Queen Anne, shortly before her death, and the jewels are either those she wore on that occasion or duplicates made especially for the funeral. Although they are of paste, it is clear that a great deal of time must have been taken to produce them. The duchess is wearing a *demi-parure*: a three-loop necklace, a pair of drop earrings, a pair of sleeve-clasps, and a brooch ornament with delicately stylized leafy scrolls, set with well-faceted crystals with enamelled backs. The general effect is very rich.

Anne I, at whose coronation the duchess appeared in this splendour, was thirty-seven when she acceded. For a great part of her life it had seemed unlikely that she would ever succeed to the throne, so she grew up in reasonable placidity, and was married off in 1683 to the indolent and vacuous George of Denmark. This good-natured and easy-to-please pair then set about having children, and Anne endured seventeen pregnancies, though in the end no child survived to grow to adulthood. When she came to the throne she was getting old, over-weight, and tired. Her life was one long confusion, never properly resolved, but in spite of her father's conversion to the Catholic faith she remained firm on one point: she was a faithful member of the Church of England, and always retained an ardent if not especially enlightened attachment to it. For the rest, she leaned on her favourites: initially she was under the capable thumb of Sarah, Duchess of Marlborough, and even when she broke off this attachment, it was only to transfer her devotion to Abigail Masham. Intrigues and party strife wore her out, her political views were muddled and easily swayed, and the quarrels among her ministers kept her in a state of perpetual worry and unrest. Her twelve-year reign had no major effect on the decorative arts.

The Crown Jewels

The Honours of Scotland: The History of the Honours; The Present
Scottish Regalia—The English Crown Jewels: Introduction; Early
Crowns and Ceremonies; Security of the Crown Jewels—The British
Coronation Rites: Crowns

The Honours of Scotland

THE HISTORY OF THE HONOURS

The names of the ancient kings of Scotland roll off the tongues of ardent clansmen and
women, scumbled together with deeds of glory, hasty flights, splendid recoveries, and power
established for all too short a period in one man's hands—to be lost and fought for anew.

The records of the early Scottish crownings are vague. Lacking reliable written
authority, historians have had to conjecture: "It is likely that . . ." and "This leads to
the conclusion that . . ." We do not know, and for our present purposes it is immaterial,
exactly what happened at the first recorded ceremony of the conferring of Scottish
kingship, when Saint Columba officiated at the accession of King Aidan, in A.D. 574.
It is, however, interesting that there is no record of the usual panoplies of kingship
being used in the early ceremonies—no crowning is mentioned, no investing with
sceptre and sword: what mattered was that the new king should take his seat at Scone.
From the accounts of the early medieval ceremonies it seems that certain hereditary
duties were carried out by the "seven earls of Scotland"; but the first mention of any
actual royal emblems comes in 1296, when Edward I of England, nicknamed "The
Hammer of the Scots", conquered Scotland, declared himself her king, captured the
vassal king John Balliol, seized the Honours of Scotland—the ancient title for the
Scottish Regalia: crown, sceptre, and sword—and carried them back to London,
together with the famous Stone of Destiny from Scone, which was taken to Westminster
Abbey, where it was incorporated into the Coronation Chair. The Honours disappeared,
and were probably destroyed during the Commonwealth; the Stone, however, survived,
and Cromwell was duly installed on it as Lord Protector in 1657.

Scotland regained her independence in the fourteenth century, and she fought
grimly to hold on to it. New Honours were in use towards the end of the century, for
Pope Alexander VI presented James IV with a sceptre in 1494; eight years later
payments to a cutler, Robert Selkirk, are recorded, for the Sword of Honour and for
making a sheath for it; and five years after that Pope Julius II presented a new Sword

of State, which may still be seen today. The sceptre was re-modelled by James V, a meddler who liked to re-fashion the royal emblems, adding more gold and jewels; the crown was also re-made by his order. The final enrichings took place in 1540, two years before his death.

The turbulent reign of James's daughter, Mary, Queen of Scots, was marked by battling between the rival parties, until at last, in 1573, the Honours were regained by the adherents of her young son, James VI. In 1585 an Act of Parliament was passed assigning them to the care of the Captain of Edinburgh Castle, and there the Honours lay while James travelled south in 1603 to be crowned King of England and to set up his court in London. His son, Charles I, was the first adult to be crowned and invested with the Honours for over a hundred years. Charles was a Scotsman, born at Dunferm-line, with all the fighting spirit expected of a Scot. He was so weakly an infant that he was unable to speak until he was five, and unable to walk upright until he was seven. But he outgrew both defects, although he still suffered from a stammer, and became a skilled marksman and a sound scholar and connoisseur. Unhappily though, he had an absolute and uncompromising view of the rights and duties of kingship, and a comple-mentary view of the right and duties of the people; his ideal was so much a part of him that he could not be false to it, though it cost him his life and led to civil war; "A subject and a sovereign are clean different things." He was crowned King of Scotland in Edinburgh in 1633, some fifteen years before his execution. Accompanied by nobles and dignitaries from the great hereditary families of Scotland, but not by his wife who disliked the Scots, he travelled in state from the castle to Holyrood, where the religious ceremony took place—Charles insisting, to the Scots' annoyance, on the Anglican ritual—and was acclaimed and crowned, wearing the royal robe of James V.

During the years of the Civil War the Honours were shifted about Scotland in an attempt to keep them safe. In 1649 Charles was executed, and the Scots leaders, who had handed him over to his English enemies, were so furious that they proclaimed his exiled son as king; Charles had, after all, been King of Scotland as much as King of England, but the English Parliament had chopped off his head without so much as a by-your-leave to their Scots allies. In July 1650 the young king came to Edinburgh with the covenanters all about him, to try to win back the kingdom beyond the border. Cromwell marched north to deal with these godfearing but "deceived" people, won a tremendous victory at Dunbar in September, and on Christmas Eve took Edinburgh Castle into the bargain; the Honours, however, were saved, and were duly used for the last crowning to take place in Scotland.

Charles II was crowned at Scone on the first day of January, 1651; Cromwell's forces held the Lowlands, but Charles's forces, a precarious alliance of different political and religious opinions, were not yet defeated. The crowning was preceded by fasting and public penitence—"I think I must repent too that ever I was born," said the young king wearily. The ancient Abbey Church had been burnt to the ground in 1559, the Stone was in England; but a little kirk had been raised over the ruins, and here Charles was crowned, the sword was handed to him, the sceptre was put in his hand, and the king showed himself to the people; the lords swore fealty, and there was a long and solemn sermon. The ceremony was rather arid when compared with his father's, but it was in keeping with the religious convictions of the people.

The Scots were defeated and their country occupied by the English forces (there is a splendidly romantic story attached to the saving of the Honours at the siege of Dunnottar); Charles marched south, deep into England, to final defeat at Worcester, and fled abroad, where he was to live for almost nine years. When he was triumphantly restored to his kingdoms in the happy Maytime of 1660, the Honours were returned to Edinburgh Castle, being duly produced according to law and custom during the sittings of the Scottish Parliament, until the Act of Union was passed, establishing a single parliamentary union of the two countries, and the last Scottish Parliament was dissolved in 1707. The Earl Marischall was called upon to surrender the Honours to the Commissioners of the Treasury; but the Scots insisted that a clause be added to the Treaty decreeing that "the Crown, Scepter and Sword of State . . . continue to be keeped as they are in that part of the United Kingdome now called Scotland, and that they shall so remain in all tyme coming, notwithstanding of the Union." So, on March 26, 1707, the Honours of Scotland were all packed up and locked away in an oak chest in the Crown Room and there, according to the H.M.S.O. booklet *The Crown Regalia*, "left to silence and seeming oblivion for more than a century", until the Scots began to suspect that the English, whom they had always fought against and distrusted, had broken the Treaty and stolen the Honours. People felt very bitter about this supposed theft, for the Honours, their legends and memories of hopes dashed in the rebellions of the '15 and the '45, were almost all they had left of their past. In 1794 the doors of the Crown Room were opened by royal warrant so that the officers could search for some missing records; they did not find the records, but they noticed the great oak chest; it was locked, and the key was missing. Even in those days bureaucracy prevented the officers from forcing the lock, so they were unable to check whether the Honours were still inside or not.

So the Honours slept on, until February 4, 1818, when the Scottish Officers of State, accompanied by Sir Walter Scott who had organized the search and obtained a warrant from the Prince Regent, entered the Crown Room. A description was written by Sir Walter himself:

> "The chest seemed to return a hollow and empty sound to the strokes of the hammer, and even those whose expectations had been most sanguine felt at the moment the probability of disappointment, and could not but be sensible that, should the result of the search confirm these forebodings, it would only serve to show that a national affront and injury had been sustained, for which it might be difficult, or rather impossible, to obtain any redress. The joy was therefore extreme when, the ponderous lid of the chest being forced open, at the expense of some time and labour, the Regalia were discovered lying at the bottom covered with linen cloths, exactly as they had been left in the year 1707. . . . The rejoicing was so general and sincere as plainly to show that, however altered in other respects, the people of Scotland had lost nothing of that national enthusiasm which formerly had displayed itself in grief for the loss of these emblematic Honours, and now was expressed in joy for their recovery."

So, after this long time of oblivion and distrust, the Honours were returned to the people, and since July 1818 have been open to public inspection, except during the two world wars when they were once again concealed. The separate office of Keeper was abolished in 1838, and since then the safety of the regalia has been entrusted to the Monarch's and Lord Treasurer's Remembrancer, the last surviving link with the ancient Scottish "Commissioneris of the Thesaurarie". (The Honours may still be viewed at Edinburgh Castle.)

THE PRESENT SCOTTISH REGALIA

Three major items now make up the regalia: the Crown, the Sceptre and the Sword of State. There are no written records attesting the history of the **Crown** before its re-modelling by order of James V in 1540, but it is by far the oldest crown in the British Isles. It was apparently re-cast from an earlier crown—there is, at least, some written evidence to support this theory in the diary of Lord Fountainhall ("The Crown of Scotland is not the ancient Crown but was casten of new by James V") and in the extant accounts of 1540, which show that John Mosman, an Edinburgh goldsmith, was paid to make and fashion the king's crown, and to supply twenty-three stones for it (there are a great many more than twenty-three in the re-modelled Crown on view today). It must have been an important re-shuffle, for John Paterson made a new case for the Crown at the same time, and Thomas Arthur made a new bonnet of velvet and satin (this has not survived).

The Crown, illustrated in Fig. 35, is of gold, which may well have come from the Scottish mines at Crawford Moor. It looks very much like an ordinary circlet, to which two crossing arches have been added at a later date and with no regard for the original design. These arches make it look unbalanced, particularly since the circlet has been heightened and enriched by ten crosses *fleury* alternating with ten *fleurs-de-lys*, which means that the lower half is very richly decorated, in contrast to the sparse upper section with its slender crossing arches ornamented simply with enamelled oak leaves. The Crown looks well enough resting on its velvet cushion infilled with the crimson bonnet sewn with pearls; but when the bonnet and its ermine band are removed, it is out of proportion. However, it is colourful enough, with its mixture of stones: there are jacinths, amethysts, topazes and rock crystals in the band, interspersed with twenty pearls—seven of which come from Scottish waters. On the crossing point of the arches stands the golden globe, or *monde*, which is enamelled in blue and adorned with gilt stars, and surmounted by a cross enamelled black and gold with terminals of gleaming pearls.

The **Sceptre** is of very sophisticated design and workmanship. It was given to James IV by Alexander VI, one of the more shameless of the Popes, in 1494, and later slightly altered by James V. Made of silver-gilt, engraved and decorated, it has a particularly beautiful head, flanked by dolphins; set between them, like statues in architectural niches, are three tiny modelled figures: the Virgin and Child, St. Andrew (patron of Scotland), and St. James (the king's own patron). They look like church portal sculptures reduced to a fraction of their original size. Above them is a globe of smoothly carved rock crystal, and above this again is a finial surmounted by a Scottish pearl.

The large **Sword of State**, presented to James IV in 1507 by Pope Julius II, is a fine piece of craftsmanship, with several allusions to the donor's identity worked into the delicate engraving. Pope Julius, a soldier churchman with a keen eye for his territorial possessions, was never slow to display his oak-leaf and acorn emblems.

In the Crown Room today there are several other items, not least among them being the oak chest. This is so large, and the doors to the room so narrow, that it was originally made in sections and carried into the room and finally assembled inside. It is of Dantzig oak, metal-bound and very solid.

The Sword of State was once accompanied by a magnificent woven lace belt and a silver-gilt buckle bearing the arms of the Pope. To keep it safe during the Civil Wars, this belt was concealed in a garden wall for over a hundred years after the siege of Dunnottar. It was rediscovered in 1790, and finally restored to the Crown Room in 1893. Also in the Crown Room are the Lord Treasurer's mace, which probably dates from about 1609, and the jewels bequeathed to George III by Cardinal Henry, the last direct descendant of James II: the Collar and George of the Order of the Garter, the St. Andrew of the Order of the Thistle, and a ruby and diamond ring.

The English Crown Jewels

INTRODUCTION

When Charles I tried to raise money by pledging or selling the royal heirlooms, he was acting in the spirit of his predecessors. In the past the sovereigns regarded the Crown Jewels and plate as a pool of reserve currency on which to draw if need be. It is quite astonishing to us, holding the Crown Jewels in reverence, to discover that past monarchs thought nothing of pawning various crowns here and there to pay for a battle or two. In 1346, the year of Crécy, one of Edward III's four crowns was pawned to Tidman de Limbergh, "a great loan contractor or money-lender in those days" according to Palgrave. In 1382 Edward's grandson, Richard II, pledged his grandfather's third crown to Matthew Cheyne, a Lombard. Even the jewels with which Henry VI was crowned King of France in Paris in the December of 1431 seem to have been temporarily released from pawn for the purpose.

But what then is the value of a crown? The estimated value of a jewel and the value it actually raised on the open market were vastly different. In 1625, when Charles I sent the marketable royal gold plate abroad for sale or pawn, an officer from the Jewel House assessed its value as £200,000 at the least. Yet within a few years, when thirty-one out of the forty items had been sold, they had only fetched a paltry £17,703. 13s. 0d.

In 1649, during the shattering Commonwealth purge, orders were given by Parliament to sell or melt down all the symbols of monarchy. Alfred the Great's crown "of gold wire-work set with slight stones and two little bells", which sounds enchanting, was sold for £248. 10s. 0d.; Queen Edith's crown went for a mere £16; anything that could not be sold was "broken and defaced". For us, a tragedy, both because of the Jewels' historical importance, and because of their priceless intangible value as symbols of the past; but if men wanted to break with tradition and were sick of all that they stood for, it is understandable that they should sell the Jewels or melt them down for the value of the materials alone.

Some pieces did survive. The tiny anointing spoon and the ampulla: the Black Prince's ruby (which was examined in the twentieth century and found to be only a spinel): Edward the Confessor's sapphire: these were somehow hidden away and kept safe by various monarchists until the restoration of Charles II. Other historic jewels which can still be seen include the Alfred Jewel, now in the Ashmolean Museum at Oxford, and the rings of Ethelwulf, King of Wessex, and Alfred's sister, Ethelswith, Queen of Mercia, which are both in the British Museum.

But a great many of the pre-Commonwealth jewels have gone forever—sold, hidden, lost, pledged and not redeemed. We can only depend on effigies, inventories, wills, royal accounts, and, in the case of the later monarchs—from Richard II downwards, generally speaking—portraits and paintings. In her *History of English Jewellery*, Joan Evans refers to descriptions of courtly jewels mentioned in pre-Tudor accounts and other documents, including, for instance, the fact that when Richard II married his second wife, Isabella of France, in 1396, he gave her an astonishing variety of jewelled items, amongst them crowns, brooches, collars, a belt of golden feathers, and a mirror in a jewelled frame; that Edward III's mistress, Alice Perrers, owned nearly twenty-two thousand pearls; that Edward II had ten crowns, two circlets and three chaplets in 1324; and that when Henry III deposited a hoard of jewels (with his sister in Paris) as security in 1272, the treasures included sixty-nine jewelled belts, an assortment of rings, and forty-five ring-brooches.

EARLY CROWNS AND CEREMONIES

So far as we know, Egbert (802–39), King of the West Saxons, was the first king to be crowned in England. The ceremony took place in A.D. 827, and it is almost certain that the only symbolic jewels used were a crown and a sceptre.

From the House of Wessex the crown passed briefly to the House of Denmark, with Canute (it was at the crowning of his son, Harold Harefoot, that the old Archbishop Elnoth put the English crown and sceptre on the altar and told the candidate frankly that he would make no attempt to stop his taking them, but he would not himself set the crown on his head, put the sceptre in his hand, nor give the blessing; Harold accordingly crowned himself). Harefoot's reign was short, his brother's still shorter, and in 1042 the last of the Saxon kings, Edward the Confessor, was crowned. A staff or long sceptre was set in his hand (a copy of it is in the present Crown Jewels) and a coronation ring on his finger. This ring was set with a very fine sapphire, which is now in the jewelled cross that tops the Imperial State Crown. (He was buried with the ring on his finger, but it was later removed from the corpse and added to the Crown Jewels.) It is probable that Edward's crown, together with the ancient robes he had worn and his ornaments, were used in the English coronation ceremonies from the time of his death until the Commonwealth.

It was Edward who instigated the crown-wearing ceremonies, which were carried out with all majesty and ritual from the year of his accession (1042) until the reign of Henry II. The king wore his crown ceremoniously in Westminster Abbey at Easter, in Winchester at Whitsun, and in Gloucester at Christmas: the purpose being to link the monarchy with the great religious feasts of thanksgiving. It also gave subjects living far from court an opportunity of seeing the king and his queen invested with the symbols of monarchy. The ceremonies, which incidentally gave rise to the belief that certain kings were crowned more than once, were eventually abandoned in 1159, by order of Henry II. He and his wife, Eleanor of Guienne, spent that Easter at Worcester; attended by their court, they processed ceremoniously to the High Altar of the cathedral that Sunday morning, and there removed their crowns and set them on the altar, vowing that they would not don them again. The Confessor's ceremony died out; and today St. Edward's Crown (which is not his actual crown, though some of the original gold may have been used when it was made for Charles II) is worn only during the coronation ceremony. The Imperial State Crown is, however, worn during the State Opening of Parliament.

The early crowns were of the simple open circlet pattern. Henry I had gemstones and pearls set around the headband to invest the emblem of power with visual richness, and John I went further, adding trefoil *fleurons*. By the time of his crowning, in 1199, there was a blazingly rich crown for State occasions and a simple gold circlet for everyday wear. It was John who lost his baggage, said to have contained at least one crown and a quantity of treasure, in the Wash (he had a good deal left, however; according to S. K. Mitchell, they found two hundred and seventy jewelled rings at Devizes after his death). Two hundred years later, Henry V was crowned, on April 10, 1413. It was at this time that the crossed arches were added to the crown, establishing the mode that has been followed ever since in the making of English crowns. These arches signify the hereditary nature and the independence of the monarchy. They are deeply depressed at the crossing-point, and this depression is said to signify royalty. In modern usage, the term "crown" is applied when these arches are incorporated in the emblem; a headband is a "coronet".

Henry is believed to have pledged his coronation crown as surety for a loan to equip the invasion forces which he led against France, in the war that was to see the siege of Harfleur, the battle of Agincourt, and eventually, the conquest of the French. *Fleurs-de-lys* were then added to the English crown to signify the sovereignty of France, and the four main uprights took the form of crosses. From these sprang the arches. The orb, or *monde*, was set at the crossing point of the arches, and this was surmounted by a cross, signifying the supremacy of the Christian faith over the earth.

The Great Seals are of interest in tracing the changes in design. The crosses *pattées* and *fleurs-de-lys* first appear on the Great Seal of Richard III, who ruled from 1483 to 1485 (earlier instances are, however, known), and the arches some years before this, on the Great Seal of 1471.

SECURITY OF THE CROWN JEWELS

During medieval times, as the monarchy became stabilized, further jewels and plate were added, piece by piece, to the regalia, and all these valuables were handed over to the abbot and monks of Westminster for safe-keeping in the Chapel of the Pyx. However, when the collection was checked in the reign of Edward I, some of the royal plate was missing. Naturally an inquiry was set up. One of the monks, Alexander de Pershore, had sold certain items to a travelling merchant named Richard de Podelicote; as a result, Abbot Wenlock and forty-eight of his monks were tried, and sentenced to two years' imprisonment in the Tower of London. The Crown Jewels and the plate were sent there too, and there, in general, have remained—though the Westminster Abbey records show that Edward III's crown was being kept in the abbey treasury as late as 1369.

The Jewels were first put in the crypt of St. John's Chapel, in the charge of an official known as the Keeper of the Regalia; but as time went by, and more and more were accumulated, there was no longer enough room, nor were they really safe. Late in the reign of Elizabeth I, in 1597, a special Jewel House was finally built—a long low flat building—where the Jewels were looked after until the Commonwealth, when orders were given that all the symbols of monarchy be sold or defaced. The Tudor Jewel House fell into disrepair and was eventually pulled down. At the Restoration, a completely new regalia was supplied by Sir Robert Vyner, the court jeweller, and a new and satisfactory Jewel House had to be built. Understandably this took a considerable time, and in the meanwhile the jewels and plate were placed in the Martin Tower, with an official guardian named Talbot Edwards, the seventy-six-year-old assistant Keeper. He was permitted to show them to visitors, charging whatever sum he could extract. As his perquisite, Edwards was given lodgings in the upper part of the Tower; the Jewels were housed in a semi-basement.

In 1671 two elderly visitors came to see the Jewels: a doctor of divinity and his wife. The lady, faint with emotion at the sight, was given a glass of spirits to revive her; and Mrs. Edwards invited her to rest and recover in the lodgings above. A few days later the clergyman came back bringing a handsome gift of several pairs of white gloves for Mrs. Edwards in gratitude for her kindness. Not unnaturally, Mr. and Mrs. Edwards told him that they would be pleased to see him and his wife at any time.

The clergyman took up the invitation and returned another day to compliment the Edwardses on their pretty daughter. He had an unmarried nephew, a young man with a tidy income—why not see if they could make a match of it? The Edwardses, overwhelmed at this unlooked-for opportunity, invited the clergyman, his wife and nephew to dinner.

They dined, and then the guests were given a conducted tour through the Martin Tower. The clergyman arranged to buy a pair of pistols from Talbot (at an inflationary price) and to collect them on the following morning—May 9—at seven o'clock. He duly arrived, with two friends and his son, all armed to the teeth with concealed daggers, pistols and swordsticks. Might they see the Crown Jewels while they waited? Trusting old Edwards willingly agreed.

The moment they had all entered the room where the Crown Jewels were kept, the men attacked Edwards, threw a cloak over his head, tied him up and gagged him with "a great plug of wood, with a small hole in the middle to take breath at, tied on with a waxed leather which went round his neck. At the same time they fastened an iron hook to his nose that no sound might pass from him that way." But brave foolish old Edwards thrashed about so noisily that one of the men thrust a dagger in his stomach and left him for dead in a pool of blood.

Then they pillaged the Jewels. One man stamped on a crown to make it less bulky, so that he could hide it under a cloak. Another hid an orb in a pair of baggy breeches. Another pocketed the Black Prince's Ruby. Someone else began to file a sceptre in half.

But, extraordinarily, Edwards's son returned home at that precise moment from serving abroad in the army. He was met at the door of the Tower by one of the conspirators, who could not very well prevent his entering his own home; as the young soldier went upstairs to his parents' lodging, the look-out rushed to the basement and warned the thieves. They decided to leave at once. Old Talbot Edwards was found by his son, the alarm was given, and after an incredibly confused chase along Tower Wharf, the thieves were caught.

Once bundled into a dungeon, the agile old clergyman was revealed as "a beardless, tall, rough-boned man, with small legs, a pock-frecken face with little hollow blue eyes". This was the notorious Colonel Thomas Blood (*circa* 1618–80), the title having been generously bestowed on him by himself: an adventurer from Ireland, who was of English descent. Everything he attempted had always seemed doomed to failure: the man was, it seemed, a born loser, who always backed the wrong side; his last desperate bid to make some money by stealing the Crown Jewels landed him in the Tower dungeon. Yet Blood's final failure turned into a most curious success. Talbot Edwards recovered; the Crown Jewels were restored (excepting one pearl and one diamond) and given back into Edwards's custody, and Charles II was so amused and intrigued by the enormity of the crime that he pardoned the outrageous colonel, returned his lands (Blood had, inevitably, been on the wrong side at the time of the Restoration) and even gave him a pension of £500 a year. In spite of the many rumours that were bandied about, this extraordinary action was not due to collusion between the king and Blood, but simply to the fact that Blood had agreed to enter the king's service as a spy. One of the most heinous crimes in the history of theft thus ended up in a most gentlemanly way, much to the fury of many in Charles's Court.

The regalia were moved to another building, near the armoury, which was thought to be safer than the Martin Tower; from the theft point of view, it was, but the choice was almost disastrous since in 1843 an explosion sent the armoury up in smoke, and the regalia nearly went with it. The treasures were immediately removed to the Wakefield Tower, secured by Messrs. Chubb, and guarded by soldiers.

The present Jewel House was opened in July 1967, a circular underground strong-room ablaze with jewels. The first sight, after the long build-up of expectancy as one descends flight after flight of steps, is not a moment ever to be forgotten.

The British Coronation Rites

The sight of the Crown Jewels often astounds the visitor; the immensity and responsibility of monarchy is symbolized by the display ("No thanks, you can keep that job as far as I'm concerned, Crown Jewels or not"); but this is a comparatively small experience when set against that of viewing an actual coronation in Westminster Abbey.

Basically, the coronation ceremony falls into four main rites. Initially, the sovereign and the people must give their mutual consent to the crowning and consecrating of the new monarch. The sovereign is therefore presented to the people for formal recognition; this given, he in his turn takes the solemn Coronation Oath to show that he recognizes and accepts the duties and responsibilities of kingship.

Secondly, there is the anointing: the solemn consecration of the sovereign. The holy oil is poured from the ampulla into the anointing spoon, and the Archbishop of Canterbury anoints the sovereign's head, breast and palms. The ampulla is shaped like a small gold eagle—it is only nine inches (230 mm) high, with a wing-span of seven inches (180 mm), and weighs ten ounces (250 g)—and was probably first used at the coronation of Henry IV in 1399. The anointing spoon is just over ten inches long, and is made of silver-gilt, set with four small pearls; the handle is decorated with thin flat granulated strapwork, closely resembling the pattern on St. Thomas of Canterbury's mitre (preserved at Sens in France), and may perhaps, as some authorities suggest, have originated from the same design-source; this would mean that the spoon dated from the twelfth century. Whatever their exact date, the ampulla and the spoon are by far the oldest objects in the present regalia, owing their preservation to the fact that they were not considered as royal ornaments, technically speaking, but rather as religious vessels.

The anointing is followed by the dramatic investing with the royal ornaments, which culminates in the crowning. These ornaments include the golden spurs, the golden armills, and the coronation ring, popularly known as the wedding ring of England. Until the reign of William IV, each monarch in turn had a new ring, which became his private property. William IV's ring has, however, been used by all the succeeding kings; it is a gold ring with a huge sapphire, covered by a St. George's Cross in rubies, this being the insignia of the Order of the Garter. Since this ring was made for a man, William IV had a new one made for his heir presumptive, Princess Victoria; it was much smaller, to fit her tiny finger, but to the same design. Unfortunately, however, chivalry ran away with itself, the ring was made far too small, and the queen suffered agonies wearing it. There is also a consort's ring, set with a large single ruby surrounded by diamonds. The ring is traditionally placed on the third finger of the right hand, where the continental wedding ring is customarily worn.

The orb is then presented to the sovereign. This is made from pure gold, a large heavy glowing ball, its jewelled cross symbolizing Christianity's sovereignty over the world; it is so heavy, indeed, that the sovereign cannot hold it for long, and a special stand is provided for it in the coronation coach, for the subsequent drive through the streets.

The sceptre, the "ensign of kingly power and justice", is then placed in the sovereign's right hand. Atop this gold sceptre flashes the enormous Star of Africa, a flawless diamond, $516\frac{1}{2}$ carats in all: the largest stone cut from the largest diamond ever yet found, the three-thousand-carat Cullinan, which was discovered in South Africa and presented to Edward VII by the South African Government (it was eventually cut into nine huge diamonds and dozens of brilliants, and the largest of the nine stones added to the sceptre as a declaration of the power and wealth of the monarchy). There are six sceptres in the regalia; the one topped by the Star of Africa was originally made for Charles II.

Finally the crown is set on the sovereign's head. The crown used in the coronation ceremonies is called St. Edward's Crown, and was made in 1662 for Charles II. Recent tests have given rise to the theory that some of the original gold from the first St. Edward's Crown, which disappeared from historical record during the Commonwealth, may have been used in its construction. It is set with four hundred and forty gemstones, and weighs over seven pounds. Being so heavy, it is only used for the actual crowning. Every monarch since Charles II has been crowned with it except for the young Victoria, who used the Imperial State Crown instead, though her Lord High Steward carried the St. Edward's Crown throughout the ceremony. There is a slight lateral spread in the crown to accommodate Charles II's flowing periwig.

The sovereign is then throned. Recognized, anointed, invested and crowned, he now accepts the homage of his subjects.

THE CROWNS

St. Edward's Crown has already been described, but there are, of course, many other crowns in the regalia. The **Imperial State Crown** is the most dramatic and compelling of them all. It is so encrusted with gems—over three thousand of them, including one Welsh pearl from the River Conway which was presented to Catharine of Braganza by her Lord Chamberlain, Sir Richard Wynn of Gwyder—that one is quite unconscious of its design, or of the fact that basically it is made from solid gold. It was first made in the reign of Charles II, with a design of oak-leaves and acorns, and re-made in 1838 for Victoria, with extra stones added. The crown is ablaze with diamonds, banded with pearls, and punctuated with enormous coloured gems. One of the most conspicuous is the great irregular *cabochon* "ruby"—actually a spinel—given to the Black Prince in 1367, and worn by Henry V at the Battle of Agincourt in 1415; it glowers away among all the sparkle like an open wound. Counter-balancing the ruby is the Stuart sapphire, almost as big, once set in Charles II's crown; James II took it with him when he fled to France in 1688, but it was honourably sold back to the English when the last surviving Stuart died. In the uppermost jewelled cross is the sapphire from Edward the Confessor's ring; in the lower band is the second of the diamond Stars of Africa, and hung between the central cross-pieces are four huge baroque pearl drops, said to have been owned originally by Elizabeth I. In spite of the staggering number of gemstones, the crown is endearingly small when compared with St. Edward's Crown, and far more familiar since it is worn by the sovereign at the State Opening of Parliament.

Since by the law of England, St. Edward's Crown may not be taken out of the country, a special **Imperial Crown of India** had to be created in 1912 when George V was crowned Emperor in Delhi. Eight small platinum and diamond arches rise to a diamond-encrusted globe; more than six hundred diamonds were used. Another crown was made for his consort, Queen Mary, with six arches instead of eight.

James II's Crown was surmounted by a magnificent aquamarine, cut with hundreds of tiny facets, and topped by a diamond cross. This splendid gemstone, much admired in earlier periods, was later found to be merely a beautifully cut ball of coloured glass. Did James II pawn the gem and replace it with glass? We will never now know.

Mary of Modena's Diadem (Fig. 36), made for her by the order of her husband, James II, in 1685, and costing him £110,000, has no arches at all. She wore this on the way to her coronation, but during the ceremony it was replaced by a **Consort's Crown**, which was very small, being designed for wearing on top of the head rather than fitting about the skull, and set with diamonds and pearls. This Queen Mary continued to wear for the State procession back to the palace. The diamonds were re-mounted for the coronations of Mary II, Anne I, George II's wife, Caroline of Anspach, George III's wife, Charlotte, and finally, William IV's wife, Adelaide, in 1831 (Fig. 36). This is the crown which is portrayed in the statue of Queen Anne which stands outside St. Paul's Cathedral in London.

Tourists are often immeasurably touched by the sight of the tiny diamond **Crown** worn by **Victoria I** when she grew old. This was made in 1870, to an heraldic Tudor design, and though in photographs it looks the same size as any other crown, when seen with the rest of the regalia it looks minute, for it is only a few inches across, as if it had been made for a little regal doll. One can imagine the frail old lady having this tiny crown gently placed on her wispy silver hair, light as a diamond feather.

The **Queen Mother's Crown** was made in 1937 for the coronation of George VI and his wife, Queen Elizabeth. It is made of platinum and the arches are detachable (a very practical factor). The Koh-i-Noor diamond is incorporated in its band. This is one of the "great" diamonds of the world. It came from India, and is traditionally said to bring bad luck to men but not to women. Following the conquest of the Punjab in the mid-nineteenth century, the Governor-General of India took the gem and shipped it home to Queen Victoria, who allowed it to be displayed at the Great Exhibition of 1851. His accompanying letter quoted a former owner's estimate of its value:

> "If a strong man were to throw four stones, one north, one south, one east, one west, and a fifth stone up into the air, and if the space between them were to be filled with gold, all would not equal the value of the Koh-i-Noor."

Unfortunately the original stone was cut several times, and rather badly. It is believed to have been about 1000 carats originally, but now is down to 106. None the less it flashes fire in the crown, together with two more of the lesser Stars of Africa. All three stones can be removed from the crown and worn as pendants or brooches. Victoria never wore the Koh-i-Noor in her crown; she wore it as a brooch; but it was set in the crown worn by George V's wife, Queen Mary, and then in the 1937 crown made for George VI's wife, Queen Elizabeth, in which it is still displayed. Elizabeth II could not traditionally wear the consort's crown, being herself the reigning monarch.

The earlier of the two **Prince of Wales's crowns** is the simplest of all. The making of a crown was sanctioned by Charles II (he had no legitimate male heir but may have considered conferring the title on his illegitimate son, the Duke of Monmouth) but it was not made until 1729 when it was created for Frederick Lewis, son of George II. The prince died before his father and was never King of England. There are no jewels, just four crosses *pattée* and four *fleurs-de-lys*, and a single depressed arch.

Far more attractive and suitable is **the twentieth-century crown** made by Louis Osman and worn by Elizabeth II's son, Charles, when he was invested as Prince of Wales at Caernarvon in 1970. It was made by the electro-forming technique—that is, the gold was "grown" in an electro-plating bath. The method was discovered in the early eighteenth century and revived over a hundred years later and had never previously been used on such a scale. It was used for two principal reasons: first, had the crown—a one-piece structure—been made by conventional methods, it would have weighed about one-third as much again; secondly, it ensured that the artist's design was reproduced with total fidelity. The crown thus created was of twenty-four carat gold, absolutely pure; none the less, it had to be stamped with the usual twenty-two carat hallmark.

Correctly speaking, this is not a crown at all, but a coronet, since it is a circlet with a single arch. The traditional crosses *pattées* and *fleurs-de-lys* are incorporated into the design, but in a completely modern idiom. The crosses—emblems of protection—are

141

built up from four "nails" of Welsh gold reinforced with iridium platinum, and held at the centres with a reinforcing motif of four small irregularly placed square-cut diamonds in platinum settings; there is another square-cut diamond at the end of each arm of each cross. The *fleurs-de-lys*—emblems of purity—are created in the same way and each held by three square-cut emeralds, the green stone representing the national colour of Wales.

The **orb** is beautifully engraved with the special heraldic attributes of the Prince of Wales and the proper mottoes, and the unicorn supporter is a neat memorial to the Worshipful Company of Goldsmiths who commissioned the crown as their gift to the Prince (the unicorn also appears in the Company's coat of arms). Diamonds are spattered across the orb: four to show the four corners of the earth, others to signify the stars in the heavens. There are more diamonds in the finial.

The entire effect of this twentieth-century crown is one of basic pure architectural form, sculptural in essence, but with a strong traditional background. It is, moreover, a young man's crown: not something designed for a flowing periwig, but suited to constructive forward thinking. The Crown Jewels have been re-modelled and re-set again and again, old ones re-fashioned, new ones commissioned, to suit the style of the day and the demands of tradition; the modern Prince of Wales's Crown is as much in keeping with new trends and traditional values as all the others.

CHAPTER SEVEN

Georgian Glitter

Introduction—Design Periods—Fashion: The World of Modes; The World of Jewels; Shopping—Diamond Cutting and Setting—Eighteenth-Century Design—*Tremblant* Jewels—Practicality in Design—The French Influence—Articles of Jewellery—Paste Jewellery: Introduction; The Making of Paste; Flint Glass; Comparing Pastes; Evaluating Paste; Coloured Pastes; Repairing Paste

Introduction

The eighteenth century was predominantly a feminine period, and the eighteenth century was fun. Many authorities have written on the domination of classicism in eighteenth-century literature, thought and art. With hindsight, they are quite right to do so. At the time most Georgians would have been astonished to hear it.

The men and women of Georgian society probably lived their lives more fully than those of any other period. There was a far greater equality of the sexes than during the seventeenth or even the nineteenth century, and they were always so *busy*. Almost too busy to stop and think carefully what they were doing. When people nowadays sigh for the "good old days", they often do not mean the early twentieth century or any time in Victoria's reign: they mean the Georgian period.

Life was enormously full under the Georges. Britain at last became as important as any other country in Europe. She kept pace: her political thinkers, her naval power, her army, made her a force to be reckoned with; her writers, poets and playwrights were read and quoted abroad; her painters were admired—from the sly political and social caricatures of Hogarth to the calm classical work of Reynolds. The new great houses being built for the rich and famous Whig landowners by Campbell and Kent were models of restrained classicism, and the delights of the decorative arts—from enamelled watchcases to Sheraton furniture—were acclaimed by all Europe as well as being exported to adorn their courts and country houses.

It was a time of wildly differing contrasts, when beauty and brutality ran in harness. The Georgians had a lust for life and squeezing every drop of pleasure out of living unrivalled before or since. They never seemed to glance back regretfully over one shoulder, instead they were always looking forward to the next pleasurable event, anything from a masked ball to a public hanging. Even if they had plunged recklessly into gambling with disastrous results, they could take the waters at one of the innumerable spas, with time off to recover financially while they ate and drank to excess and flirted with every available pretty girl. Charles James Fox, for instance, had lost £140,000 before he was twenty-four, which did not stop his leading an extremely satisfying life then and afterwards. Sir John Bland, on the other hand, lost the whole of his estates—which included the entire city of Manchester—on the turn of a card in 1755, and he shot himself, which was rather more final. The greatest degradation in the eighteenth century was to be patently penniless.

England was progressing in every possible way, and was expanding with remarkable speed. In the year 1700, just before Anne, last of the Stuart monarchs, came to the throne, the population of London was 674,500; by the time George IV died in 1830 London had 1,654,994 citizens. Other cities fared the same. In 1725 Birmingham was a village of no account; in 1778 it was a city. Bristol was the second largest city in Great Britain and the second largest port outside London: the merchant vessels that lined her quays came from Russia, the northern European ports, the Mediterranean, the New World and the East. Everywhere there was hustle and bustle and expansion and trade. No one dallied or lingered except deep in the country. Society, trade and industry were travelling faster and faster, cutting the roads to ribbons with their horse-drawn vehicles. Stage coaches and mail coaches swept regularly from London to the major towns: horns blowing, horses sweating, leather harness gleaming, and trunks and boxes piled high among the jaunty travellers. The coaches carried everything new—from furniture to fashions—from London to the provinces, so that the quick and astute in Dover or Durham, Norwich or Bath could appear in the London styles at virtually the same time as they burst upon the capital. Heavy goods went by cart or by canal—the Georgian era was the greatest period of canal-building in England. Telford, Smeaton, Jessop and Cubitt made their names as canal-builders. Watt and Boulton went into partnership towards the end of the century, and set up steam-engine works near Birmingham ("I sell here what all the world desires," Boulton told George III: "Power."). The first steam-boat was plying on the Clyde in 1812; four years later Stephenson's locomotive was puffing along the tramlines drawing trucks of coal; by 1825 the first passenger railway was open, with an engine that could draw ninety tons at a rate of eight miles an hour; and by 1830, the year George IV died, a railway linked Manchester and Liverpool, and the Georgian industrialists could speed along it at a terrifying pace—over thirty miles an hour.

Everyone seemed to be travelling. Young men were sent off on the educational "Grand Tour" of Europe—one reason being that the English universities were such dens of vice; ladies travelled to the spas or to visit their relatives; families travelled up to London for the Season, then back to the country again, having arranged a suitable match for one of their many daughters; and foreigners travelled to England to see for themselves exactly what was going on.

They were amazed at what they saw. The freedom of the English social scene was astonishing when compared with that of other European countries. Possibly what staggered the visitors most was the liberty of free speech, an endearing and enduring English characteristic that has never been lost. They took themselves off to the theatres as well, where the fashionable *ton* and the rising middle class watched comedy and farce, burlesque and spectacle (in 1700 there had been only two theatres in London, by 1750 there were five more and an opera house as well, plus half a dozen more in the provinces, and by 1800 the number of provincial theatres had swollen to over three dozen). They came to listen to the operas, the new orchestras and the musicians. (George II gave a thousand pounds to found a Royal Academy of Music, and old Handel was secured as one of the composers; the Londoners grew quite used to seeing him shuffling along the Strand on his way, perhaps, to rehearsal in the Haymarket; when he died in 1759 they buried him in Westminster Abbey among the kings.) But above all, they came to look. To look at the buildings, the fashions, the shops. To look at the countryside, with its magnificent estates and farms, its well-fed plough-horses and productive cattle. By the end of the era, the well-ordered countryside of England was an example to all Europe.

But the foreigners also came to look at society—and especially at the society women. They were so beautiful, so graceful and charming, and they had such presence, all of them, from the lovely Duchess of Devonshire to the naughty Lady Hamilton. They were frivolous and generous, delighting in luxury and extravagance whenever possible; some of them, indeed, were uncaringly depraved and immoral. Beauty, money and charm were the only things expected of a Georgian woman. One asset out of the three was acceptable; all of them guaranteed success, whatever one's birth. A woman had to marry and produce a male heir; once she had done that, she had earned her keep for the rest of her pleasure-filled life, and she had gained complete emotional freedom. Married women had lovers and were often mischievous enough to parade them openly. Sometimes a husband might be pushed into asserting himself and his rights, but action like that was resented: it upset the accepted order of life. The wife of Sir Richard Worsley openly paraded thirty-four lovers before he finally felt moved to divorce her; Lord Frederick Baltimore, on the other hand, had eight wives all at the same time and travelled all over the world with them without shocking anyone very much.

Whatever happened, no one in society ever gave up. They attended the social events, followed the fashions slavishly, experimented with every form of cosmetics. Paint and powder and patches, wigs and hoops covered absolutely everything, whatever one's age. No one dreamed of appearing in public with an unpainted face, and as a result several society women died from white lead poisoning, two notable beauties who did so being Maria Gunning, a lovely provincial who caught the Earl of Coventry, and pretty Kitty Fisher, the daughter of a German stay-maker, who married a Mr. Norris. A fine portrait of Kitty Fisher, painted by Sir Joshua Reynolds, hangs now in the Grinling Gibbons Gallery of Petworth House in Sussex. She was only twenty-six when she died, in 1771.

The Georgian era also saw the appearance of Wesley and his Methodists. There was no room for John and his brother Charles in the Church of the seventeen-thirties; his fellow-clergymen thought him a madman, and he had to organize his followers into a religious movement that lay beyond the bounds of the established Church. It was the poor who flocked to him, crowding together into his congregations. Society was rather amused, rather shocked by such zeal and enthusiasm; it never dreamed of following suit. "To speak the rough truth," Wesley said, "I do not desire any intercourse with any persons of quality in England." They responded in kind.

Yet in spite of the lack of religious principle, in spite of the frivolity, extravagance and luxury, how is it that the artists and craftsmen of the Georgian era seemed never to put a foot wrong? Just about everything made during the eighteenth century, from a Palladian mansion to an ivory-sticked fan, seemed to be imbued with a feeling for design, a sense of style, and an impeccable judgment. Throughout this entire period, which stretches from the early decades of the eighteenth century through a clear hundred years, everything is in keeping with its high regard for order and harmony.

Design Periods

In discussing the eighteenth century and its decorative arts, it is easiest to divide the period arbitrarily into three distinct sections. The first is the period from 1702 to 1760, covering three reigns: Anne I (reigned 1702–14), whose period was marked by military glory, but whose married life was passed in quiet domesticity with her heavy Danish husband; her successor, and distant kinsman, George I (reigned 1714–27), a heavy Hanoverian who did not even speak English, and whose court lacked a queen, since he had divorced his wife and left her closed up for over thirty years in Schloss Ahlden; and his son, George II (reigned 1727–60), obstinate, lacking in wit or intelligence but

Queen Charlotte Sophia of Mecklenburg-Strelitz, wife of George III, from the Studio of Allan Ramsay: this portrait, now in the National Portrait Gallery in London, is believed to date from about 1762, and shows the Queen in the full glory of Georgian jewellery. Her stomacher, tapering from the neck to the waist of her gown, is a blaze of jewels. It was designed and made especially for this occasion, the stones—which were immensely valuable—being hired from the Court Jewellers, Garrards, and subsequently returned to them for storage until next they were needed. Georgian jewellery was stiff with diamonds, brilliant, dramatic, but always practical: this lavish stomacher was designed so that the weight, which must have been considerable, was carefully distributed, and the pieces sewn in place without pulling the fabric out of shape. The Queen is wearing a diamond *aigrette* in her hair and a choker necklace—the Arcot diamonds—about her throat. Beautiful strings of matching pearls are knotted on the shoulders of the gown, looped about the sleeves, and allowed to cascade along the line of the pointed bodice; more are twisted about her wrists. Serenely self-assured, clad in the glitter of Georgian diamonds enhanced by the lustre of matched pearls, here she stands in her stiff brocades and rich ermine, one hand resting negligently on the jewelled emblem of Royalty: exemplifying the age's sense of display and drama, allied to its practicality and its absolute assurance.

By courtesy of the Trustees of the National Portrait Gallery

clever enough to know his power, and fortunate enough to be married to, and to appreciate and trust, Caroline of Anspach (who died in 1737). It was a period of settled stability, centring on a court which, for the greater part of this time was ruled by heavy Hanoverians; a period which belonged to the older generation.

The second period may be said to open in 1760 with the accession of George II's grandson, George III, then a young man of twenty-two. He was to rule, in name at least, until 1820, though towards the end of his life his son, the Prince Regent, ruled as king, when illness drove the old king mad.

The third period dates from 1789, midway through George III's reign. It was triggered off by the French Revolution, and characterized by the neo-classical movement; and will be dealt with in greater detail in the next chapter.

Fashion

THE WORLD OF MODES

Throughout the entire century, fashions in England seemed to be just one step behind the French and one step ahead of the Germans. In France the inspiration came from the monarch's wife or mistress; in England it was heavily influenced by the stage— the dresses that Mrs. Abington or Mrs. Siddons wore were eagerly examined by every

Fig. 35: the Crown from the Honours of Scotland, by far the oldest now surviving in the British Isles, was re-modelled by order of James V in 1540. It is of gold, which may well have been taken from the Scottish mines at Crawford Moor: a simple circlet which has been heightened and enriched by ten crosses *fleury* and ten *fleurs-de-lys*, with slender crossing arches apparently added at a later date, giving it a rather unbalanced look. It is extremely rich, the gold band being set with jacinths, amethysts, topazes and rock crystals, interspersed with pearls (some of them Scottish), the *monde* enamelled in blue and adorned with gilt stars, and the surmounting cross enamelled in black and gold with pearl terminals.

Fig. 36: the diadem on the far left was made for Mary of Modena by order of her husband, James II, in 1685; it cost him over £100,000. She wore it on the way to her coronation, but during the actual ceremony it was replaced by a tiny crown made to sit on top of the head rather than circle the skull. The diamonds and pearls with which this crown was set were re-mounted for successive queens, some regnant, some consort—Mary II, Anne I, Queen Caroline, Queen Charlotte, and finally, in 1831, Queen Adelaide, who wore the crown shown here.

By courtesy of the Controller of H.M.S.O.: Crown Copyright

female in the audience and quickly copied or adapted. Mrs. Siddons (1755–1831) was painted by Gainsborough: a dominating portrait of her in a big plumed hat, blue-striped dress, fichu and furs, *poudrée* and serene, hangs in the National Gallery in London; anything further from a painted theatre hussy it is harder to imagine.

Very broadly speaking, when the eighteenth century began fashion meant a fuss of fabric, folded, pleated, swirling round the female body, concealing any deformity and exposing only the head, neck and forearm. By the end of the period, the whole body was exposed in a titillating manner, with flimsy fabrics cut in such a fashion that the figure beneath was the focus of attention, suggestive and exciting. The English never went quite as far as the French, who at the height of the Greek style of fashion appeared virtually bare-breasted—but it was a near thing. The charming and extravagant Miss Chudleigh, for instance, attended one masked ball "dressed" as Iphigenia at the altar— "So naked," said Lady Elizabeth Montague a trifle tartly, "that the high priest could very easily inspect the entrails of the victim."

The more one reads about the eighteenth century, the more plays and films and television productions one sees, the more one is conscious that a myth has grown up about the dresses of the period. They are made to look so elegant, so refined and so delicate—and so they were, on top. Everything that was on view, everything on the surface, was simply beautiful, and wonderfully arranged—the tiny fans, the fairy-like laces, the enchanting textiles, and the delicate embroideries. But very little value indeed was attached to what could not be seen. A common thread of sheer bourgeois practicality ran through the entire century. Soft satin ball-gowns embroidered in silver thread were lined with coarse linen and hemmed with huge uneven stitches. Whalebone and wire frames were constructed in such a way that they must have felt like coats of armour. The luxurious gown that George III's wife, Queen Charlotte, is wearing in the portrait facing page 146 was so heavy that she could not lift the skirt; a mechanical device is concealed behind the rich fabric. Underwear too was virtually unknown. When an eighteenth-century gown arrives in a museum there are sighs of admiration from the public and sighs of sorrow from the staff who have seen, and concealed, the inside. It is all too true that for a very long period, until the appearance of the spotless and supremely elegant Beau Brummell (1778–1840), whose rule as the arbiter of fashion covered the opening years of the nineteenth century, the dictum firmly believed by the whole nation, from society butterflies to simple dairymaids, was "Wash the hands often, the feet seldom, and the head never."

THE WORLD OF JEWELS

In the early part of the century fashion moved slowly—indeed, all the arts moved slowly under the ponderous early Georgian kings. But after the accession of George III matters began to quicken, and fashions in modes, jewels, and almost everything else in sight changed far more swiftly.

Fashions in jewellery parallel fashions in dress during the century. The early styles were florid, fussy, following the scrolled designs of the magnificent woven damasks, heavily baroque in style. By the end of the century, however, the gemstones were exposed, lightly held in settings that were apparently as fine and fragile as gossamer. Just as the emphasis in dress changed from the display of fine textiles to the display of flesh and figure, so the emphasis in jewellery changed from the setting to the stone itself.

During the eighteenth century the harmony of dress and jewels was of supreme importance. They were considered as essentially complementary. A Georgian lady had a full costume designed and made for one particular occasion: while the outfit was being collected, stitched and fitted, the matching pieces of jewellery were also being created. The diamond stomacher that Queen Charlotte is wearing in the portrait facing page 146 was designed and made for this particular portrait, which dates from about 1762; the stones themselves, valued at £275,000, were hired from Garrards, the court jewellers, and returned as soon as the portrait was complete; they could then be removed and put away until next they were needed, and the settings melted down. (Garrards' accounts for this period are still in the library at the Victoria and Albert Museum, and make fascinating reading.) At no other time has precious jewellery been made and re-set as often as during the eighteenth century, particularly the latter half.

Shopping

The ladies of the Georgian era loved shopping, and London was full of tempting *modistes*, milliners and so on. New Bond Street, an extension of the original street, was first rated in 1721; within a hundred years it had become a paradise for the fashionable shopper. This is Wilhelm Bornemann describing Bond Street in the year 1818, in his book *Einblicke in England und London*:

> "Here elegant ladies appear in different costumes for every hour of the day, changing them as simple folk do for the different seasons, displaying the latest creation of the restless world of fashion, buying and paying for everything twice and three times as much as would be charged in other parts of London. Everything must be bought in the shops of this renowned street if it is to find favour with refined taste."

The goldsmiths and the jewellers were nearby. In medieval times they had set up shop in the area around Foster Lane and Goldsmiths Row, but in the fifteenth and sixteenth centuries they had begun to move westward, until by 1720 the Haymarket was the centre of the trade. One of the most important of all the houses was Garrards. The excitement caused by the collapse of the South Sea Bubble had scarcely died away when George Wickes, citizen and goldsmith, opened his doors to sell "all sorts of jewels and curious works in gold and silver made after ye best and newest fashion and at reasonable prices". By 1735 the Prince of Wales had appointed Wickes his "Goldsmith, Jeweller and Silversmith"; many of the nobility naturally chose to patronize the same man. In 1792 the business came into the hands of Robert Garrard whose sons, Robert and James and Sebastian, subsequently took over as Garrard Brothers. Royal patronage continued. Queen Charlotte bought her gold toothpicks there, the Duke of Wellington his coronation coronet (it cost him £26). The Koh-i-Noor was entrusted to them for re-cutting. Queen Victoria patronized them, Queen Alexandra, Queen Mary. After the Second World War they amalgamated with the Goldsmiths and Silversmiths Company; they are still established in London, and still, as they have been since 1735, Crown Jewellers; an unbroken tradition of which they are rightly proud.

Diamond Cutting and Setting

During the course of the seventeenth century, the diamond had become established as the most fashionable and precious of stones. Supplies of the finest quality were brought into Europe from the diamond mines of India, along the Godavari river: they changed hands in the great trading city of Golconda, which stood at the meeting point of the Indian trading routes and was built like a mighty fort, its walls being seven miles around, with eight gates set in them and seventy bastions. Dozens of the most famous jewels in the world changed hands there; and until the early eighteenth century, when diamonds were discovered in Brazil, every famous diamond in the history of jewellery was bought and sold there, many of them being purchased by Tavernier for Louis XIV of France.

The European monarchs acquired some of the larger diamonds; their courtiers followed suit, decking themselves in the smaller stones. Pattern books were printed, showing designs for diamond-set jewellery, with the facets clearly marked and with a back-view of the mount as well: Herbst's *A Book of Severall Jewelers Work*, published in London in 1710, is such a book.

The standard form of cutting the stone was the rose cut, which was to dominate the entire seventeenth century. As has already been described, a rose-cut diamond was cut with a flat base, rising to a central point which was surrounded by triangular facets, regularly arranged; the finest rose cut had twenty-four facets, but there were other variants, having less. The base was often covered with black paint in an attempt to reflect back the light. Alternatively, the diamond could be backed with reflective foil. (The paragraph on page 166 goes into rather more detail about foiling; briefly speaking, a "foiled" stone has a thin leaf of metal placed behind it to heighten its brilliance; in the ancient European regalia coloured gems and pastes are often backed by a piece of coloured foil of the appropriate shade.) Each stone was treated individually, whether oval, oblong or circular, the number of facets being carefully calculated.

Then, towards the very end of the seventeenth century, Vincenzo Peruzzi from Venice perfected the brilliant cut. It is aptly named, for it makes a magnificent and expert use of all the crystalline properties of the stone. The general theory of the brilliant cut has not been improved on, and Peruzzi's style, with minor modifications, is still used today. At the base of the stone is a point or "culet"—this is not really a point at all, for that would splinter, but a tiny flat facet. At the top is the "table", the surface facet. The widest part of the stone is called the "girdle". Above this are thirty-two facets, and below it a further twenty-four. Thus, adding in the table and the culet, a brilliant-cut diamond has fifty-eight facets.

The brilliant cut was far better than the rose for revealing and releasing a diamond's fire, but it was also much more expensive and difficult to do. The two fashions of cutting were to run alongside for over a century.

As lapidaries grew more experienced and more confident, so settings shrank. This was a very gradual process: diamonds were so expensive and precious that few early eighteenth-century jewellers dared to rely on an open mount—the diamonds had to be held fast and safely. For the first fifty or so years of the eighteenth century, they were still mostly rose-cut, backed, foiled, and tightly gripped in claw settings. Then, slowly and cautiously, jewellery began to open out. Brilliant-cut diamonds were introduced, in claw or coronet settings, with the jewel lifted and held above the base. By the end of the period the jewellers had at last become sufficiently self-confident to open up the backs and experiment. They were even bold enough and expert enough, by the time of the Regency, to use *pavé* settings (the stones being set as if in a pavement), which were particularly suitable for the display of a group of small stones—as in a brooch, for instance. The metal frame in which each stone is set is hardly visible at all.

This advance in setting techniques, together with the great popularity of the faceted diamond, had a second effect on the metalwork. At the beginning of the century, when the metalwork was still of great importance, with the stones added to brighten the design, gold was generally used. By the end of the century the emphasis had shifted to silver, sometimes backed with gold for added strength. Silver was cheaper, for one thing; more important than this, however, it flattered the diamond. Gold contrasted, silver complemented. The silvery reflective gleam suited the sparkle of the faceted stones.

Eighteenth-Century Design

Styles in jewellery, like styles in dress, moved slowly in the first decades of the century. Between 1702 and 1760, jewellery design did not alter very much or very swiftly. Herbst's pattern book, published in London in 1710, has already been mentioned. A quarter of a century later, in 1736, Thomas Flach published *A Book of Jeweller's Work Designed by Thomas Flach in London*. The designs differ, of course, but not radically. The earlier work is far more delicate: Herbst's engraved designs could be made up in gold and set with diamonds to create a light and pretty brooch, or, just as easily, be enamelled on the back of a gold watchcase or a *châtelaine*. In the later work, however, the designs are opening up: the patterns are bigger, and there is a far broader scope. But in both cases the patterns show scrolling, formalized leaves, formalized flowers; nothing is naturalistic. The designs could as easily be used for silver, textiles or furniture of the same period. It was not until later in the century that patterns and designs for jewellery were drawn up specifically *for* jewellery, and could be used for nothing else: a change that was partly due to the shift already mentioned, from creating jewels made of precious metals with a few stones set in them to brighten the design, to creating jewels in which the stones were of supreme importance and the metal setting gradually tailored to vanishing point.

For the first three-quarters of the century, jewellery designs featured anything which was completely non-controversial. Flowers, for instance, offended no one; neither did ribbons and bows. It is interesting that in these least-of-all religious times designs were grouped around feminine interests; bows and flowers and curving scrolls. But then, almost the entire century was focused on the female.

At the beginning of the century the designs were formal, and continued so for several decades. By the end, however, they had become naturalistic. This change in emphasis can easily be traced by examining the treatment of the flower motif, which had flourished throughout the seventeenth century. By 1700 the Dutch influence, which had been of supreme importance in popularizing the floral motif in the earlier decades of the seventeenth century, was fading. The French were leading Europe, and the Dutch delight in exact detail and careful naturalistic portrayal was fashionable no longer. The formal classical style was in vogue.

At the start of the period the flower looked rather like a lazy daisy in a child's embroidery. It had five or six petals and a single-stone centre, all of diamonds, and was placed arbitrarily in the design, with no leaves or buds or stalks, evenly and flatly displayed against scrolled foliage. These diamond flowers were rather heavy, being in solid metal settings and backed with foil. The sheer weight and size of the jewel was such that the design had to be kept as open as possible, or the fabric to which it was pinned would sag and might even tear. Anything really large, like the stomacher Queen Charlotte is portrayed wearing, had to be designed so that the weight was distributed evenly, either by sewing the jewel into place, or by incorporating a series of fitments at the back.

Gradually, however, the floral motif began to acquire leaves or stalks of its own. It lost its star-like formalized look and began to look more like a real flower which had grown from the earth—not necessarily a recognizable rose or tulip, but at least a complete entity, with stem, flower, leaf and bud. There is an excellent example of this in a diamond flower brooch in the Cory Bequest, at the Victoria and Albert Museum in London.

In 1768 Joseph Banks travelled with Captain Cook on their memorable expedition to Australia and the South Seas. On his return in 1771, Banks brought with him sketch-book upon sketch-book of perfectly lovely drawings of botanical specimens (one of the reasons Australia's Botany Bay got its name was because Banks was so enthusiastic about the flowers and plant-life there). This was to result in a wave of enthusiasm over nature, and especially over accuracy in depicting it. The "flowers" of Georgian brooches had now to look like the real thing. Not only that, but the leaves must be right as well, and the bark or stem must be textured. Bouquet brooches, made up of a small bunch of diamond flowers, also underwent a change: wheat-ears and grasses were added, the stems were bound with ribbon to form a proper little posy, and as often as not a tiny dragonfly or butterfly hovered overhead, placed on knife-edge springs of gold or copper wire that were cunningly hidden so that the insect trembled in the air above.

At the beginning of the period a design of flowers had been flat, formal and two-dimensional; now it was produced to look as natural and three-dimensional as if a real bouquet of hedgerow flowers had crystallized into diamonds at the wave of a wand, with the *tremblant* butterfly above them still quivering as if alive.

Tremblant Jewels

The *tremblant* effect was not entirely new. For a long time jewellers had been using the same treatment on large motifs within a design of diamonds, so that they would shimmer with every breath taken by the wearer and catch every nuance of candlelight. Every movement one made in the eighteenth century was considered as an attention-catcher. Every graceful sweep of a powdered head burdened with, perhaps, a ship in full sail, was rehearsed in a looking-glass before the ball: so was every minute movement of the fan, from the phrases of a wordless conversation (complete little manuals were written on the "language of the fan") to its spreading open, which could, if rightly handled, sound like a pistol shot. Many a shy young beauty had her entrance ruined by the crack of an opening fan wielded by an older rival, which caught the assembly's attention; and it was this catching of attention which concerned society. *Tremblant* diamonds in a froth of lace or catching up a smooth satin hem would catch the attention if they winked and shimmered even when the wearer was standing as still as a statue; breathing evenly and quietly was quite enough to activate the springs.

Practicality in Design

Many of the jewels made in this era were created in sections. It is this intensely practical attitude which one must remember all the time; it typified the Georgian society. If one went to the expense of having diamond jewellery created for one, they argued, then it should be designed so that it could be separated into sections which would make up into several completely different pieces—preferably without one's rivals noticing and commenting on the fact, when one wore the "new" jewels at a later event. A design incorporating several large flowers, for instance, could be taken apart to serve as a set of brooches with matching earrings; formal leaves could be fastened together as a spray brooch; smaller leaves and scrolled stalks could be linked to make a necklace and matching bracelet. Above all, the money (and it really was a question of a very great deal of money indeed) must be thoroughly well spent.

There was no nonsense over wasting beautiful craftsmanship by enamelling the reverse of the jewel; it was simply never seen, they reasoned, so why bother? Attention was lavished only on what was on view—just as with the beautiful dresses; anything that would not be visible was left absolutely plain.

And once one had got the full use out of a jewel, one sent it back to be re-set. The diamonds themselves were immensely costly and must be treasured; but labour at that time was very cheap indeed. The precious and expensive diamonds could be re-set again and again, almost endlessly, the same stones being re-used in different designs, the precious metal simply melted down and re-worked. The Georgians might be extravagant, showy, and bent on enjoying life; but they were also extremely practical. Common sense was highly prized. Money, craftsmanship, time: they wasted none of it.

The French Influence

As the Georgian Age drew on, from its slow Hanoverian beginnings into the flowering of the latter half of the century, so the accent in all the decorative arts, from furniture-making through textile-weaving to silver-work, swung further and further from the masculine to the feminine, from dark rich colours to pale shining ones, from the heavy and ornate to the light and delicate, from draped velvets to revealing gauzes, from the broad to the slender. The leaders in the movement were the French: the French court ladies, French fashions, French makers of furniture and textiles and especially porcelain. But the English craftsmen, and notably the English silversmiths and jewellers, became equally adept: challenge a leading jeweller in England or Scotland today to tell you the difference between two pieces of eighteenth-century jewellery, each with no known history, and he cannot assign them definitely to either side of the Channel. He may say, "It is *possible* that this piece is French because . . ." or "It is probable that this other piece is English because . . ." but if there is no mark, and no known provenance, then there is simply no real way to tell. Many of the designers' books from France were used in England, and vice versa; many a gift was made in Paris for a lady in England; it was even perfectly possible for stones cut in Antwerp or Amsterdam to be used in a piece made up in London from a French design. If the original velvet-lined case has been lost, if the original bill has vanished, there is no real way of telling. Some of the finest Georgian jewels were made for the gentlemen's mistresses; naturally, then, the details were kept quiet. Yet, if the work was of fine quality, does it really matter all that much if it is French or English? After all, they were the best.

Articles of Jewellery

The articles of jewellery in general use during the eighteenth century often have French names, a fact that reinforces the importance of the influence from the French court. It became fashionable to own a *parure*—that is, a complete set of matching jewellery. (A great many *demi-parures* were also made, for reasons of economy; far more, indeed, than complete sets.) The *parure* would probably be made up of a necklace, two bracelets, a brooch, a pendant, a pair of earrings, and possibly a small diadem or an *aigrette*. (A *demi-parure* only included three or four of these pieces.) French *parures* were more opulent and more colourful than the English ones, but they were both equally at home in either country.

In considering the various pieces, one may as well begin at the top and work one's way downwards. In the hair jewels called *aigrettes* were worn: sometimes singly, sometimes scattered amongst the powdered curls. The largest, often *tremblant*, would be worn either in the central part of the coiffure at the front of the head, or to catch up a cascade of curls at the back. Smaller ones would be placed with a deliberately careless effect, almost lost in the curls, at other points of interest in the elaborate hair-style, drawing attention to the coiffeur's expertise. *Aigrettes* were almost always of diamonds set in silver. The design was curled and flowing, like a feather, deliberately creating the effect of movement. Some were so large that they could be separated into smaller jewels. Various motifs, such as flowers or wheat-ears, could be worn as *aigrettes* or, if one wished, detached from their stems and screwed into place in a small diadem or a tiara (minute box mounts with screws being supplied for this transfer); the be-ribboned stems could then be used as a small brooch or a lace-pin.

From the ears hung fairly elaborate earrings known as *girandoles*. These were pendant, and looked a little like the great chandeliers so necessary for reflecting the light in the ballrooms of the era. They were made for pierced ears, and the thin—but strong—gold wire which was fastened through the lobe of the ear was very long and sometimes bent back on itself for the sake of safety. Generally there was a counter-balance of one large stone set against the lobe of the ear, with three large drops hanging from it. These three dangling drops were known as *briolettes*, the central one being considerably longer than the others. Because the effect the jeweller aimed for was to reflect the light and to create an earring which quivered and shimmered as much as possible, *girandoles* were often minor miracles of workmanship. Small connecting rings were used: from one ring, set at right angles to the gem on the ear-lobe, would hang the mount for the three drops; they, in their turn, would also hang from tiny rings, moving independently; sometimes each *briolette* was a small diamond frame with a separate diamond swinging in the centre. In this way, the entire *girandole* swung and quivered, and so did each separate part of it, while the whole jewel remained securely attached to the ear. The effect achieved was virtually that which the makers of *tremblant* jewels tried to copy but could not attain, since a *tremblant* stone was mounted on a spiral of wire, not suspended. Finely made *girandoles* were masterpieces, excellent at catching the attention; *tremblant* jewels were the next best thing.

Until the end of the century, choker necklaces were fashionable, fastening at the back of the throat with velvet ribbons. At each end of the band of stones was a loop or a pair of cylinders, set parallel with one another so that a ribbon could be threaded between them. The velvet ribbons, chosen to match or complement the gown, were threaded through this fastening and tied at the back. Many of these necklaces were later re-set with snaps, or even adapted into bracelets, and it is rarely that one finds an eighteenth-century necklace with the original thin gold loops or cylinders. Queen Charlotte (page 146) is wearing a diamond choker necklace, presented by the Nabob of Arcot.

Another form of necklace worn by Georgian ladies was a very long string of matching pearls. Gone were the days when pearls were valued for a baroque distortion of shape, and set individually as the centrepiece of an enamelled jewel. Now they were strung together and valued for their spherical form, their matching size and colour. A string of pearls was threaded on silk, sometimes with a knot between each pearl, and then draped across the body. In the portrait of Queen Charlotte facing page 146 there is no question of her wearing her pearls as a simple necklace; they are taken up from under the arms, casually knotted several times upon the shoulders of her gown and fastened there. Further pearls are peeping through the tier upon tier of delicate lace around her elbows; others are passed around her waist and fall to the point of the stomacher; yet more are looped at her waistline and cascade in double strands down her skirt to finish in a gleaming tassel. It is quite probable that these are the pearl strands seen in State portraits of Charlotte's predecessor, Caroline of Anspach (1683–1737), now in the royal collection (Fig. 31). Other portraits of the time show strings of pearls held at one shoulder, falling to a point almost at the waist, and then gathered up together to one side of the breast and fastened there by a huge brooch. By the end of the century pearl necklaces of this kind were gradually being replaced by lengthy gold chains. The short graduated pearl necklace as we know it in the twentieth century was never dramatic enough to be worn by the Georgians. (At this time pearls were also used for framing miniatures; tiny seed pearls were used for framing mourning rings as well, and very pretty they looked too.)

False pearls were still being made by the thousands in the eighteenth century, just as they had been for several hundreds of years. The French had a neat way of making them by using tiny glass beads filled with wax. Another method used small shells and fish-scales for lustre. The Georgians, like their predecessors, had absolutely no feeling of guilt at wearing counterfeit pearls. Guilt over wearing "fake" items only came into being in the latter half of the nineteenth century, with the advent of "antique shops".

Up until then, no one dreamed of collecting antiques. One might have heirlooms, of course, cared for from a sense of family duty, or one might bring back a few loads of classical remains from the Grand Tour; but having old things in the house generally simply meant that you were too poor to re-decorate. Once antique shops arrived, however, people began to question whether the antique they were buying was genuine or a copy. (Most of the time they seem to have been either copies or clever constructions using some parts that were really old and some that were brand new; the discovery of this was to give those early antique shops rather an unpleasant reputation.)

Buyers of modern jewellery, especially from Germany, often buy jewels which incorporate acrylics, used because by this means the jeweller can achieve some special effect he needs. These buyers do not think of acrylics as being "fake" stones or metal; just as materials which create a completely different effect. So it was with "French pearls", and indeed with pastes, which are dealt with later in this chapter; the French pearls were not intended as fakes, they were merely different—and cheaper; what could be more sensible? Real pearls and French pearls were used by the great ladies of English society from Queen Elizabeth in the sixteenth century to Queen Charlotte in the eighteenth. In the inventory of Sarah, Duchess of Marlborough, who died in 1744, there is listed, for example, a necklace of French pearls and turquoises.

Of all Georgian jewellery, brooches probably achieved the widest variety of designs. Until the final quarter of the eighteenth century, they were set with diamonds. Coloured stones were occasionally used—less in England than in France—but even so they were incorporated in a diamond setting. The coloured stones one sees most in Georgian jewellery are sapphires and rubies, both of which come from the same source, a material called corundum (this is colourless; add a little chromium oxide, and you have a ruby; add a little titanium oxide, on the other hand, and you have a sapphire), and both of which have the same type of facets since their crystalline formation is similar. Corundum is second only to diamond in the scale of hardness; this does not, however, mean that rubies and sapphires are only a trifle softer than diamonds, since the gap is a considerable one—they are actually eighty-five times softer than diamonds, but still harder than any other stone in the gemstone ladder. But diamonds were by far the most popular stones.

Echelles are brooches of a kind exclusive to the Georgian era: a set of matching brooches of precious stones (generally diamonds), made with either one or two pairs of loops at the back so that they could be sewn on to a garment. The designs are flat and formalized. In the Victoria and Albert Museum in London there is a set of forty-eight leaf-shaped diamond *échelles*, all exactly the same; they were used to alter the appearance of some grand ball-gown. They could, for instance, be sewn all around the hem at graduated intervals for one occasion; then, for the next ball, could be applied in parallel lines down the front, from neck to hem. In Fig. 31, Queen Caroline is wearing an enormous set. Some match in size, others graduate from large to small. They begin at the shoulders of her low-necked bodice and continue round the neckline; more *échelles* graduating from large to small are sewn to the front panel of the bodice, from the bust to the waist. On the skirt of the brocaded satin gown below there are ten huge *échelles* sewn from waist to hem, and glimpses of further sets sewn parallel to these around the skirt. Altogether thirty-seven matching *échelles* can be seen in the painting, although by their very arrangement it is clear that a further eight to ten must be concealed by the folds of her train. Fig. 30 shows a close-up of three such *échelles*.

The Georgians also wore bow brooches known as *sévignés*, made from diamonds. At the beginning of the period these brooches were rather flat, voluptuous and baroque; their only resemblance to a real bow lay in the general outline, a formalized "bow" shape. In time, however, the designs gradually altered to become far more feminine and naturalistic. The bow became three-dimensional. It began to have body to it, like a real ribbon bow. By the end of the period it was so realistic that it looked like a ribbon of silver spattered with diamonds and lightly tied by the fingertips, curling in and out of the knot, the ends carelessly turning over on themselves as real ribbons do, and the sides no longer exactly sized up—after all, few bows of ribbon are absolutely precise; uneven loops and trailing ends looked far more realistic. These brooches were used to loop up a string of pearls and hold it in place, or to fasten a bunch of real ribbons, a flower, a froth of lace: yet another Georgian attention-catcher.

Stomachers were huge brooches worn across the bodice. Unlike *sévignés*, which were designed to draw attention to the pearls or lace they held, stomachers were meant to draw attention only to themselves. They were worn across the front of the gown, starting at the neckline and often descending almost to the waist, in a tapering V shape, big, scrolled, and made of gold with a good deal of openwork (otherwise the weight of the brooch would have pulled the bodice out of shape). Set into the metal were gemstones, placed in such a way that the general design was not obscured. As they were so prominently displayed, most English stomachers were set with diamonds, or with diamonds mingled with rubies, sapphires or emeralds. They cost a great deal of money, kept their value, and advertised the wearer's wealth. Few remain today, for the fashion is over, and has been over for about a hundred and fifty years. We can still, however, see them in portraits of the period, or in design books—there are several stomachers in Thomas Flach's *A Book of Jeweller's Work*. As the fashion for them gradually died away, at the close of the eighteenth century, they were sent back to the jewellers', so that the metalwork could be melted down, and the stones re-set, or the piece broken up into separate sections and used as *aigrettes* or as smaller brooches. This was fairly easy to do, for most stomachers, with typical Georgian good sense, were not designed and made as one solid entity, but in sections: a wide brooch-like section at the top, a small one at the bottom, and graduating sections in between, linked by connecting rings; these also made it possible for the wearer to move and bend with rather more ease.

Although many pieces of eighteenth-century jewellery have been broken up and re-set, it is still possible to see examples of Georgian *aigrettes*, *girandoles*, chokers, strings of pearls, *échelles*, *sévignés* and stomachers, together with bracelets and tiaras and other pieces, in contemporary portraits, good jewellers', and the best museums. The Lady Cory Bequest in the Victoria and Albert Museum in London contains a wonderful range of Georgian jewels. By studying the pieces in the Victoria and Albert Museum, one can also contrast English eighteenth-century jewellery with continental counterparts. A comparative study makes it clear that the further south one travelled, the more people liked colour in their jewels. Spanish and Portuguese jewels of the same period are filled with colour; the cooler north preferred the glitter of diamonds set in silver. It is also possible to compare workmanship: standards varied from country to country, even when the same design was used. The Russian court pieces, for example, are much heavier and coarser.

Towards the end of the century, a new fashion came in which resulted in the advent of a new jewel. Gossamer *fichus* were in vogue, draped around the shoulders and fastened with a lace pin. These pins are small and are generally set with diamonds. The jeweller had to give full consideration to the type of material the pin was to fasten: since this was delicate lace, the brooch had to be tiny and light, with a maximum amount of openwork. The folds of lace might obscure the pin by drifting gently across it, so to organize the greatest impact jewellers used stones which would shine through the lace-threads: diamonds were obviously preferable to, say, pearls.

The lace pin was an intensely practical jewel, even though it was so small; it also had to be intensely efficient. There were no safety chains in Georgian days, so the gold pin at the back of the brooch was made especially long, so that it would remain secure even when fastened over several folds of lace. Many a small diamond brooch worn today began life as a lace pin: one can generally assume that if the brooch is curved with a long straight pin at the back (to gather in as much lace as possible as securely as possible) it may well have been originally designed to fasten a fine *fichu* around a lady's shoulders. There is a Gainsborough portrait of Countess Howe which is now in the Iveagh Bequest at Kenwood House in England, in which the countess is wearing a lace *fichu* in this style (she also has a choker necklace tied at the back of her throat with a satin bow).

Among other brooch forms worn during this period are the magnificent jewelled Orders which gentlemen wore during the evening hours. Picture an exquisite wearing a jewel-coloured satin coat, a fall of point-lace at his throat set here and there with lace pins, and a diamond-set Order on his breast. Here, more than almost anywhere else, one can see the effect that every jeweller was trying to attain, with *pavé*-set diamonds blazing away, winking and blinking in the candlelight. Many of these eighteenth-century Orders still remain in family collections centuries later, exactly as they were made, the present owners diffident at the thought of breaking them up. There are glass cases filled with jewel-set decorations in dozens of British stately homes: Wilton, for example, or Blenheim Palace, or Harewood House. If, by any chance, a wealthy man were not entitled to wear any of these Orders, he could easily have something similar made up—a diamond cross, for instance, looking rather like the eight-pointed star of the Order of St. John of Jerusalem—and wear this instead: not to pretend to an honour he did not possess, but rather to complete his costume. Such a piece would look very dramatic.

In the better jewellers' of England and Scotland, one may sometimes come across flat leather cases lined with velvet in which are sets of matching diamond buttons. If these buttons are original, they should have the original single attachment loop at the back (in a few cases, this may be double). The most expensive ones were silver or gold covered with diamonds, but many other types were made as well, including large buttons of faceted crystals. In the Victoria and Albert Museum in London there are examples of diamond buttons, and a magnificent collection is on view at Waddesdon, showing the vast range that was made.

Eighteenth-century buckles, either for the belt or the shoe, and either set with diamonds or with paste, have often been adapted for use as brooch fitments in the inter-vening centuries. Occasionally one comes across a buckle with the original long teeth, but they are rare nowadays. Much time was originally expended on the making of these buckles. Surviving specimens often have interesting bright-cut work on the metal-work (they were usually made of silver, strengthened with gold). It is a good idea to search for details, such as textured gold borders and beading.

Châtelaines, which were made and worn throughout the eighteenth century, were essentially daytime jewels. One rarely sees an eighteenth-century *châtelaine* which is set with sparkling diamonds—making them the exact opposite of diamond buckles and buttons, which were only worn during the evening and were therefore designed and worked to catch the candlelight. They were generally made of gold, beautifully wrought, embossed and *repoussé*, enamelled or chased with scenes to suit contemporary taste. A *châtelaine* was one of the very few items of eighteenth-century jewellery which was decorated as beautifully on the back as on the front, for it hung from the belt—being worn either by women or men—and as it swung freely against the garments could easily swing round to display the reverse. The front was sometimes quietly be-jewelled as well.

From the *châtelaine* dangled several gold chains, terminating in hooks rather like those found on modern dog-leads. These gold chains could also be enamelled. The most elaborate were constructed of small gold plaques linked by connecting rings; these plaques were also enamelled, and occasionally framed with pearls or diamonds. Several practical items were suspended from the hooks: keys, for example, or a watch, or an *étui* (a little case containing, perhaps, scissors and thimble and needle, or a small manicure set, or a miniature writing set). These items were created as a matching set; a watch, for instance, would be in at least one protective casing—sometimes more—and this case would be enamelled to match the *châtelaine*; the watch was also designed so that it could be read with ease, without unhooking it from the *châtelaine*.

Châtelaines are particularly interesting in that they illustrate the changes in design which were affecting many of the decorative arts during the eighteenth century. In the early decades they are baroque, echoing in miniature the carved and gilded furni-ture of William Kent (a fine example of this style is the watch-*châtelaine* made for Queen Anne in 1705 and now in the Fitzwilliam Museum in Cambridge). The rococo style, which came to England from France, was deliberately asymmetrical; it probably made its greatest effect on silverware, but it was also a particularly sympathetic style for *châtelaines*—frivolous and capricious, but with an underlying sense of purpose. Rococo *châtelaines* were very feminine, delicately fussy, French in essence and asymmetrical in appearance. One unusual *châtelaine* dating from about 1760 is now on view in the London Museum: although the *chinoiserie* movement seems to have had no effect on eighteenth-century jewellery—though its effect on furniture, wall coverings, and silverware was very great indeed—this particular *châtelaine* has a little anglicized chinaman and a miniature pagoda. By the end of the century, stern neo-classicism was straightening out the enchanting feminine scrolls; now everything was to be severe and simple in line.

Luckily many fine *châtelaines* are still on view in private and public collections. One reason they survived was that there was no practical point in breaking them up. They are charmingly evocative of the way in which beauty and common sense were linked during the Georgian era.

There was a great affection for finger rings during this time, and they were worn both by men and by women. Generally speaking, the styles that were made were those that had been in use in earlier periods, but a new fashion did come in after 1760. This was the *marquise* ring (there is one in the group of rings in Fig. 27), shaped like a slender oval with pointed ends. The centre was sometimes set with one stone framed in diamonds; alternatively the bezel might be of enamel, possibly set with a small diamond or pearl in the middle. The shape is very kind and flattering, it makes a plump hand look shapely and a slim hand look ethereal; the white hand of the eighteenth-century aristocrat must have looked especially elegant adorned with a *marquise* ring.

Beautifully cut single stones framed in diamonds were also worn at this period. Gentlemen sometimes preferred a glowing ruby set in scrolled gold. A moss agate was also very popular. Other rings incorporated tiny miniatures painted on ivory or vellum and protected by glass or crystal, framed in diamonds or sapphires; these were sometimes memorial rings, others merely showed details from contemporary paintings. In the main, the earlier rings were less personal. The designs were formalized, with backed and foiled stones. As the century wore on, the mounts were opened up and became much lighter. Gold gave way to silver, strengthened with gold. Claw settings and *pavé* settings were used.

Towards the close of the century, hardstone intaglios and cameos became extremely fashionable. So too did seal-rings with personal coats of arms. The neo-classical period introduced a wealth of these cameo rings, for they exemplified the vogue for classical learning and Greek styles; none the less, one must remember that copies of Greek cameos and intaglios were being worn for quite some time before the shock of the French Revolution and the full flowering of the neo-classical mode.

Paste Jewellery

INTRODUCTION

Why do some people sneer at the word "paste" and decry it? Generally out of sheer ignorance. *Antique Paste Jewellery*, written by M. D. S. Lewis, a leading expert, and published in 1970, is a magnificent book which makes it perfectly clear that paste is an art-form in its own right. It is absolutely essential to consider it in these terms, and never, ever, as a means of counterfeiting other stones. Far from being jewellery set with fake diamonds, paste jewellery was made to achieve certain effects which could *not* be achieved by using diamonds, or to be used in circumstances when it was not practical to use diamonds. From a technical standpoint, paste jewellery was often a good deal more sophisticated than diamond-set jewellery, but it was purchasable for a good deal less.

The maker of paste must be knowledgeable about crystals and light and their relationship to one another, and must also understand the gemmological properties of refractive indices, dispersion and hardness: an appreciation of all these is essential to a proper understanding of paste techniques. Surely, even from these few phrases, it is clear that the making of paste jewellery is not merely a question of sticking some odd little pieces of glass into a setting, to look like diamonds?

The refractive index is the measure of the extent to which light is refracted (or bent sideways) when it shines into a stone, and how much is reflected back from the surface. A diamond has one of the highest refractive indices of all stones. The term "dispersion" is really self-explanatory: it means the extent to which light is dispersed or broken up into the separate colours of the spectrum when it penetrates the stone—it does not, or should not, remain colourless, but should instead splinter into red, orange, yellow, green, blue, indigo and violet, in the rainbow sparkle which is called its "fire". Diamonds have magnificent qualities of dispersion—the most expensive have a glorious fire which is an ever-changing permutation of flashes of brilliant colour, whereas cheap little stones merely throw back a white light. Hardness is calculated on Mohs' Scale (page 270), a kind of pecking order which arranges stones according to their hardness; the diamond is the hardest of all, and other stones are calculated in relation to it. The hardness of a stone determines what can be used to cut it (only diamond will cut diamond) and also how high a polish can be achieved. A hard stone will take a high polish, whereas a soft gem, such as coral or turquoise, is scarcely polished at all. Being the hardest stone of all, diamond can take the most brilliant polish.

The cutting of a faceted stone is never left to chance or inspiration. A faceted stone is cut with a flat facet on top called the "table"; in modern cutting, this facet is generally large. Light penetrates the table, disperses into colours in the heart of the stone, and is reflected back from the lower facets which are cut at very carefully calculated angles. If these lower facets are cut incorrectly, the light rays escape through the bottom of the stone or emerge through the sides, but if they are cut with great geometrical precision and then polished as highly as possible, the light bounces back and forth in the stone and finally emerges through the table again.

Light is the operative word. Without it there would be absolutely no effect at all. Paste jewellery has been known from very early history, but the eighteenth century saw immense advances in technique and popularity. During this period men and women began to live all the most enjoyable parts of their lives during the evenings and far into the night. Until then a good many social activities had taken place during the day, lit by sunshine; now, however, with quantities of fine wax candles, and far better glass for chandeliers, pier glasses and so on, social life was promoted in the evening hours. When the era began, candles were generally set in single sconces with some reflective silver backing; as it progressed, however, these sconces burgeoned into great branches. Looking-glasses, which were small plates of glass set in carved frames at the beginning of the period, were huge shining glass panels covering whole sections of wall by the time it was drawing to its close. If one placed a branch of wax candles in front of, or to either side of, a vast area of looking-glass, the room was filled with twinkling candle-light reflected backwards and forwards, just like the light inside a beautifully faceted diamond. The effect was magical. The whole eighteenth century is filled with similar flashes of dramatic light and colour.

The early baroque houses, like Blenheim Palace in Oxfordshire, or, rather later, Holkham Hall in Norfolk with its fine interiors, were built as a spectacle, classically inspired, with saloon after saloon provided for the parade of society: a stage on which the men and women of the eighteenth century could enact their parts in public. The elaborate fashions—high heels for men, hooped skirts and towering powdered coiffures

A Group of Georgian Diamond Jewels: the Georgian era was very much the era of the diamond. Techniques of faceting had been greatly improved—both the brilliant cut and the rose cut were now in use—supplies were readily available, labour was cheap, and with the dramatic fashions, the powdered *coiffures* of the middle decades, the elegant room settings and the delight in display, diamonds came triumphantly into the very forefront of fashion, glittering in the light of a thousand branched candlesticks, reflected in the new pier glasses, and supremely suited to the needle-sharp wit and gaiety and whole-hearted enjoyment of the era. The feeling was pre-dominantly feminine, and for the first time real attempts were made to create ladies' jewels of equal importance with men's and to suit designs to current fashions. Many incorporated the bows, flowers and frivolities popular at the French Court; and gradually, as the age drew on, English craftsmen began to produce designs portraying leaves and flowers in a newly naturalistic style, rather than as formal two-dimensional motifs.

The graceful necklace seen here shows a high standard of diamond-setting. The flowers are not, as one might expect, mere repetitions of one another, the bow is looped like a real ribbon, and the linked leaves would flow about the bare neck. The Georgian brooch at the top left is earlier than that on the right, and they contrast well, the former being more stylized with its stones deeply embedded in the metal, and the latter more delicate and fluid, with stones much more confidently set and spaced separately in the design. The swallow and the butterfly, both *pavé*-set, are characteristic of the age's liking for novelty and of the popularity of Nature motifs.

The Georgian interest in stars and comets was sparked off by the studies of Edmund Halley, who correctly forecast the reappearance of his famous comet in 1758 (the next viewing is due in about 1984). Star-burst jewels occasionally featured a coloured central stone, surrounded by diamond rays and trailing a long diamond tail. Smaller ones were worn in the hair or sparkled in a lace cravat; larger ones, like the one shown here, blazed like Orders on the breast of an exquisite's satin coat, completing his *ensemble* with panache: in this dramatic and lavish era the men still held their own, though within a few decades they were to rely simply on the excellence of their tailoring to impress Society.

By courtesy of N. Bloom & Son

Fig. 37 and Fig. 38: the mid-Victorian age saw a resurgence of interest in diamonds, popular as an indication of the solid financial standing of the purchaser, but set with impeccable craftsmanship as befitted an era passionately interested in machine perfection. Their costliness and glitter married with the rich fabrics, the heavy gleam of polished mahogany, the glow of silver-gilt tableware under hissing gaslight, the fatly stuffed furniture, the crowded curio cabinets, the walls thronged with pictures. The fixed bangle on the left has been cleverly designed to highlight the massive stones, and the back opened up to keep the weight minimal. The diamonds are set in gold (platinum was not yet in use) and blaze like a thoroughly satisfactory Bank statement. The brooch on the right dates from early in the period (about 1848) and is marvellously light and delicate, and wholly nineteenth century, each segment hung on articulated wires (knife-edge work) so that it is a separate entity within the main fuchsia-buds-and-flowers design, swinging and sparkling independently. The *tremblant* effect popular in the Georgian era has thus been developed into a new form: technically known as *pampilles*—"waterfalls"—this was initiated by the French in about 1825–1830, and immediately taken up by the English. A good many examples were shown at the Great Exhibition of 1851, including Lemmonier's *parure* for the Queen of Spain, probably exhibited simply because it exemplified this technique—excellence and novelty hand-in-hand, to attract the overseas buyers.

By courtesy of N. Bloom & Son

Fig. 39: during the neo-classical period, and particularly with the Directoire and Empire and Regency styles which flowered from it, the arts of pre-Christian periods came back into fashion. Antique cameos of gods carved in gemstones and simply mounted in gold were erudite, "classical", and, in their modesty, particularly popular after the cataclysm of the French Revolution. Huge interest was also aroused by the excavations at Herculaneum and Pompeii and the artefacts found there. Beautiful cameos were made, carved from shell—a new departure—or coral or even lava from Vesuvius, as well as the traditional hard gemstones. Intaglios were also popular. The earlier pieces were correctly simple and set in plain gold surrounds, like the pendant on the upper left or the ring on the right. Later, however, as the Greek simplicity of the Directoire style gave way to the Roman enrichment of the Napoleonic Empire, the settings became more elaborate, like that of the brooch on the lower left. Settings of pearls were historically accurate—the Greeks had used them lavishly—but the use of enamels, as in the brooch on the lower right, is entirely a mid-nineteenth-century innovation and a curious marrying of Renaissance and antique. The necklace, which portrays Louis XV and his family, each cameo correctly set in a simple gold framework, is both unique and magnificent.

By courtesy of Cameo Corner Ltd

for the ladies—were all designed to suit the chosen part within the play—but the play was, of course, continually changing, and the styles of dress and jewellery changed with it. An enormous proportion of eighteenth-century diamond jewellery was continually sent back to the jewellers for re-setting because of the intrinsic value of the stones. Paste jewellery, however, was much cheaper (not ridiculously cheap, but certainly far less expensive than diamonds) and so it was merely put aside when the fashion had run its course, rather than being broken up for re-use. Paste cuts were tailor-made for one setting, and for that setting alone. As a result, quite a few pieces of eighteenth-century paste survive today, strong, tough, with the original fastenings. They are well worth collecting.

THE MAKING OF PASTE

What is paste? This depends on the period in which it was made.

The early paste, used by the ancient civilizations, was primitive coloured glass made from soda, lime and silicate, with metallic oxides added to give colour. Many of the early civilizations, from the Egyptian to the Byzantine, delighted in colour (there are examples of pastes in the treasures of Tutankhamun, and in the Roman and Byzantine jewellery in most leading European museums), and since gemstones were valued more for their magical or medicinal powers than their monetary value, it made perfectly good sense to use paste if suitable stones were not available.

The passion for colour began to lessen in the seventeenth century A.D.; and a major factor in this change was the improvement in the methods of faceting diamonds, already described in this and the preceding chapters. A diamond is an octahedron, so that theoretically at least there are a great many possible permutations in cutting the stone; but the general theory of the brilliant cut, evolved in the closing years of the seventeenth century, has never been improved upon. At about the same time another important discovery was made, this time in England. This was the creation of flint glass.

Flint Glass

In about 1675 George Ravenscroft was experimenting with glass-making techniques, in the hope of improving them and making England independent of the European markets. In effect he changed the general recipe for glass and added large quantities of lead oxide: and English flint glass was born. It is especially lovely and easily recognizable, being colourless (no mean feat for those days), heavy and lustrous; it takes a high polish; and, best of all and most significant for the paste-maker, it has a high refractive index and really good dispersion.

All Europe was excited by the introduction of this new type of glass, and many ideas were put forward for its best use. It was a splendid material for the making of paste jewellery. Stone-cutters knew by now how to cut diamonds, and were competent and confident in doing so. Half a century of the supremacy of the diamond had overcome the old prejudice against colourless stones. Best of all, the artistic climate of the eighteenth century suited the making of paste jewellery.

It may sound from this as though England alone was the discoverer of paste jewellery. This was not so. The manufacture of paste jewellery was developed in several European countries: besides England, it was under way in France and in Spain. Very fine, inexpensive jewellery was also made in Portugal, but there chrysoberyls, white topaz and crystal (colourless quartz) were used.

Paste jewellery is often referred to as "Strass", especially on the Continent, because of the prolific output of Georges Frédéric Strass, a jeweller from Strasbourg, born in 1701, who came to Paris in 1724, already fully trained, and there joined a jewellery business run by a Madame Prévost. Their small shop on the Quai des Orfèvres immediately began to flourish, Strass producing paste jewellery as well as diamond-set work. Within ten years he was appointed jeweller to the king. When he died in 1773 he left a fortune to his heirs and a celebrated name to posterity. A portrait miniature of him shows a man with bird-bright eyes who appears to have an enormous sense of humour—in dealing successfully with the French court in the eighteenth century, he would need one.

COMPARING PASTES

It is extremely difficult to assign a piece of paste jewellery to a country of origin. From the evidence presently available, it appears that the output of eighteenth-century paste jewellery made in France in the decade 1730–40 antedated anything manufactured in England or Spain. To give the briefest and most general summary, one might say that English paste jewellery is simpler and less fussy than the French. The stones, which are made from English flint glass of finer quality than anything then available on the Continent, are larger, and the mounts are therefore slightly thicker and flatter. But the range of designs is more limited, even though the quality of the eighteenth century English work is considered unsurpassed, even by the French work. Spanish paste is inferior to both: the cutting of the stones lacks invention, being generally uniform, and the colours are predominantly green and white, emulating the South American emeralds and diamonds which the Spaniards loved. Their paste jewellery is, on the whole, larger and coarser than the English or the French. None the less, their best pieces can be very fine indeed.

EVALUATING PASTE

Paste jewellery was so much cheaper than diamond-set jewellery because the labour and the materials cost so little—the price of flint glass was infinitesimal when compared with the price of diamonds.

How can the amateur tell the difference? Basically, there are two quick rules-of-thumb. One looks first at the shape of the stones, and secondly at the settings.

Diamonds are cut in conventional shapes—rounds, ovals, oblongs—so that they can be used again and again if their mounting wears thin or breaks, or merely if the fashions change and the owner becomes bored with the design and wants the piece re-set. Being so durable, they will last far longer than the metal in which they are mounted, and a huge proportion of eighteenth-century jewellery has been re-set over and over again in the intervening generations.

In view of their shape, conventionally cut diamonds could not be set closely together in eighteenth-century work; the jeweller either had to leave a small gap between the stones, or allow the metal mount to show through. When eighteenth-century fashion decreed that a piece of jewellery should consist of an unbroken mass of gemstones, it was difficult to achieve a satisfactory effect using conventionally cut diamonds; instead the piece was made up in pastes, which are soft and easy to cut, and which can be cut in absolutely any shape the lapidary wishes. Unlike a diamond, glass does not have a crystalline formation, and so imposes no restrictions on the designer. Thus the moment one sees a piece of jewellery set with stones which have been cut in shapes differing from the conventional diamond styles, one knows that there is a possibility it is paste.

The second point to consider is the setting. Up until the eighteenth century, all the gemstones used in jewellery, generally speaking, were enclosed and foiled, even diamonds. (The foil was a very thin piece of metal sheet, either silver or coloured, which was set behind the stone and which reflected the light back through the stone, rather like a looking-glass. Many a stone seen today in an ancient crown would be almost colourless were it not for the foil. One may well be looking through a transparent stone which has lost its colour completely; but the foil set behind it reflects back the colour— ruby red, for instance—which one expects to see. In the Schatzkammer Residenz in Munich there is a delicate pinnacled crown which belonged to the Princess Blanche of England; several of the stones set in this are colourless when looked at sideways; seen full on, however, they shine with the appropriate colour, because the light is being reflected back from the coloured foils behind them.) During the eighteenth century, however, the lapidaries had made great improvements in cutting and the jewellers were becoming increasingly confident about setting faceted stones, even the precious diamonds; and they began to open up the mounts of diamond-set jewellery. Eighteenth-century paste, however, *had* to be enclosed and foiled. If the backs were not air-tight, air and damp penetrated the setting and corroded the foil. In the best pieces, each individual paste had a "cut-down" setting. This meant that the paste was backed by a thin piece of bright metal sheet and the setting metal worked round the glass so that the foil was air-tight. If corrosion did take place, it was simply not worth the bother and expense of taking the piece apart to replace it.

During the nineteenth century improvements in paste settings were made, so that this particular guideline can only be applied to work carried out in the late eighteenth century, when precious stones were being set in open settings of the claw type, whereas pastes were still foiled and set in air-tight mounts. But assuming that one is considering a piece of jewellery which, on stylistic grounds, is said to date from the eighteenth century, one can make two immediate checks: are the "stones" irregularly cut, and are they foiled and set in air-tight mounts? A combination of both means that it is probably paste.

There are also other clues. The best eighteenth-century paste was mounted in silver, and the mount very rarely carries an assay mark because it was so thin (pastes being much lighter than diamonds). Gold was used for additional decoration or to increase the strength of fastenings.

The weight of the piece should always be taken into account. Eighteenth-century makers went to great lengths to keep paste jewellery as light as possible. Each stone was hand-mounted in the thinnest metal. Reproductions tend to be cast, to save expense, and therefore come much heavier.

One should not, however, assume that a piece is a reproduction simply because small moveable parts have been replaced; these are, after all, the parts of a jewel that wear out quickest. An expert can tell whether a fastening has been replaced by looking at the method of soldering used. It is perfectly possible, for instance, that the long wire fastener on a *girandole* earring might have snapped in the intervening decades, and been replaced with a screw-type fastening (these were never seen during the eighteenth century); or that an eighteenth-century choker necklace might have been adapted to take a more modern fastening. Such alterations are naturally permissable.

In especially good quality work one can look for added refinements. Generally speaking, for instance, an eighteenth-century paste necklace or bracelet should not have more than two connecting rings between each motif. The addition of a third ring suggests that the piece is either a reproduction or has been deliberately lengthened. If an extra chain has been added to a necklace, this too suggests that it was lengthened at a later date. Knife-edge work, in which the metal is turned on its side so that only the thin edge can be seen when it is worn, was never used for connections during the eighteenth century (this work looks unbelievably thin until it is examined closely, when one can see that it is in reality both stronger and thicker than it seems at first glance). Turn the piece over and look at the backs of the stones: in good quality eighteenth-century paste the back of each paste is individually covered—rounded, smooth, and without ornamentation. Reproduction paste has cast or flat-backed mounts which have obviously been stamped out by machinery.

But the main feature that determines good eighteenth-century paste jewellery is the way in which the stones are cut. They should always look as if they have been individually "shaped", unlike the conventional diamond cuts. The greater the variety of shapes, the better a piece is, all fitting closely together like *tesserae* in a pavement.

Finally, there is the "black spot" test. Fine eighteenth-century paste has a tiny spot of black paint on the culet of each stone (nineteenth-century pastes were cut to a point and thus have no culet). This black spot is fair evidence that the piece is of good quality, and is certainly well worth looking for in eighteenth-century work.

COLOURED PASTES

Colourless pastes look like diamonds; but there are also several colours which are used in paste jewellery. Foiled deep blue paste can easily be mistaken for enamel; but red pastes can hardly be taken for rubies or garnets, nor can green pastes be taken for emeralds; even apart from the question of shape and cut, they look quite different. Aquamarine pastes and topaz pastes can, however, be misleading, and if one is anxious to know whether a piece of aquamarine or topaz jewellery is set with gemstones or with pastes, it may be necessary to have it tested by an expert.

Among the most curious forms of all is the opaline paste, which was made in the period 1780–1820, both in England and in France. One of the largest and finest collections of opaline paste is now in the Victoria and Albert Museum. The experts made a milky-looking glass with an opalescent effect, which could be cut into stones and mounted over rose-coloured foil. The resulting pastes resembled no known gemstone, but can look most effective, especially when set with contrasting pastes as a border.

REPAIRING PASTE

It is almost impossible to find anyone who would be willing to repair eighteenth-century paste, and even if one could do so it would be immensely expensive. A missing or damaged paste would have to be replaced by one cut by hand to fit—and where would one purchase the matching paste? Corroded foils cannot be restored, for the eighteenth-century colours are no longer available. The only repair one can hope to make is the mending or replacing of connections or catches; and even this is not always possible. On the whole it is far far wiser never to buy damaged paste jewellery. Fine quality eighteenth-century paste in good condition is, on the other hand, a very good investment indeed.

CHAPTER EIGHT

Neo-classical Restraint

Introduction: Neo-classicism; Neo-classical Jewels—Classical Studies: The Grand Tour; Herculaneum and Pompeii—Fashions: Revolution to Regency—The Craftsmen and Their Work—Cameos and Intaglios: Cameos; New Materials; New Subjects; New Settings; New Craftsmen, New Patrons, New Fashions; Intaglios; Craftsmen and Fakers—Cut-Steels—Hair Jewellery—James and William Tassie—Josiah Wedgwood

Introduction

NEO-CLASSICISM

Empire and Regency jewels were strongly influenced by the neo-classical movement which had been steadily gaining ground throughout the eighteenth century.

Neo-classical designs were based on what contemporary designers knew, or thought they knew, about the antique. This was not very much on the whole, although some of the classical motifs were still to be seen in surviving architecture and sculpture and could be copied. Thus there was a tendency to concentrate on perfect proportions and a simplicity generally associated with the Greeks (it was difficult for the people of this period to distinguish between classical Greek and classical Roman), and to use the known classical motifs which included garlands of fruit and flowers (animals were garlanded before being led to the ritual slaughter, and once the sacrifice was over, the heads were hung high on the temple walls with the garlands set gracefully between them), the antemion (or honeysuckle), the palmette, the shell, and sea-creatures—whether real, like dolphins, or legendary, like tritons. Additional motifs were the scroll (often called the Vitruvian scroll) and the Greek key pattern. As next to nothing was known about the furniture and ornaments used in classical times, designers and crafts-men made up contemporary furniture and applied whatever decoration they considered appropriate (the excavations of Herculaneum, Pompeii and Paestum were to prove them, in some cases at least, remarkably accurate in their guesswork).

NEO-CLASSICAL JEWELS

In spite of their dominant neo-classical flavour, however, early nineteenth-century jewels were extremely feminine. Most of the decorative arts were now built up on strict proportions and a straight line, sometimes giving the feeling that the classical control which determined their design was almost throttling them as well. There were some curves, it is true, and the gentle sweep of the arm or leg of a Sheraton chair is exquisite. But much was straight, severe and balanced. Yet the jewellery of the neo-classical period retains its femininity: of all the decorative arts, it is the least dull, the least cold, the most inventive and quite the prettiest.

"Liberty, equality, antiquity": the slogan of the neo-classical jewellers and designers in post-Revolution Europe echoed the famous slogan of the revolutionaries themselves. Before the Revolution the women of the French court went decked in diamonds—as many diamonds as they could possibly muster; then, in 1789, unbelievably the mob stormed Versailles. When the terror and destruction and levelling of the Revolutionary years were over at last, and a court re-established under the new emperor, Napoleon I, the aristocrats were dead or exiled, the diamonds sold. A woman of the new society did not go about ablaze with diamonds or dress her hair in a powdered coiffure a yard high or wear a gown of silk brocade interwoven with gold and silver threads and spread over an enormous hoop: to do so would be dangerous, stupid, unpatriotic, and quite possibly an invitation to theft and murder.

The shock-waves of the revolution spread throughout Europe: the new fashions caught on—dresses in simple, classical Grecian styles, made of flimsy muslins and batistes and embroidered Indian cottons which would have torn under the weight of the great old-fashioned diamond jewels. Fashions in dress were changing very rapidly, largely due to the emergence of fashion plates and the printing of the first of the women's magazines, whose fashion columns gave the English gentlewoman a blow-by-blow account of changing styles and prices every month. Fashions in jewellery changed more slowly, simply because a jewel cost so much more than a muslin dress, but novelties did appear which foreshadowed the costume jewellery of the twentieth century. Empire and Regency jewels were by no means all grand pieces, although the grander ones did tend to remain intact a little longer. Grand or not, they certainly never shouted "wealth" at the spectator.

Craftsmen looked to the past, making a conscious effort, where possible, to return to antiquity, sometimes copying extant pieces of classical jewellery, but more often emulating, as best they could, the ancient techniques. They did not have a great deal to go by: most archaeological excavations have taken place in the last two hundred years or so, and a good many of those in the latter half of the period—the Gold Room of the Hermitage Museum in Russia, for instance, is filled with classical treasures found during the first decades of the twentieth century; it is only during the last fifty years or so that art historians have begun to build up a body of work dealing with classical jewellery, and only very recently that European museums have begun to catalogue their collections. This may be due to an old prejudice dividing the arts into "major" and "minor"; a silly division, and an ignorant one since in Hellenistic and Roman times the goldsmith and silversmith took precedence over the painter and sculptor.

But though they looked to the past, and occasionally did so very successfully, jewellers also looked to the future. A greater range of materials was being used than ever before. Shell cameos were introduced, cut-steels and Tassies; pinchbeck (already described on page 54) was in use for settings; the resulting pieces cost far less than diamonds set in silver or sapphires set in gold, and even people of modest means could afford to buy and wear them. The standards of craftsmanship, however, remained high; this was especially true of the English craftsmen—the splendid French jewellers had understandably withdrawn into the shadows, and the Revolutionary and Napoleonic wars kept Europe in a state of confusion and uncertainty.

The jewels they produced could be charming: elegant, superbly made, new materials creating pieces of classical simplicity and beauty. Although they may have lacked the modern art historian's knowledge of classical jewellery, they caught perfectly the mood of the Homeric Hymn to Aphrodite, assigned to the seventh century B.C.:

> *"She wore a dress brighter than the flames of fire,*
> *Spiral bracelets, gleaming flower earrings,*
>   *and beautiful necklaces on her delicate neck,*
> *All of gold, superbly wrought."*

From this one can see how feminine and flattering the jewellery of classical times was made to be; fortunately the Empire and Regency jewellers realized this and created neo-classical jewellery in the same spirit. The other decorative arts were very purposeful and serious, jewellery seems to be the exception.

Classical Studies

THE GRAND TOUR
The wealthy young men of the eighteenth century who went on an educational (in all its aspects) tour of Europe had to have something to show for it when they came home, both because of the expense entailed, and as an outward and visible sign of the classical education thus acquired. Greek and Roman statuary came flooding into England in the wake of these Grand Tours. Many a fake was collected by these young men, as well as some exceptionally fine pieces (often acquired through a knowledgeable agent); these were crated up and sent home by sea, and when they reached England many months later, the young owner was occasionally horrified at the amount he had chosen, and was faced with the problem of providing a suitable place for their display. The third Earl of Egremont, for instance, inherited his father's entire collection which had never even been unpacked. The solution he conceived was brilliant: he built a special gallery to display the collection by infilling a loggia at the end of his family house at Petworth.

Other young men had a whole house built with a classical collection in mind: Coke of Norfolk, for instance, and his property at Holkham Hall, or Lord Burlington who, together with William Kent, designed a charming villa on the lines of Palladio's *Villa Capra* at Vicenza and built it in the grounds of his Jacobean property at Chiswick, just to house his library and his statuary. The Jacobean house was pulled down in the last century, and many a visitor who goes to see Chiswick Villa today simply cannot understand why there are no bedrooms and "usual offices". Should they read the scholarly guidebook, they would realize that the house in which Burlington lived with his wife and Kent has gone, though the erudite Palladian villa remains in its beautiful setting—but too few do.

The pieces of statuary that could not be fitted into the houses were placed outside at focal points in the gardens where the ladies and gentlemen went walking. Some of the loveliest Georgian gardens in England are still adorned by these statues, often half-hidden amongst the foliage.

All of this statuary gave men an extra interest in the classics, and gave the histories of the Roman emperors and the myths of the Greek gods a new dimension. On the whole, the Georgians were becoming fairly well educated. Many people were able to read and write and went to school—the haphazard charity school movement, though conservative in the extreme, provided education for the children of artisans and the like; there were also grammar schools, as well as the public schools and the private tutors. A lower middle class was emerging and expanding; its educational standards and its technical skill led into the Industrial Revolution—Wedgwood came from this class, and the pottery cameos he made, classically simple, were within reach, price-wise, of the class among whom he had grown up, though beautiful enough for any duchess. Men were beginning to equate being well-educated with being successful. The rewards for an educated man seemed to be endless, though it was far from easy to gain a proper education if one had no money. As a result, education was an attainment in itself, an enthralling treasure hunt, a thing that no one decried.

HERCULANEUM AND POMPEII

Without doubt one of the most important events in the history of the decorative arts was the excavation of the cities of Herculaneum and Pompeii. It was not a sudden affair. No one went in with bulldozers (fortunately) and five years later presented to the world an excavated and documented city. The excavations took years and years, hundreds of tragic mistakes were made; indeed, the work is still going on, though now it is carried out with all the care modern scholarship can muster.

Herculaneum and Pompeii lie on the western coast of south Italy. The cities were developed during the Greek occupation, and towards the end of the second century B.C. were taken over by the Romans as quarters for retired soldiers; they also built luxurious country houses there where the wealthy could holiday by the sea. In A.D. 63 Pompeii was partially destroyed by an earthquake, but was rapidly rebuilt. Then in A.D. 79 Vesuvius erupted, completely engulfing Herculaneum, Pompeii and Stabiae. Warnings had been given shortly before the volcano erupted, so the wealthy were able to get away in time; the poor, however, remained *in situ* and were engulfed in lava as they worked or slept.

There were at least another six eruptions in the ensuing centuries, notably one in 1631. New layers of lava spread and hardened over the hidden cities—which was one reason why it took so long to find them. It was almost seventeen hundred years before the first statues were recovered by tunnelling into the buried city of Herculaneum, in 1711. The discoveries so excited the connoisseurs and scholars and collectors of western Europe that a systematic excavation of the cities was eventually begun in 1748.

Until the time of these discoveries, architects had been able to study and copy the remains of the ancient buildings, baths and temples, and thus to reconstruct in ideal form the architecture of the classical world, much as Palladio had reconstructed Vitruvius's work in the sixteenth century. Inigo Jones and the other architects of the Palladian school had built magnificent new homes for the wealthy and erudite of

Europe, based on this classical ideal; but there was absolutely no clue to the fashions of decoration and furnishing that had been followed by the classical artists *inside* their severe and beautifully proportioned buildings. Did they have chairs, for instance? Did they paint the walls or cover them with textiles? Were the walls faced on the inside with brick or stone or covered with plaster? Simply no one knew. As a result, the pre-1748 Palladian masterpieces, like the splendid Double Cube Room at Wilton House (furnished by William Kent), were decorated in the grand sixteenth-century Italian baroque style, with velvet on the walls and huge solid pieces of furniture built-in as part of the architectural scheme. It looked magnificent with all the richly lavish gilding and scrolling, but what a strange contrast to the clear clean symmetry and the perfect proportions.

The excavations revealed how men and women had lived in those small Italian provincial towns: their culture, their art, the small details of their private lives. In the past, when a civilization collapsed its cities were sacked, its villas looted: paintings were destroyed or abandoned, bronzes and metalwork melted down, marble sculptures burned for lime. But at Herculaneum and Pompeii, everything had been encased in lava, completely protected century after century. It had engulfed the towns so swiftly that there was no time to grab a handful of coins and run: everything was swallowed up, just as it was.

The development of the decorative arts revealed in the excavations dated back for about a hundred years before the eruptions. There were pieces of furniture; cups and plates; a shop counter, a till for money, a dog stretched across a threshold; frescoes and graffiti and mosaics. The paintings (many of them copies or versions of older Greek pictures) are flat, enigmatic and two-dimensional with beautifully fresh colours—sometimes earthy ochres, greys and black, more often pale pinks, blues and greens. Greek key frets are in evidence, together with scrolling, and fan and shell designs. There were charming statues, fountains, bronze portrait busts, and papyrus rolls of the writings of otherwise unknown philosophers. It was one of the most exciting discoveries ever made.

The designers immediately took up these decorative forms and employed them in the creating of furniture, ceramics, silver and glass and textiles. But the excavations took a very long time. Naturally the bigger things—the statues, the fountains and busts, the mosaics—were found first; smaller things, such as jewellery or coins, were not found during the early excavations—or if discovered, were probably stolen by the amateur archaeologists. But fortunately the French were granted the concession to excavate Pompeii properly between the years 1806 and 1814, and it was then, during the Napoleonic Empire, that most of the jewellery was discovered. In the Campana Collection in the Louvre today there are about twelve hundred pieces of Greek, Etruscan and Roman jewellery, most of which were ferreted out in Pompeii.

For the very first time people could see specimens of the kind of jewellery worn by ordinary folk in classical times—not the great grand works of art buried in the tombs of the rich and high-born, but the ordinary rings and bracelets, earrings and chains, worn by the woman next door. It was a revelation; and coming as it did, on the heels of the French Revolution and the deliberate levelling of the class structure, it made fine political material. Men and women could see what their counterparts had worn seventeen hundred years before, and quite naturally they proceeded to copy or adapt the designs and the antique techniques which had been used. It was extremely difficult but they did it very well, and the fashion that grew up was in perfect accord with the political and social and cultural climate of opinion at that time.

Fashions: Revolution to Regency

The French Revolution shook everyone in Europe and had a profound effect on the political and cultural history, the manners and morals and fashions, in every European country. The French court, which had set the fashions for all Europe, had vanished—apparently for ever. What had happened in France might all too easily happen again elsewhere; the strength of the power invested in the middle and lower classes was driven horrifyingly home to the privileged: they reacted in various ways. Some were for immediate and complete repression of any signs of radical revolt (the radical movement was growing fast in the industrial north of England in the decades that preceded the Regency); some were for compromise and cautious political reform; some believed in a simple evangelism which would ensure a diligent and sober working class, neither exploited, nor brutalized, but properly content with a Christian society, re-organized on decent principles; and some, particularly in the literary world, greeted the early days of the Revolution—before the terror and murder broke out—with sheer joy.

The poets and writers of Europe had been acclaiming the virtues of simplicity and freedom and feeling for some time. Blake and Burns, for example, both wrote in simple language of a world which, whether rural and fresh or imbued with its own strange terrors, was far removed from the urbane and civilized and formal world of the early Georgians. The language of feeling, the language of the heart, poured out with a new freshness. Philosophers, notably Jean-Jacques Rousseau, wrote of the basic freedoms which were denied to so many ("*Man is born free, but everywhere he is in chains*"). Rousseau died in 1778, seeing little significant result to his appeals. Marie-Antoinette had her "farm" at Trianon and played milkmaid there with the ladies of her court, but anything farther from the realities of peasant life could hardly be imagined.

In England the general atmosphere was not nearly so artificial. The English liked their out-of-doors life, and whereas the French lords and ladies viewed exile from Versailles as perpetual imprisonment, and cut off from all that made life worth living, the English nobility had its country estates and spent a good deal of time on them. The English have the type of humour which ridicules any attempt at playing the shepherdess: farms were there to be productive, not to provide a theatrical backdrop for high society games.

In the last decades of the eighteenth century, clothes were becoming practical. Hoops were abandoned, except for court use. Men seemed to renounce their gay beautiful clothes and to dress with quiet elegance, as if the old "fancy dress" differentiation between the ranks were fading at last. Powder went out of style: anyone old-fashioned enough to appear *poudré* after 1795 had to pay a fine of a guinea for doing so (a rule which gave rise to the phrase "a guinea-pig"). Out went colour, ornamentation and extravagance. Out went jewelled accessories, such as diamond buttons and sapphire bows. Women loosened their corsets and affected a "natural" look, with simple dresses, breeze-ruffled curls which had never been within a salon's length of the great out-doors, less obtrusive make-up; it was as if the English aristocracy tried to show its sympathy for their French fellows—many of whom were now living in England as *émigrés*—by affecting a more modest appearance. The jewellery followed suit. There is a portrait at Polesden Lacey in Surrey which is a fine example of the portraiture and the dress of the period. Sir Henry Raeburn (1756–1823) here portrays Mrs. Simpson— of whom we sadly know nothing. She is seen in a flimsy gauzy dress, tightly gathered under a high bustline, with small sleeves. Her hair is cut as short as a boy's, curling forward over her forehead in the most careful Revolutionary disarray with no trace of powder. She sits in a landscape setting, her hands calmly and quietly folded in her lap, young and serene with no vestige of jewellery or worldly wealth about her. The blaze of Georgian diamonds faded and was gone. Few diamonds were worn for about fifteen years—but they did not melt into thin air, their owners simply tucked them safely away to wait until they came into fashion again.

Gradually, however, women compromised with the severe classical simplicity of the Directoire style. They re-discovered the delights of looking thoroughly and deliciously feminine rather than severely correct. Although their dresses, like their jewels, were still "classical" in line, there was a capricious swerving towards frivolity and femininity.

The stabilizing of political life in France under the supreme power of Napoleon Bonaparte (1769–1821) meant the re-establishment of the French court. Napoleon, one of the cleverest tacticians in history, knew that the countries of Europe were accustomed to looking to France for a lead. Away went liberty and equality and fraternity. Antiquity survived, but this too was updated: from the basic simplicity of the Greek style, as interpreted by the revolutionaries, to the richness of the Roman Empire, as seen by the new emperor. Jacques-Louis David, the Revolutionary artist who had studied in Rome and there won the *Prix de Rome*, painted the coronation of Napoleon and Josephine in 1805. The painting, which hangs now in the Louvre in Paris, shows the new social scene. Napoleon decided that no one from the Church was worthy to crown him: he set the crown upon his own head, and then himself crowned his empress. He is shown wearing a long red velvet Roman toga, thickly embroidered with heavy golden bees, his hair in a Brutus cut bound with a wreath of golden laurel leaves, and Josephine kneels in front of him, in a dress which imitates the Grecian style but suits her new imperial dignity. Her gown is of white satin, with a high waist and long sleeves, made with a small puff at the shoulder and then tight to the wrist; there is lace at the neck, gold embroidery on the puffs. A rich red train, adorned with gold and ermine, flows from her shoulders. Her hair is *en Grecque*. She wears a diamond diadem and a pearl bracelet with a cameo clasp. The courtiers in the background shimmer with diamonds and pearls: their appearance, and its faithful reproduction in paint, was a deliberate and forceful gesture, setting a new standard of splendour as grand as in the days of Louis XIV, symbolizing the New France and Napoleon's ambition to be the first man in modern times to rule the whole world. Where the emperor led, others followed; the gulf widened again between rich and poor—save that now the rich were often a new breed, ennobled by the emperor, and the poor were the old aristocrats from whom everything had been stripped.

By 1806 there seems to have been a passion for jewellery. Uzanne described the French ladies of fashion in the Second Empire (*circa* 1810):

"They decked themselves to such a degree with jewellery that the women looked like walking jewellers' shops. On every finger several diamond rings glittered, one above the other. Gold chains were wound around the neck as many as eight times. Their ears were pulled down by heavy massive pendants; their arms surrounded by chased bracelets of wonderful workmanship. Pearl collars and pearl fringes adorned the hair and often fell down to the shoulders. Long gold pins sometimes held the hair together, and the gold hair-combs set with diamonds and pearls represented fortunes."

But reaction was quick to set in, and ladies of taste dressed more quietly and restricted the number of jewels they wore, leaving a jeweller's-shop style of display to the *nouveaux riches*.

For a great part of this period England was at war with France, Napoleon's ultimate defeat at Waterloo, and departure into his second exile, not occurring until 1815. None the less the fashionable world kept in touch with the changes of French fashion, modifying them to suit its own taste. Under the influence of Beau Brummell and his followers, men's tailoring had reached exquisitely refined heights—even the French travelled to London to acquire the beautifully cut coats of the Regency era. A man showed his wealth through the perfect cut and quiet good taste of his clothes, rather than an array of jewellery. Brummell's influence over the Prince Regent came to an unfortunate end in 1813, but men continued to follow the lead he had set. The Prince Regent's own "style" was never emulated in England as Napoleon's had been in France. No disciple attempted to convert a country estate into a Royal Pavilion, like the extraordinary affair the Regent had built in Brighton. No disciple squandered a tenth of the money he threw away on trifles and fantasies. Gradually the man caricatured himself, and when he died in 1830, after nineteen years of ruling England—from 1811 to 1820 as regent for his father, and for ten years after that as king in his own right—it seemed that scarcely anybody cared. The ladies had no real arbiter of fashion either, from whom to take a lead: the young Queen Charlotte who had stood, decked in diamonds, for her portrait (facing page 146) was ageing now: in her late sixties when her son took over the regency, and over seventy when she died in 1818, she had borne fifteen children, her husband, the king, was ill, if not mad; she was hardly willing to make an all-out attack on the fashions of the capital. The Prince Regent, with a string of dubious stage-ladies to his discredit, had made a disastrous marriage in 1795 to Caroline of Brunswick; the couple separated within a few years, after the birth of their only child, the Princess Charlotte, and Caroline took herself off to travel on the Continent; society was agreeably scandalized by the stories of her exploits abroad. The Princess Charlotte herself died tragically in childbirth in 1817, when she was hardly in her twenties. An extant portrait of her, painted by Dawe and now hung in the National Portrait Gallery in London, shows her in her late teens, dressed in the pure English neo-classical style. Her hair is *en Grecque*, with pearls twisted in it. She wears a simply cut dress in a dark fabric, its lace sleeves caught with small pearl brooches. There is a triple brooch of cameos at her bust, and one small ring on her hand. But she lived out her short life in retirement; until the young Victoria came to the throne in 1837, there were to be no real leaders of fashion in England.

The Craftsmen and Their Work

English craftsmen were as good in a technical sense as any in France, and their settings were often finer or better made, particularly during the Regency period, and indeed for several years before that. As soon as Napoleon began his lengthy campaigns, the amount of money available for jewellery faded away. The French sometimes used flimsy machine-made settings stamped out by the dozen, and the resulting pieces lacked any true unity of craftsmanship. In England, however, where there was a far greater general prosperity, jewellers continued to make their pieces most beautifully by hand, and the difference is obvious.

One new fashion which the English and their craftsmen did promote in the opening decades of the nineteenth century was the use of the topaz and the amethyst. These stones came into fashion at the time of the Revolution, and continued to be worn right through the Napoleonic and Regency periods. They had not been seen very much in the past, except for ecclesiastical jewellery, but the darker textiles and the severe classical lines suited them—and they fitted in well with the Revolutionary colours of purple, white and gold. Other gems which were not as costly as diamonds (one must never call them "semi-precious stones", it is like saying that someone is semi-dead or semi-pregnant) were also introduced at about this time: foiled pink topaz, for example, dark red garnets, and the peridot or olivine. Seed pearls were also popular—picking up the third Revolutionary colour, white—and were frequently used (Fig. 44). The tiny gems, each weighing less than half a grain in weight, were attached to a perforated mother-of-pearl background with white horsehair or silk thread.

These newly fashionable stones were lightly held in silver settings strengthened with gold, and had an elusive air of fragility. A popular motif was the Bacchus bunch of grapes and vine-leaves, perhaps with pearls for grapes and leaves in several shades of textured gold to give a richer effect. The grape-and-vine-leaf image was frequently used in the silver of the times, patricularly in the work of Paul Storr, one of the royal silversmiths.

At the time of the Revolution and in the years that immediately followed it, these settings were exceptionally light and delicate; they had to be, worn as they were with Grecian-style dresses in light gauzy fabrics; but they were adapted to the changing fashions that followed—and in the Regency period, fashions were changing very quickly —until at last, in the heavily corseted mid-Victorian times, they were over-large and coarse.

But the Regency itself ended on a note of feminine prettiness and charm. The most entertaining novels have been written about the period; in its own way it was, like the whole-hearted Georgian era which had preceded it, a time to enjoy, if one were lucky enough to be born in reasonable affluence. Regency ladies strove, in a charming and ingenuous way, to make the best of themselves; and even if a lady had no diamonds of her own, and could not afford to buy any, it was both possible and, in terms of fashion, permissable for her to wear cameos, topazes set in pinchbeck, or one of the novelties of the jeweller's trade, such as cut-steels, Tassie's pastes, or Wedgwood's ware.

Cameos and Intaglios

CAMEOS

Cameo-cutting had reached its peak of craftsmanship and beauty during the Hellenistic period of the Greek civilization. The Romans took up the art and continued it, and both Greek and Roman cameos have been found in the lands they conquered and colonized. These early cameos are like sculpture in exquisite miniature, the gemstones being expertly carved in relief.

During the fifteenth and sixteenth centuries, at the time of the Renaissance, there was a revival of interest in the cameo. Genuine classical ones were mounted in contemporary settings, the precious metal being sometimes enamelled, sometimes set with additional gems. Many a copy was made as well; and Renaissance craftsmen also carved cameos of their own, portraying classical or contemporary subjects in their own style.

A new surge of interest arose in the latter half of the eighteenth century with the rise of the neo-classical movement. Copies were made of the Renaissance cameos as well as the classical ones which had survived the centuries, and new types were also carved to neo-classical designs, influenced by the spate of Greek and Roman statuary which came flooding into England in the wake of the travellers returning from the Grand Tour.

Gradually, however, the eighteenth- and early nineteenth-century craftsmen began to develop their own distinctive cameo style, using new materials, new subjects, new settings. The simple classical severity was softening into a light-hearted and feminine frivolity: cameos were mounted and worn as ladies' brooches or rings, and naturally the style of the setting, and of the cameo itself, was influenced by the shifts and changes of fashion; Fig. 39, facing page 163, shows this very well.

New Materials

The Greeks and the Romans had carved their cameos out of hard gemstones; the Georgians, however, faced with a great demand for cameos, and no doubt influenced by their own practicality and liking for novel and unusual materials, tried working in shell as well.

Generations before, during the Renaissance period when anything unusual and rare was valued, some great shells were brought to Europe from the warm tropical seas: among them the nautilus shells, which are found in the Indian and Pacific Oceans. These were beautifully mounted, set or worked by the craftsmen of the time for their patrons, all eager for luxuries and rarities. The body of the beautiful sixteenth-century Pelican-in-her-Piety covered cup, now in the Victoria and Albert Museum, was originally a nautilus shell, peeled and polished and set in gold; when this broke a copy was made up in gold and substituted for the fractured shell. In the same museum there is still an eighteenth-century nautilus cup, made by the French craftsman Jean Martin in 1770; this is mounted in gold, and the metalwork is studded with colourful classical gemstone cameos.

Shell-carved cameos gradually replaced the classical gemstones. They were cheaper, for one thing; it was possible to make larger pieces of jewellery, and to make matching sets; and the range of colour available (shell cameos can be carved from at least ten recognized types of shell) intrigued the discerning public.

Each of the types of shell used in cameo-carving is made up of three definite layers, giving the craftsman three different colours with which to work—though the outer layer, which may be mottled, or very dark, or even, on occasion, yellow, is generally completely removed with some sort of file. Below this is a white layer, and below this again a coloured layer which can vary from the chocolate brown of the Black Helmet shell, through violet and port wine, to the familiar pink of the Queen Conch. The white layer is carved in relief against the contrasting background of the coloured layer.

New Subjects

As the extreme severity of the neo-classical and Revolutionary cameos gave way to the work of the Napoleonic and Regency eras, so the type of subject began to alter. In the earlier cameos one finds beautifully restrained reproductions of Greek or Roman ruins; then portrait heads of the classical gods; then complex historical scenes which were carved in several depths, and sometimes with such extreme patience and skill that the craftsman managed to achieve a "veiling" effect, with gauzy draperies blown across glowing limbs. Then, and most unfortunately, people tried to bring cameos up-to-date. In their respect for the qualities of the classical age, they tried to emulate the classical scene; and cameos were produced which bore portrait heads of the new emperor, Napoleon, and the new "arbiter of taste", the Prince Regent, as if, by portraying the questionable leaders of the present in the fashion of the past, one could invest them with classical glory and provide, as it were, a built-in reputation. Gradually cameos became debased, their purpose negated.

New Settings

The nature of the setting determined the price of a shell cameo. Some were set in gold and framed in diamonds or sapphires; others were set in simple pinchbeck. The Greek simplicity of the early gold mounts gave way to the greater richness of the Napoleonic period, and by the eighteen-forties they were lavishly set with full Roman elaboration.

It is extremely difficult to date a cameo jewel since many a gold mount was subsequently melted down, or handed over in time of war or national emergency (a shell cameo itself has no intrinsic value, what one is paying for is the craftsmanship; thus the cameo would often survive, being re-mounted later on) and all that one can safely say is that a cameo is either contemporary with or older than its present mount. Very few were signed.

New Craftsmen, New Patrons, New Fashions

Carving a cameo takes time, patience and very few tools, whether one is working on the relief carving itself, or on cutting away the surround to reveal the coloured background. The key to a cameo's quality is the depth of undercutting and the tonal nuances the craftsman has achieved; neither of these is properly copied in twentieth-century work.

The principal late eighteenth- and nineteenth-century carvers of cameos came from Italy and Sicily, and set up work in the regions around Naples and Rome, partly because the materials were available there (sea-shells, corals, lava from Mount

Vesuvius), and partly because of the enormous interest in the excavations at Herculaneum and Pompeii.

The patrons of the Napoleonic period were dressing in the classical style, and wanted jewellery made to match; shell cameos fitted in beautifully. Complete *parures* were made from shell cameos mounted in gold: a frontlet or *tour de tête* worn across the forehead like a little diadem, sometimes with a comb attached (the Empress Josephine, her daughter and her sisters-in-law were fond of wearing these), a necklace, earrings, a brooch, a pendant, bracelets, perhaps a ring. Each cameo was either shaped like an oval (a *garbo*) or a circle (a *perla*) and was generally carved with a mythological design. They were linked together by simple rows of fine gold chain or filigree gold. Some of them were very beautiful, especially those made in the early period, between 1770 and 1805, when they still had a marvellous Greek simplicity. Richness and frivolity, however, inevitably crept in, and the old classical and Renaissance seriousness, dating from the times when cameos were honoured, even revered, both for their own elegance and craftsmanship and for the moral or philosophical significance of the subject they portrayed, gave way to frivolity and fashion.

INTAGLIOS

In the history of jewellery intaglios antedate cameos, for the Greeks—and other civilizations before them—were engraving gemstones in intaglio before ever they began carving them in relief. The Romans took up the craft from the Hellenistic civilization, and it was again revived by the Renaissance craftsmen and given a new thrust forward by the neo-classical movement. Among the finest of the eighteenth-century craftsmen were the master-and-pupil team, Burch and Marchant, who were working in England at about the same period as the Pichler family was engraving in Rome and Jacques Guay in Paris.

Edward Burch (1730–1814) began his career as a wherryman but eventually won admittance to the Royal Academy schools and became an A.R.A. in 1770 and a full R.A. in 1771. Seven years later he was appointed medal engraver to the king and the Duke of York. His work was early praised for its "great delicacy, truth and finish". He became one of the most famous of the British gem engravers, and was in addition a painter and sculptor.

Nathaniel Marchant (1739–1816), Burch's pupil, was of better birth than he. In addition to studying under Burch, he was able to work and study in Italy for fifteen years, sending home impressions of ancient intaglios to the Royal Academy. He was elected a full R.A. in 1809, becoming official gem-engraver to the Prince Regent shortly afterwards. His work was greatly prized. In addition to normal classical subjects, he made splendid portraits in intaglio of living men and women. The Duke of Marlborough sent gems out to him in Rome to engrave, and many of his pieces were placed in famous collections, among them Sir Richard Worsley's. Although his work was rated so highly during his lifetime, modern connoisseurs are said to find it "too fine and finicky". It seems a strange comment about something worked in miniature.

CRAFTSMEN AND FAKERS

When the Georgian era began, gem engravers were fraudulently copying antique specimens as well as composing modern portrait heads in the classical style. The latter half of the century, however, saw the neo-classical movement gaining ground rapidly, and the engravers began to take more care over their work as the public itself became better educated in classical styles and techniques. They spent less time turning out frauds and more attempting a genuine imitation of the antique which was not an actual copy. It was Winckleman who eventually persuaded the trade to reverse the process, so that artists and craftsmen began to create accurate copies rather than imitations.

Johann Joachim Winckleman (1717–68) was the son of a German archaeologist, who worked at Herculaneum, Pompeii and Paestum, and who, in 1736, was made Superintendent of Roman Antiquities. He published a number of treatises on ancient archaeology, notable among them being his *Treatise on the Imitation of Greek Works in Painting and Sculpture*, which came out in 1755, and *History of Ancient Art*, his masterpiece, published in 1764.

The eighteenth-century artists and craftsmen became so successful in their copying that Robert Adam remarked patriotically that the reign of George III "might fix an era no less remarkable than that of Pericles, Augustus or the Medici". The remark is a revealing one: the patrons Adam named belong to different countries and widely different periods, yet he lumped them together in the splendour of the "antique" past. Past ages were still hugger-mugger in men's minds, and only the scholars managed a proper and careful differentiation between the Greek and Roman styles.

Rather than be accused of fraud, eighteenth-century craftsmen who made meticulously accurate copies of classical engraved gems now began to sign their own work. It is true that they signed in Greek letters, but this was merely so that the signature was in keeping with the subject, not a deliberate attempt to mislead the customer—in general at least, though there are always some rotten apples in any barrel and some fakers were working busily away, signing their work with ancient Greek signatures, and selling the pieces as originals. These men went to enormous trouble to make their cameos and intaglios look genuinely old, sometimes scratching them, chipping them, and forcing them down a turkey's gizzard—a process which ensured that the stone acquired the dull chalky look associated with antique gems. One notorious and highly successful faker was an English art dealer named Thomas Jenkins, living in Rome. A contemporary English sculptor and Royal Academician, Joseph Nollekens (1737–1823), described Jenkins's trade

> "supplying the foreign visitors with intaglios and cameos made by his own people, that he kept in a part of the ruins of the Coliseum, fitted up for 'em to work in slyly by themselves. I saw 'em at work though, and Jenkins gave a whole handful of 'em to me to say nothing about the matter to anybody else but myself. Bless your heart! he sold 'em as fast as they made 'em."

Fortunately there were craftsmen like Burch and Marchant as well as fakers like Jenkins, and engraved gems continued to be created well into the nineteenth century, some of the finest work being done in the Regency period. The gemstones used were onyx, sardonyx, cornelian and agate, in harmony with those used by the ancients. Some people wanted to have the more expensive stones, such as sapphires and rubies and even, on occasion, diamonds, engraved for them, but these were not in the true spirit of the age with its eager classical reconstructions.

Cut-Steels

Amongst the less expensive jewellery worn by the emergent middle class was cut-steel work (Fig. 50). In spite of its surface similarity to marcasite jewellery (which enjoyed a great vogue during the eighteenth century, and is still made today), it is quite different, and the two should never be confused. It is true that marcasite and cut-steel are both a dense dark grey in colour, that marcasite jewellery and cut-steel jewellery are not set with precious gems, that both will sparkle if turned to catch the light; but there the likeness ends. The name "marcasite" is generally applied to iron pyrites, which is cut down into a quantity of minute little stones, like grey diamonds; these are then mounted individually in claw or coronet settings, and framed or set in silver. Modern marcasite jewellery of good quality is extremely expensive, considering the cheapness of iron pyrites, so it is clear that one is paying almost entirely for the high labour costs.

The technique of cut-steel jewellery was quite different: a metalworker's craft carried out in miniature, with patient and expert riveting. Basically, a design was conceived and drawn. The main parts were then cut out in thin sheets of metal—brass, silver alloy or tin. These sections were generally shaped like rosettes. The secret of cut-steel jewellery was to pack each rosette with as many steel studs as possible. The rosette was then riveted on to a base plate. (The use of rivets is the key to cut-steel jewellery; marcasites are never riveted to their mounts in this way.) The mounted rosettes were joined together by curved sections which were also packed with studs or by links, and which were often strengthened on the reverse if the motifs used were particularly large or heavy. This, however, was rare in the early work since the designers of cut-steel jewellery were aware that too solid a piece would be daunting, depressing and heavy. They strove for an effect of lightness and femininity, using sparkling little rosettes like tiny flowers, spaced apart and joined by undulating curves or openwork scrolls. Gradually, however, as the early decades of the nineteenth century gave way to the Victorian age, cut-steel designs became heavier, and cable bracelets, heart-shaped locket clasps, and representations of butterflies, lizards, stars and crescent moons replaced the light and delicate stylization of the earlier work.

Cut-steel work was not invented in the late Georgian and Regency period, though it was then that it was most in fashion. Anne Clifford's book *Cut-Steel and Berlin Iron Jewellery* traces references to it from the sixteenth century onwards. She gives many interesting details about the centre of the English trade which was, unexpectedly, Woodstock in Oxfordshire. Birmingham or Coventry might seem a more feasible centre, and indeed cut-steel jewellery was made there at the height of its popularity, but the work of the finest quality originated in Woodstock.

It was by no means cheap, though within the range of the independent lower middle class. Cut-steel scissors could cost fifteen guineas a pair, whereas an ordinary pair of plain steel ones went for fifteen pence. The range was considerable. Brooches, bracelets, buckles, bangles, necklaces and earrings were made, and can still be found today, now selling at well below their original price. So were tiaras and "stars for the nobility"—

rather difficult to wear nowadays. Examples of these stars, then selling at twenty guineas apiece, can be seen on display at Claydon House in Buckinghamshire. A cut-steel chain which was made in 1813, weighing merely two ounces, was sold in France for £170 according to the Victoria County History of Oxford. A great many cut-steel *châtelaines* were made (the material was both practical and suited to daytime wearing), some of them very elaborate. Several now on view in the Victoria and Albert Museum in London incorporate small Wedgwood-style medallions modelled by James Tassie. There are other samples of eighteenth-century cut-steel work in the Victoria and Albert, together with some Regency watch-chains which are allied to the blue and white jasper ware.

The English trade was the first to become established, and much of its work, like the £170 chain just mentioned, was exported abroad: even when the fashion in England died out, the firm of Hipkins continued to supply the court of Spain with buttons and buckles ornamented with cut-steels. The redoubtable Matthew Boulton (1728–1809) of Birmingham, who entered into partnership with James Watt, propped him up with his own energy and enthusiasm, and nearly bankrupted himself before the steam-engine became a commercial success, also had a finger in the cut-steel trade. His exports of cut-steel buttons—by no means cheap—to Holland, Russia, Spain, France and Germany were formidable; and it was he who persuaded Josiah Wedgwood to supply the trade with cameos, which were used in pieces as diverse as brooches and snuff boxes.

A crisis came during the Revolutionary wars, when France stopped importing from England. Pitt had half-crippled the country with taxes, but this did not have the effect of making people buy fine cut-steel work—the new bourgeoisie ignored cut-steel craftsmanship and went all out for sparkle instead. But the industry weathered this particular storm and by 1845 there were 3,700 people working in the jewellery trade in Birmingham; we do not know what proportion of these were workers in cut-steels, but it must have been fairly considerable. Unfortunately it was this centralization in Birmingham and this expansion of the trade which killed it. The passion for machines and the vast pool of available labour made mass-production irresistible. Experiments were carried out with unworthy materials, and the results proved to be flimsy trash.

It was a great pity. Cut-steel jewellery was peculiar to England, and "progress" stamped it out. At the height of its popularity and excellence, it had fitted the mood of the time: severe rather than sparkling, which suited the more sombre neo-classical style; delicate and feminine, which suited the dresses of the period and women's striving to achieve a classical quality, and dark in tone, which made it suitable for mourning jewellery (so many young men were killed in the struggles of the Napoleonic wars that much mourning jewellery was worn).

Stray pieces of cut-steel jewellery can still be picked up in country jumble sales for a few pence, and at the better auction sales for well under £50. It carries no marks, so there is nothing to indicate the place of origin—nothing to say, for example, that one necklace was made in Woodstock, another in Birmingham; or even that one was made in England and another in France (though French work is later, more representational, and tends to be based on an oval rosette rather than a round one). Nor is there any exhibition of the best Woodstock and Birmingham work which one can examine. But it is effective, amazingly delicate, and unexpectedly strong, and the twentieth-century public, accepting the primacy of quality over glitter, might well like to look out for surviving pieces. It would be a fascinating antique to collect.

Hair Jewellery

Mourning jewellery has been known at each and every period, but a reasonably new form appeared at about the turn of the century: this was hair jewellery, whose popularity was to last well into the Victorian age. It caught the imagination of the Empire and Regency ladies, and of the Victorians who followed them, to such an extent that various pattern books were published from which they could choose the designs that appealed to them. A particularly fine example, published towards the very end of the vogue, is the five-shilling (25p) catalogue which William Halford and Charles Young published in 1864. This contained "*A Great Variety of Copper-Plate Engravings of Devices and Patterns in Hair; suitable for Mourning Jewellery, Brooches, Rings, Guards, Alberts, Necklets, Lockets, Bracelets, Miniatures, Studs, Links, Earrings, & etc etc.*" There were 164 patterns in all, and although one might associate mourning jewellery with some small feeling for religion, especially during the nineteenth century, only five Christian crosses are shown. Hair jewellery is essentially sentimental, and the phrase

Whose hair I wear, I loved most dear

probably sums it up as well as any.

One may divide hair jewellery into two basic groups: the classical and the frankly sentimental. The latter, unless desperately personal, generally lacks both beauty and intrinsic value, and is never worth acquiring or keeping; but the former can have historical value, and some indications of style and intricate craftsmanship, and is worth keeping for its interest. Both were produced in quantity in the period that lay between the French Revolution and the mid-Victorian age—from about 1790 to 1870—and then mercifully died out.

The better quality jewels incorporate a neo-classical scene: a miniature pastoral play, where hair is used to create the leaves of a weeping willow, a stiff little poplar on a skyline, or the feathers of a swooping pair of bluebirds. Almost always visible is a boxlike tomb, a classical column or a Grecian urn (presumably marking the resting place of the loved one's remains whether bone or ash) and generally there is a lake as well, or a little stream. Heaven, or at least its entrance, was always kept in view; and somewhere, somehow, the deceased's initials had to be worked in, perhaps as a gold monogram, together with the date of passing on. Oceans of grief were conjured up with scenes of disconsolate widows, mourning children, and tiny little seed-pearl tears. It was a peculiarly English invention, but was much admired and copied in France even after England had exhausted the fashion.

A typical scene is Number 16 from the Halford and Young Catalogue. This is a design for a brooch 2 inches wide by $1\frac{1}{2}$ inches deep (about 50 mm by 35 mm), oblong in shape but with rounded corners. In the centre is a classical column on a square plinth topped by two hearts pierced by one long arrow. Above this is a swallow swooping down from the sun's rays holding a wedding ring in its beak. All this takes place in a country scene:

two or three different types of trees dot an undulating park and a large country house lies to the right. The space is minute, and filled with detail, yet there is a good feeling for the three-dimensional nature of the scene. Various materials would have been used in its creation: seed pearls apart, the maker would need ivory for the column and gold for the ring and the arrow, as well, of course, as hair. Once completed, it was covered with a piece of glass or rock crystal, and given a protective gold backing to keep it secure and to shut out the damp—always a final destroyer. This back was inscribed with, for example, the initials of the departed and those of the betrothed, the dates of birth and death, and possibly also a line from some poem the lovers had cherished.

This scene did at least attempt to be artistic as well as sentimental. It is when a mourning jewel consists simply of a plaited background of hair, or perhaps a small curl, set in gold with a heavy black enamel frame, that it becomes sub-romantic and grisly. It was a genteel way of keeping a relic. No Georgian or Victorian would dream of cutting off a toe or a finger-tip (as the medievals did with the bodies of their saints), encasing it in gold and black enamel, and wearing it as a brooch to pin a lace *fichu*; yet they were quite prepared to do this with someone's hair. It seems a strange and eerie taste.

Naturally, while they were at it, and ideas and hair seemed so plentiful, they eventually set about making hair jewellery which had no mourning connotations at all. In the Victoria and Albert Museum there is a necklace of hollow beads made entirely of intricately woven hair, with a tiny gold fastening; it is an amazing sight. (A vase made out of hair was even exhibited at the Great Exhibition of 1851.) The Halford and Young catalogue shows an endless variety of brooches and pendants in the most curious shapes: tightly plaited and woven hair is twisted into harps, into bows and arrows and quivers, into writhing snakes. The snake, is, indeed, a perennial motif in hair jewellery, slithering and wriggling from the neo-classical period clear through the Victorian age. Made of plaited hair over some hard core, the Halford and Young snakes twist into knots, bite their own tails, and even, in the case of Number 152, manage to dangle a small gold locket from their fangs at the same time. Coiled snakes, created from hair mounted on multitudes of springs, writhe up a slender arm: their heads are made of gold studded with small gems (turquoises were especially popular), and set with evil little ruby eyes. Numbers 106 to 114 are fine examples of this style. Even the harmless-looking plaited hair necklets give one the feeling that one of Cleopatra's asps is quietly hissing in the background, awaiting its cue.

James and William Tassie

An Empire or Regency lady in mourning, who wanted to wear something suitable but whose taste did not run to hair jewellery, might well decide on a classical cameo or intaglio with a suitably sombre scene; if the originals were out of reach of her pocket, the next best thing was probably a Tassie paste.

James Tassie (1735–99) was born in Scotland, served an apprenticeship as a stone-mason (his tombstone in memory of his parents in Eastwood Churchyard is the only known surviving work of his in stone) and then studied draughtsmanship and modelling for three years at the Foulis Academy of Art in Glasgow. In 1763 he visited Dublin, where he became a friend of the distinguished physician and connoisseur, Dr. Henry Quin, King's Professor in the School of Physic. Together they invented a vitreous paste which was perfectly adapted to the making of moulds and casts of antique reliefs; Tassie was also to make use of it when casting his own portrait medallions of contemporaries, modelled from life in wax.

In 1766 Tassie moved to London where he opened a shop in Leicester Square. Here he sold, among other things, paste reproductions of classical gems and medallions. (He was also a serious artist and portrait-medallist, and presented samples of his work at the Royal Academy every year from 1769 to 1779, and again from 1781 to 1791.) He was working during the culmination of the neo-classical period, and people were extravagantly eager to obtain the ancient gemstones; originals were very hard to come by and very expensive, so Tassie's beautiful reproductions, faithfully created in vitreous paste and coloured to match the originals, were in great demand. In 1775 he issued his first catalogue listing a great quantity of gemstone impressions, both cameo and intaglio, modern and antique, which included 3,106 different items assembled from collections all over Europe. Tassie medallions became so popular and so famous that Catherine II of Russia paid for a complete collection of his "pastes in imitation of gems and cameos", and many private collections of antique gems and reliefs were made available to him for reproduction. In the catalogue of his work published in 1790 by Rudolph Eric Raspe more than 15,800 Tassie reproductions are listed.

The catalogue was published in Edinburgh on April 16, 1790 and was entitled "*Descriptive catalogue of a general collection of ancient and modern engraved gems, cameos as well as intaglios, taken from the most noble cabinets in Europe and cast in coloured pastes, white enamel and sulphur by James Tassie, modeller.*" Raspe wrote a foreword in which he said:

> "In the arrangement, I have therefore nearly followed the plan of the late learned Abbe Wincklemann, in his description of the Gems of Baron Philip Stosch: not that his arrangement is unexceptionable, but because it is as good as any hitherto imagined; and perhaps as well connected as our imperfect and not sufficiently digested ideas of ancient Mythology, Iconology, Fable and History seem to admit of."

A foreword to a book, like the introductory lecture to a series, is often the key to the whole subject, and thus it is with Raspe. As a result, he begins his descriptive (and it is extraordinarily descriptive) catalogue with Egyptian gems and takes it through eight stages to the Greeks and Romans. The prices alone are staggering. For intaglio pastes, of a suitable size for seals and rings, one paid from 1s. 6d. to 2s. 6d. (from 7½p to 12½p). For cameos, according to their size and craftsmanship, from 10s. 6d. to 2 guineas (from 52½p to £2·10). *Appliquées* (that is to say, "heads or figures glued to false grounds") were said to be "only Deceptions, unsafe to use as Rings, Bracelets and etc unless they are set under Glass, being liable to fall off and break, therefore only proper as pleasing Ornaments or Furniture; may be made from 5s. (25p) and upwards according to size". If one bought the entire collection as impressions in "red or other coloured Sulphur, with neat gilt Borders" they would cost only 3d. each (just over 1p).

Each mythological god rates a special section describing his exploits, which is followed by further information about the particular gems on which he is performing.

The following example, taken from the section on Priapus, the god of gardens, is Number 5728. It is said to show:

"A sacrifice to Priapus by five persons, among whom we distinguish a young lady newly married, who takes off her girdle; and an old Faun, kneeling, who seems to promise her great pleasure in her new state; at least he harangues upon a large vase which is near the altar at the foot of the sacred term. It is not only probable that those newly married presented themselves to the god of Lampfacus; but we shall very soon prove that they sat upon what was most terrifying to young girls and their prudish governesses."

The following pages are subtitled

"Hitherto we have seen Priapus, or the fecundating principle of Nature, in the form of a term, greatly resembling Pan, and his sacrifices covered with symbols of chaste allegory: we now come to see him less dignified, and his obscene worship without a veil. *Procul est profani!*"

The descriptions which follow are eye-opening even to the reader of the late twentieth century. Latin, Greek and French phrases abound amongst the old-fashioned "ff"'s; it is all extremely entertaining, in spite of the way one stumbles about in sentences filled with "phalluffes". There is a pleasing freshness in the comments, such as "A modern engraving in bad taste yet not altogether without merit" (Number 5720) or "A very curious engraving" (Number 3564, in the section on the theatre). One has the impression that the author and his circle thoroughly enjoyed their studies of the classics. Two hundred years further on, we look back at this interest in the classics from a viewpoint of informed opinion; we study the museum exhibits and admire them; to us they look coldly perfect. If we could only remember how lustily the Georgians viewed life in all its aspects, we might better recapture their approach to the classics: they found them novel, fresh, enormously satisfying, and above all, highly enjoyable. The exploits of the ancient gods and goddesses found echoes, after all, in the Georgians' own behaviour at times, untrammelled as they were by future Victorian morality.

James Tassie's portrait medallions, which date from as early as 1768 (when the portrait heads were displayed against a glass ground), represent his more creative work. They were mostly based on contemporary portraits which he modelled in wax, from the life, and then cast in paste. Both he and William his nephew, whom he had taken into the business and who was almost as fine an artist as he himself, signed their portrait work. James, the originator, signed either "Tassie F" or simply "T"; William signed "W Tassie F". Both charged modest prices for portraits (reproductions from 5s. to 1 guinea—from 25p to £1·05 in modern terms), and both were prepared to accept commissions to work for others, notably Wedgwood.

William, who was fifteen years younger than his uncle, survived him by many years. On his death the bulk of his surviving stock-in-trade was willed to the national galleries of Scotland, including a complete set of twenty thousand Tassie gems in vitreous paste together with their moulds, as well as his own collection of contemporary portrait medallions. They can still be seen in Scotland; in addition, there are some examples at the Victoria and Albert Museum.

Josiah Wedgwood

Wedgwood and Tassie were almost contemporaries, the former living from 1730–95, the latter from 1735–99. Although supremely a potter, Wedgwood influenced the jewellery trade considerably. He was a man of great artistic perception and a passionate love of experiment, who was always seeking to try out, to improve, to perfect. His work was beautifully finished—the lids fitted, the plates could be stacked—and made to clean restrained designs. Among the famous wares he perfected for his ornamental pieces were his cream ware (called queen's ware, because of Queen Charlotte's patronage); black basaltes; marble ware; and his famous jasper ware. He drew ideas for designs from many sources, including engravings and casts from antique and Renaissance gemstones, and his plaques and cameos (Fig. 41) enjoyed great popularity in the closing decades of the eighteenth century and in the Empire period.

It was the vast output of people like Wedgwood and the Tassies that brought exact and faithful reproductions of classical art into the homes of people who had little money and less education, but who appreciated the vigour of a Tassie relief and the serenity of a Wedgwood cameo. There could hardly be a more palatable way to be fed on classical art; the purchasers were delighted with it.

CHAPTER NINE

Victorian Sentimentality

Introduction—Fashions in Dress and Jewellery—Popular Victorian Gemstones: Introduction; Turquoises; Corals; Diamonds—Enamels—Types of Jewel; The Flower Motif—Victorian Eclecticism: Classical Techniques; Castellani; The Giuliano Family; Other Styles—Victorian Gothic; A. W. N. Pugin—Victorian Sentimentality: Mourning Jewels; Jet; Souvenir Jewellery; Commemorative Jewellery—Victorian Jewellery Exhibits

Introduction

Queen Victoria was necessary to Britain. The country had had enough of the Georges and needed her moral stability, the Germanic thoroughness and precision of her husband, and the autocratic atmosphere of confidence under which, decade after decade, her people were to shelter, as under a huge umbrella. Her aura of energetic resolution was reflected throughout the entire country which, during her reign, was to achieve tremendous development and economic growth, striving after improvement in all fields ("I *will* be good"). Rule Britannia! Victoria was a simply magnificent public relations officer for her country and all it stood for. She was as solid as a rock, a female deity with both small feet stamped firmly on the ground, an institution, never, surely never, due to die. Bossy and interfering, capricious and wilful, she developed into a hawk-eyed martinet who encouraged diligence and professionalism; and it is an insult to say that "the Queen was not amused", for she very often was.

Victoria was born on May 24, 1819, the only child of George III's fourth son, Edward, Duke of Kent, and his wife, Victoria Maria Louisa of Saxe-Coburg. On June 20, 1837, her uncle, William IV, died, and she was crowned almost exactly a year later, on June 28, 1838 ("I shall ever remember this day as the *proudest* of my life"); nearly two years after her crowning, on February 10, 1840, she married Prince Albert ("My DEAREST DEAREST DEAR"), younger son of the Duke of Saxe-Coburg-Gotha. A satisfactory total of four sons and five daughters was born to them in their almost twenty-two years together. By the time she died, Victoria seemed to be related by blood or by marriage to just about everyone of any consequence in the royal houses of Europe and had written some of her mighty letters to them all—whether close relatives or not. Her emotional tentacles were octopus-like in their sinuous grip; even the man in the street whom she never saw was afraid to displease her and thought of her as if he knew her personally.

"Her court was pure; her life serene;
God gave her peace; her land reposed;
A thousand claims to reverence closed
In her as Mother, Wife and Queen—"

wrote Tennyson; and Lord Salisbury wrote after her death:

"I have always felt that when I knew what the Queen thought, I knew pretty certainly what views her subjects would take, and especially the middle class of her subjects."

Bourgeois Britain loved her. In spite of occasional impatience and criticism, they watched their queen-spider busily spinning a web of duty and affection and determined improvement about herself—a web whose threads did not snap, but rather clung more tightly still, in the long shut-away period of her widowhood—and they loved her, admired her, copied her: her clothes, her jewels, her way of life, her devotion to the family, her eager interests. They followed her every move like detectives, in newspapers and magazines, in fashion plates and photographs. They identified with her, sharing her joy and love and confidence; sharing too her grief and disappointment. In spite of the fact that she was the queen, in spite of the long widowhood that followed the grief of Albert's death on December 14, 1861, she was always one of them.

Victoria's taste was for gay colours (until her widowhood, at least), splendour and warmth, the gleam of pearls and the flash of diamonds from dear India combined with some nicely embroidered pansies, sprays of English grass, and a wreath of beloved Albert's favourite convolvulus, tangible memories of the family crowded about her, cosiness and novelty. Balmoral, "a pretty little castle", was crammed with tartan: tartan curtains and wallpaper, tartan chair-covers and linoleum—but while there, she could visit all her tenants in the most snug and charming way, and delight in their unaffected Scottish simplicity (later in life Balmoral became a much stricter duller place, and the family suffered sadly). Osborne, also sacred to dear Albert's memory, was full of pincushions and photographs, miniatures and memorials, statuettes and busts and casts of the children's hands and feet. "The Emperor remembers every frock he has ever seen me in!" she remarked naively to her Foreign Secretary; it would certainly not be surprising if he had. For her State visit to Paris, visiting Napoleon III and his empress, the stylish Eugénie, she wore a dress embroidered with geraniums and a vast bonnet, and carried a bright green parasol and a bag embroidered, in compliment to the French, with a white poodle. When she drove to her Diamond Jubilee Thanksgiving in 1897 someone from the crowd shouted, "Go it, old girl!" and in matters of taste, and in so many others, she assuredly did, with a rampaging royal domesticity.

Above all, her reign was one of plenty. Industry was roaring ahead, the old class structures were being shaken up, there was an all-pervading air of bustling business. Many a person has a sinking heart at the word "Victorian", but this should not be so; it springs from considering the period in a purely negative way. The Victorian Age was an atomic bomb explosion of enterprise, enthusiasm and inventiveness scarcely seen before or since on such a scale. It was unquestionably the most practical time imaginable, partly because so much was expected of man and machine alike. Industry, a sense of purpose, and open-minded inventiveness led to prosperity, to expansion in trade, to the winning of international competitions, to the spread of the Empire. It led to an increase in world-wide prestige: Albert's Great Exhibition of 1851 was planned as a picture of the development mankind had so far achieved, and as "a new starting point from which all nations will be able to direct their future exertions". It led especially to money. Money, as we all know, breeds money, and in the nineteenth century it bred faster and more fully than ever before. There were better homes for more people (Albert designed some model houses for the labouring classes to show builders that it was possible to build cheap but decent dwellings); better furniture, better clothes; better education. A new class of men went travelling across Europe to check on what their competitors were doing and to sell their own wares; a young man called Thomas Cook (1808–92) set up as a travel agent, and from a discreet Victorian beginning— he organized the first publicly advertised rail excursion, the "treat" was a temperance meeting—soon developed a vast organization, which eventually moved a whole army to Egypt. Travel was an education in itself, and a marvellous excitement for the inquiring mind. People began to wonder about other countries, their histories, crafts and habits. In learning about the rest of the world, they were continually and happily reassuring themselves how important Great Britain was herself, and how many advantages they had in comparison with other people.

It was all extremely romantic and sentimental, and writers have been criticizing the long roll and surge of emotion ever since; yet the Victorian tapestry was woven of hard work, confidence and ability, and by their efforts they put Great Britain on such an economic footing as she had never known before, until most of Europe and much of the world admired and envied her.

Fashions in Dress and Jewellery

During the Victorian age, just about everything that could be worn was full, fussy and exaggerated. Even if a garment was designed to be relatively simple, the Victorian bourgeoise simply could not leave well alone. Reading through the various fashion magazines, catalogues and advice to the uncertain, one sees a bewildering series of changes in costume and jewels. This is an early Victorian reference, taken from *The World of Fashion* of September 1844:

> "Bracelets are now considered indispensable; they are worn in the following manner; on one arm is placed the sentimental bracelet, composed of hair and fastened with some precious relic; the second is a silver enamelled one, having a cross, *cassolette*, or anchor and heart, as a sort of talisman; the other arm is decorated with a bracelet of gold net work fastened with a simple *noeud*, similar to one of narrow ribbon; the other composed of medallions of blue enamel, upon which are placed small bouquets of brilliants, the fastening being composed of a single one; lastly a very broad gold chain, each link separated with a ruby and opal alternate."

Sleeves, bodices, bonnets and trimmings all changed according to the prevailing mode, but for a good fifty years the accent was primarily on the skirt, its size, and, eventually, the styles of draping its fullness. In the early years of the queen's reign, skirts were reasonably abundant. The flimsy delicate fabrics of an earlier era—frail embroidered muslins and batistes—had given way to wool and satin and silk, supported by petticoats and starched calico. Skirts gradually became wider and fuller; starched petticoats were replaced, in the forties, by underskirts incorporating stiff horsehair (called in French *crinolin*), and then, in the fifties, by hoops of whalebone or covered wire, over which the skirt was stretched. According to the *Punch* cartoons of the time, these hooped skirts reached gigantic proportions. Skirts of such a size were difficult to steer, and a lady wishing to preserve a proper modesty needed to wear petticoats underneath—making the costume still more voluminous and exaggerated—and finally, decorative drawers as well. Towards the end of the sixties it became clear that the skirt could get no fuller or wider, and the great swathes of fabric were drawn towards the back: the crinolette superseded the crinoline, and in turn gave way to the complicated bustle; this eventually subsided in the seventies, though skirts were still drawn back and intricately draped; came back in the early eighties; and by the nineties had finally yielded place to draping and goring.

The dress of Empire and Regency times had been styled with deliberate simplicity, to display a certain emotional sympathy with the revolutionary principles and in addition, to make some kind of gesture towards economy in times of war. But the lady who lived in the High Victorian times lived in a period of peace and prosperity, and was intent on showing the difference between herself and her daughters, living on a comfortable income, and the less well-bred, less hard-working, or less able. The fuller the skirt, it was reasoned, the richer the owner and the less likely it was that she need work. The principle was exactly the same as that which lay behind the wearing of high red heels by Louis XIV's courtiers, or the way the ruling classes of China once grew their finger-nails many inches long.

The Victorian lady also longed to show off the exciting new imports from abroad. She would wear cashmere shawls sent by soldier-relatives in India, carry fans imported from China or Japan, and display ostrich feathers from South Africa. Her laces came from Malta, Chantilly or Honiton; her ribbons from Lyons or from one of the new weaving factories in the north of England; her jewels were probably bought across the counter in London or any of the large provincial cities.

No longer was there such an emphasis on commissioning special pieces of jewellery, though this was still done by many; now that shops were all the vogue, a husband could buy an anniversary present, or perhaps a surprise gift, across the counter, simply picking a ready-made piece he liked. It was so much easier and so much less embarrassing than consulting with a designer, ordering a piece well in advance, showing up one's ignorance of present fashions and techniques; all one had to do was pay the money asked. Such a man might be a factory-owner, a lawyer, a doctor, a businessman. Shops no longer looked exclusively to the nobility, the rich and well-educated, to buy their goods; they merely wanted customers with well-lined pockets. One could be astute and wealthy even if one could not read Homer in the original Greek. The purchaser picked something he liked—possibly something that would stand out, not merely pleasing his wife but impressing the family, his friends, and his own business contemporaries too, who could tot up the probable cost of the jewel and estimate the income the donor must be enjoying. It was public relations work at its most basic, and it worked beautifully.

In the early Victorian period jewellery was feminine and delicate, sometimes erudite, with wreaths and garlands of flowers and foliage, like that described on page 196. By the seventies, however, it had become florid and rich and voluptuous, deliberately contrasting with the textiles of the period, whereas earlier work had complemented flatteringly the satins and laces of the young queen's heyday of happiness. Jewels had to be showy when worn against the richer, darker, shinier fabrics of the mid-Victorian period. Shot-silks, for example, became very popular because they shouted "wealth" at the spectator. Fashion also decreed richly patterned brocades and smooth velvets. Black was often worn, not necessarily for mourning but also because it was flattering and dramatic. Delicate black lace was draped over the head or around the shoulders, and it looked charming against a contrasting pearly white skin. Every effort was made to texture fabrics and to adorn the garment itself; the fashion magazines are packed with the words "draping", "flouncing", "pleating", "ruching", "printing", "piping", "fringing". To get the full effect, one may visit the Costume Museum in Bath where there is a magnificent array of Victorian dresses, as well as garments worn by the gentlemen and the children of the era. There are also examples at the Victoria and Albert Museum in London and at provincial museums, and some very elegant settings in the Bowes Museum at Barnard Castle in Yorkshire. The fuss, fuss, fuss of the dresses was emphasized by the over-decorated bonnets, hats, turbans, laces and morning caps, and enhanced still further by the parasols, bags, reticules, and all the other paraphernalia of Victorian dress. By the eighties the exuberant femininity, whether of the fashionable young matron or the stately widow, was almost overwhelming; thereafter the general style became far less exaggerated, though the effect was still rich and stately.

How in the world could one place a jewel so that it would show up against such a bewildering background? Where could one position a brooch amongst all that whale-bone, pinning, tucking and frilling?

The answer was three-fold: size, rich metalwork, and contrasting colour. Jewels became far larger. The delicate classical jewels of the Empire and Regency periods, the prettiness of the early Victorian years, no longer made any impact unless created as a *parure*, or matching set, in which case its essentially repetitive quality could give it importance. Gold settings were used because they looked richer than silver, and this richness was enhanced by using various shades of gold; one was scarcely enough, they wanted to wear three or even four. The gold had to be textured too, engraved or granulated or filigree (Giuliano's work in this field is described on pages 200–1). Dark fabrics, moreover, meant a need for new stones—it was here that jewellery changed, perhaps, most radically—with a few diamonds set round them as a splendid contrast, to make them stand out even more excitingly.

POPULAR VICTORIAN GEMSTONES

Introduction

The topaz and the amethyst, both of which can be found as large stones, were extensively used, with or without diamonds. So was the green peridot or olivine—the nineteenth century is, in fact, unusual for its use of green and blue stones. Carbuncles were great favourites, glowing richly in their port-wine depths (these are unfaceted garnets cut and polished *en cabochon* and can be extraordinarily large). Two other materials used for their novel and penetrating colour were the turquoise and the coral, which deserve rather fuller descriptions: both were especially popular because they were considered "suitable" for the young as well as for the middle-aged—this was particularly important at a time when fashion magazines, domineering in their advice about what it was "suitable" for each age-group to wear, were consolidating the autocratic control that was to be imposed on the average woman all through the nineteenth century and well into the twentieth.

Turquoises

Turquoises were mined in Persia and imported from India, so the British ladies of the Victorian Empire naturally thought it patriotic to wear them. They have always been reasonably easy to mine, since they do not lie far beneath the surface of the earth, and so can be extracted without using complicated and expensive machinery; this keeps the price down to a sensible level. The best collection of turquoises in the world is in the Crown Jewels of Iran, where the true blue of the fine turquoise stone is displayed; the greeny shades are considered inferior. Being opaque, they were a foil to the glitter of other faceted gems. Tiny turquoises were set in the heads of the gold snake bracelets and matching necklaces that coiled about the arms and necks of opulent ladies. As the use of turquoises increased, lines of them were incorporated, down the length of the snake's body; and at last, inevitably, after the queen became Empress of India in 1876, the entire trinket was made of them. There are examples in the Victoria and Albert Museum, and many a shop window staging a display of Victorian jewellery shows turquoise-studded snakes, hearts, lockets and flowers. A fine Victorian turquoise set is shown facing page 195.

Corals

Coral, like turquoise, had been in fashion at earlier periods, but such a wealth of coral jewellery was made during the Victorian age, and coral is at present so out of fashion,

Fig. 40 : this magnificent brooch is signed by Carlo Giuliano, whose work is described on pages 200–1 and dates from about 1870. The piece is approximately 2½ inches (63 mm) high, and is of gold with *cloisonné* enamels, incorporating the head of an Egyptian deity or king with a diamond headdress set with a ruby, flanked by two white enamelled horses' heads, and with a lotus motif and three pearl drops. It shows the enormous Egyptian influence, a direct result of the widespread interest in contemporary excavations and the work on the Suez Canal, which according to Vever (Vol. II, page 277) was very evident in most of the jewellers' work displayed at the Paris Universal Exhibition of 1867.

By courtesy of Wartski Jewellers Ltd

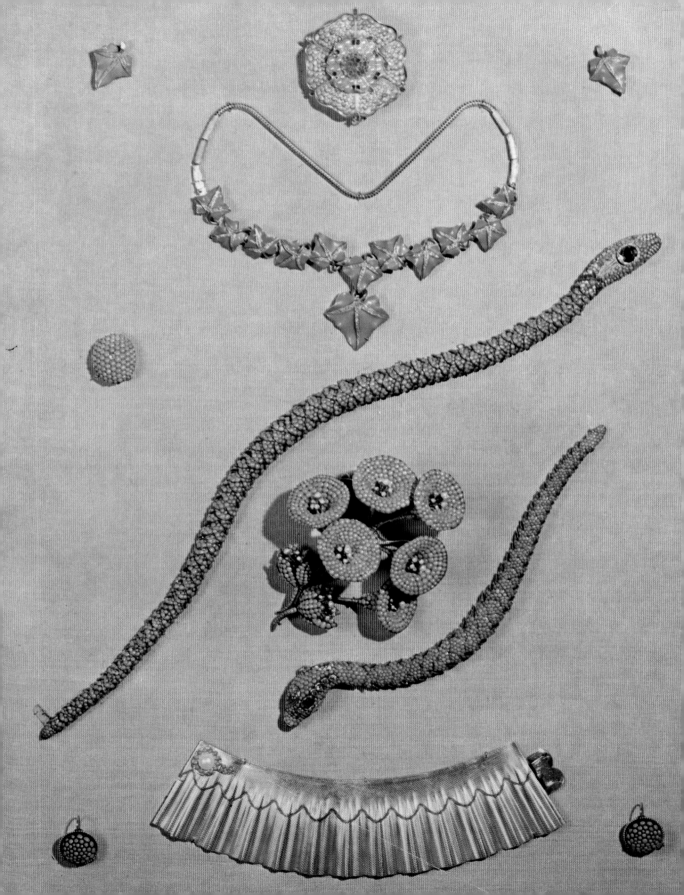

that coral and turquoise jewellery stand out for re-sale. Like turquoise, coral is reasonably soft, is opaque, and can be carved. It has been found in the warm Mediterranean, especially around the coast of Sicily, for thousands of years, and its use goes far back into history. It can be set in its own original shapes, mounted in silver or gold; or alternatively, carved and polished and used as beads. The great Victorian interest in craft, as opposed to art, meant that many ladies were delighted to wear carved coral beads, set as earrings, necklaces or bracelets. Robert Phillips, a London jeweller of the Victorian period, spent so much time encouraging the Italian craftsmen and so popularized coral jewellery in England, that in 1870 the King of Italy decorated him for improving trade in the poor areas around Naples.

Diamonds

During the Victorian age, diamonds were being set more brilliantly than ever. There was, for example, a great deal of knife-edge work, which enabled a jeweller to create a sparkling fall of diamonds so mounted that they looked as if nothing but the thinnest silvery hair held each in place (the fuchsia brooch in Fig. 38 is a fine example). But diamonds were also, for the first time, being set with the "common" gems. Until now a diamond was, as it were, a superior stone either mounted with other diamonds or

A Group of Victorian Turquoise Jewels: wealthy mid-Victorians did not necessarily always rely on a parade of diamonds or on the use of rich dark enamels and deep-coloured gemstones; they found novel stones and a massing of colour almost as effective. Two of the pieces shown here are startlingly clever and surprising: the snake bracelet and the snake necklace, each hinged to lie sleekly about wrist or neck, their wicked heads set with diamonds and furious ruby eyes, their bodies studded all over with matching turquoises. Each jaw is so designed that the snake will grasp its own tail in a vice-like grip when looped about arm or throat. Snake motifs had come into popularity in the neo-classical period—there were obvious Egyptian connections— and Queen Victoria seems to have had a liking for them, though hardly because of the erudite Cleopatra-and-asp connotations which had appealed to her predecessors; perhaps they reminded her of India, a part of her Empire for which she had a particular fondness. Albert gave her at least one ring in the form of a snake, but his own favourite motif was the gently drooping and curling convolvulus—a very large bunch of convolvulus blooms encrusted with turquoises forms the central brooch of this set. It is noticeable that the Victorians do not here attempt to portray an actual convolvulus flower, an actual snake: it is the technique that enthralls them, the novelty, the gay bright colours, the cleverness. With the buoyant and crowded eclecticism of the age, Victorian jewels took some extraordinary forms.

By courtesy of the Trustees of the Victoria and Albert Museum

o   195

occasionally set with the top three gemstones in the hierarchy: rubies, sapphires and emeralds. Now, however, diamonds were mingled with every other stone imaginable. A Victorian design for a basket of flowers or a cornucopia of Nature's bounty would show them all mixed up together, gaily winking and blinking in a kaleidoscope of colour and sparkle.

Enamels

Rich dark jewellery could also be achieved through enamelling. Experts could now enamel anything of almost any shape in almost any colour; by the end of the century Carl Fabergé was to produce a pattern sheet of over a hundred shades. A dark blue was particularly popular. There are examples at the Victoria and Albert Museum of large matching pieces of jewellery enamelled almost navy blue and set with diamonds; and very effective they must have been too. They were not pretty—prettiness was left to the young unmarried girl; they were handsome statements, evidence of highly satisfactory personal finances.

Types of Jewel

Fashions in dress and hair-styles changed so quickly in the first fifty years of Victoria's reign that it is impossible to list the pieces worn without going into a blow-by-blow account cataloguing the endless variations. Generally speaking, the fashionable Victorian lady needed to change her jewels to suit the style of gown and hair. If the hair was drawn back or dressed high, earrings came into favour; if it was looped down over the ears or worn in braids or ringlets, earrings were out of fashion. A high-necked day-dress could be relieved by a long chain of intricate workmanship, made of gold, and often worn with a portrait locket attached. A low-necked evening gown could be set off by a necklace fitting closely about the throat and set with sparkling faceted stones and coloured enamels. If the fashion was for long sleeves, one could wear heavy gold bracelets—perhaps, for evening wear, mounted with coloured gems, diamonds or pearls. In the earlier decades of the Victorian era, women wore rigid bracelets called "bangles" (Fig. 37); later, however, they favoured a wide mesh and heavy stone-set clasps.

THE FLOWER MOTIF

The flower motif had been popular from the earliest times, and never more so than during the early Victorian era. The great blossoming of Victorian Gothic, with its enormous debt to Pugin (page 204), the fondness for Nature which had degenerated from the fierce strangeness of earlier decades into a sentimental prettiness, the Victorian taste for cleverness, preferably combined with nostalgia (a huge chandelier was hung at Osborne, with green glass leaves and pink glass convolvulus flowers, reminding dear Albert of his childhood home in romantic Thuringia): all contributed to the outburst of flowery jewels and trinkets (Fig. 43). There were pretty flowers, curious flowers, garlands of nuts and fruit and leaves delicately enamelled and set with stones. There were single flowers—especially sweet peas, roses and columbines. There were complete jewelled bouquets. Each flower was supposed to be representational, and very often a tiny bee, butterfly or even dragonfly hovered overhead on a *tremblant* spring. Leaves and stalks were enamelled to look "real"; diamonds were used in profusion for dewy glitter. The young unmarried girl might wear a few of these romantic pieces: a brooch designed like a flower and set with unpretentious stones (never, on any account, a display of diamonds), a heart-shaped locket, a branch of coral set in silver; the pretty married matron, like the young queen herself, could deck her hair with a jewelled wreath and pin a jewelled bouquet to her bodice.

Victorian Eclecticism

There were no true artistic innovations in Victoria's long reign, no marked change in creative sympathy. Crafts there were in plenty, though here too, in the mid-decades, between the loss of Albert and the rise of the art nouveau, there was a lack of purpose: a kind of "low pressure zone" of silliness and stereotypes. The development of machinery was fantastic, but creative art gave way to an energetic and determined eclecticism. So much had happened in the nineteenth century to make the ordinary mid-Victorian aware of the past and its importance that each new fashion was taken up and followed slavishly.

CLASSICAL TECHNIQUES

The discoveries made at Pompeii during the French excavations of 1806–14 had excited European jewellers to an exaggerated degree. Until then they had merely been making gold ornaments "in the antique style" with some hopeful Greek key frets, and hardstone or shell cameos. Now, however, they could copy the authentic pieces, and examine the classical artefacts for evidence of the techniques used in their creation. A leader in the field, whose influence cannot be stressed too much, and whose work can fortunately still be seen in abundance in the better jewellers', was Fortunato Pio Castellani.

Castellani

Italians are passionately nationalistic people, often bound by every nerve and sinew to their own particular part of their country. Castellani was just such a person; his family was so fierce in its opinions that both of his sons had to leave Italy because of their political sympathies. Born in 1793, he lived and worked in Rome, an extremely competent and respected goldsmith, and was present in an advisory capacity at the excavations of the Etruscan tombs; his astonished admiration of the finds shaped his whole future life.

Occasional pieces of Etruscan work were found in Italy during the earlier centuries, but only aroused a little local interest; then, in 1827, some tombs were opened at Corneto and some remarkable wall paintings discovered. The Etruscan territory lay on the western coast of Italy, within the loop of the Tiber as it flowed south-west to the sea, in the strip of land stretching, generally speaking, from Elba down to Rome. Other tombs were found: part of the cemetery of the ancient city of Vulci, the Regolini-Galassi tomb at Cerveteri (in 1836), the Campana tomb at Veii (1842), the Grotta dei

Rilievi, again at Cerveteri (in 1850). The jewellery and metalwork found in these tombs were sumptuous, some showing a marked oriental influence: granulated and embossed earrings, for example, shoulder clasps with gold granulated sphinxes, fine gold filigree work.

Many a writer on nineteenth-century jewellery gives the story of how Castellani heard a rumour that there was a family in some remote mountainous area which had never caught up with the nineteenth century and which was still somehow carrying on the ancient Etruscan goldsmithery techniques; and how he searched and searched until he finally discovered them and persuaded them to leave their village and join him in Rome to teach his own employees. It is certainly true that he found some such people, it is even known that they came from San Angelo in Vado, but the thought of any successful Roman goldsmith-cum-archaeologist actually scouring the primitive countryside in person takes a rich imagination; even in the twentieth century it would be questionable. It is a rare Roman who does not send someone to do his work for him.

Castellani had already spent some considerable time studying the ancient Etruscan techniques. Unfortunately we have no original written information about these techniques—or at least, none we can comprehend. Some Etruscan inscriptions do survive, and so does one long liturgical text (wrapped round a mummy in Zagreb), but no one has yet been able to decipher any lengthy passage, although a few dozen words have been translated—among them, significantly, *zamathiman*, "golden brooch". Castellani had, however, been able to read some of the other classical texts on the working of gold—Pliny, for example, and Theophilus—and the work of the Renaissance master, Benvenuto Cellini, and had experimented with their recipes. He had also studied the contemporary filigree-work of Genoa, Malta and India, and the classical jewellery of the Etruscan, Greek and Roman civilizations, meticulously distinguishing between them instead of lumping them all together as "antique". It was necessary for Castellani to take as much trouble as he did because he was determined to be taken seriously as an authentic archaeologist and expert. There were so many fakers of classical jewellery, selling their pieces surreptitiously as originals for enormous sums, that the last thing he wished was to be considered a fraud.

The Etruscans had been virtually working gold in miniature. The degree of fineness they achieved in their granulation and filigree work was almost, but not quite, impossible to recapture. Like Castellani, Cellini too had tried to copy the Etruscan use of minute beads or granules of gold decorating and enriching the surface: a most sophisticated effect. In filigree work, thread-like decorations of gold or silver wire are woven by hand into a pattern like a precious cobweb (later filigree work was machine-made and cast, and is easy to distinguish; Victorian posy-holders were often made of pliant tin from the Combe Martin mines in Devon, stiffened with an alloy and assembled with virtually invisible solder).

Castellani experimented until he had perfected his techniques, using his large collection of authentic pieces as a source of continual inspiration. His reputation in his lifetime was without equal, and has remained so from that day to this. One anonymous nineteenth-century writer and journalist commented on his work in *Notes and Sketches of the Paris Exhibition of 1867*:

"The Castellani exhibit is of a duplex nature. The first category is formed of that wonderfully beautiful 'Etruscan' jewellery, from antique models, in the production of which he has long held the first rank among Continental goldsmiths. The characteristics of this ware I have already described, as accurately as was in my power, in the notice of the goods shown by Mr Phillips of Cockspur Street. Among Castellani's special examples of Etruscan art, the most dominant is a sumptuously worked coronal or diadem of 'dessucated' and 'reticulated' gold—an extraordinary specimen of design and workmanship, which has been purchased by the Earl of Dudley, at the price, I believe, of a thousand guineas. I much doubt whether the intrinsic value of this ornament exceeds a hundred pounds; but there cannot be any cause for complaint in the price asked and paid. The marvellous excellence of the workmanship would warrant the exaction of even a higher price than that quoted.

The second moiety of M. Castellani's display is devoted to a very curious and suggestive collection of the gold and silver ornaments worn by the Italian peasantry and lower middle classes—ornaments which are rarely seen in the shops of fashionable Italian jewellers, but which form the principal stock-in-trade of the dealers who keep the poky little shops on the Ponte Vecchio at Florence, and in that sombre colonnade at the southern foot of the Rialto at Venice. Among the queer coarse trinkets brought together by M. Castellani are great knobbed silver pins not much smaller than life preservers, and others, in the forms of daggers, arrows, anchors and javelins, to transfix the 'back hair' of the Contadini. There are bracelets as heavy as handcuffs, brooches like frying-pans, and lockets as big as hand mirrors. The earrings are especially exorbitant, and of amazing variety of quaint and uncouth design."

This "second moiety" of peasant jewellery was virtually a political statement on Castellani's part. He wanted it known where his sympathies lay. Everyone who had a political conscience was fighting for freedom in nineteenth-century Italy, and he fought as hard as anyone. But his peasant jewellery did not catch the English imagination. England lay too far, in miles and in sympathy, from those sunburnt Roman hills and the hot-blooded people who toiled there. The Victorians might be titillated, even shocked, by heavy elaborate gold earrings and great gold bangles, but they simply did not dare to wear such barbaric splendour.

Castellani's copies and adaptations of Renaissance jewels were not nearly as successful as his Greek and Etruscan jewellery. Perhaps he was too close to them. He was so determined that they should be perfect that they lacked the one ingredient, personality, that one expects from fifteenth- and sixteenth-century jewels. In the Renaissance era a designer knew the person for whom he was designing the jewel, and even, perhaps, the occasion on which the jewel would be worn. Jewellery was caught on the wing, so to speak, brilliant, original and completely personal fantasies made as fast as life was lived. Castellani, on the other hand, was using his brains rather than his emotions. He was making jewels for an ideal, not for a patron. The magic quality was lacking, and this showed.

His Greek and Etruscan work was marvellously classic and cold. He had worked on their techniques for so long that when he made jewellery in the image of theirs it was precise, erudite, small, surprising and perfect. A long stretch in time lay between him and those early craftsmen, giving his work dignity and distance. On each and every occasion, he took it seriously. His adaptations of classic jewels were small and exact and intricate, he seemed to piece them together like jigsaw puzzles from a thousand tiny sections. He worked in small areas of gold, rarely leaving any large space of undecorated metal. Gold was almost always the basis of the jewel, with granulated gold or filigree decoration, a sparing use of enamels, small stones cut *en cabochon* (of the right historical period), and occasionally pearls. When working in this idiom, he made nothing that was vulgar, nothing that was really large. He re-created a school of craftsmen working in the mosaic techniques for which Italy has always been famed.

These mosaics Castellani first saw on the walls and floors of Pompeii. One must stress immediately that wall mosaics are different from those laid underfoot. Ground mosaics are coarser, tougher, less picturesque, more patterned. Wall mosaics were often created to surround fountains, those magic givers of life and symbols of plenty, and were finer, often showing colourful pictorial scenes from mythology.

When Castellani copied these mosaics, he copied them in miniature. Two schools grew up to emulate him: the Roman school, which worked with minute *tesserae* fitted together to create a classically inspired scene; and the Florentine school, creating mosaic jewellery by the far smoother *pietra dura* technique. The *tesserae* method was more correct when one was dealing with work inspired by the classical ruins of Pompeii, but the traditions of *pietra dura* had long been associated with Florence and its stone craftsmen. The Roman school created classical scenes, ruins, temples and gods; the Florentine, further away, concentrated more on the tourist market and, since all tourists were universally interested in motifs drawn from nature, they gave them flowers and leaves, smoothly inserted in a border of granulated gold. The making of mosaic jewellery for the tourist market still persists in these areas of Italy, a hangover from early Victorian times. Nowadays it is about as nasty as it can be, but Castellani's was beautifully made, directly inspired by the newly discovered mosaics, and positively instructive for many people who had never had the opportunity to visit Pompeii for themselves.

Castellani meticulously instructed his two sons in his techniques. Like him, they signed their jewels with two *C*'s in monogram. He trained them well, and they became almost as well known as their father. Augusto, it seems, was more of a designer, and Alessandro the salesman based in England (the British Museum commissioned him to buy for them). Both sons were more than craftsmen; they wrote books, they gave lectures, and when they died, left personal collections of authentic Greek and Etruscan pieces to national museums.

Many a man was influenced by Castellani and his sons: in England, for instance, there were such people as Robert Phillips of Cockspur Street, Carlo Doria, John Brogden, Richard Green and the Giuliano family. Their work can be seen at exhibitions and at the Victoria and Albert Museum in London. It is seriously executed, historically accurate, and technically superb.

The Giuliano Family

Of all the craftsmen perhaps Carlo Giuliano, brilliant and successful, stands out at the head. He was born in Naples, but during the eighteen-sixties, when Italy was going through a particularly turbulent period of her history, Robert Phillips persuaded him to work in England. He died there in 1912; his two sons, Federico and Fernando carried on his business in Piccadilly.

What Carlo Giuliano managed to do was to adapt the classical techniques and designs to suit the Victorian lady. He was not nearly as severe as Castellani had been in his Etruscan work; moreover, he was working later in the century, when the exuberant crinoline was giving way to the bustle, and bolder, more striking jewellery was in vogue. Unlike Castellani, Giuliano combined Etruscan techniques with Renaissance individuality, and always had his customer in mind. There was no working in limbo for him, his was a truly personal service.

Giuliano's work was exceptionally light, delicate and feminine. He used gold as a base, but plenty of enamels too, and white enamels at that. Each jewel was made up of dozens of tiny sections, no more than a quarter of an inch (7 mm) across, contrasting in colour and treatment, linked into a single piece of jewellery but existing as independent creations within it. These tiny sections might be infinitesimal spaces of coloured enamel, or translucent stones polished *en cabochon*. But then he drifted away from the classic traditions by inserting a faceted diamond in a central position, giving a focus which was lacking in Castellani's jewels.

One of Giuliano's most splendid jewels is shown in Fig. 40; another, a really charming "Renaissance" jewel, is at the Victoria and Albert Museum. In the centre is a cameo of Marie de Medici signed by Bissinger. This cameo, in profile on onyx, is Greek in treatment, but carved with a neo-classical technique, to give the effect of colour glowing through a gauzy veiling. The framework of enamelled gold is so infinitely delicate that it looks like a precious cobweb, and pendant from it are two pearls, the upper one circular, the lower one baroque.

In the better jewellers' shops there are still plenty of jewels which were made by the Castellanis or the Giulianos; but they are becoming scarcer as people begin to consider them as works of art, which they are, rather than merely as pieces of Victorian jewellery. During the first half of the twentieth century, when people preferred the glitter of over-exposed stones, jewels of this kind were consigned to safes and not worn; but when people began to evaluate jewellery with a more discerning eye, they came back into demand. Lucky is the woman who has a piece by either of these two great craftsmen.

OTHER STYLES

The imitation of past styles continued unabated throughout the first half of Victoria's reign. The Greek and Etruscan work, the Renaissance styles—exemplified by most delicate copies of adaptations of Holbein designs (Fig. 47, for instance)—coexisted with the Assyrian style, the Celtic style, the Scottish style (Queen Victoria's hand was heavily behind this one). There seemed to be no end to the enthusiasms. Each in turn was eagerly displayed, eagerly bought across the counter, worn as long as the fashion lasted, and then tucked away in the appropriate velvet-lined leather case.

One reason why there is so much Victorian jewellery on the market is that so much was actually produced to keep up with all the changes in dress, hair-styles, and eclectic enthusiasms. Moreover, the type of stone employed was, on the whole, not worth resetting. A carbuncle, for instance, set in textured gold, might well go out of fashion; it was hardly worth having the stone removed and the metal melted down for its intrinsic value—better to wait and see if the old fashion returned later on—after all, modes were spinning like roundabouts. And in any case, the donor would have been hurt had the trinket been altered; and such an act was impossible in so sentimental an era.

Victorian Gothic

The Romantic Movement had flourished at the close of the eighteenth century and the beginning of the nineteenth. Natural scenic beauty had then replaced in favour the earlier cult for the carefully organized "picturesque", and the contemplation of Nature herself became of paramount importance, as can be seen in all the paintings of the time. The instinct which sent people out to visit a famous beauty-spot was the same as that which sent them to worship in church on Sunday, for as they contemplated the beauties of Nature they reminded themselves that her architect was God. The admiring of views and the taking of sketches became a cultivated interest. The fashionable Regency lady, viewing some celebrated burst of country, arranged her thoughts and emotions as painstakingly as if attending church.

The contemplation of Nature, so charged with its own vital presence for the artists and poets of the Romantic era, came gradually to represent a looking-back to a simpler life, serenely untroubled by the complications of the Machine Age. And the past too came to look more and more attractive and worthy: so full of certainty, calmly set apart from the turmoil of the present—though that same present, with its manifold skills and triumphs, could copy and improve the past's techniques.

The Victorian religious instinct was very strong. They discussed every nuance of the moral teachings of the Bible, every possible alternative ritual. (Should the dear children kneel to say their night prayers, Victoria wondered with real anxiety, or might they sit up in bed?) This religious revival was to become one of the most important social and artistic forces of the century, absolutely characteristic of the period and taken up with immense fervour. On the one hand there were the Scots, resenting the system of lay patronage and refusing to accept the queen as head of the Church (she thought them very tiresome on this point); in 1843 nearly five hundred Scottish ministers threw up their livings and formed the Free Church of Scotland. On the other hand there was the Oxford Movement, led by a number of Oxford writers, with Newman, Pusey and Keble prominent among them, which was a High Church Movement within the Anglican Church, intended to revive "the true conception of the relation of the Church of England to the Catholic Church at large" and to show that the true doctrines of the Anglican Faith were those which had been taught in earlier ages. Their *Tracts for the Times*, published between 1833 and 1841, set out their beliefs; and their great deep reverence for the medieval teachers and mystics led them to emulate with fervour the practices of earlier times. No two movements could have been set farther apart in the religious spectrum, yet there was a strong link between them: religion mattered, it had a life of its own distinct from the State, its proper observances—whatever one felt these were—were of vital importance. Victoria herself was a woman of simple piety and wide tolerance (though strict in family observance); like many of her subjects, she had a strong moral sense and a high regard for the liturgy, and liked the thought of a comfortably "established" church, though she had no exaggerated respect for churchmen—religion was very much a family affair, learnt at the parent's knee—and deplored the bigoted outbursts on both sides of the Roman Catholic/ Protestant divide, once remarking in her journal that she had been more moved by the Great Exhibition than by any church service.

The early Victorian architects revived the Gothic style in the teeth of much opposition, but in the honest belief that it had been the greatest period in English history. Perhaps it was because they knew so little about it, on the whole, and enjoyed the treasure-hunt of discovery. Certainly their greatest difficulty was to find suitable medieval churches to copy which were worthy of their ideals. Exteriors had survived, but what they really wanted to find were interior furnishings and decoration. These had almost all been destroyed in the various religious purges that had followed the Reformation: metalwork had been melted down, sometimes being re-cast into simple communion plate; wall paintings had been whitewashed; statues had been smashed. A few fonts and screens had survived, but they were generally damaged and had to be carefully restored, work which demanded a high degree of scholarship.

However, they went ahead enthusiastically, recreating their image of the medieval church: solid clustered columns, elaborate screens, stained glass windows, and intricate carving of stems, leaves and flowers. One of the richest sources was Southwell Minster in Nottinghamshire, with its beautiful thirteenth-century sculptures of leaves, fruit and flowers, showing the piercing exactitude of native medieval work, which was paralleled by the Victorian interest in botany.

In the end, by the late eighteen-seventies, the few genuine examples had been done to death, the early inspiration had evaporated, and the Gothic had become respectable, dull and vulgarized. But in its time, it was a tremendous force, profoundly influenced by the Cambridge Camden Society. Many people came to appreciate a "medieval" style of ceremonial, conducted in a distant chancel beyond a "Gothic" screen—the ritualistic details concealed from the faithful in the nave, which added to the sense of awe—bathed in the rich gloom of stained glass or lit by small dim lamps placed against dark painted walls; perhaps a cloud of incense too, and candles burning in a shrine to the Virgin Mary or twinkling on a gilded "medieval" reliquary. The colours most frequently used were those of the liturgical year: the white, red, violet, green and black which had their place in the elaborate ecclesiastical scheme of colours for the vestments and hangings appropriate to Advent, Christmas, Epiphany and so on. Woven into the same pattern was the music, much of it equally fascinating, and the hymns, specially written for every possible occasion:

> *"Pleasant are thy courts above*
> *In the land of light and love;*
> *Pleasant are thy courts below*
> *In this land of sin and woe."*

It was all awe-inspiring, mystical and emotional, and the High Church Victorian loved every moment of it.

Brighton is filled with churches built during the mid-nineteenth century and inspired by the Oxford Movement. The Church of St. Michael and All Angels is one; another is St. Paul's, built in 1848 by the father of the priest-in-charge, the Reverend

Arthur Douglas Wagner, who several times got into trouble for his Tractarian views. Others can be seen in Yorkshire, where there is a small group either adapted or actually built by George Edmund Street, R.A., St. Peter's Church at Helperthorpe (1871–73) being of especial interest. The architects who built these new churches furnished them too, so that everything was in keeping with the general decorative scheme. Expense was never spared, and these new Victorian Gothic churches were all of a piece, rich, and overpoweringly holy. But in spite of the painstaking research that went into their decoration and furnishing, there is absolutely no question of confusing the genuine with the imitation.

A. W. N. PUGIN

One of the chief protagonists of the Gothic Revival was Augustus Whelby Northmore Pugin (1812–52), son of a French architect. Pugin trained as an architect, but in the course of his career was also an antiquary, a writer, and a designer who designed anything asked of him, from churches to jewellery. He is probably best remembered for his work on the decoration and sculpture of the new Houses of Parliament, in 1836–1837. As a designer, Pugin simply drew up the designs and then put them into the hands of the manufacturer, who carried them out under his supervision. Hardman's of Birmingham, a firm of ecclesiastical metalworkers, normally executed his designs and were eventually persuaded to produce his jewellery as well. His association with them dated back to 1838.

At the age of twenty-three, Pugin was converted to Roman Catholicism, and from then onwards worked mainly, though not exclusively, for the Roman Catholic Church and for Catholic patrons. Throughout his career, his religion was the mainspring of his being.

Jewellery was a difficult subject to fit into the Gothic scheme. Where could Pugin and his followers get their inspiration? All they had to copy were the pieces shown in stained glass windows and in illuminated manuscripts; and of course, the illustrations looked flat and two-dimensional. As a result, no matter how hard they tried, Pugin and his disciples designed jewels which looked old but lifeless. His designs are very light interpretations of medieval inspiration, drawn with a working architect's sense of scale; the manufactured metalwork looks thin and machine-stamped.

Amongst other Pugin jewels on show at the 1851 Exhibition were some pieces made for Jane Knill, who was to be his third wife: a necklace made from nineteen four-lobed sections held together with links and weighted by a pendant cross, a brooch incorporating a mandorla, and a cross with trefoils of pearls at each terminal. The colours of these jewels were very dramatic, and ecclesiastical in tone, with stones *en cabochon* and enamels.

Pugin was largely responsible for the revival of enamelling techniques, which he used for much of his metalwork. He promoted three techniques: *cloisonné* and *champlevé*, which have already been described, and encrusted enamels, which had been used in Renaissance jewellery. In encrusted enamelling, the surface is not engraved; instead the enamels are applied to the surface in high relief. Pugin's encrusted enamels, whether showing flowers, leaves, or other motifs, portrayed the object in its natural colours. The effect is similar to painting, much in the style of Limoges, and was very popular in the nineteenth century. Pugin's enamelled flowers, for instance, had gracefully shaded petals.

Enamelling, which had been out of favour in England for almost two hundred years, had all the charm of novelty, as well as richness, colour, and an agreeably "antique" look—whether Gothic, Renaissance, or Tudor (Tudor styles were known as "Holbeins" and would have surprised Holbein very much indeed). Enamelled jewels had an agreeably rich and heavy look, particularly popular as the century wore on. Jewellery lost the movement and rhythm of the Georgian eras, when diamonds had been set in silver, often on *tremblant* spirals, to create an effect of glittering lightness; it settled down gradually into a static, comfortable calm.

Pugin took such trouble with his designs, and cared so passionately that others should do the same, that in 1848 he produced an influential pattern book of his own, *Floriated Ornament*, which owed much to a German book of 1590, *Eicones Plantarum*, in his possession. This showed Gothic ornament based on natural forms, and traced and identified the plants used in early Gothic architectural decoration. Its effect on the floral jewellery of the period was very great.

In the Victoria and Albert Museum there are some pieces of jewellery which Pugin designed for his third wife, Jane, and created shortly before he died, insane, at Ramsgate in 1852, the year after that triumph of virtuosity, the Great Exhibition, at which his work had been displayed. A set is shown in Fig. 45.

Victorian Sentimentality

The emotion generated by the religious revival, the importance of "feeling", the gentle pervasive nostalgia for the past, the devotion to the family: all these found their expression in the jewellery of the period. Presents of jewels were given for every possible occasion, and just because they were bought for some especial occasion, each was suitably inscribed. This ruined the chances of re-sale, but given the atmosphere of the time, the question of re-sale was purely theoretical anyway. Wedding gifts were engraved, so were christening gifts, so were engagement presents and anniversary presents; and mourning jewels were the most obvious targets of all.

MOURNING JEWELS

For the first time since the Reformation, religious jewellery was being worn openly, as an everyday affair. There have never been so many crosses worn, created from so many different types of materials, and adorning women of so many classes. Religion was not merely respectable, it was important; above all it was a family affair. The family occasions—christening and confirmation, wedding and anniversary—were celebrated with suitable commemorative jewellery: a small cross set with pearls, an engraved bangle, a locket. But the supreme occasion on which religion and family met together was the death bed, and mourning jewellery was at the height of its vogue.

Never before had there been a time when the ordinary woman in the street could so closely copy the monarch's dress and jewels. When the queen was widowed in the December of 1861, she draped herself in mourning; naturally the court followed suit, that was *de rigueur*; but so did almost all the country. For a time at least, the woman in the street chose voluntarily to deck herself in mourning jewellery; and though formal mourning for the Prince Consort did eventually end, the fashions set for widowhood endured and were stringently followed. Etiquette was rigid: the period of full mourning, the jewels that might be worn in half-mourning, the depth of black edging on one's writing paper, all were strictly observed. One London shop, Jay's, founded in 1841, sold *nothing* but mourning attire. Whitby jet came into fashion and its popularity lasted for decades.

Jet

Jet has been in use for decoration for thousands of years: Pliny (A.D. 23–79) refers to it, as does the Venerable Bede (A.D. 673–735). A very ancient ring, possibly carved during the Roman occupation, was discovered in a cairn in the parish of Inchinnan in 1753, and was preserved at East Kilbride as an inestimable specific in diseases "more valuable than many tons weight of medicine". Magical and medicinal properties have long been attributed to jet: Ibnu'l Baitar, one of the most important Arabic writers on stones, wrote that it would drive away venomous beasts; a late thirteenth-century manuscript at Pembroke College, Cambridge (MS. 87, fol. 193) recommends it as an anaesthetic; and Marbode, Bishop of Rennes from A.D. 1067–81, examined it fully in his lapidary.

What is jet? A form of driftwood. Like coal, it is a hard substance formed by the decaying of vegetation over hundreds and hundreds of years. The wood has lain for centuries in stagnant water, gradually rotting, and finally flattened by enormous pressure. The deeper it is found, the harder it is. Scrape a piece of jet with a knife, and you can clearly see the annual rings in the pale-brown wood that lies beneath the black surface. If you put a piece of worked jet on to a cloth or sheepskin and rub it with a paste made from its own dust and some drops of fine oil, it will again assume its deep black shine. If you break a piece, the room will fill with the smell of oil.

The best English jet is found in the cliffs near Whitby on the east coast, generally in wedge-shaped horizontal seams which are from an inch to six inches thick (from 25 mm to 150 mm). The strata lie below the alum rock and above the ironstone. They are hewn from the cliffs with handpicks—and all too often a rich-looking seam is a tease, which quickly dies away into commoner rock. Because of the geological changes in the area, however, by no means all the jet lies in cliff-face seams, and old Victorian jet workings can be found some distance from the sea.

It was a totally unmethodical industry. The jet was mined and taken into Whitby, where the dealers sold it to the manufacturers. Some had quite large factories, others ran a one-man business. The work was exceptionally dusty, because the jet had to be ground, and exceptionally dirty too, because it had then to be polished; and the craftsmen must have looked very grimy in their blue smocks. None the less, during the nineteenth century they also looked very cheerful indeed, for there was plenty of work to be done. Queen Victoria took an especial interest in the Whitby jet industry and wore many of the fashion accessories they created, and naturally other ladies followed her example. The Whitby workshops turned out carved beads for necklaces and rosaries, cameo rings, brooches, bracelets and earrings, ornaments for the hair, and delicate falling fringes. When the queen plunged into mourning, she naturally wore more jet than ever; and not only did she take it up, but so did some of the courts of Europe.

Jet had many advantages. It was dark and glittery, so useful for mourning jewellery, relatively cheap, and splendid for the craftsman (as opposed to the artist). In time some magnificent edifices were created, with carved foliage hung with carved fruit, on which perched the most delicately carved birds, butterflies and insects. Probably the best things made, however, were the small jet busts of serious politicians.

At the height of Whitby's success, in 1870, a completely different type of jet was introduced from Spain: this was a hard brittle easy-to-fracture glass imitation. France too exported a new type of "jet": first black wax covered with glass, then black glass mounted on stamped black metal backs. The Whitby industry was unprepared for this piracy, and between this and the sudden change of fashion the jet trade died out by the turn of the century.

There is still a museum at Whitby which has some fascinating examples of the jet craft; and fashion being the ephemeral will-o'-the-wisp that it is, the vogue may even yet revive and the old workshops be opened again. In the meantime it is worth considering collecting jet. It was an historic craft, indigenous to Britain, and clever examples can still be found; the search for them is itself intriguing.

SOUVENIR JEWELLERY

The Victorian taste for commemorative jewellery did not stop at mourning jet and engraved anniversary presents. There was a great liking for souvenir jewellery, especially novelties. Ladies too were touring Europe now, and they liked to bring back something to prove to the stay-at-homes how fascinating and enjoyable it had been and to remind them of all that they had seen. (The Countess of Arundel had accompanied her husband and Inigo Jones on some of their Italian journeys in the early seventeenth century; they brought back classical marbles; she, with a liking for the novel any Victorian traveller would have approved, brought back a gondola.)

They bought coral cameos from Naples, cameos carved from the lava of Mount Vesuvius, shells carved in Rome, mosaic jewels from Rome and Florence, "authentic" pieces of Etruscan or Greek goldwork. Ivory lockets came from China, pure silverwork from the Far East, and tigers' claws set in gold from India. (These last pieces must have looked curiously incongruous set upon some maiden aunt's shoulder; but she no doubt treasured them for their rarity, they looked different from the trinkets less fortunate ladies were wearing, they made her feel important in her own right, a "somebody"; and, of course, she treasured them for the sake of the donor, a dear soldier-nephew serving the queen.) Women brought home jewellery from their own "expeditions", showing off the fact that they, like their menfolk, were cultured and educated: cairngorms set in silver from a sketching holiday in the queen's beloved Scotland; "Scotch" pebbles or fresh-water pearls from a geological tour; pieces of Irish bog-oak set in Wicklow gold from a sightseeing tour in Ireland; copies of the Tara Brooch which had been found there in 1850. It was a striving and reaching out as adventurous in its way as any of the grand explorations which sent determined Victorians pacing across the continents, apparently without much concern for anything that got in their way, intent on discovering something—anything—new.

COMMEMORATIVE JEWELLERY

Whereas many of her subjects bought their jewellery across the counter, relying on inscriptions to give it individuality—adding, perhaps, a small photograph to a heart-shaped locket, or mounting a wisp of childish hair in a brooch—Victoria and Albert could commission jewels which were specially designed to commemorate an occasion. Victoria had an amazing taste for commemorative jewellery: in 1857, for example, she was presented with a diamond brooch (she did not actually commission this, but she had a good deal of say in its design) which was shaped like the entrance to the Mersey Tunnel opened by herself. In 1845 Albert designed a jewel which was made up by Garrards as his anniversary gift to her in February 1846: made of engraved and frosted gold, porcelain and enamel, so incredibly delicate that it looked as if it would collapse at a touch (it is still, however, in existence), it was a wreath of "orange blossom"—she had worn sprigs in her hair at their wedding; in delicate allusion to the fruits of their marriage, four small enamelled oranges were incorporated. (This allusion was, indeed, so delicate that the expected arrival of a fifth "orange", the Princess Helena, born three months after the anniversary, was not indicated.) This feeling for commemoration, for family affections and harmony, for nostalgia, pervades Victorian jewellery, though few surviving pieces are as charmingly personal as this wreath, created in celebration of a true union of sentiments.

Victorian Jewellery Exhibits

The settings in the Victorian Gallery at the Victoria and Albert Museum are curiously unsympathetic because the items displayed there are all in pristine condition; most of them were designed and made for the Great Exhibition and were transferred to the museum as soon as it was built. They have never been used, nothing is bent or chipped or dented or cracked, it is all in splendid condition and, naturally, overpowering. The cosiness of the Victorian age, exemplified in the room settings of the Castle Museum at York—with the dog in its basket, the child's doll, the fretwork on the pianoforte—is somehow lacking. The jewels, however, are most beautifully displayed in the Jewellery Gallery at the Victoria and Albert Museum.

A great deal of Victorian jewellery survives today and is, indeed, perpetuated. "It looks like something Granny used to have—*dear* Granny." "It reminds me of the locket Great-Aunt Kate left me, the one I lost, she would have liked me to replace it." No new forms were evolved, no new ways of wearing jewellery; yet Victorian trinkets had, it seemed, an appeal of their own, apparently fragile but in reality as tough as the Victorians themselves.

The Great Exhibition

Family Feeling—The Great Exhibition—An Unending Harvest

Family Feeling

Our image of middle-class Victorian England is one of pious Pugin's Gothic churches packed with dutiful church-going folk, fathers and mothers, children and servants. The Sunday procession forms: wife and aunts in their "best" clothes and finest daytime jewellery, children and nursemaids and governess paraded like so many noughts in a bank account, the man of the household strutting proudly ahead like a major-domo showing off his tangible assets: and all, once in their pews, singing that most Victorian-seeming of hymns:

> *"From Greenland's icy mountains,*
> *From India's coral strand,*
> *Where Afric's sunny fountains*
> *Roll down their golden sand,*
> *From many an ancient river,*
> *From many a palmy plain,*
> *They call us to deliver*
> *Their land from error's chain—"*

and then home again to roast beef and Stilton, perhaps giving sixpence to an old soldier by the churchyard gate.

With hindsight it looks constricting and sad, but it gave many people a sense of belonging that they do not know today. Family feeling was a great glue of stability, a stability which was the foundation of confidence, and on this confidence they created their great British Empire, in poignant contrast to the uncertainty and instability of later eras.

The Empire was not all that great in the beginning, the economic stability of each new acquisition had to be built up slowly, and one of the surest ways of doing this was by the promotion of Empire trade. Britain imported goods for use in her factories and in her homes, but apart from these there were also Empire luxuries such as valuable gemstones: pearls and turquoises from India, moonstones and sapphires from Ceylon, opals from the newly discovered opal fields in Australia, diamonds and gold from South Africa. It was no coincidence that Victoria wore so many of these stones and sent others as presents to her relatives; her use of them was copied throughout court and country, and the Empire grew wealthy as a result.

The Great Exhibition

The deeper one delves into the history of the Great Exhibition, the more one realizes what an extraordinarily dramatic event it was, entirely in keeping with the spirit of the age. So very much went into its staging, and even more came out of it in results. It was the success story of the century: bold, enterprising, a carefully calculated risk involving thousands of people and, indeed, thousands of pounds.

The 1851 Great Exhibition was the very first international exhibition to be staged in England, but it was not by any manner of means a complete plunge in the dark. As a preliminary exercise Prince Albert and his collaborator, Henry Cole, put on a National Exhibition in 1847; it drew twenty thousand visitors, so the next year they staged another, which drew seventy thousand, and the year after that a third which pulled in a hundred thousand. The English, liking novelties, curious, and eager for self-improvement, seemed to be taking to the idea; the prince and Cole decided to risk a full-scale international affair.

Prince Albert was enormously hard-working, as often as not he was up at five in the morning to get on with the organization—for he was on every one of the three hundred and thirty Exhibition committees. He was vastly practical and painstakingly meticulous, in a thoroughly Germanic way, and was prepared to take on all the risks of this, the first-ever international exhibition to be held in England.

Cole, a man of powerful vision, was perfectly confident that British could be Best. He helped Rowland Hill to launch the penny postal service, he was involved in the introduction of standard gauge railway tracks, he set up the Royal College of Music, built the Albert Hall, and was in overall control of the affairs of the Victoria and Albert Museum for twenty years; yet today he is forgotten.

The most remarkable feature in the organizing of the Exhibition was the speed with which it was done. They did not decide to have one at all until June 1849. The prince and Cole decided on the title:

THE GREAT EXHIBITION
OF THE WORKS OF INDUSTRY OF ALL NATIONS
1851

and on the site; they first chose Leicester Square, but then, soon realizing how enormous the Exhibition was going to be, agreed on Hyde Park instead (there were protests from the riders in Rotten Row). They also decided to allocate half the available space to Britain and the Empire, and the other half to foreign nations; to forbid smoking. dogs, alcohol and Sunday opening (it was a *very* improving Exhibition); and to vary the entrance fees to suit all purses. And they decided on the date for the opening ceremony: May 1, 1851, two years ahead.

The committees were set up and the work began. So did the arguments. Critics and newspapers set upon the prince and Cole with a viciousness far greater than any twentieth-century "comment". The greatest objections were about the choice, and

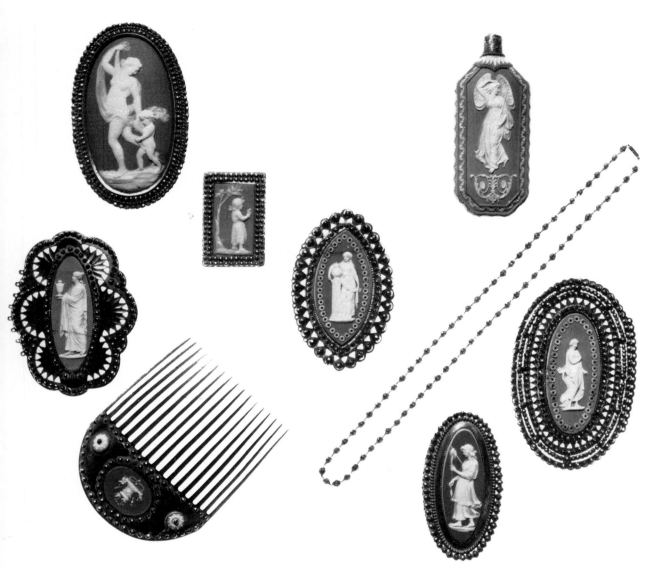

Fig. 41: A selection of early Wedgwood "jewellery" in jasper ware and cut-steels, from the Wedgwood Museum at Barlaston. The steel comb to the lower left, with three blue and white jasper ware cameos mounted in cut-steel, is marked *Wedgwood*, and was made in 1786; it is 4″ long. This comb, the cut-steel necklace, and the six Wedgwood medallion brooches were all mounted by Matthew Boulton in about 1790. The scent bottle to upper right, in pale blue and dark blue jasper ware, is marked *Wedgwood 1785*. Wedgwood had successfully produced the white body for jasper ware by 1776, and put it quickly into production, but at this early period he only used it for cameos, seals and small portraits, since further investigation and experiment were necessary before larger masses could be fired with safety. Undercutting preceded firing; and after firing the ware was put through a lapidary process for polishing.

As with all Wedgwood's ware, these designs are breath-takingly accurate. His precision and craftsmanship brought classical culture within the range of the more modest incomes.

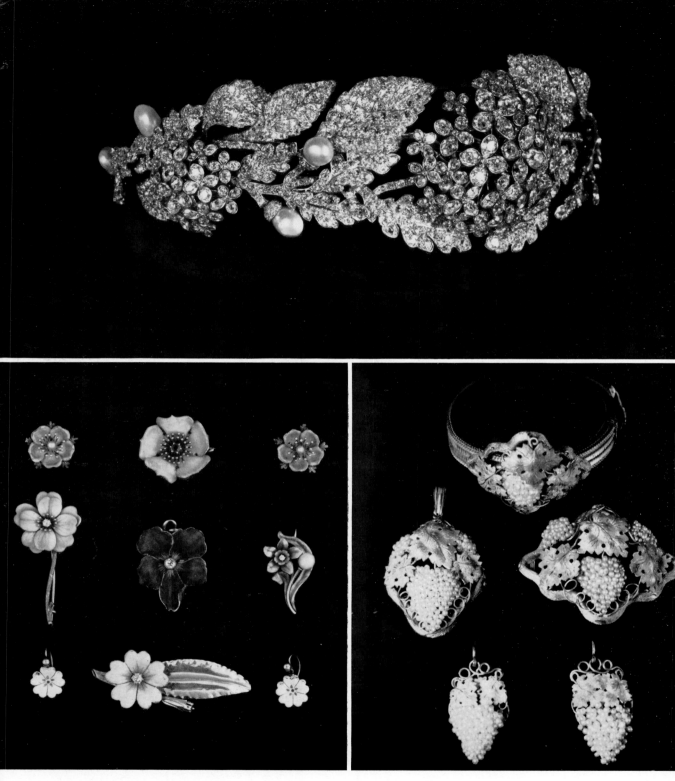

Fig. 42: A diamond tiara, early 19th century, worn low across the brows. *Fig. 43:* Some 19th century enamelled work exhibited a fresh and delicate naturalism. *Fig. 44:* A *demi-parure*, dating from 1830, in seed pearls with a vineleaf motif—both popular at the period.

Fig. 45: "Gothic" jewellery by A. W. Pugin, exhibited at the Great Exhibition of 1851, now in the Victoria and Albert Museum; though technically clever, accurately made up by Hardman & Co., it completely lacks the vigorous and vital craftsmanship of true Gothic.

Some Victorian jewels: the *rivière* shown in *Fig. 46* (facing page, above) and the brooch-pendant in *Fig. 48* (facing page, below right) show the floridness characteristic of many mid-Victorian pieces, which had to be designed to show up against a background of frilled, tucked, shirred, draped and embroidered fabrics, often in rich dark colours. For much of this era the emphasis was on the skirt, and jewels such as these, with bright over-exposed stones, would also have helped to balance the fuss of crinoline or bustle. *Fig. 47* (facing page, below left) illustrates the tremendous eclecticism of the era. New styles were constantly appearing —the Gothic, for example, or the Scottish, or, as here, the Tudor. This is a "Holbein" pendant and chain, dating from 1850, enamelled and set with emeralds, pearls and diamonds: it would have surprised Holbein very much indeed. The brooches shown above in *Fig. 49* are all tiny—about the size of postage stamps. They illuminate the sentimentality of an era which cherished keepsakes and souvenirs. This set of brooches is now in the Victoria and Albert Museum.

Fig. 50: Towards the end of the eighteenth century, and throughout the nineteenth, technical advances, changes in social structure, and the expansion of trade, all helped to bring jewellery within the reach of the middle classes. Illustrated here are six modestly priced Victorian pieces, each with a butterfly motif. None of them are set with gemstones—that would have sent the price soaring; instead they depend for their effect on craft and cleverness and the play of light on metal. The pinchbeck and porcelain bracelet dates from about 1840, the lower of the silver bangles from 1865; the flexible bracelet was gradually to increase in popularity during the period, while the rigid bangle correspondingly declined. The silver drop earrings were made in about 1875. The two cut-steel brooches illustrate the great popularity of this craft, which was at its height in the early decades of the century but persisted none the less into Victoria's reign. The lightness and femininity of Regency cut-steel work, which was essentially a metal-working craft carried out in miniature, was gradually lost as the heavier Victorian styles of design were introduced.

Fig. 51: A "prospector's" brooch, dating from the period when great deposits of opal were found in Australia. This one is of textured gold, with the Australian states in different shades of opal, and is believed to have been made in about 1875 (here seen twice the actual size).

Fig. 52: Mid-Victorian richness and expertise are immediately apparent in this flexible gold bracelet set with a floral motif of large emeralds and diamonds, separated by black enamels. The motif can be detached and worn separately as a pendant.

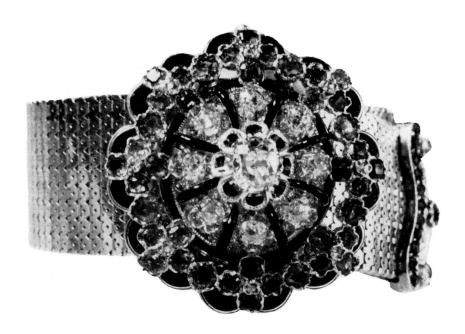

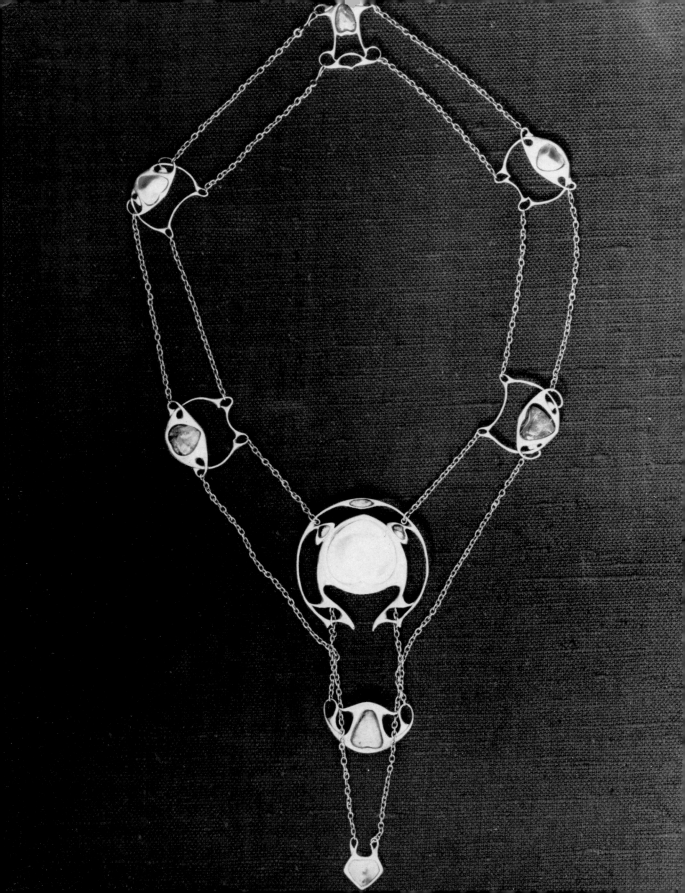

Fig. 53: The delicacy of the hand-set necklace on the facing page, created by the Art Nouveau craftsman Archibald Knox, was in deliberate stark contrast to the huge lustrous ropes of pearls and the formal brooches bristling with diamonds set in platinum that were worn at the Edwardian Court. Turning against machine-made settings, duplicated designs, a blaze of gemstones and a deliberate display of wealth, the Art Nouveau craftsmen-designers in England—often anonymous—produced individual and feminine jewels like this necklace, beautifully made, understated, and echoing, in the fluidity and relative simplicity of their design, the new eagerness to adapt Japanese art forms to a European context.

Fig. 54: The dragonfly brooch shown above is set with opals, diamonds and garnets, and dates from about 1890. Opals were extremely popular towards the end of Queen Victoria's reign, though her successor, Queen Alexandra, disliked them, and they therefore went out of Court fashion after the turn of the century. The dragonfly pre-figures the Edwardian popularity of insect motifs and the coming division between a formal blaze of diamonds and pearls for evening wear and smaller lighter jewels for daytime wear—some of them neat and sophisticated, others sportive "joke" pieces—glittering against pale floating fabrics or accentuating the more severe tailored styles.

Pearls were very popular during the Edwardian era, and fresh-water pearls in particular suited the soft floating fabrics in their delicate Edwardian shades of cream and ivory, lavender and grey and off-white. At the turn of the century, over a hundred pearl-fishers were working the Tay in Scotland; by 1972 there was only one, Bill Abernethy, seen above in *Fig. 55*. The method he uses in fishing for mussels in the river-bed is essentially the same as that used for two thousand years or more. The soft subtle sheen of fresh-water pearls can be seen in the modern brooch in *Fig. 56:* made by Messrs. Cairncross of Perth.

In contrast, the Art Deco jewels of the twenties and thirties were deliberately bright and crisp, often angular in design. Two brooches and a pair of earclips are shown on the facing page. The brooch illustrated in *Fig. 57* is an aquamarine set in diamonds, dating from about 1925. Beside it, in *Fig. 58,* is the Varney & Batt brooch, exemplifying the craftsmanship and style of the mid-thirties. Made up of diamonds and emeralds set in platinum, with a fine lunette diamond in the centre, it is boldly geometric in design, the apex of the triangle being accentuated by perfectly matched full swinging bars of calibre emeralds. The ruby and diamond mulberry earclips in *Fig. 59* date from about 1930. Like the brooches, they are bold, dramatic, glittering, and completely impersonal.

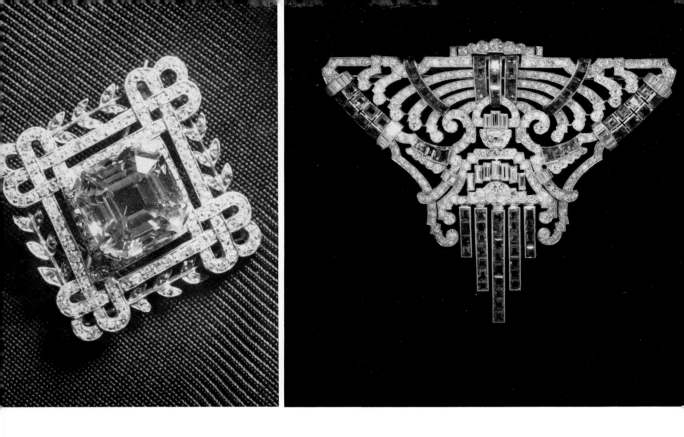

Fig. 57 (above, left), an Art Deco aquamarine and diamond brooch, Fig. 58 (above, right), the Varney & Batt brooch, and Fig. 59, a pair of Art Deco earclips, are all described in more detail on the facing page.

Fig. 60: John Donald's sculptured brooch with its unconventionally-cut green tourmalines suspended in cavities accentuated by brilliant-cut diamonds, incorporates all the vigour and craftsmanship of the best modern work, making it far more alive than any Georgian *tremblant* earring.

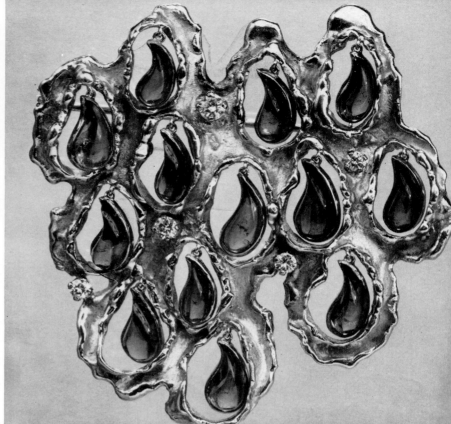

Fig. 61: This pin, designed by Gilian Packard and consisting of a delicate crystal of rose-quartz framed in gold fronds, each tipped by a marquise diamond, won a De Beers Diamonds-International Award in 1964; it exemplifies the sense of movement and life, and the feeling for the crystalline, that characterizes much of the finest present-day work.

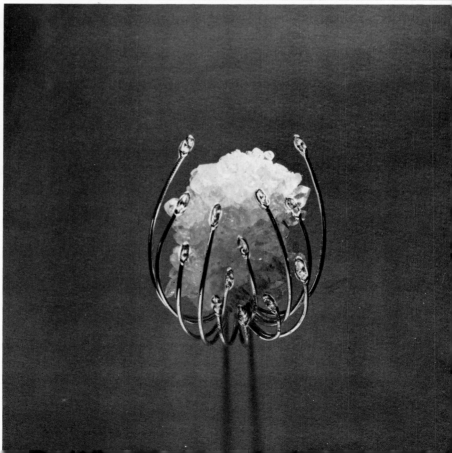

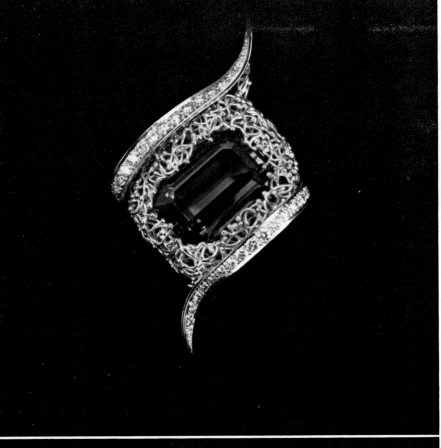

Fig. 62: Many modern jewellers, asked to set a large rectangular stone for a patron, are faced with the difficulty of bringing it to life. Lawrence Wheaton does it brilliantly in this brooch: the central peridot is set in yellow gold, with diamonds in a flowing sweep of white gold.

Fig. 63: A flower-like ring created by an exceptionally fine goldsmith-jeweller. David Thomas uses yellow gold, preferring its warmth, set with brilliant-cut diamonds. His designs, like this one, often create images reminiscent of some mysterious undersea life. Although they look so delicate, his jewels are miracles of lilliputian engineering.

Some of the techniques used by Richard Bonehill and Lynne Bradshaw are shown in the group of small personal jewels illustrated above in *Fig. 64*. The polished yellow gold of the brooch contrasts with the twisted yellow gold wire used in the ring on the left and with the enamelled gold in the flower ring on the right. This deliberate experimenting with textures extends to the gemstones, which range from the faceted citrines and spherical pearls set in the brooch to the echoing striations of the large round rhodocrocite set in the left-hand ring. These pieces show a versatility of technique and an originality of design perfectly suited to the creation of individual jewels commissioned by private patrons, as well as the making of competition pieces, medallions, enamelled badges of office, and so on.

The brooch shown above in *Fig. 65* is a sparkling, lively jewel by Frances Beck and Ernest Blyth. It is clean-cut but totally harmonious. The unconventionally-cut diamonds are so set that they create a sense of depth, a feeling of varying levels. Like so many of the finest twentieth century designs created in the applied arts, this one is built up on an architectural form. Here, in a tiny jewelled space, mathematical concepts are accurately carried out in miniature. The brooch has pace and style. It is not simply a crisp geometrical piece of decoration; instead it has depth, vigour and balance.

Fig. 66: Another award-winning jewel characterized by the present-day feeling for depth and curling, living fronds of metal. It is made in yellow gold and set with brilliant-cut diamonds.
Jane Allen, its creator, won her first Diamonds-International Award in 1971.

Fig. 67: Susan Barfield designed this award-winning necklace when she was still a student. It is a magnificently individual design, the fluid gold strands rippling round the neck, spraying up like water against the throat, and spreading bib-like down across the breast. The watery effect is heightened by the small diamonds with which it is set.

size, of the site—sixteen acres! It would be larger than Buckingham Palace! There were other criticisms too, especially financial, and the prince had to organize private guarantors to cover the cost.

The building itself was one of the greatest headaches, especially because of fire risks and lighting problems. Then Joseph Paxton produced a master stroke. Bearing in mind his designs for the revolutionary Chatsworth conservatory of 1837, he designed a vast soaring creation of steel and glass. But he was truly inspired in refusing to submit his design to any one of the many committees (who would surely have thrown it out); instead he arranged for it to be printed in *The Illustrated London News*, so that the general public could judge it. They went wild about it. Everyone thought it was absolutely brilliant, the building committee was virtually forced to commission it, and *Punch* christened it "The Crystal Palace", a name which stuck.

In August 1850, nine months before it was to be officially opened, they laid the concrete foundations. By September the first columns were up, and by the end of January 1851 the construction was complete, although the floors had still to be laid, the galleries erected, and so on; and on May 1, 1851, in pink, silver and diamonds with a "little crown", Queen Victoria opened the Exhibition dead on time, to the accompaniment of cheering, organ music and, of course, the Hallelujah Chorus. Winterhalter's *May the First* served a double duty, commemorating both the opening of the Exhibition and the birthday of the baby Prince Arthur, just one year old. The queen wrote:

> "This day is one of the greatest and most glorious days of our lives, with which to my pride and joy, the name of my dearly beloved Albert is for ever associated! It is a day which makes my heart swell with thankfulness."

She continues for page after page with the most minute details of the journey to the Exhibition, what the family wore, what they all did, ending rather endearingly with the words:

> "Was rather tired, but we were both too happy and full of thankfulness for everything."

The Exhibition was open for under six months, but it made a solid profit of £186,000 and a name for itself for ever. In those months over six million people came to wonder and stare; Mr. Cook organized special excursions, and London was crammed with visitors, from overseas buyers to families up from the country to see what Britain and her empire had achieved. There was an amazing variety of exhibits, ranging from the Sportsman's Penknife made by Rodgers and Company—with a multiplicity of eighty blades—to the Medieval Court fitted out by Mr. Pugin. The canoes and furs from Canada intrigued the whole family, and the imports from China astonished them— such a lack of progress! They saw foreign buyers ordering the goods the British had made. They saw their own manufactures competing on equal terms with the goods, machinery and technology of the rest of the world. They saw the riches of the empire. In spite of its tremendous international outlook, the Exhibition was still a family affair, with the people of Britain and her empire united under their queen and confidently taking on all comers.

Victoria went many times, in order to be sure she saw everything, and worked her way steadily through the displays of the different countries. She put her finger on the pulse when she wrote in her journal on July 16:

"After lunch we went to the Exhibition. . . . The whole of the Indian section beginning with the rare products—including the splendid jewels and shawls, embroideries, silver bedsteads, ivory chairs, models, is of immense interest, and quite something new for the generality of people, these latter articles having hitherto only come over as presents to the Sovereign."

Among the exhibits was the Koh-i-Noor diamond which disappointed everyone because it was badly cut and lacked fire. The engraving in the catalogue shows it lying on a velvet cushion inside a parrot's cage, on top of which rested a replica of the Imperial State Crown.

The comments made on the exhibits were tart and to the point. The queen's cradle, carved in Turkey boxwood by W. G. Rogers, was put on show:

"A most dainty and delicate piece of workmanship; he must, however, be on his guard against his finikin tendencies: the lime tree and boxwood doubtless invite detail, but the British oak is not to be tickled with penknives."

Even Pugin's Medieval Court had fairly rough treatment:

"The illustration of a style of decoration now almost totally neglected except in Roman Catholic churches. . . . On his entrance the visitor was struck with the awe which is so often felt in a sanctuary; the place was, as it were, set apart from the rest of the Exhibition, looking dark and solemn for the display of the taste and art of dead men."

Apart from the Koh-i-Noor, the Hope diamond was also on display, and a huge lump of gold from California. The jewellery exhibits included the jewels Lemmonier had created for the Queen of Spain—a tiara of sapphires and diamonds, a brooch of pink pearls and diamonds, a bracelet and head ornament of emeralds and diamonds. Victorian jewels were always imposing, but court jewels such as these were positively spectacular. Astonished families gazed at the costly fan (over £1,000) made by Duvelleroy for the Emperor of Morocco and studded with gems; the jewelled hawk belonging to the Duke of Devonshire, its wings and body covered with rubies, turquoises and emeralds, and a golden loving cup nestling in its plumage to commemorate the ending of a Dutch feud; the Indian exhibits, which included the Lahore diamond, two necklaces of oriental pearls, a necklace of gold and rubies, a coat of cloth of gold with pearl epaulettes and gold embroidery overlaid with pearls and rubies and emeralds, a girdle of gold studded with huge emeralds; and the high spot, a carved ivory throne presented to the queen by the Rajah of Travancore, used by Prince Albert in the closing ceremony. The illustrated catalogue is fortunately preserved at the Victoria and Albert Museum, and there is also a fascinating descriptive booklet by Charles Gibbs-Smith.

An Unending Harvest

The Exhibition was a miracle of ingenuity and contrivance and organization; what they did with the profit was a still greater one, benefitting later generations even more than the Exhibition itself had benefitted its contemporaries. They bought eighty-seven acres of land in South Kensington, and there they built the Victoria and Albert Museum, the Science Museum, the Natural History Museum and the Geological Museum. Then they went further still, building the Imperial College of Science and Technology (which incorporates the Royal College of Science, the Royal College of Mines, and the City and Guilds Engineering College), the Royal College of Art and the Royal College of Music. They invested what was left so well that over the years about £1,800,000 has been given away in scholarships and bursaries, and there is still a capital of £900,000 and a sizeable annual income. None of it would have come to pass without the vision of Albert and Cole, and the supreme Victorian confidence in British ability and British products. The Albert Memorial, as staunchly confident as the prince himself, showed him holding the catalogue of his Great Exhibition; and when a year after his death a new international exhibition was opened, Mr. Tennyson celebrated the memory of the original inspirer:

> "*Where Science, Art, and Labour have outpour'd*
> *Their myriad horns of plenty at our feet.*
> *O silent father of our Kings to be,*
> *Mourn'd in this golden hour of jubilee,*
> *For this, for all, we weep our thanks to thee!*"

CHAPTER TEN

The Art Nouveau

Introduction—The Japanese Influence—The Paris Style: René Lalique—
The Art Nouveau in French Jewellery—The Art Nouveau in British
Jewellery—Ruskin, the Pre-Raphaelites, William Morris—British Art
Nouveau Jewellers—Liberty's—The *Avant-Garde* Woman—Summing-up

Introduction

By the mid-Victorian period, the consolidation of the prosperous middle class had
created an expanding market for consumer goods from all over Europe, mass-produced
by machine to satisfy the rising demand.

The machine was becoming the master, stamping out a hundred articles in the time
it would take an artist/craftsman to produce one. It stood to reason that this brought
down prices, and resulted in a far greater volume of products, well within the reach of
a great mass of the population. The charm and vitality of hand-carved decoration
could now be purchased by the yard, flawlessly reproduced. This perfection of finish
was itself a novelty, for the products of decorative arts displayed in the modern museums
are in general the best of their kind; in reality much contemporary work was poorly
finished, uneven, and badly matched. To be able to buy a set of anything, from tea-
spoons to chairs, which was exact, perfectly made, and not prohibitively expensive, was
a revelation. Why then should anyone take the retrograde step of preferring uneven and
poorly finished work just because it was hand-made? Most of the craftsmen were working from the same pattern books anyway, and thus creating nothing that was really
original.

This was also, of course, true of machine-made goods in the nineteenth century. No
original new designs were being produced for the machine-made product; instead
designers ferreted away, adapting those of the past. Every single period was relentlessly
examined, and any appealing decorative motifs were copied and slapped on to nineteenth-century work, generally without any pause to consider what one was doing or
why—merely making quite sure there was enough to make a good show. Strip any
"Gothic" wardrobe of its applied decoration, and you have nothing left but a plain
solid oblong box.

A few critics did warn that a dangerous gap was opening between art and industry,
and condemned the low standards of design. Writing in 1852, Matthew Digby-Wyatt
contrasted classical work with contemporary examples in his *Metalwork and Its Artistic*

Design, and scorning "those heavy bracelets, simulating uncomfortable snakes or ponderous fetters, and earrings decorated with unmeaning shellwork" wrote:

> "If the mechanical facilities of production are perfectly comprehended in the present day, an almost total ignorance of the just principles of special design is no less generally prevalent."

The machine had come to stay, and this being so, men of vision pointed out that new forms and materials should be devised for, rather than in opposition to, the machine, thus dividing goods into two separate categories: those made by machine because the consistent standard of machine performance suited the design of the product, the material used, and the purpose the product was to fulfil; and those made by hand because machinery could not achieve the same results as the craftsman—yet, at least.

In the art world it was a trying time. Fewer and fewer artists, designers and sculptors could find a reasonable amount of work to do; they were forced to turn to other employment. Original sculptures could now be reproduced by the Collas process in scaled-down copies made in almost any material, especially gilt bronze—every fashionable drawing-room in Europe had its small bronzes littering tables and desks, and most of the "modern" electric lights were perched on sculptural reproductions; original sculpting commissions were harder and harder to come by. In the other arts a similar situation prevailed. To a certain extent this sifted talent, since only the most determined struggled on, but the future was a depressing prospect for them all.

And then, astonishingly, men found a new source of inspiration which fitted perfectly into the spirit of the time with its eager interest in novel other cultures and its enthusiastic imitation of their forms.

Japanese art arrived.

The Japanese Influence

In A.D. 1637 Japan had closed her doors to foreigners and refused exit permits to her nationals as a result of a civil uprising against brutality and misrule in which many of the Christian population unfortunately joined. The insurgents hoped for foreign help: instead they were slaughtered, and any possible foreign influence firmly and finally ended. (A Portuguese embassy was sent in 1640 to re-open contacts, and the greater part of its members executed to discourage further attempts; it was an effective warning.) Only one nation, the Dutch, was allowed to retain a trading post on one of the off-shore islands, thus keeping Europe and Japan in very precarious touch with one another. A few pieces of decorative art did find their way to Europe via the Dutch traders, and were promptly confused with Chinese art by the Europeans. On the whole Japan rested in isolation, developing her arts and her crafts in strict seclusion. But at the end of the eighteenth century and the beginning of the nineteenth, foreign ships began to appear off her coasts; and in 1854, under the threat of an American mission commanded by Commodore Perry, Japan was forced to sign a treaty which, with subsequent negotiations, brought to an end her isolation and her comparative lack of material progress. Catapulted into competition with other nations if she were to retain her independence, she was forced to trade.

England, America and Russia were all temporarily occupied with wars and similar disturbances and could not, at that particular time, take advantage of what Japan could offer. France, on the other hand, was temporarily at peace, and jumped in at once. She poured money into Japan to build shipyards, docks and iron foundries, and Japan in turn exported decorative artefacts to France, sending prints, embroidered textiles, pottery, lacquer work, inros and netsukes (there were no pockets in a kimono, so the Japanese used an inro—a set of tiny boxes fitting into one another, capped by a lid, dangling from two cords which passed under the wide belt or obi, with a counter-weight, the netsuke, which was generally carved to portray a mythological scene; this was smooth so that it would not snag the smooth silk or satin of the robe). As soon as these artefacts appeared in Paris, enthusiastic connoisseurs and dealers went rushing out to Japan to see for themselves and to buy up their own consignments.

First Paris, and then all France, became fired by this totally new phenomenon. The re-hashing of past European styles was quickly considered decadent by the French *avant-garde*. First on the scene of Japanese art, they were determined to make the most of it. No one tried to copy Japanese art exactly, it would not have been very popular if they had; as usual the French extracted the essence of the style, as they saw it, and adapted it to the expression of their own ideas in their own materials.

Much of the work that came from Japan was based on designs drawn from Nature and the natural world, which the Japanese revered with an absolute empathy unknown in Western art; this fitted in very well with nineteenth-century ideas, though there was none of that sense of separation, of feeling oneself distinct from the natural world, which had so often characterized Western thinking. Floral designs were bolder, yet a single flower sufficed where the English or the French would have used a repetitive design. Instead of attempting to portray an exact and objective scene, the Japanese artists showed, perhaps, a single significant image; it was a refinement that yet remained accurate and full of life. Because Japan had been so long in isolation little of her art was a comment on other civilizations, but rather a comment on life in Japan—life itself, not the way of living it; a life in which everything had its own being, its own personality, its own soul, from a squirrel in a pine-tree to a rocky boulder. The Japanese artists studied Nature without sentimentality, intent to perceive this inner reality. They saw with a penetrating eye; and they translated what they saw, what they thought, into the barest essentials in paint or line, reproducing the central core, the essence, and that alone. They looked beyond the surface to the secret within, the quiet and hidden places in Nature, the continuous rhythms of the seasons, the mysteries of plant life.

Colour became extremely important. The Japanese artists created colours which fused in an entirely natural-looking way and which were, moreover, translucent, the light seeming to be filtered through them in a mysterious and beautiful way. The "holy" colours used by Pugin and his followers had been rich, dark and opaque, with a dense flat look: the ruby red of a sanctuary light, the deep sapphire blue of a stained glass Madonna's robe; and the neo-Gothic lighting, though it too was coloured and, in its way, mysterious, came from some external source, falling on and revealing the object. Japanese blues fused gently into greens, yellows into reds, golds into silvers, and all were irradiated with light, as if a luminosity existed deep within the object and shone effort-lessly out. An inanimate object shimmered and gleamed as if it had a real inner life of its own, possessing that soul which the Japanese knew to be present in all things.

The French artists found the new colouring a great relief, and as they worked at it, found it easier to create colours with the luminous Japanese effect. The potters and, especially, the glass-makers became supremely skilled in the necessary techniques.

The ability to single out a solitary flower and leaf and transfix this image in space in a believable manner was far harder for the Western artists to acquire. They were sometimes successful when creating textiles or pottery in this style, or when using it as a form of applied decoration; but when normally brilliant designers like Charles Rennie Mackintosh (1868–1928) created a chair which stood on four spindly legs (strengthened by stretchers) with a single tulip on a long straggling stalk to support each arm-rest— these frail flowers being a part of the actual structure, not an applied decoration—it was understandably a miserable failure.

Many Japanese designs feature water as part of the natural scene: water which is linked to the mountains, trees and flowers: itself a natural flow of movement. Everything is interlinked in Japanese mythology and philosophy, even good and bad are two sides of the same coin. So it is in their paintings and designs, there is a flow of movement, a continuous linking thread which is never broken.

The European artists retained this continuous flowing line, this unbroken movement —a linking thread which was tortuously turned and wound through the design, but never came to an end. They retained too the interest in Nature, turning their backs on sentimentality, considering the natural world fairly and squarely, and seeing that it could indeed be a cruel place.

The new style of design was sinuous and sensuous, often rousing a half-formed apprehension of something concealed and sinister, the line curling round and back without end. The mysterious shifting colours persisted, strengthening the concept, as did the mysterious inner silvery sheen—silvery because it was generally a moony translucence rather than a golden glow. The heavy golds quickly went out of fashion and silver came back: it was even interwoven with textiles. Anodized metal was used— that is, metal treated electro-chemically to thicken the protective coating that forms on exposure to air; the finish can be extremely decorative, particularly if dyes are added to give a silvery sheen of colour. Instead of the heavy onyx, dark marbles and mahogany that had previously been used for lamp-standards and sculpture plinths, artists working in the new style tried pale marble or chunks of rock crystal. When they used gold at all, they did so sparingly. And above all, throughout the decorative arts there quickened a feeling for movement.

A certain "plant hierarchy" had become ingrained in the European mind: one compared the lady to a rose, possibly to a daisy, but not to a dandelion. The Japanese, however, had never differentiated between "exceptional" plants and "lowly" weeds: in their philosophy, all was interlinked and, generally speaking, equal in value. The European designers, following this lead, began to use far more everyday plants and flowers in their designs, especially those which had coiling tendrils, delicately pointed petals, tongue-shaped leaves. They used the hedgerow vetch, for example, straggling chrysanthemums, and iris; the sinuous convolvulus—Prince Albert had loved the delicate pink-and-white trumpets, the new designers loved the endless clinging tendrils and the soft secretive droop of leaf and flower; orchids—the small greeny-brown flowers found in secret marshy places and shadowy woods; and silvery moon-lit honesty, whose

French name is *la lunaire*. A choker necklace by Wolfers Frères, dating from 1899 and created of gold, rubies and enamels, is based on a design of vetch clinging and twisting close about the throat; a wrought-iron staircase by Louis Majorelle, dating from about 1900 and now in the Musée des Arts Decoratifs in Paris, has a balustrade of delicate honesty clusters (some of the finest art nouveau ironwork is still in daily use in Paris— Hector Guimard (1867–1942) created the cast-iron railings and pavilions of the Metro in the art nouveau style).

The Paris Style

The *avant-garde*, searching for new sensations, had been quietly experimenting with drugs for some time: not simply as an escape from reality, but as a means of new experience. The erotic and sensuous dreams with their strange implicit logic were sometimes, though not always, counter-balanced by sick disgust, and sometimes, though again not always, flowered into poetry and prose of extraordinary beauty. Drug-taking was as sensuous as any Eastern design, as sinister, as never-ending.

In the new concept of art, drugs, sex and the world of Nature were inextricably linked, in direct contrast to the comfortable decencies of Victorian middle-class life, with its church-going, its sober virtues, and its conventions. (When Victoria was thinking over the kind of education her children should receive, she decided it ought to be "good, moral, religious"—but not "bigoted or narrow-minded"; all the same the Prince of Wales was almost seventeen before his tutor explained to him "the purpose and the abuse of the union of the sexes".) The middle-class Victorian ladies would have been shocked to death by the *avant-garde* life in Paris; the man of the family very probably knew what was going on and would, if he had sufficient money and a good enough excuse, go over to take a look for himself, but he would not dream of telling his wife. Women—wives, daughters and sisters, at least—must be kept in their proper virtuous place.

In Paris, however, it was a different matter entirely. There the entire new movement had found its focus in the image of woman as a mysterious goddess rather than a pure and dutiful creature who was the core of family life. There the new dress salons paraded *haute couture* clothes to startle and thrill the wealthy and admiring public. There grace and brilliance, splendour and beauty were glorified. There women were decked like works of art in all that was finest and luxurious, a perfection of quality.

Who were the leaders of the cult? They were the stars of the theatre, the dancers, the opera singers, women who lived in the public eye so that everything they said or did or wore could be observed and copied, just as in the past people had copied the monarch and the court. There was no queen in France now, but one by one the "public" women set the style—leading fashion in their own right, rather than as wife or mistress. Sarah Bernhardt was among them, that queer odd elongated genius, herself a sculptress and the patron of several rising craftsmen. Loie Fuller was another: the American dancer whose art was based on a thorough understanding of the beauty of movement and the quality of light. As she danced, with a few diaphanous veils drifting about her, the lights were made to shift and float so that she was a creature dancing in a dream— and for every man who watched the dream was different: a flower unfolding, a dipping

218

butterfly, a flickering flame, a twist of smoke curling slowly like the fume from an opium pipe. Cléo de Mérode was yet another—also a dancer, who had trained in the classical school and danced for the Paris Opera Ballet. Men called her the most beautiful woman in France. Every other woman wore her hair fashionably coiffured close to her head in little curls and crimps or swept into a shining *chignon*, but Cléo let her lustrous golden hair fall in a breaking wave about her classically beautiful face so that it wafted about her as she danced. Women were leading the entertainment world: Yvette Guilbert and Mistinguette at the Music Hall, the famous trio of Jane Avril, Anna Held and La Goulue in Montmartre.

Among the famous courtesans in the *demi-monde* were women who promoted every possible exaggeration: Liane de Pougy, for instance, Emilienne d'Alencon, and Caroline Otéro—they drew their own particular kind of audience. There was a sense of excitement at any fashionable party as people waited to see which of these questionable ladies would be present—one was quite good value, but two or three was better by far, since there was a great deal of rivalry between them (the magnificent collections of jewels bestowed by their lovers were a special bone of contention). What would they wear? How many jewels—and whose?

One of the most famous works of art created in the art nouveau style is the Clément Massier iridescent plaque, made in about 1898 and now in the Luigi Visconti Collection in Ischia. A sculptural nude woman is here portrayed, her nakedness shining and pulsing through incandescent draperies which are woven through with her long waving hair; her eyes are half-closed, she is drugged and dreaming, her head turned away from the onlooker as if she searches for some other world. Pinks, blues, turquoise and silver fuse together into a muted and luminous silveriness. The flowing shimmering endless line gathers light and colour into the most sensuous and relaxed of images.

The image of the woman, the feeling for movement and fusion, the sense of mystery is everywhere apparent, as if art were here reflecting in light and line and colour the images and meanings of some secret other world. Pictures and clocks are framed in nudes whose draperies flower into petals; a woman's face lies deep in the heart of iris or water lily.

The artists and designers of the time were great experimenters. Rather like their counterparts in England, the church architects, they turned their hands to all the applied and decorative arts. A man like Georges de Feure, for instance, designed furniture and textiles, porcelain and theatrical costumes; he was supremely versatile—his posters, like Mucha's, are a joy. There was something to work at, something new and different; it affected all the decorative arts, but its finest creations are seen in the posters, the pottery and glass, and the jewellery, since in none of these is construction of great importance. They do not need to withstand weight, and so in their designing fantasies could be played out to the fullest possible extent.

Emil Gallé's glass is one of the best examples. He experimented using opaque and coloured glass with enamel decorations, the colours being milky and opalescent. Gallé superimposed several layers of differently tinted glass, then, with acid or a grinding tool, cut away the layers to reveal a design in several shades. His techniques are said to have been inspired by the Chinese snuff bottles which were then being imported; in their turn they inspired every glass artist in Europe. All his motifs were taken from the natural world: flowers—the Japanese chrysanthemum, for instance—and insects, such as the dragonfly, a favourite image at this period. His colours muted and fused together, and all his forms were sculptural.

RENÉ LALIQUE

René Lalique is today famed for his glass rather than his jewellery, but he only turned to the designing of glass when the art nouveau movement had collapsed into vulgarity—its original designs reproduced by imitators and sold at cheap prices. His jewels, created in its heyday, were extraordinarily beautiful.

Lalique was born in 1860, in Marne, and lived a very full eighty-five years, dying in 1945. He was well into his thirties before he achieved personal fame, with a strong foundation of training and experience to build on. At the age of sixteen he had been apprenticed to a Paris jeweller and silversmith, named Louis Aucoc. During the period of his apprenticeship he also studied at the École des Arts Decoratifs. He then attended an art school in England for a further two years before returning to Paris where he became a freelance jewellery designer. At twenty-five he became manager of the Détapes workshops.

Lalique was commissioned to create stage jewels for Sarah Bernhardt, and the extraordinary success of these prompted him to exhibit his work under his own name at the Paris Salon of 1894. He caused a sensation. From 1894 onward he showed his work at exhibitions all over Europe, and staged occasional one-man shows as well. His work was also on show at the central showroom in Paris which had been opened by Samuel Bing. This was at 22 rue de Provence and was called *L'Art Nouveau*. Until Julius Meier-Graefe founded *La Maison Moderne*, this was the only showroom in Paris which specialized in promoting the modern designs.

Lalique's pieces were dramatic and theatrical, especially those designed for Sarah Bernhardt, which are quintessentially art nouveau—motifs drawn from Nature, flowing nudes, sensuous, luminous, full of sexual images—women being swallowed, spiked, stung—deliberate, cruel, completely unreligious, always surprising. The design sets out to shock; the materials are chosen with the same aim. Lalique mixed enamels with diamonds, horn with gold, ivory and glass with carved jade. A Lalique hatpin dating from 1900, now in Copenhagen, shows a carved opal sunflower with five black-and-gold diamond-winged wasps swarming about it and sucking out its nectar, framed in an elongated wing-shape like a sycamore seedhead, made from spiny thistle leaves; gold and silver, diamond and opal, horn and glass all went to its making.

Among his brilliant jewellery were many pieces commissioned by Calouste Gulbenkian and now on view at the Gulbenkian Foundation in Lisbon. There today is his famous dragonfly corsage, commissioned by Calouste Gulbenkian and lent to Sarah Bernhardt who wore it on stage. It is huge—the wingspan of the dragonfly is 10½ inches (over 250 mm)—and magnificently and deliberately unbalanced, amazingly beautiful and cruel, with as many nuances of meaning as any Renaissance masterpiece. Gold, enamels, chrysoprase and diamonds were used in its creation. The long thin flexible body narrows at one end into a spiky double sting; at the other the mouth is stretched painfully wide to take a last swallow of Agnes Sorel, the medieval French courtesan, nude save for her head-dress. Her eyes are serenely closed; the lines of her arms flow into the dragonfly's lacy wings and are lost in the transparent delicacy where darker patches of enamel emphasize the shape and accentuate the width, in complete contrast to the three heavy gold-and-enamel nailed claws. The whole jewel is frighteningly beautiful, and the longer one gazes at it, the greater its mesmeric power.

The Art Nouveau in French Jewellery

Generally speaking, it was in France that the art nouveau found its finest expression. Among the designers, men like René Lalique, Georges Fouquet, Eugène Grasset, Lucien Gaillard, Paul and Henri Vever and several others were creating brilliant work. Philippe Wolfers in Brussels became almost equally famous, and Georg Jensen in Denmark was later to carry on the movement successfully in a completely different idiom.

Enamelling was of great importance, especially in the French work. Various enamelling techniques were being used in Europe—*champlevé, cloisonné*, "encrusted"—but in France they preferred to develop the *plique-à-jour* technique, in which the enamels are set, like gemstones, in a metal framework which has no back; thus they are held like the fragments of glass in a stained glass window, translucent and glowing (no religious motives, however, affected the French designs). The technique meant that a jewel could be permeated with light; a dragonfly's enamelled wings, for instance, could be given a certain iridescence of which the designers made full use.

As the movement developed, the colours of the jewels grew lighter and lighter. From gold to silver, from sapphires to moonstones, from emeralds to opals, from rubies to blister pearls, from glowing enamels to paler and more luminous ones, and thence, eventually, to colourless glass engraved with insects or flowers. This gradual development can be seen very clearly in Lalique's work.

Another characteristic of French art nouveau jewellery is that the focal point of the jewel was often carved, perhaps in chrysoprase or jade, ivory or glass (the Lalique hatpin, centring on a carved opal, has already been cited), and modelled in the style of Rodin or Degas.

Because their curious and astonishing designs appealed to a limited number of customers, the French art nouveau jewels were mainly hand-made, although some craftsmen did use machines where possible—unlike England, there was no feeling that it was morally right for the artist to reject the machine.

The Art Nouveau in British Jewellery

When Lalique gave his first London exhibition of jewellery at the Grafton Galleries in 1903, the catalogue commented:

> "There is, at times, something almost sinister in this wondrous beauty and exquisiteness; in this super-subtle fancy that disdains the common earth and seeks to tear out the heart of Nature's beauty—but also her never-ending pain and struggle."

The commentator was quite right, in his way, but he made the jewels sound far too pompous and heavy. Lalique created beautiful works of art, but he never entirely forgot that they were to be worn—that they must be personal, and that they must be fun. His designs did incorporate motifs from the natural world, but the general style of his images was triumphantly sexual. Scarcely a piece that he made lacks a sculptured female bust or a sculptured naked couple. Like everyone else in Paris he was enjoying the new cult and its new means of expressing sexual fantasies. Unhappily it was an unwillingness to acknowledge sex that prevented the British jewellers from creating any supremely fine art nouveau jewellery. They were ready enough to make beautiful under-stated hand-made jewels with Nature motifs—but that was as far as they could go. Anyone who wanted a free and fashionable expression of sex must go to Paris for it, there was too tight a moral and religious grip on English designers—and even had they made and sold the jewels, few ladies would have been bold enough to wear them in public. British art nouveau jewellery lacked that one essential ingredient, and this was tragic; Britain had the designers, she had the skills, but she lacked the courage and the customers.

Ruskin, the Pre-Raphaelites, William Morris

John Ruskin (1819–1900) was probably England's greatest art critic and certainly one of the most original thinkers of the Victorian era—possibly because he had hardly any formal education. Three people had had a profound influence on his character and his way of looking at and thinking about art: Sir Walter Scott, William Wordsworth, and J. M. W. Turner. From them he had derived a love of romantic medievalism, a love of nature, and an appreciation of pictorial art's vision of the world. From a very tender age he was taken travelling round Europe: looked, drew, evaluated, and then soberly wrote down his comments and criticisms. Soberly, but not without feeling—"I believe the right question to ask respecting all ornament is simply this: was it done with enjoyment? Was the carver happy while he was about it?" He was, however, using happiness in the creative sense, there was nothing mechanical about it—none of the "three-square-meals-a-day-and-money-in-the-bank" style of happiness. Labour, sorrow and joy are all bound up together; and there is a firm line of demarcation between the designer and the workman: "No person who is not a great sculptor or painter *can* be an architect. If he is not a sculptor or painter he can only be a *builder*." And again: "Fine art is that in which the hand, the head and the heart of man go together." Unlike the Grand Tour travellers, to whom Italy was Mecca, Ruskin and his parents preferred the clean cantons of Switzerland, the valley of the Rhine, and the cathedral cities of northern France. "I expected to be *disappointed*," he wrote of St. Peter's; "I was *disgusted*. The Italians think Gothic architecture barbarous. I think Greek heathenish."

Ruskin had an enormous influence on the Pre-Raphaelite Brotherhood, formed in 1848 by James Collinson, William Holman Hunt, John Everett Millais, Dante Gabriel Rossetti, William Michael Rossetti, Frederick Shepherd and Thomas Woolner. They named their society the "Pre-Raphaelites" because they genuinely believed that the paintings of the earlier masters, who had preceded Raphael, surpassed those of the Italian schools. They wanted to restore the craftsman to his medieval status as a valued member of the community. Their knowledge of history was rather shaky but their zeal considerable; they selected and portrayed a list of heroes, starting with God and travelling down via Shakespeare to an assortment of philosophers and poets. Many a Bible today is filled with reproductions of Pre-Raphaelite biblical scenes, created by pure imagination, loaded with symbolism, and carried out in the most minute enamelled detail. In the Tate Gallery in London hangs Dante Gabriel Rossetti's *Monna Vanna*, painted in 1866; it shows his sitter, Annie Miller, icily aloof, almost Bronzino in essence, wearing beautiful fabrics and jewellery which is painted in minute detail—far more attention is paid to these adornments than to the sitter herself.

William Morris, born in 1834 and educated at Oxford, was also deeply impressed by Ruskin, and although not a member of the Pre-Raphaelite Brotherhood was counted among their friends. More fortunate than many, he had a comfortable private income of £900 a year. Although he tried to paint and draw, he ultimately discovered that his true bent lay in pattern-making rather than creating the huge medieval and religious scenes of his collaborator, Burne-Jones (who worked with such extraordinary, lingering, happy precision that one painting, begun in 1869, was not finished until 1898). Partly because of his marriage to Jane Burden, a social misfit in the milieu in which he had been raised, and partly because he absorbed the Pre-Raphaelite principles, Morris became a Socialist. Hating the machine-made monstrosities of the Great Exhibition, hating the new industrial cities and the wholesale destruction of old buildings and tranquil countryside to make way for the new roaring thumping factories, he longed to return to the "ideal" life of the Middle Ages, when all (he thought) was gentle, peaceful, and worthwhile. He began to re-use the old medieval motifs—the Gothic leaf-and-flower being prime among them—making them the basis of his patterns. In 1861 he inaugurated the firm of Morris, Marshall, Faulkner & Co. which created the furnishings used in his Red House at Bexley Heath in Kent—everything in it was hand-made, hand-woven, hand-beaten. He designed nothing that was new, he never progressed, he took art not one inch further forward, he merely re-hashed the anonymous medieval work in a repetitive pattern that stretched out and on for ever. His patterns were so generalized that they could as easily be used, and indeed were, for wallpapers as for chintzes, for embroideries as for carpets. He made no jewellery, but his pattern motifs, interlaced with a continuous flowing line, and carried out in muted and shaded blues, greens and browny pinks, were to have a tremendous influence on jewellery, as on all the decorative arts. His leaves and flowers, creeping round the tree-trunks, folding back on themselves in trefoils and quatrefoils of foliage, curled into patterns so full of un-natural nature that there was space in the room for nothing else; even the owner was unnecessary.

British Art Nouveau Jewellers

The art nouveau jewellery created in Britain was hand-made, single individual items being made for the few *avant-garde* patrons willing and able to commission them. It was in complete contrast to the elaborate gold-and-diamond commercial products in their machine-made settings. An art nouveau jewel was designed and made by the same artist-craftsman, on proper Morris principles, in a deliberate effort to restore the medieval system with its emphasis on craftsmanship; a conscious rejection of machinery.

Unfortunately this very exclusiveness, which gave it its character, was also to kill it. Hand-made pieces became very expensive, too much so for the ordinary customer (paradoxically, English art nouveau jewellery had a kind of exaggerated modesty about it—the quiet perfection of craftsmanship rather than the flash of diamonds—and this made it look far more inexpensive than it was, alarming the customer still further).

A craftsman could only make a few jewels in a year, whereas a machine could stamp out a hundred in a fraction of the time; who was to pay the butcher's bills meanwhile? Designers often worked in several of the decorative arts, rather than specializing in one, and this no doubt helped to bring in a little money. They might, for example, design a jewel for one customer, a piece of silverware for another, pottery or glass for a third. None the less the art nouveau craftsman, whether male or female (women were beginning to enter the trade), was entirely practical. He or she had been trained to keep the qualities of the materials always in mind. It is noticeable that whereas the French art nouveau jewellery makes considerable use of precious gemstones, including diamonds, the British paid more attention to the working of the metal and the use of enamels—which again served to give the jewel a rather more modest look.

The French delighted in creating jewels to enhance the appeal of the women who wore them, with subtle colours, sexual motifs, and *plique-à-jour* enamelling to give an extra luminosity, a hint at some inner core of life—almost an extra dimension of fluid light. The English, on the other hand, were far more successful and confident at creating jewels for the Church. Such jewels were sexless, rich with religious symbolism—the English artists of the time seem to have breathed most happily in a heavily religious atmosphere—yet still dramatic (they had to be: a jewelled chalice or a cloak clasp made in gold and set with gemstones had to have impact if it were to shine out through the "censer-made mists" and flickering candlelight) and carried out in deeper colours and glowing enamels.

Sir Alfred Gilbert (1854–1934) made some of the finest of the British art nouveau jewels. He had considerable advantages, being both a sculptor and a metalworker, and having spent two extremely important years in Paris in his early twenties, studying at the Ecole des Beaux Arts (1876–8). Among his pieces is the stunning Preston mayoral badge and chain, made in 1888 and carried out in silver-gilt with enamels and moonstones. Its beautiful gilded convolutions curl and loop in an unending richness of line.

Charles Robert Ashbee (1863–1942) was educated at a public school and at Cambridge, and was then articled to an architect; in his spare time he took evening classes at Toynbee Hall in the East End of London, which was supported by his old university. Living as he did at the time when the Socialist movement was growing in England, he too looked around him at the multiplicity of factories gobbling up the small workmen, the one-man and two-men firms, the individual craftsmen; comparing the quality of life so many of his fellows experienced with that of an idealized past drove him almost desperate. In 1888 he founded the Guild and School of Handicraft, which was to help people to recapture the old skills and to encourage individual talent; ten years later it became a limited company, and four years after that was moved out to Chipping Camden in Gloucestershire, right away from London (by 1907 it was at an end, and the art nouveau movement was itself dying). Ashbee did not merely lead, he encouraged.

The peacock is a motif which Ashbee used several times; not surprisingly, since so beautiful and harsh a bird, with its cruel screech and splendid jewelled tail, is itself as exaggerated as any art nouveau fantasy. He worked in gold and in silver, using blister pearls, jade, and turquoises, and dangling the whole delicate jewel from quite the finest possible hand-made chain; the pendant facing page 226 is a magnificent example of his work.

Alexander Fisher (1864–1936) spent two years as a National Scholar at South Kensington, and followed this by visiting France, where he concentrated on the study of the various enamelling techniques and proved to be so promising and enthusiastic that he was awarded a scholarship to continue with his studies in France and Italy. By 1888 he was back in England, where he set up his own studio as well as becoming a teacher of enamelling, and influencing some of the best craftsmen in England at that time. His work was shown at the Royal Academy, the Arts and Crafts Society, and several international exhibitions. At the Victoria and Albert Museum in London one may still see his enamelled girdle showing scenes from Wagnerian operas: a huge and magnificent nineteenth-century masterpiece of the enameller's craft. Among his distinguished pupils was Nelson Dawson (1859–1942), who in turn taught his own wife Edith, and another couple working on the same lines, Arthur Gaskin (1862–1928) and his wife Georgina.

But it was Henry Wilson (1864–1934) who made crystal clear the techniques of British art nouveau jewellery, summing them up in his textbook *Silverwork and Jewellery* which was published in 1902. The Introduction to this book was written by W. R. Lethaby (1857–1931), an artist-craftsman who eventually became Professor of Design at the Royal College of Art, and who helped to found the Art Workers Guild. Lethaby stressed the importance of design: "The true method of design is always growth, not rootless egoism"—a radical change of principle from the eager eclecticism of a few generations before. He warns the readers sternly against the "new art", writing:

"Of the two vulgarities—that of commercial dullness, and that of the blandishments which assume the name of 'new art'—the latter is likely to be by far the worse."

Yet strangely enough, Wilson's own art nouveau silver and jewellery was among the most original in England.

The book itself makes fascinating reading. Wilson is immensely practical, he leaves nothing out at all, giving every possible direction (and the reason behind it) as well as dozens of detailed diagrams. His lesson is quite clear:

"If the student will study methods, materials and natural forms, perfect his skill in handiwork, feed his imagination on old work, attend faithfully to his instincts, his personality can safely be left to take care of itself. It will infallibly find expression."

Wilson ended a brilliant career as architect, silversmith, sculptor and jeweller by being elected President of the Arts and Crafts Exhibition Society for 1915–22. In the true tradition of English art nouveau, he made modest and gentle jewellery for women (Fig. 69 shows one of his tiaras), but blazingly exciting and original religious jewels and plate. The Wilson chalice owned by St. Bartholomew's Church in Brighton is outstandingly lovely: partly silver, partly carved ivory, partly enamelled, it could only have been made by a sculptor.

Liberty's

Arthur Liberty (1843–1917) was a draper's son from Chesham in Buckinghamshire. At sixteen he had his first taste of employment at a lace-manufacturer's warehouse in Nottingham; migrating to London, he worked at a draper's in Baker Street, and finally joined Messrs. Farmer & Rogers in Regent Street. The growing interest in Far Eastern arts led Farmer & Rogers to open an extension next door to their main store, and call it *The Oriental Warehouse*. Arthur Liberty became its manager, and remained so for twelve years. It was stocked with *objets d'art*—Japanese prints and lacquers, porcelain, bronzes, silks, fans and *bric-à-brac*—most of the very highest quality (many of them left over from the 1862 Exhibition). The Pre-Raphaelites used to wander in to discuss

An Ashbee Peacock Pendant : this peacock and chain by C. R. Ashbee shows the restraint one can expect in British Art Nouveau jewels. Made of two colours of gold, with opals, blister and baroque pearls, and a generous sprinkle of diamonds, it seems almost austere when compared with the sinuous, sometimes sinister, and undulating lines of the peacocks created by Lalique, Grasset and Vever in France, or the modulated and impressive peacocks of Jensen in Denmark. The gentle progression from the rounded body of the diamond-crowned bird through the etched gold feathers to the openwork of white gold and diamonds is a poem of restraint : the hand-made fine gold chain to lie about the neck and the supports for the triple baroque pearl and diamond groups finish off the jewel with delicate balance. It is evident that the design is here all important, the gemstones being set *within* it, rather than the gems being of greater importance than the metalwork, as was the case with so much Edwardian diamond jewellery.

During the fifteen or twenty years it was in fashion, at the end of the nineteenth century and the beginning of the twentieth, Art Nouveau jewellery became paler and paler, partly to complement the gentle nuances of Edwardian fashion (the blush pinks, silvery greens, cloudy lavenders, and cool pale greys) and partly to avoid clashing with the galaxies of diamond stars and the milky ropes of pearls then fashionable at Court. The gemstones in vogue at this time were the products of the expanding British Empire: opals from Australia, pearls from the India regions, moonstones from Ceylon and diamonds from South Africa, cementing the inter-dependence of the overseas dominions and the mother country. In using these colours, marrying them with *plique-à-jour* enamels (a technique rather like stained glass in miniature—translucent and subtle), the *avant-garde* designer-craftsman created jewels with a Japanese luminosity, their inner glow shining out, gently and subtly iridescent, in contrast to the tennis-match sparking of light to and fro across the facets of the great Court diamonds.

By courtesy of the Trustees of the Victoria and Albert Museum

Fig. 68: this brooch, designed by C. R. Ashbee in about 1900 and executed by the Guild of Handicraft, is typical of the English Art Nouveau style, both because of its hand-made appearance and because of the carefully inoffensive motif—a French or Belgian brooch would have featured something sexy or sinister, but the English kept sex, vice and terror carefully under wraps.

Fig. 69: the illustration below shows an Art Nouveau tiara designed by Henry Wilson. The Edwardian Court was a stage-set for magnificent displays and rituals: when the young girls were presented, they had to appear in the required modest gown, family jewels blazing, ostrich feathers in the hair—a clip to hold such feathers can be seen at the back of this tiara.

By courtesy of the Trustees
of the Victoria and Albert Museum

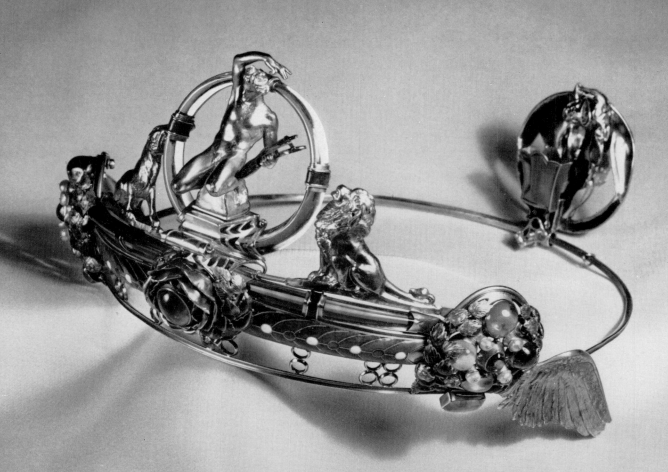

with Liberty the fine nuances of Japanese art, and to collect in a quiet way. Another customer was the American artist James McNeil Whistler, who had trained in Paris before crossing to London. Whistler was fascinated by Japanese art—he designed and decorated some exquisite Japanese fixed fans and painted scenes showing a "Japanese" way of living—and the English nicknamed him "the Japanese Artist".

By this time Japanese imports were entering Britain in sufficient quantity for collectors, artists and connoisseurs to make comparisons and evaluations, but the style was still so new that it had not yet been taken up, copied, and vulgarized by the factories. By the time Liberty felt experienced enough and confident enough to open a half-shop at 218A Regent Street, with a minimum of staff and, he hoped, a maximum of turnover, he was deeply involved with the aspirations of many contemporary artists and wished wholeheartedly to improve design, to improve public taste, and to consolidate both improvements by coming down heavily on the side of fine craftsmanship. His taste and acumen made the shop a great success, and within a year he was able to buy the other half.

In the early eighteen-eighties Liberty became dissatisfied with the quality of the Oriental silks and textiles now being imported; the manufacturers in the Far East, aware of the huge European market, were trying to make their goods more commercial, so that they would appeal to a wider public, and their efforts to achieve this resulted in a deepening of colour and a coarsening of design. He decided to take a huge gamble and to manufacture and sell his own fabrics, made in Britain, and coloured with subtle experimental dyes. Thus the Liberty colours were born. The soft fabrics fell naturally into folds like silken sculpture, and were so popular that his firm became enormously famous in England, and perhaps even more famous in Europe. (The art nouveau is still called the "Liberty Style" in Italy.) The British prejudice against the "New Art" had meant that the work of some designer-craftsmen had been virtually ostracized. Charles Rennie Mackintosh, for instance, of the Glasgow School, had designed all-white rooms in astonishing contrast to normal Victorian dark fussiness; his stark honest straight lines and his exaggeration of forms set him fifty years ahead of his time, even though some of his experiments went awry; Europe went wild about his work, and his influence on the Continent was considerable, but Britain remained unmoved and aloof. Now, however, it became all the rage to go to Liberty's; George du Maurier's gentle caricatures in *Punch* were splendid extra publicity.

But Liberty's influence on the new styles did not stop here. Unlike Morris and his sympathizers, Liberty believed that it was sensible to use the enormous resources of the mechanical world wherever possible. Accordingly, although he revived ancient dyeing and weaving techniques, he went off to the factories and stood over the workmen while they tried to re-create his designs and colours by machine methods, experimenting and experimenting until the result was perfect, and virtually showing the factory-owners what their machines and workers could achieve.

He insisted, moreover, on selling everything under his own name. Fabrics were by *Liberty & Co.*; so was furniture, so was *bric-à-brac*, so was jewellery. When Liberty set out to sell silver, for instance, he commissioned a designer—Arthur Gaskin perhaps, or Archibald Knox (Fig. 53 is by Knox)—to create a full range; he sent the designs out to a factory; and he sold the goods under the simple trade name *Liberty & Co.* No label saying *Designed by Knox*, not even a small ticket saying *Manufactured in Birmingham*. There was, for example, the Cymric range of silverware and jewellery launched in 1899, and the Tudric range of pewter which followed in 1901; both beautifully created in the general art nouveau style toned down to suit English taste, and both anonymous—no clue at all to the designer. (A recent exhibition of the work of Archibald Knox, held at the Victoria and Albert Museum in London and featuring designs and finished pieces, was a revelation; it showed that this designer—very underestimated for much of the twentieth century—had been one of the principal designers for the beautiful early ranges of Liberty's metalware.) The decision was a sensible one, even inspired, from the salesman's point of view, though cruelly hard for the designer. He worked, he was paid, he ate, he did what he really longed to do, but he got no credit for it, he was an anonymous part of the manufacturing process. In many artists this can eventually kill the creative instinct; success and publicity go hand in hand, and anonymity brings self-reproach and despair. But in his way, Liberty too was right. A mass of names would only have confused the public; as it was, he managed to create whole ranges of beautiful, finely-made, high-quality goods that were art nouveau in inspiration, without alienating his customers or falsifying his own *avant-garde* ideals. Liberty's could supply quality goods for the whole household, from drawing-room lamps and dining-room silver to evening dresses in soft-coloured fabrics. But for absolutely everything there was just one trademark: *Liberty & Co*. It was famous all across Europe, and it inspired confidence.

The Avant-Garde Woman

What did she wear, the turn-of-the-century girl, with her Socialist principles, her flowing Liberty fabrics, and her art nouveau jewellery? Almost certainly she had some kind of jewel in her hair: an elaborate comb, a complicated hair-pin, or even the latest style of *aigrette*. She usually did not wear earrings, since these would detract from the focal jewel in her hair and would in any case probably be hidden by her flowing hair-style, but she might have a fine gold chain around her neck terminating in an art nouveau pendant (this might well be detachable, with a fitment at the back so that it could also be worn as a brooch). She lavished attention on her hands, with rings swarming up her fingers, sometimes linked by slim chains or spiral-sprung snakes to a sinuous bracelet coiling around her wrist: Sarah Bernhardt was often pictured wearing a most elaborate confection of snakes by Lalique which twisted from finger-tip to mid-forearm.

Summing-up

Fifteen years comprised the whole of the true and original art nouveau in England; a very short period in any history of design. During those few years—from about 1895 until about 1910—all the better work was produced. The only men who managed to make any kind of lasting commercial success were those who adapted their designs to suit machine-reproduction—Jensen in Denmark, Liberty in England. The other brave attempts perished: they were too expensive, too exaggerated, and eventually, when people became desperate to make them commercially viable, vulgarized.

Art nouveau jewellery does not yet rank as antique, and there are thus not many pieces on show, although the Victoria and Albert Museum has a collection. However, Sotheby's of London has now opened a salesroom for Victorian work and art nouveau work, a public acknowledgement of the growing interest in and importance of these periods, and art nouveau jewels are increasingly coming on to the market and inspiring prices which can, at first sight, seem amazing, until one recalls that these are not ordinary mass-produced jewels but rather works of art. They are eminently worth acquiring, dating as they do from a period which was a turning point in the history of jewellery, and can, if undamaged, be both valuable and a sensuous form of decoration.

CHAPTER ELEVEN

The Twentieth Century

The *Grande Toilette* Gemstones: Diamonds; Pearls; Opals—Edwardian Fashions—Shop-keeper and Designer—The World of the Arts, 1900–1920—Dress and Jewels, 1900–1920—The Social Scene Between the Wars—The World of the Arts, 1920–1939—Jewellery, 1920–1939: Cultured Pearls; Mid-Thirties Jewellery—The Post-War Years—Diamonds: Natural Diamonds; De Beers Consolidated Mines Ltd.; Synthetic Diamonds—Johnson Matthey & Co. Ltd.

The Grande Toilette Gemstones

DIAMONDS

It was in 1867 that the first diamond was found in South Africa, five hundred miles inland from the Cape of Good Hope, near the source of the Orange River. The story is as romantic as any of the flashpoints in history which have changed the direction of men's lives. A passing pedlar noticed some children playing with a handful of stones on the floor of a farmhouse. One of the stones seemed to have its own inner glow, and he suggested taking it to a nearby mineralogist for testing; it was a diamond. The pedlar sold the stone to the governor of the Cape Colony who had it exhibited at the Paris Exhibition of 1867. The great diamond rush began.

Frustrated diggers roamed over the African countryside, plunged into rivers and streams, and scratched every likely patch of dry earth. By 1875 there were about ten thousand prospectors in Kimberley, some successful, some not; and by 1888 De Beers Consolidated Mines had been formed. Stones of differing sizes, shapes, colours and degrees of clarity were sent to London. The larger ones were set singly—the *solitaire* ring, set with a single beautiful stone, was introduced at this period—and the smaller ones massed together in the glitter of the *grande toilette*. They were generally set in platinum, which acted as a silvery foil to their brilliant light.

There are photographs extant showing Queen Alexandra, wife of Edward VII, at her coronation in June 1902. Her jewels are as plentiful as any worn by Elizabeth I in her heyday: row upon row of choker pearl necklaces, the Arcot diamonds (a royal heirloom; Queen Charlotte wore them too—page 146), more diamonds, five huge ropes of pearls cascading down the front of her gown, pearl and diamond earrings, several wide bracelets, *échelles*, chains, brooches and Orders. (Many of these jewels later passed to her daughter-in-law, Queen Mary, and were subsequently shortened or scaled down to a more reasonable size for Elizabeth II.) This almost frightening display was obviously arranged to enhance the splendour of the coronation, itself a State occasion and a supremely rare and important event; perhaps too, after the long, crape-decked seclusion of his mother Queen Victoria—forty years mourning for her Albert—Edward VII may have wanted to show that court life was again a brilliant and splendid affair. None the less, it is extremely difficult to find *any* illustrations of Queen Alexandra which show her wearing just one or two pieces of jewellery. The Edwardian Court was a place of rigid formality, and whenever the queen was painted or photographed it was necessary to plaster her with jewels like a gilded icon. Her private inclinations are said to have been towards a more modest style of dress, but her public image was carefully arranged to promote exactly the opposite impression. Her elegance was considerable; even with diamonds and pearls streaming all over her, she still managed to look serenely beautiful.

PEARLS

Oriental pearls, fished from the salt waters of the Persian Gulf, the Bay of Bengal, and other noted salt-water pearling banks, had been popular in Europe for hundreds of years, but as the traders travelled out across the world, opening up new shipping routes and linking together the new settlements and colonies, other sources of supply were found: the Australian waters, for example, the islands of the South Pacific, the Gulf of California and the Gulf of Mexico.

Fresh-water pearls were also worn—one, a pink pearl found in New Jersey in 1857, was eventually sold to the Empress Eugénie; it weighed nearly 2 ounces (over 45 g). The River Tay in Scotland had been fished for fresh-water pearls before the Romans came over the border, and at the turn of the century there were over a hundred full-time pearl fishers pearling in the Scottish rivers. By 1973 only one man, Bill Abernethy, maintained this ancient tradition. The system he followed was essentially the same as that used for hundreds of years before his day.

A pearl is a concretion formed by a mollusc, and consisting of the same material—nacre, or mother-of-pearl—as the mollusc's shell; thus the wonderful radiance of prismatic colour that one sees in mother-of-pearl is the same as that glowing from the surface of a pearl. A particle of grit lodges in the mollusc's fleshy mantle, and the creature secretes nacre which slowly forms in layers around the irritating speck. A spherical "perfect" pearl grows in the soft tissue areas of the mollusc's body; a baroque pearl, of the kind so prized by the Renaissance artists and craftsmen, is deformed because the invading speck lodges in muscular tissue, where the resistance is greater; a blister pearl grows so close to the mollusc's shell that it forms as a half-sphere, flat on one side. (There are four other shapes for grading pearls: *boutons* (these are also flat on one side), seed, the elongated houndstooth, and pear.)

When Abernethy fishes for fresh-water pearls, he searches for mussels. Unlike the sea variety, which attach themselves to rocks, these roam in the river bed, anchoring themselves by protruding a tongue into the gravel, in clean flowing water. They can be up to 6 inches (150 mm) long. Holding a glass-bottomed jug in his teeth, Abernethy looks down through the water with its changing surface reflections. (Fig. 55 shows him at work.) He grips the mussels with a forked stick and throws them into a sack on his back (if the water is too deep for wading, he tosses them into a boat). As soon as he has a satisfactory collection, he retires to the bank to open them. He can open five hundred in an hour, and is extremely lucky if just one amongst them all contains a pearl of gem quality.

The lovely soft subtle colouring of Scottish fresh-water pearls is quite distinct from that of their oriental cousins. They are like fruit still on the tree, untouched, rather than fruit which has been plucked, polished, and displayed in a shop window. Their scarcity and beauty means that their value approaches that of oriental pearls. It is rare to find a necklace of matched spherical fresh-water pearls since the shape can so easily be deformed as the mollusc builds up the layers of nacre round the irritant.

Most Scottish fresh-water pearls are thus uneven in shape, and the *boutons* and pear-shaped pearls are used in brooches, earrings, pendants and bracelets and rings designed with especial care to reflect the qualities of the pearl and the essential characteristics of the Scottish countryside. Messrs. Cairncross of Perth make a speciality of high-quality Scottish fresh-water pearl jewels, which have immense charm and gentleness and are not ruinously expensive. One is shown in Fig. 56. When Elizabeth II opened the Tay Bridge in October 1960 she was presented with a lovely brooch of Tay River pearls, partly because it was so appropriate a gift, and partly because she was known to love pearls and often seen wearing them.

The find of the century was made in 1967 when Abernethy brought up a relatively small shell from a pool above the village of Stanley on the Tay. This yielded the most wonderful Scottish pearl seen in living memory. It weighed 44½ grains and measured ½ inch (12 mm) in diameter, completely spherical, with a flawless lustre. Being unique, its commercial worth was difficult to assess; but its beauty was beyond question.

OPALS

A novelty stone which came into favour in the last quarter of the nineteenth century was the opal. It had been known before this, but until the opening up of the great opal fields of Australia had only been rarely used. Now, however, the British jewellers and their customers were shown some fantastically coloured gems. The introduction of the Australian opal on the British gemstone market was marked by the creation of some curious historic brooches, known as "prospector's brooches", which are shaped like the map of Australia, its States marked out in different coloured opals set in textured Australian gold (Fig. 51).

Opal is a mineral consisting of amorphous silica and varying quantities of water. Many different kinds are known, a few of which are called collectively "precious opal". Common opal lacks iridescence and fire, but precious opal holds such a brilliant kaleidoscope of colour that it looks as if there is a living fire in its heart—yet no two gems are ever exactly the same.

Precious opal has been found in Czechoslovakia (the principal source for opals in ancient times), India, the western United States, and elsewhere in the world, but the true "opal country" lies in Queensland and New South Wales in Australia: fifty thousand square miles of dry sandstone where once there was sea, 120 million years ago. Opals were first found in Queensland around 1870. The biggest source today is the

Coober Pedy fields of South Australia; the name stems from the Aborigine phrase meaning "men in the holes", and is a graphic description of a desert township, treeless, bitter in the winter when the temperature can drop well below freezing, unbearable in the summer when it can leap to 130 degrees Fahrenheit, riddled with sandstone tunnels and disused galleries where men can make their homes in relative safety from the cruel extremes of temperature on the surface.

Opals are especially curious in that all manner of things can become opalized; quite a collection can be seen in museums—a cat's skeleton, a gatepost opalized at the foot, dog-shark, shell-fish, sea-lilies, shells, and other sea-creatures, and one splendid discovery of immense interest to the scientist, a plesiosaurus (an extinct sea-reptile), well-nigh perfect, in glorious opal. Dinosaur's bones have also been found, and at Lightning Ridge, in New South Wales, part of a crocodile's jaw and teeth. The black opal was first discovered there in 1905. Other seams of magnificent blue-black opal were found later, including one at Andamooka, discovered in 1915, whose finest stone— 203 carats, and valued at a quarter of a million pounds—was given to Elizabeth II when she visited Australia in 1954.

Entertaining stories about the crazy characters who prospected for diamonds in South Africa have slid into history; similar stories came, and come still, from Australia— stories of opal prospectors like men possessed, gambling with life and death in a cruel part of the country, in a highly Australian concentration of independent and individual characters. They sound more incredible than most but it seems that the majority of them are true, and the tales of lost hoards and secrets buried with the dead prospectors still drive men on, like a fever, to search unendingly for yet another opal.

Opals appealed tremendously to the art nouveau jewellers because of their elusive quality of light, their never-ending permutation of colour; they were also very popular with Queen Victoria, who set a fashion for wearing them which was followed by many of her subjects in different social classes. Queen Alexandra, however, appeared to dislike them, and during the first fifteen years of the twentieth century the fashion for them slowly died away, though it was revived in the between-the-wars period and after the nineteen-sixties. Many a glowing opal was set in an Edwardian tie-pin, and surviving examples of those pins—set with an opal, or a brilliant diamond, or a black pearl—are now very highly prized. They have an air about them, a quality, which recaptures the essence of the elegantly tailored man of the Edwardian era, much as the formal blaze of the *grande toilette* jewels recalls his lady dressed for an evening ball.

Edwardian Fashions

The Victorian style, concerned with effect rather than intrinsic quality, yielded gradually to the new modes of the Edwardian era.

During the eighteen-seventies, the homes of the Victorian *nouveaux riches* (who really made use of their riches) reflected the fact that here lived people of importance: they were comfortable, crowded, displaying the latest novelties and the latest styles to impress the guest. People often decorated different rooms within the house in different ways: a drawing-room in the Renaissance style, for instance, a bedroom in the French rococo, a smoking-room *à la Turque*. It was decorative chaos, but it made a showy splash in direct contrast to the all-of-a-piece vogues of the aesthetes and the art nouveau.

Much the same haphazard behaviour affected dress. By 1870 the vast crinoline had given way to one of the most exaggerated styles ever created for women's wear, manipulating them into sartorial caricatures: the bustle. A woman's skirts were dragged back and positively upholstered on springs and pads of horsehair, falling in long intricate folds and swathes of fabric as elaborate as the curtains and drapes of her drawing-room. She was corseted to achieve a most constrictingly unnatural high bustline emphasizing the tiny waist below, and her silhouette became one of the strangest in the history of dress, for she and her contemporaries looked exactly like ducks. Through the succeeding years fashions came and went, with draping and goring and trimming and padding, but by 1895 the waddling ducks had straightened up into butterflies, still corseted, still controlled, but presenting a different silhouette. The head was kept very small, with the hair either dressed in curls or smoothed round in a *chignon*, always close to the skull. The neck was elongated and accentuated by chokers, velvet ribbons, or high tailored collars. The bust was high, tapering to a tiny waist, the hips smooth and gently rounded, the skirts falling to the ankles without puffing into great billows of fullness, the bustle non-existent. Graceful and slender, the ladies grouped together at the theatre or the *soirée*, their gauze or lace scarves fluttering from their shoulders like the transparent wings of butterflies. Though fluttery, the style was never slipshod, for the conventional lady dressed with immense care, matching her beautifully tailored husband, and pointing the contrast between herself and the aesthetes in their looser robes, uncorseted, with flowing or braided hair. The luminous butterfly effect was heightened by the use of diaphanous pale pretty fabrics: pearly greys, dusky pinks, the pale blush shades of the heart of the rose, lavenders, and the softest silvery greens. The Liberty colours were also in vogue—the "greenery yallery" shades, plenty of rich Devonshire cream colours, and snowy white. Much of this was due to the introduction of electric light which had now been adopted in many places of entertainment, hotels, and richer homes. The heavy Victorian colours looked perfectly well by candle light or gas light, but outlandishly garish in electric light, so paler tones were a natural solution—and served, moreover, as yet another subtle class distinction. There was a new feeling for texture: a gown made in a single colour could still look rich if one considered the possibilities of different materials—cream satin, for instance, with cream net frilling at the neckline, pin-tucks and ruching down bodice and skirt, and pleated cream lace around the hem. Satin was pulled tightly to the body, which moulded and sculptured it, whereas laces and gauzes were required to float.

Although bright colours were considered terribly vulgar, a lavish display of jewellery was an absolute social necessity—in court circles, at least, where the ladies wore their *grandes toilettes*, roped in long strands of pearls and bristling with South African diamonds. The new stiff court style was so expensive that only a small proportion of the people could adopt it; a few families were astoundingly rich, but the majority could not afford to deck their womenfolk in the grand jewels that Queen Alexandra wore— diamonds and rubies and sapphires and emeralds, more and more diamonds and huge great rounded pearls. (She did not follow the art nouveau style, although Edward VII spent much of his time visiting the fascinations of Europe, especially those of Paris, and must there have seen the finest flowering of the new mode: one vogue for the *demi-monde* and the entertainers of Paris, another for wife and queen.) Britain had spent too long without a royal arbiter of fashion; with Victoria in virtual retirement—though still grasping the reins as tightly as ever, and allowing her eldest son very little say in the affairs of the nation—people had grown out of the custom of slavishly copying every detail of the monarch's dress. By the time Edward VII acceded to the throne, in 1901, he was fifty-nine and his wife Alexandra three years younger; they were rather too elderly to be exciting leaders of society.

A new and important change had also begun to affect the jewellery world: the division between evening jewels and daytime jewels. The first were as grand as possible, blazing with diamonds; the second were much more modest, smaller, but always novel —perhaps sporty, perhaps a sophisticated joke; and the two could not be interchanged. Women, now taking a much more robust and active part in outdoor life, wore fox mask pins, brooches shaped like riding crops or even bicycles. There were small diamond picks to commemorate a rock-collecting holiday, small gold boots or shoes to commemorate a mountaineering expedition, and gold or diamond horseshoes to celebrate some hunting exploit. Wishbones, tigers' teeth and tigers' claws mounted in gold were worn; the ever-sentimental "honeymoon brooch", with a crescent moon and a tiny bee, came into fashion; and charm bracelets arrived—all a part of the quest for novelty.

Shop-keeper and Designer

In formal Edwardian jewellery—and in spite of the sporty daytime novelties, this was the majority—stones were mounted with no metal showing, sometimes on high galleries. The "invisible" settings gave the effect of diamond lace. The pieces were rather delicate in composition, and very pristine and impersonal.

The places where they were sold were impersonal too, for this was the period of the rise of the big jewellers' shops. Bond Street and Regent Street seemed packed with branches of the Parisian jewellers, as well as the better British ones; many of them are there to this day. Horse-drawn hansom cabs deposited the wealthy buyer and his lady (who often had to be anonymous as well), and they would look through the plate glass windows at tray upon tray of glittering diamonds, and then disappear inside to talk about prices—but not about designs.

The designer was absent, forgotten, ignored. Shop-owners had taken their lead from Liberty; their pieces were sold under one name only, the name of the shop. It is extraordinarily difficult to study the history of the better-class firms in Britain established at this time; the names of their designers were simply not recorded. And the same attitude often persists: "We are all working for the one concern, it is the shop that counts"; "We only use artists for special commissions so that the customer can see what the design would look like in different coloured stones"; "Stockpile jewellery is taken from our own standard designs"; "We never name designers."

Perhaps this attitude had its origin in the fact that by the early years of the twentieth century, artists and designers were distinct from the general community—a small sect, many of whom were considered "not very nice" by those who could not understand their work. Certainly the strides taken by art and sculpture during those years were greater than during almost the whole century before. Art came out of the doldrums and began to forge ahead with frantic vitality. The conventional person was shocked out of his wits.

The World of the Arts, 1900–1920

In the first two decades of the twentieth century, which included the four-year holocaust of the First World War (1914–18), the political and social structures of the world underwent rapid and radical change. There were marked parallels in the arts—literature and music, painting and sculpture and architecture: all were affected by the political and social changes, the development of science and technology, the general shifting climate of opinion. These trends quickened into a nervous energy which was eventually to culminate in the staccato fireworks of the nineteen-sixties and seventies.

By the beginning of the twentieth century, painters had earned a certain freedom from conventional influence—abandoning the past, as it were, looking coolly and analytically at the present, and groping enthusiastically towards the future. The developments that took place in styles and techniques and modes of creative expression were not restricted to any one country, they were increasingly international; and although the leaders came from specific national backgrounds, their dedicated followers gathered from all over the world. Fauvism and Cubism, for example, arose in France, Futurism in Italy, Synthetic Cubism in France again, Expressionism in Germany and De Stijl in Holland: yet none was restricted to the country of its origin; their influence spread world-wide.

In 1912 Picasso composed a picture which incorporated a piece of oilcloth: it was the beginning of the collage movement which proved to be a new breakthrough in the decorative arts. Artists of the highest and most enviable reputations took up this new style, introducing texture into the composition by applying alien materials to a "painting". Such a move had never been envisaged before by serious and recognized artists, and it broke away from the conventions of earlier art. Texture became as important as colour. The compositions of Braque and Picasso created in this idiom appear rather to have been assembled in limbo than painted on the canvas. This abstract construction, together with the use of collage, meant that the subject was indicated rather than reproduced in paint. For the first time since Turner, people were expected to use their imaginations when they looked at a painting. The past became anathema: the treatment must be entirely original—the healthiest trend possible in any art.

Braque's fascination with materials found a fresh expression in 1961, towards the end of his life, when he began to create jewels. It is almost surprising that he had not tried this before, for he used to collect pebbles from the beach and assemble them into sculptures, and to experiment with conglomerate stone—saying on one occasion, to John Craven, "I should have been a sculptor, to be able to fight constantly with the material." He devoted the major part of those last two years of his life to the creation of jewels like miniature sculptures: it was his last brilliant metamorphosis as an artist. Among the stunning jewels he made were a number based on myths: there is one, for instance, representing in abstract style the story of Hyas, who was killed while out hunting, and his sisters, the Hyades and the Pleiades, who grieved for him so bitterly that Zeus in pity turned them into stars: an exciting *mélange* of diamonds is fixed in a starry blaze to a pinky-brown orbicular rhodocrocite framed in gold.

Opinions vary as to whether sculpture developed faster than painting in the early decades of the twentieth century. Certainly it was as deeply concerned with textures as painting with form. The sculptures of this period came increasingly to look as though they had been assembled from bits and pieces rather than carved out of a solid block. Woods were used, galvanized iron, terracotta, bronze, stone and reinforced concrete. The Constructivist Movement developed out of these new concerns and idioms. The feeling for space as an integral part of any composition was expressed in 1920, when the brothers Antoine Pevsner and Naum Gabo wrote in their *Realistic Manifesto*: "Space and time are the two elements which exclusively fill real life."

The early twentieth-century architect was also possessed by a feeling for texture, form and space. Significantly Le Corbusier in France, Mies van der Rohe in Germany and Vladimir Tatlin in Russia were all working along the same lines, using iron and glass and concrete, weighing and considering function and structure and their relationship to one another.

Dress and Jewels, 1900–1920

A feeling for function and structure rather than simple decoration began gradually to affect women's dress; an attempt was even made in pre-war Germany to create a new type of clothing which was hygienic, aesthetic and practical, and based on medical opinion of the capabilities of the female frame. For the first time in centuries a woman's health was considered to be more important than her looks. The doctors proved conclusively that squeezing the body into tight corsets was a serious health hazard. A woman's clothes, it was suggested, should be as light as possible. The centre of gravity of the dress should lie on the shoulders, which technically, at least, bore all the weight.

The result of the careful German theorizing and experiment was a type of clothing which was hygienic and comfortable, but unfortunately ugly and unpopular as well. Gradually, however, the strictly corseted look did give way to a more natural appearance. The pouter pigeons disappeared, and women began to dress in fabrics which were rather more serviceable and lasting. But there was still an outlet for frivolity: enormous hats were worn, covered in ostrich feathers or swathed in spotted tulle, occasionally even adorned with complete stuffed birds. Women were living far more practical and active lives. Many of them no longer had sufficient time, money or patience to wear foolish and extravagant clothes, however pretty, or a clutter of accessories. A tailor-made costume and a long fur stole were simple, elegant, and comfortable. This trend towards practical clothes suitable for wearing to the office or on social work among the poor was greatly speeded by the war, when women were working in the factories and the hospitals alongside the men. Floor-length skirts sweeping the ground were completely impractical for factory work; and long grim corsets were no use to the V.A.D. who was bending to help a wounded soldier from his stretcher.

Jewellery too became more practical-looking, at least for daytime wear, to match the severe tailored suits. The art nouveau look with undulating lines coiling and looping nowhere gave way to a squarer design with corners and angles. The butterflies fluttered away, the bees and the snakes were gone; in their places came the abstract shapes with which the artists and sculptors were experimenting. The clear pale translucent *plique-à-jour* enamels yielded place to the darker richer opaque ones. The soft fuzzy colours gave way to harder and sharper shades. The new fashion for onyx and diamonds summed up the prevailing feeling for bright dark angular work with a sense of solidity and crispness about it.

This was also the time when many of the richest collections of family jewels were made for evening wear: tiaras and diadems, matching necklaces and brooches, and the new flat flexible bracelets which clasped the wrist—many families are wearing them still. The old Georgian heirlooms thick-set with diamonds were brought out and the stones re-set, sometimes in pieces made in the new style, sometimes in scaled-down copies of the old Georgian designs which could be worn with contemporary clothes. But even the great firms used anonymous designers for this work. Collingwood of Conduit Street, for instance, had been granted the royal warrant in 1837, twenty years after they were first established, and have held it continuously from that day to this because of the high quality of their work and the impeccable nature of their service; nowadays they name their craftsmen-designers (many conservative firms still do not, and still use the old dull and anonymous designs of those early decades—"People expect it of us, our customers don't like changes"), but in those opening decades they followed the conventions of the time, and their sketchbooks, filled with designs for royalties and for ducal houses, never carried a designer's name.

Although members of the British royal family rarely sell their jewels, the Earl of Harewood did sell, at Christie's in London, twenty-eight items which had originally belonged to his mother, the Princess Royal, George V's daughter, and which dated from approximately this period. "It is," he said at the time, "a combination of their being worth some money, one's not needing so many jewels, and of finding the right occasions to wear them." None of them were by named designers; it was an anonymous collection of tiaras, brooches, necklaces and bracelets from famous shops, with a mass of over-exposed diamonds, without real artistic merit or historic value; the purchasers may well have broken up the pieces and re-set the stones at once. Jewels from this period, made up to conventional designs, lacking individuality or character, have no artistic value, and marketing them is often the wisest thing to do.

The Social Scene Between the Wars

The holocaust of the Great War had killed an appalling number of people and had left the living to struggle through a series of economic crises, fighting now to cope with peace—a peace that seemed desolate and empty. Currencies were devalued, buildings laid waste, men thrown out of work. As the years drew on towards the late thirties, a sense of new impending havoc made things yet worse.

Women had won relative social freedom, in the upper social strata at least; they were free now to make the same mistakes as the men. Skirts became shorter and shorter, fabrics as wild and brash as the young men's check plus-fours, clothes cheaper, make-up more exaggerated. Women copied the modes of their favourite film stars, much as earlier generations had copied Sarah Siddons or Elizabeth I, but now, because of the splintering of social structures and the spread of communications, changes in fashion affected more people than ever before. The sophisticated flapper era of the twenties came too quickly because of the war, it was wildly exaggerated and out of control, but it could not possibly be reversed.

It was not all jazz, however. The world was never to be the same again. The artificial splendour of the pre-war court style, the hint of slyness that lay beneath the art nouveau's stress on personal significance and the importance of craftsmanship: these things were gone. Men and women, artists and patrons, were forced to try to come to terms with this new existence. There was a turning back to basic principles. People began to consider the importance of actual structure. The concept of space was gradually introduced into design. For years and years jewellery had been regarded as applied decoration; now, very gradually, people began to consider the materials of which a jewel was, or might be, made. Instead of being a reflection of the wearer's social position, jewels came at last to be viewed once more as works of art, creations; the basic nature of the materials had now to be taken into account, and designs developed that basic honesty which is the hallmark of the best modern jewellery, with its feeling for space and depth and the natural structure of a gemstone. It did not come all at once, of course; but once begun, it could not, thankfully, be halted.

The World of the Arts, 1920–1939

In the between-the-wars period painting seemed to lose its sense of direction. It went virtually nowhere and it did even that in a muddle. The cosmopolitan artists, concentrated in Paris, traditional centre of their world, seemed curiously unsure; no longer tied to a specific national context, they seemed now to belong to nothing, bereft of that sense of identity which had shaped earlier men living and working where they were born, bereft even of a linking climate of established and accepted opinion. When they looked for help, for masters to guide them, they found none: the professors could only offer theoretical teaching, not practical experience. Suspicious of the alien intellectuals, they fell back on personal preference. Their spare lines and forms merely hinted at reality, creating a composition that had meaning only for them. They affected a loss of interest in the human form as a subject for painting. They played with colour. They were in limbo, their work tentative and half-afraid.

But the sculptors were not groping at all, they were grasping the opportunity to express the new values in three-dimensional form. Their work was on a new scale: massive timeless abstract themes born of a fantastic dialogue between the sculptor and his material. The eternal theme of the reclining nude, for example, was treated in a completely new way and from a completely new viewpoint by such giants as Henry Moore, whose originals showed supreme strength and confidence. Enigmatic structures, with a pristine cleanliness and a high finish, complemented the new architecture—and here a magnificently honest appraisal of function and structure was being made. "The house is a machine for living in," said Le Corbusier in the nineteen-twenties; and fifty years later some people still do not understand exactly what he meant.

A brilliant band of international architects concentrated on light, space, texture, basic forms, a sense of movement; they used new materials, often composing a structure so that one was reflected in another to increase the three-dimensional look. They worked in concrete, of course, in marble, in chromium-plated steel and onyx and ebony. Their designs were in the abstract geometrical style, but married to a rational concern for function: hygiene, comfort and economy were basic requirements.

The most influential school was the famous Bauhaus. This had its beginnings in the Weimar Art School, under Walter Gropius, but moved in 1919 to Dessau, where the Bauhaus Building was constructed in 1925–6 under his direction. Every design incorporated in the Bauhaus was based on spheres and right angles, and all the colours used were the primary ones. It was to be an experimental laboratory in which engineers, architects, painters and sculptors and designers worked as a team on formulae and standards which could be applied to create goods that satisfied modern requirements and could be standardized, prefabricated, and mass-produced. They were working, as it were, in co-operation with the machine, and their designs had therefore to be completely practical. Everything they made was useful and functional, any superimposed decoration was minimal and was never allowed to interfere with function. Their work ranged from metal chairs and plate-glass tables to angled chess-sets, and many of their original designs are still best-sellers today because they were essentially clean and practical. The straight-forward clear honest approach was echoed in similar movements all over the world; yet in a sense it too was limited. People, it seems, cannot live long without some form of decorative beauty about them, and the simple practical beauty of those grids of straight lines and bright primary colours had obvious limitations.

Jewellery, 1920–1939

The jewellery of the period also became impersonal, abstract and functional, with a great emphasis on straight lines and an over-exposure of the diamond, as can be clearly seen in contemporary women's magazines and journals. This was the time of the Art Deco jewel (Figs. 58, 59, 70, 71): abstract shapes, geometrical designs, all lines and angles to harmonize with the clothes and furnishings of the time. The new fashion for stainless steel and ebony in the home encouraged the use of hard bright gems and deep enamels. Diamonds were in favour, of course, but so too were the deeper-coloured stones: the ruby, the emerald, the sapphire. Topazes came back into fashion, aquamarines and amethysts, amber, jade, and, in the nineteen-twenties, a wealth of coral. Enamelling was in bright hard colours—orange, for instance, or acid green—and a good deal of black enamel was also used, especially to set off the glitter of diamonds. Jewels had a loud look, and, like the stainless steel or ebony now in vogue for furnishings, a smooth surface and a high polish. They were practical: women were wearing wrist-watches now, sometimes set in a diamond bracelet; larger pieces were made up of separate components which could themselves be worn as smaller jewels—a brooch, for instance, could be split into two identical clips to be set at the neckline of a black cocktail dress, or the central motif (never a bird or flower, always a crisp geometric figure) could be detached and strung on a chain—a loop was incorporated—and worn as a pendant. A set of Art Deco jewellery is shown facing page 243.

It was a difficult period for jewellery designers, since the current emphasis on structure and function had little reference to their art. A jewel is not basically a practical structure: it is naturally required to withstand wear, but not compression or tension—not in the same terms as, say, a concrete pillar. Its function is simply to decorate. The best jewels are essentially personal creations, true works of art: not abstract and anonymous webs of metal and stone. Thus the Art Deco jewels are poor shadows of the individual designs created in other fields of the arts. The materials that went to their making were used simply because they were "fashionable", not because the designer was engaged with them as a Renaissance craftsman, for instance, was engaged with a fine baroque pearl. They played no part in the creation of a jewel which had an individual character of its own.

Yet the honesty and the clear-sighted approach of the between-the-wars designers did have its effect, and was to contribute towards the later brilliant development in jewellery design; and the emphasis on practicality and symmetry played a great part in the new popularity of the cultured pearl.

CULTURED PEARLS

The natural creation of salt-water and fresh-water pearls has already been described on page 231. In the closing decade of the nineteenth century the Japanese had perfected a method of growing a "cultured" pearl by introducing an irritant into an unfortunate oyster and watching over it while it patiently secreted layers of nacre which slowly covered the irritant and grew into a perfect spherical pearl—that at least was the theory. In practice it proved to be extremely difficult to find an irritant which the oyster did not automatically reject. Eventually, after many tests, it was discovered that tiny particles of the pig-toe clam shell, brought from the Mississippi Valley in the United States, were acceptable to the oyster. These shells were, and still are, brought to Japan in bulk, and cut into strips and then into spheres—very small ones, varying in size from $\frac{1}{10}$ to about $\frac{1}{4}$ inch (2·5 to 7 mm)—which are carefully introduced into the molluscs. The subsequent growing of the pearl is a long, complicated and risky process, lasting from one to four years dependent on the size of the pearl, and beset by endless hazards—some oysters go on strike, some eject the irritant, some are sucked right out of their shells by eels, some are killed by a change in the temperature of the sea (it must be at least 25 degrees Centigrade), some are swept away by tidal waves or hurricanes, some are stolen by pearl thieves. Even when the oysters are finally harvested and brought ashore, only 5 per cent of the pearls are of true gem quality, and less than 40 per cent of those are marketable. The process was invented by Kokichi Mikimoto, and the Japanese held a monopoly of the trade for the early decades of the twentieth century; the present centre is Ago Bay. Japanese cultured pearls are now auctioned monthly under extremely strict conditions—since 1957 the Japanese Government has prohibited the export of any but those of the highest quality, in order to protect a vitally important national industry.

In the nineteen-twenties the fashion was for symmetrical, lustrous pearls of fine matching colour. (A pearl derives its colour from the water in which its oyster lives: in general, creamy pearls come from the Persian Gulf, white ones with a bluish or greenish sheen come from Australia, brown ones come from Panama, black from Mexico, rosy-coloured ones from Ceylon, creamy ones from Japan, and white with a pinkish overtone, from Burma.) Women took to cultured pearls at once—the oriental pearl business was virtually at a standstill between the wars partly because a series of natural disasters devastated the pearl banks; moreover, women liked the matched size and colour of cultured pearls and their quiet "good class" gleam. People who could not afford cultured pearls wore very large fake ones instead. All sorts of supposedly "practical" schemes were introduced, notably the add-a-pearl idea, much publicized by the presentation of add-a-pearl strings to the young princesses, Elizabeth and Margaret Rose. The idea that pearls would increase in value with age was a myth, its adoption reflecting the general economic uncertainty of the time (it is very difficult indeed to sell a pearl necklace today at anything approaching its original price, unless the pearls were of really exceptional quality; which goes to prove that gems should be worn and enjoyed, not used as a hopeful investment).

MID-THIRTIES JEWELLERY

In the mid-thirties people began to gather their riches together again. Gold jewellery came in once more. It was a heavy, extravagant look, plenty of different gemstones set in gold and mounted in cocktail party designs. Women exhibited their jewels deliberately, like walking show-cases, often wearing black which made a good dramatic background: large gold and diamond rings worn over long black gloves, for instance,

Fig. 70 and Fig. 71: Australian opals had been used in many of the Art Nouveau jewels created early in the century for patrons with *avant-garde* tastes. During the Art Deco period between the two world wars they were taken up by every wealthy customer and virtually done to death. Magnificent opals were then arriving in Britain, every single one unique, every single one different in the shimmer of colour that played within it as the light struck the gem. Many, like the fine brooch seen here, were mounted in a geometric diamond framework. The bracelet, which is of gold set with diamonds and five large individual rubies, shows all the trends of the age. Its lines are strictly geometrical, but a really clever hinging technique has been used so that it swirls fluidly round the arm. The Victorian jewellers had used springs to create a clinging bracelet instead of a rigid bangle, but this new concept of incorporating a mass of interlocking units gave a simple bracelet a suppleness of movement hitherto unknown. Bracelets like this one occasionally contained a tiny watch, set into one of the sections and covered by a gem-set motif which performed the double duty of being decorative and protective. Jewels like these are the kind of ornaments worn with a "little black dress" at a cocktail party, or in the bars of the International grand hotels of the between-the-wars period.

By courtesy of N. Bloom & Son

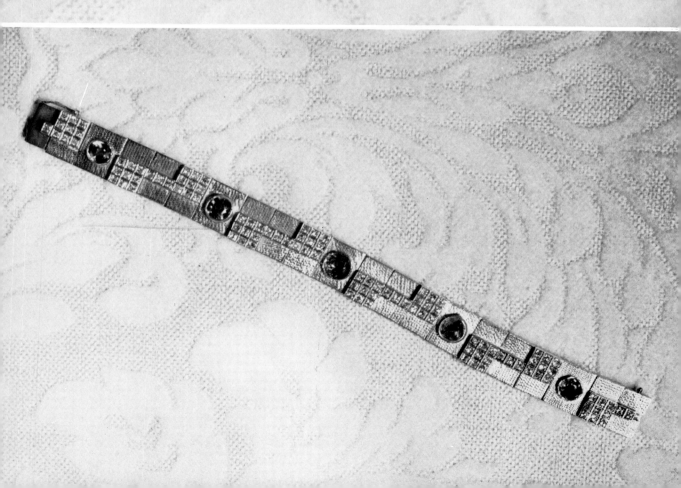

wrist-watches mounted in ornate gold and diamond bracelets, the tiny watch-face shining among a profusion of stones, often itself being covered with *pavé*-set gems. As 1938 and 1939 drew nearer, and people realized that there was, almost certainly, going to be another war, there was a great burst of buying precious jewellery as an investment against the future. Too many people could remember the devaluations that had followed the First War, this time they meant to have something in reserve.

The Post-War Years

The Second World War was fought with a fierceness which almost wiped humanity off the face of the earth. Men and women, fighting side by side on equal terms, were

A Group of Art Deco Jewels : the Art Deco jewellery of the between-the-wars period has several distinct characteristics: the stones are often over-exposed, the colours often deep, the designs often "amusing"; above all, the lines are straight or angular, and the finish smooth and polished. The three brooches seen here are set with citrines, topazes and diamonds. The largest of them is sectional, and can be split into two clips. The use of carved ivory in the rose brooch is typical of the twenties and thirties, and the addition of the enamelled ladybird is a deliberately "cute" touch, as is the appearance of the little dog. The cocktail watch exemplifies the sharp slick style of the period, with its chromium-plated furniture, its syncopated jazz, its endless black-and-silver colour schemes for interior decoration, for *haute couture* dresses and for jewellery. Wristlet watches were relatively new for women: for the past three centuries they had used watches dangling from *châtelaines*, but the First World War changed this, as so many other things, and a more practical style came into vogue. Some watches were, however, still made as decorative pendants and pinned to the shoulder of a short-skirted dress; these had a careful protective cover.

The angular and geometrical lines typify the crisp practical style of the time. At the Bauhaus in Germany designers were working on furniture that was stackable and economical, with the same sharp clean lines—suitable too for pre-fabrication. Here, as so often, jewellery mirrors the current trends in the other arts.

This was also a time when many a British family was living in India, following the Army or working with the Civil Service to build roads and railways and to set up schools. When they came home on leave, they brought with them topazes from India and Ceylon, elephant ivory, tiger's claws set in gold. The stones were cheap and plentiful, so large pieces of jewellery could be manufactured at not too great a cost, with a scattering of diamonds to add value even if they were not absolutely essential to the design.

Characteristically again, these jewels are totally anonymous. Who designed them —for whom? We do not know. They were simply bought across the counter in some grand shop.

By courtesy of N. Bloom & Son

fighting for their own freedom in a war in which, for the first time, all were personally involved—civilians and combatants, men and women and children. The first burst of terrifying nervous energy which flared up in the peace—an intensity of relief that it was over, a great compassion for those who had suffered most horribly, a vow that it should never happen again—this soon burned out, and life was organized again for a tired and worn-out nation. The drab wartime uniforms gave way to mean dull clothes; rationing and clothes coupons, introduced as wartime measures, went on for years. People longed for a little glamour. Many of them had donated their jewellery to the war effort; now, trying to brighten up old depressing clothes, they bought inexpensive mass-produced jewellery, or second-hand pieces from the local jeweller's shop, the Red Cross sales held to raise a few comforts for the disabled servicemen, and the antique shops which began to multiply at a great rate. Women had sold much of their jewellery, to raise a little money and because it seemed unlikely that social life would ever flower again.

The present looked so uncertain that most people treasured what they had left. They peered into the antique shops, re-read old books, listened to nostalgic programmes on the radio; emotionally worn-out, they preferred to buy trinkets made in the old-fashioned styles that reminded them of the past. New goods were simply not coming into the shops, and utility furniture was dismally terrible; better buy something from the antique shop round the corner, or even refurbish junk pieces, painting them in the gay colours recommended by the magazines. Adult education came galloping in: the rooms were warm, the fees low—they still are—and there was a companionable atmosphere which smacked a little of the friendliness of the war years. Those who treasured the past could here learn about the history of art and antiques; the popularity of such courses has increased steadily, out of all proportion and beyond all expectation. The only tragedy was, and is, that so many classes took their studies as far as the end of the nineteenth century and then shied away in horror, preferring to call a halt in Victorian days; and this made a nonsense of the natural continuity of art which is, and must be, a living thing, not something existing solely in the safe isolated context of the past. Yet at that time such studies had a real emotional value of their own, and this was particularly true of the creative classes, where people practised painting and sculpture, for instance, pottery and woodwork, gaining immense pleasure from their efforts—the pride of completing the first six matching wooden egg cups was so great that it had to be seen to be believed—a new serenity, and sometimes achieving, in addition, a very high level of workmanship.

With the late fifties and the sixties, everything seemed to steady down. Manners changed—some of the old gentle ways seemed obsolete; morals changed—people were questioning the old conventional standards, especially in regard to sex; religion side-stepped into questions, with or without answers; tolerance changed almost overnight from a deadly sin to a virtue; dogmatism, on the other hand, was out. People seemed intent on "getting back to base". The practical attitude was, if anything, more evident than ever before; and synthetics, which had already been introduced into the jeweller's world, made a new and much publicized impact with the arrival of the synthetic diamond.

Diamonds

NATURAL DIAMONDS

One of the main reasons for the twentieth-century faith in the genuine diamond is the virtual certainty that it will keep its price and even, quite possibly, increase in value. Loose diamonds are probably more reliable than any form of paper currency now in circulation; but they are only useful as an immediate investment if, in addition to being loose stones, they are of absolutely top quality and fairly large—at least two or three carats. Diamond-set jewellery comes into a rather different category: it is, or should be, beautiful to look at and lovely to wear; its intrinsic value is a secondary consideration, and unlikely to increase for at least ten years. When a customer buys, for instance, a diamond brooch, he is paying a good deal more than the original cost of the un-mounted stones. The jeweller bought those stones at a carefully estimated value, cut them (in the course of this process the size and weight of each stone may well have been reduced by half), had them set by his craftsmen to a chosen design; his selling price must take all those factors into account, together with his own overheads, his own profit, and any taxes imposed by the government. Diamond jewellery cannot be thought of as an investment like stocks and shares; loose stones bought from a reliable dealer, however, are quite another matter.

De Beers Consolidated Mines Ltd.

The standard of diamonds offered for sale, the prices they command and the balance of supply and demand are fortunately very carefully regulated; this is in large measure due to De Beers Consolidated Mines Limited, whose history is bound up with the history of twentieth-century jewellery. The original firm was formed by Cecil Rhodes in 1888, its far-seeing purpose being that of imposing control on the mines themselves, the mining interests, and the output. The hard work and sheer enterprise of Rhodes and the Oppenheimers culminated in the forming, in 1929, of a De Beers subsidiary called the Diamond Corporation. (A fascinating and painstaking book, *Diamonds*, by Eric Bruton, is full of excellent stories about Cecil Rhodes, Barney Barnato and Sir Ernest Oppenheimer in those early years—as well as everything else one could want to know about diamonds.) A year later the Central Selling Organization was formed, and a sensible and functional formula devised for the buying and selling of South African diamonds.

Eighty per cent of the world's genuine diamonds now pass through the C.S.O. There are ten annual "sights" when a controlled selection of the diamonds for sale is sorted into parcels, each of a certain value, which are shown to and bought by a number of recognized and reliable buyers. Obviously each buys a quantity that is far and away above his own needs, for he is usually representing an area; he then divides the stones out fairly amongst local purchasers. About two hundred dealers are allowed to buy rough diamonds direct, everyone else has to buy through these sights.

The value of the diamonds sold through the C.S.O. is almost beyond comprehension. In 1969, for instance, it was about £300,000,000; three years later it was £655,474,410 (an indication of fantastic demand that year, not of a simple doubling of the intrinsic value of the diamond—which usually rises at roughly the same rate as the economy).

When considering fluctuations in demand one must remember that diamonds are used for industrial purposes as well as for jewellery. A stockpile of diamonds is always kept in reserve—generally about two months' supply—and in years when the demand for diamonds is unusually low (1958, for example, or 1970) any residue is added to the reserve.

SYNTHETIC DIAMONDS

It takes millions of years to form a natural diamond; the synthetic gem produced by modern technology is created in much the same way—recipes vary, but generally speaking, carbon is subjected to immense heat and then left to crystallize as it cools—and in a fraction of the time. Where are the differences?

The first is in the price. Synthetic diamonds were first successfully produced in Sweden in 1953, in America two years later, and in South Africa soon after that; the early gems were about twice the price of natural gems, but within ten or twelve years of the initial successful synthetics being made, the cost had dropped below that of the natural stones, and by 1971, when a considerable campaign was set up to publicize them, they were not cheap, but still considerably cheaper than real diamonds.

Like all synthetics, they need to be cleaned with extra care. If a film dulls the surface, dimming the stone's lustre—dirt perhaps, or scent or hair lacquer—the piece must be professionally cleaned.

Another problem is that some synthetic diamonds are very hard—8 or $8\frac{1}{2}$ on Mohs' Scale—and therefore difficult to cut properly. A crystal lacking the full fifty-eight facets of a brilliant cut loses some of its fire and flash.

Lighting can also be a difficulty. Displayed in shops under the correct lighting—Halogen bulbs, for instance, which are particularly good, or low-voltage spotlights—they look wonderful; out in the daylight they may look rather different. It is true, however, that this particular drawback is common to most stones, not merely synthetic diamonds.

When new, set in 14 carat or 18 carat white gold or yellow gold by experienced craftsmen, synthetic diamonds are difficult to differentiate from the genuine stones. People still seem to feel tentative about buying them; it seems almost wasteful to spend a fair amount of money on something that is not "genuine", even if it is craftsman-set in hallmarked gold in Hatton Garden; and many shops too are cautious about selling them, preferring their customers to buy "the real thing" whose lasting quality can be confidently guaranteed. There is, however, one certain market: synthetics can be used to make up copies of real and valuable pieces, which can then be safely deposited in the Bank.

Perhaps we will be able to evaluate synthetics better after another fifty years or so, when the continuing experimental work on them has gone still further, and the gems have acquired some tradition of quality and service. It is early yet; feelings take a long time to change.

Johnson Matthey & Co. Ltd.

So much jewellery has been made and sold at every price level in the twentieth century that there might have been a serious danger of the market getting out of control, had it not been stabilized by firms like De Beers, regulating the diamond trade, and Johnson Matthey, Europe's leading refiners and engineers of precious metal, and the sole refiners and distributors of platinum metals from the Rustenburg Platinum Mines in South Africa, the world's largest producer.

Johnson Matthey, founded in 1817, has, for over a century, held appointments as Official Melters, Refiners and Assayers to the Bank of England and the Royal Mint. Its head office is, appropriately enough, in Hatton Garden in the City of London, but it has associated companies world-wide: in France and Holland and Italy, in Sweden and Belgium and Austria, in the United States and Canada, in India and South Africa, in Australia and New Zealand. Its reputation has come to be as world-wide as its concerns, its name being accepted as synonymous with tested quality. The firm makes a bewildering number of goods, from the metals used in fine jewellery to the components for facial surgery, and its success may be gauged from the published figures for invoiced sales in 1970: £98,900,000.

A major development in the world's platinum industry took place in the early nineteen-twenties when large deposits of platinum-bearing ore were discovered in South Africa. Rustenburg Platinum Mines Ltd. was eventually formed to work these deposits, Johnson Matthey being associated with them as smelters and refiners of the output and distributors and fabricators of the metals. Together they guarantee to industries throughout the world that there will be a controlled, adequate and continuing supply of these metals.

Johnson Matthey also market a complete range of metal alloys which can save jewellers a great deal of work. Carat golds are available, for instance, in a range of forms which includes grain, sheet, strip, blanks, wires and tube. One of the trickiest of materials is solder (the Assay Office tests solders as well as metals in silverware or jewellery), and this too they produce in several forms. The new designer-craftsmen who are creating the beautiful present-day jewels can thus supply themselves with metals and components of tried and proven quality; and ultimately the customer too must benefit.

CHAPTER TWELVE

The Present Day

Introduction—New Approaches to Jewellery—Patronage Today—Present-day British Designer-Craftsmen: Andrew Grima; John Donald; David Thomas; Other Modern Jewellers—The De Beers Competitions—Exhibitions and Showrooms—The Years to Come

Introduction

Where today is the centre of the art world? New York? London? Rome? Paris? The creative artist-designer is no longer strictly confined within national frontiers, nor bound to live and work in any one place which is a current centre for artistic innovation and experiment. Nor is he bound by the need to live within reach of his patrons: the globe has shrunk like a badly washed sock, he can travel almost anywhere by air within a couple of days, his work is shown at international exhibitions, he competes in international competitions, no longer relying on word-of-mouth to spread his reputation. His patrons travel too: they may well belong to the jet set, zooming from one air-conditioned villa to the next.

The old conventions of past artists and craftsmen have not been overthrown or abandoned, but rather adapted to serve a scientific and technological age and a new climate of opinion that sidesteps many of the old beliefs. New techniques have been evolved: the most gigantic leap forward, for example, has been made in the weaver's craft. New approaches have been tried: embroidery, for instance, is an age-old art which is adapting itself to the use of new textiles and modern designs—some of the finest embroidery in the world is being created in the Britain of today. New art forms have been accepted: photography, for example—the advances made in this fascinating medium over the last fifty years are astonishing, technology marries with craft and optical illusion to create something which is far from those smudgy early mechanical portrayals. But of them all, jewellery is the most exciting, the freshest and the most unconventional.

New Approaches to Jewellery

The brilliant British designer-craftsmen of the present day get right down to the basic truth of the materials they are using. How was the gemstone originally formed? The scientific developments of the twentieth century have helped enormously here; at the close of Queen Victoria's reign there were relatively few gemmologists and mineralogists, and those there were worked on strictly academic lines; now, however, the jewellery world is rich in qualified professionals, and has, in addition, new machinery with which to test gems and pearls, and a new knowledge upon which to build. No ruby comes out of the earth polished as a star-formation; no emerald formed by Nature is baguette-shaped, no diamond brilliant-cut; the stones must be man-handled to achieve the conventional shape and glitter. What of a gemstone's natural shape, its sharp clean crystalline lines: might they not be used in the creation of a design? And what of the other treasures within the earth? Many minerals which have never before been used in jewellery have an intrinsic beauty of their own. Generally speaking, the present-day craftsmen-designers do not use any new mineral or new gemstone which is too soft to wear well, preferring those which are over 7 in Mohs' Scale of hardness; but given this limitation, there are plenty of new stones and new minerals being used nowadays which have a luscious range of colour and a strange beauty of formation suggesting hidden depths. Agate, for instance, once thought dull, can look fabulous in a modern jewel, its multiple striations of colour revealed by the designer. So can green malachite, with its great swirls of green and white, its beautiful markings which are themselves a natural and fluid composition. So can iron pyrites: there is, for instance, a brooch made by David Thomas, with iron pyrites set in gold like a miniature Giant's Causeway, as spikily and irregularly beautiful as any natural formation.

How should these new gems be treated? In the past gemstones were shaped and moulded by the conventional cuts; nowadays each is treated individually. It is another Renaissance. There is no point in faceting, say, malachite to achieve sparkle; it is the natural colour, the natural shape that are important. The stones can be used exactly as they are; they can be polished; they can be carved; they can be cut—but not neces-sarily in the old conventional patterns of facets; a new jewel can be designed to incor-porate a new cut. Baroque pearls have come back into fashion; so have opals—no two the same in size, shape or colour.

Just as gemstones were mixed in the best jewels of the art nouveau period, so now they are again mingled arbitrarily, in open flouting of the old conventions (it was once held, for example, that only diamonds should be set with rubies). Each stone is considered individually. One might find, for instance, a jewel centring on a singularly large ruby which has been carved—not conventionally faceted—into some strange individual shape, perhaps an image that has particular meaning for the patron, with a smaller diamond set right into the ruby's surface; Andrew Grima has done this. Alternatively a designer-craftsman might study a flawed emerald, polish it *en cabochon* (another revival of an ancient technique) to reveal the beetle-skeleton inclusions within, and add textured gold "legs" with *pavé*-set diamonds to turn a wayward trick of formation into an intrinsic feature of the design.

Dealing with gems in this way gives jewellery a new quality which has until now been lacking: a strange sense of stones, minerals and metals as having an implicit life of their own, as if living Nature were here caught in the close meshes of a net that still pulsed with the life within. The new craftsmen-designers treat the newly discovered marvels of the natural world with honour and respect, rather than imposing their

249

own conventions and manipulating these materials to suit their own pre-conceived ideas.

The same quality can be seen in the metalwork. The metals in principal used today are gold, platinum and palladium (which is about half the weight of platinum). Present-day settings feature lightness, strength, and texture. Here again there have been tremendous developments in techniques and in the making of new and sophisticated machines. Casting, for instance, has become much sharper and more accurate. Electro-gilding has been greatly improved: (this is a process whereby a piece of silver jewellery is hung in a solution which contains gold, potassium and cyanide; when a current of electricity is passed through the solution, the gold is deposited on the silver, forming a coating): whereas the gilding used to be very soft, and was only obtainable in a single colour—yellow—it is now much harder and more reliable, and different decorative shades have been developed. Electro-forming is another relatively new technique: a sensitized wax mould is immersed in an electrolytic bath on which gold is gradually deposited; by this means Engelhard Industries Limited "grew" the crown designed by Louis Osman for the Prince of Wales in 1970.

The surface of the metal is often textured to give a three-dimensional effect. Andrew Grima, for instance, took casts from real leaves and made them up in gold, which he then sand-blasted to take away the natural smooth shine of the metal's surface, covering it with minute pitting to re-create in metallic terms the delicate suedy look of the original. Another Grima jewel exemplified the present-day feeling for depth; he constructed it from layer upon layer of gold until he had a chunky twig-like shape, set diamonds at its heart, and wrapped round it a sheet of sculptured gold peeled back, like bark from a woody twig, to reveal the diamonds and the feathery soft delicacy of its core.

There is an ingrained and natural tradition of reverence for the Etruscan gold-workers, with their magnificent mastery of their craft; yet the sophistication of the new techniques married to the expertise of the craftsman and the brilliance of the designer is producing jewels which equal anything the Etruscans created. Present-day work has a finish and lustre that is incomparable.

In modern British jewels the new ways of treating minerals and metals and gemstones are complemented by the skill of the designer-craftsman, forming marvellously inventive shapes unlike any dreamed of in jewellery before. Many are abstract designs based on the shapes and forms of the natural world; many reflect the images of the atomic era; all are alive—*how* some jewels pulsate with an inner life—and all are individual. The creator of modern jewellery is again both designer and craftsman. He or she is thoroughly educated and trained. The resources of modern technology are adapted to develop the age-old techniques; erudite individuality is the theme, just as it was in the old Renaissance days, but here expressed in the modern idiom. No two uncut stones were, are, or could be exactly the same; it was man who made them match, imposing his arbitrary and conventional facets on the natural crystalline formation. No two baroque pearls, no two blister pearls, no two opals were, are, or could be identical twins. The designer-craftsman allows his material to command the character of his work; it is a supremely honest approach. He has a long training behind him: he may well have begun as an artist or a sculptor, then trained in metalwork, and finally turned to the creation of jewellery. Nothing is skimped (the Worshipful Company of Goldsmiths would see to that, even if his personal integrity did not do so), his work is never slipshod or unworthy.

Nothing is more fascinating than to watch a working jewellery-designer twist and turn a gemstone in his fingers, consider it, cherish it; then fetch in a piece of metal, jot down idea after idea, and finally evolve a full-scale working drawing. He may well try out a whole series of variations on a theme: in 1970, for instance, after Susan Barfield (Fig. 67) had won her first Diamonds-International Award, fifteen full-scale drawings made by her in the course of the creation of the prize-winning jewel were displayed at the Hornsey College of Art: they showed how a running stream-like theme evolved into the rippling flowing lines of a beautiful necklace. Present-day jewellery designs have the fluid modelled look of sculpture by Henry Moore or Barbara Hepworth; the applied splatter effect of collage is fortunately out of fashion.

For whom are these designers working? Some of them still work anonymously for the conventional shops, creating designs which can be mass-produced commercially while yet reflecting the modern idiom—the angles and spikes and clean sharp lines of a natural crystalline structure, "new" gemstones, an emphasis on depth, a feeling for texture and finish. Others create their own individual designs, perhaps for competitions in which the finest designer-craftsmen in the trade compete to design some award or commemorative medallion; perhaps for tender, again in competition, designing a new chalice for a cathedral, a new mayoral chain for a city; perhaps, and very probably, for personal patrons. Jewels are no longer created to echo dress fashions, which nowadays change almost overnight; new gimmicks no longer have time to die away, instead they are sharply elbowed aside for something new. Few people still have clothes designed especially for them—it is too expensive, for one thing, and the shops and boutiques are full of up-to-the-minute clothes and accessories at off-the-peg prices. Jewels are still costly, however; and more than this, they are now true works of art. In the past, jewellery fashions have see-sawed between a tremendous display showing off the wearer's wealth and social standing, and, conversely, a feeling that it was vulgar to parade one's jewels—as vulgar, in fact, as to mention one's bank balance, which was simply indicated by one's style of dress, perhaps enhanced by a perfect string of pearls. Present-day jewels do not shout "Wealth", like a Tudor gold chain or a Georgian diamond *parure*; they say "Art" instead, and say it beautifully.

Patronage Today

Who are the patrons today? In the past they were the kings and queens, the popes and princes of the Church, the dukes and connoisseurs. Now, however, times have changed, and changed for the better. Money is spread around more evenly, education too; there are plenty of well-to-do people, plenty of educated people—and the patrons *are* the people.

Since the first antique shops appeared at the end of the Victorian era, people have become more and more conscious of the past. Nostalgia has become a cult, urged on by all the media. Bound up with this nostalgia, and with an increase in education, was a fear that the "national heritage" was being obliterated. This was particularly urgent when it came to architecture: paintings, sculpture, furniture, silver, porcelain, glass and jewellery could all be preserved in the great museums and the stately homes; but architecture was, and is, different. One cannot put a Palladian mansion in a glass case. People began to fight for the preservation of old architecture, and all the other "old" things came in for much the same treatment.

During the eighteenth century, the erudite and wealthy land-owners had become the true patrons of the artists and craftsmen of their times. They had new houses built and furnished in the most modern style, never looking back to the past—it did not occur to a Georgian gentleman to keep a "nice Jacobean chair" in a drawing-room designed by Adam, adorned with painted decorations by Angelica Kauffmann and furnished with

Two brooches by Andrew Grima: the two jewels illustrated here show surprising variations of technique. The upper one is a star-burst quite as dramatic as anything made in Georgian times, but completely modern in its unconventional approach to the setting of its emeralds and baguette diamonds. The textured gold wirework is Etruscan-fine, the facet on the central topaz so sharply cut that it sparkles as brilliantly as the other stones. This is a theatrical jewel, personal, dramatic, eminently suitable for wearing by one of today's brilliant and creative women. The lower brooch, in contrast, is very different and enormously inventive, featuring carved gemstones—a fashion Grima revived after it had lain dormant for generations. Hard gems were carved in classical times, both Greek and Roman, when they were valued for their magical and medicinal virtues and often engraved with a symbol or sigil; they were of immense personal importance to the wearer, who sometimes regarded the possession of such a stone as the only line of defence between him and the hostile forces of the outer world. The old technique was revived during the Renaissance when great showy cups or bowls were carved out of hard stones and framed in gold and pearls, displaying the patron's wealth and standing, and smaller stones carved in the antique style and valued by their owners much as the men of classical times had treasured talismans. In the nineteen-sixties, with a new jewellery Renaissance centring on Britain, Grima revived the fashion yet again; this brooch, an exemplar, incorporates carved rubies and a pale carved emerald, in classically simple leaf and flower motifs. Only the *pavé* diamonds are faceted. All the stones are set in textured gold, bark-like, nubbly, with a rounded rather than angular line. This is true carving, true modelling, not a "throw-at-the-wall" collage. Both brooches exhibit the "secret ingredient" of a splendidly successful present-day jewel, for they have that extra dimension, that feeling for depth, characteristic of today's finest jewellery. There is a fine stepping up and down in texture, a classical approach translated into the newest possible idiom. Both are here seen larger than life-size, technically perfect, modern as tomorrow, but still totally timeless.

By courtesy of Andrew Grima Ltd

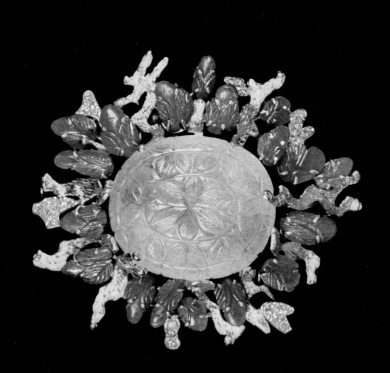

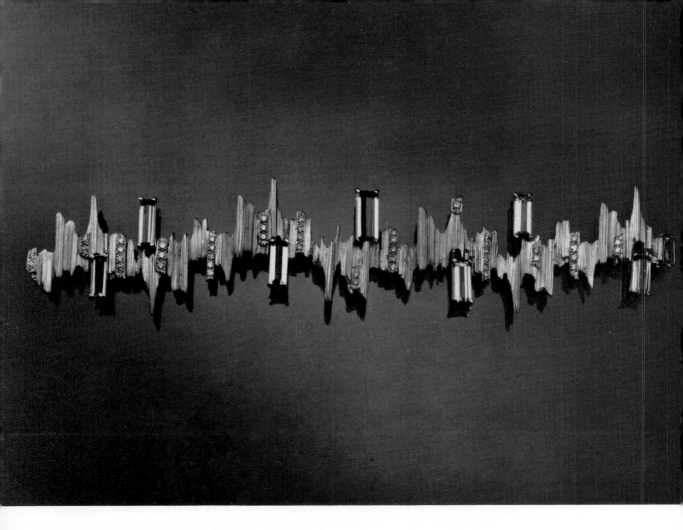

Fig. 72: foremost among the British craftsmen-designers who in the post-War Renaissance have produced supremely and exclusively personal designs, executed with marvellous craftsmanship, innovatory and beautiful, is Andrew Grima, who can and does produce jewels at both ends of the financial spectrum, always original, always exciting, and famed throughout the world. The bracelet shown above has that same all-important extra dimension as the brooches featured on the previous page: a feeling for depth, created by the brilliance of the design and the variety of materials and techniques—layers of texturing, polished stones, faceted stones, polished gold, textured gold, all combined in this elegant and angular jewel. Made of gold, diamonds and peridots, it is an exercise in symmetry, balance and architectural form.

By courtesy of Andrew Grima Ltd

pieces hand-made for him by Chippendale; the old chair was banished to the attics. (English craftsmanship at this time was so superb that bulk consignments of furniture were exported abroad, and hardly anything imported at all, except a few paintings and some antique sculpture.) Regency elegance led into the enormous prosperity and wealth of Victorian England; now it was the machines and the engineers that were un-paralleled, and the Victorians were fully and proudly aware of it. By the end of the century, the wealthy men were often those who had little or no artistic education, and to whom the vitality of new creative work made as little appeal as the refinement of some of the earlier masterpieces. With no family tradition of connoisseurship at their backs, they seldom risked buying too much that was new; the old pieces were safer. The artists had to find new patrons, and they turned now to the dealers and the galleries, where a one-man show might arouse interest in their work. The patron was simply the man who came in off the street to buy something ready-made, much as he might buy a bag of sugar across the counter; the art world seemed to turn in on itself, each artist painting out of his own inspiration and hoping that the result would appeal to the passers-by sufficiently for someone to buy it. The old personal relationship between the artist and the patron was gone; their link now was a very tenuous and delicate one, seeming to consist merely in a flicker of shared liking for one external work—and even that was not essential. The two world wars did nothing to help a situation in which patron and artist were out of sympathy with one another, and often linked only by a shared lack of respect.

Since the Second World War, however, a tidal wave of artistic production has broken over us. We are still too close to it to evaluate it wisely. The sheer volume is frightening. Art galleries put on show after show, the International magazines are filled with reviews; and the general public pays little heed to it all, impatient with a set that talks a language of its own and seems wrapped in its own rituals. Yet *we* are the patrons today, it is up to us to visit the shows, to talk to the students, to buy the new work, to demand better grants—the vibrant interest in the arts in present-day Germany, for example, is a measure of the Government's sponsorship, grants which seem huge compared with our own—to help the National Art Collections Fund or the National Trust, which are preserving many of the old treasures, but also to help keep art a living reality by becoming personally engaged in it. Personal interest, personal communication, is something no art school can give its students: art school existence, brief though it is, can promote the feeling that one is on a tube train travelling round and round, some-times flashing briefly into the light, mostly rushing through the dark, while a different world goes quietly about its business in the daylight far overhead. The magazine critics do their best for artists trying to make their way after art school, in a way they have taken the place of the old-style teachers, but a review is a flat criticism when compared with true personal contact.

Today's designer-craftsmen jewellers are thoroughly trained, technically superb, always looking for new ideas and new treatments without being *outré* or slapdash, and, at their best, have achieved a fine balance between creating original work that satisfies themselves and creating commissioned work that pleases a customer. A successful business depends on satisfying the customer—however brilliant the design, he or she does not want to be kept waiting for it—and the present-day jewellers are very successful indeed.

If one wished to commission a jewel and had never before approached any of the independent designer-craftsmen, and wanted to be sure that one were commissioning someone of proven reputation, why not obtain the lists of past competition winners? There are now a good many competitions, both national and international; few of them are run by commercial firms (and even so, are judged by outside experts trained in the subject), the majority being organized by the Worshipful Company of Goldsmiths and De Beers Consolidated Mines Ltd. A craftsman-jeweller who succeeds in any of these very tough competitions has more than proved his worth.

Most of the present-day craftsmen-designers who are established in their field have shops of their own (the address list in Appendix G gives a small and arbitrary selection, it is by no means comprehensive). One can thus study the pieces displayed in the shop window, or in the show cases within; or visit the showrooms and exhibitions mentioned at the end of the chapter; then, when one has found someone whose idiom appeals, spend a while talking to the designer, explaining the price limit, the type of motif one has in mind, who it is for, what sort of colours and gemstones might be suitable. Designers who undertake commissioned work swiftly develop an astonishing depth of sympathy with their patrons. This might, indeed, be said to be the distinguishing characteristic of contemporary British work, the quality that has lifted it into a class on its own. Present-day German work has a marvellous precision, which may be traced back to the Bauhaus inspiration; Scandinavian work has a characteristic simplicity and economy about it; the Brazilian can and does draw especial creative inspiration from the superb quality of indigenous gemstones; the Americans have done striking work in the field of visual impact; but British work has a personality about it that derives from the designer's ability to put the patron first, and his own feelings second. As Gerald Benney, one of the leading British silversmiths, said, "There is something very impersonal about going into a big shop and laying bare your soul to some casual salesman." How much better to patronize one of the modern craftsmen-designers, the very motive of whose commissioned work is to create something individual, something uniquely suited to patron and occasion. The design the artist suggests takes into consideration the life-style of the wearer. One might perhaps commission a brooch for a birthday present—John Donald designed just such a piece in white gold set with alexandrites. It was made up of a number of small starry motifs, as delicate and spiky as snowflakes, emblematic of the recipient's love of flowers. For another patron, who brought him a heavy gold cigarette case left by her husband, from which she asked him to create something entirely personal, he designed and made a flexible bracelet of autumn leaves, perfectly suited to the autumnal golds and browns she liked to wear and to her liking for an outdoor life.

Usually such a designer-craftsman will prepare a number of sketches for the patron to consider; then have the chosen one costed, allowing for time, materials, and so on, and including his own mark-up. He may have his own stock of gemstones, but will generally be prepared to use stones which the patron wishes to have re-set, provided these are of a reasonable size; usually, however, he will buy in his own metal—the autumn leaf bracelet was a special case. The work should be ready within a few weeks.

It is often also possible to commission fourth-year students in art colleges: their craftsmanship is superb—their time is given up to learning and practising, rather than nibbled away by commercial demands—and their ideas usually decidedly *avant-garde*. The work is very carefully watched by the tutor, guaranteeing an extremely high standard of performance. It is an exciting thing to go to any art school's annual exhibitions (one can apply to be put on the mailing list of the local ones), pick out work one particularly likes, perhaps buy a little, watch the students' subsequent careers, discover—it can be extremely stimulating—whether one's early choice was a good one, and if it was, continue to buy, thus building up a personal collection which has a continuity of its own. The personal interest is vital, this is something no institution can give; the encouragement of creative work, the encouragement of artists, is not a right, it is a duty; if we treat modern work as "a load of rubbish" and new artists as "not nice to know" it will be our loss in the end.

Present-day British Designer-Craftsmen

ANDREW GRIMA

Foremost among the men who have established the reputation of British designer-craftsmen, working initially at a time when people accepted the craftsmanship of British jewellers but were sceptical of their ability to produce supremely and exclusively personal designs, was Andrew Grima, now a man of international standing; two of his brooches are shown facing page 252, and a bracelet on the following page.

Grima was born in 1921, of Maltese and Italian parentage. He trained as an engineer and then went to war, where he spent much of his time repairing vehicles in Burma. When the war was over he spent a short time "helping" in his father-in-law's jewellery business, and became so enchanted with the medium that he never left it. In 1946 he founded the manufacturing jewellers, H. J. Company Limited, and over the years made himself a driving force in the modern approach to minerals. One of the very few successful jewellers of the present day who has not had a full goldsmith's training, he concentrated on design, hating the old conventional styles, and did it so brilliantly that he won eleven De Beers Diamonds-International Awards and dozens of other competitions.

Grima's present London shop is an intensely personal place with a startling fortress frontage, magnificently baroque, yet supremely modern, its two levels linked by a spiral stair of transparent acrylic steps winding round a stainless steel shaft—Cinderella's shoes must have been made of material like this—and crowded like Aladdin's cave with a wealth of original pieces. Every single piece on sale, including the watches, was designed by Grima and made up by his craftsmen; the overall control is his alone.

The originality and panache of his designs have won him the Royal Warrant, an international *clientèle*, quantities of awards—including, in 1966, the Duke of Edinburgh's design award, and a reputation so high that he has travelled world-wide, setting up overseas branches of his business, giving personal shows, accompanying exhibitions mounted by the Worshipful Company of Goldsmiths.

Grima virtually started in Britain the fashion for using crystals in their natural form. It is said that he was the first jeweller to use crystallized agate, a seductive whorl of grey stone overlaid with a shattering of silver effervescence. He has used a whole range of gemstones: opals and baroque pearls, quartz, citrines, tourmalines, and many many more; tried out all the opposites; carved rubies where one would expect them to be faceted; cut a new style of faceting on other stones; perched one precious gemstone on another; set them all in richly textured gold. His watches, with Omega movements set under slabs of aquamarine or rutilated quartz, amongst other gemstones, with sculptured gold bands textured in fashions before unknown, have sold world-wide. The driving force seems always to be "Design before monetary value", so that he has created some pieces which are of enormous intrinsic value and others, equally beautifully designed, where the stones themselves are of little intrinsic worth but of great beauty. Some of his jewels are designed with such originality and created with such individual flair that they rank with the fantasies of Cellini or Fabergé. Year after year he creates new and still surprising work, always fresh, and always exciting. His work and his efforts have broken through the old conventions and given modern British jewellery its international status.

JOHN DONALD

John Donald was born in 1928, studied graphics at the Farnham School of Art, and won a place for further study at the Royal College of Art, where he concentrated on jewellery. By 1961 he had his own workshop, and by 1967 his own City of London shop, deliberately kept fairly small in order to maintain personal control and the true personal touch. His craftsmen still work alongside him, as craftsmen traditionally did in the old days, casting and polishing, soldering and setting stones and so on.

John Donald's work is wholly personal. It is difficult to know which comes first in his life, his own meticulous craftsmanship or his ability to design. He has designed all manner of things in the industrial field as well as jewels—hand luggage, for instance, and spectacle frames. His most memorable public commissions are probably the jewelled badges of office he has made: several for industrial organizations, others for the Wardens of the Worshipful Company of Goldsmiths (a competition which he won), and one for the Sheriff of Nottingham which was especially timeless in its style of design, and very finely made. His private commissions show great empathy: truly personal jewels which take into consideration the customer's general appearance and life-style—his perception is extraordinary—and flatter the wearer; these beautiful pieces, each created for an individual customer, yet reflect the creator's unassuming and understated courtesy.

John Donald's interest in gemstones is so absorbing that there have been occasions when he was reluctant to set a particular stone because he so enjoyed fingering and admiring it. The stones are set with an innate respect for their shape and colour and beauty, a reverence, as it were, for these natural creations, but are still subordinate to the design itself. His recent jewels have an individuality as marked as any signature. Fig. 60 shows just one beautiful piece. He has used textured golds in shorn-off spaghetti shapes; rough and polished pendant gold cavities with faceted gems or baroque pearls swinging inside; drums and ovals of white or yellow gold inside which are set gemstones balanced on slender stalks at differing levels. One ring made in this idiom had a circular pierced drum-shaped frame set at right angles to an oxydized white gold shank, with small rubies and sapphires recessed within it, each on its own stalk, like a ripening blackberry. The effect of depth thus achieved gives that extra dimension which is a distinguishing feature of the best present-day jewellery.

DAVID THOMAS

David Thomas, born in 1938, studied at the Twickenham School of Art, graduating to one of the highly-prized places at the Royal College of Art in London. By 1960 he had his own workshop where a small group of craftsmen work full-time to produce his designs; he still makes as many jewels as he can himself and, like John Donald, keeps his business small, ensuring personal attention for his customers.

David Thomas is supremely a goldsmith—a modern Etruscan master, working with the thinnest of gold wires soldered together and linked by tiny gold globules. The seeming fragility of his goldwork belies its strength. If one cups a Thomas brooch in the hand one can feel its balance, like civil engineering in miniature, Lilliputian scaffolding in its most precious form. Fig. 63 shows a single sample.

He has worked with all the gemstones, whether well- or little-known, from rubies and diamonds—poised on the tip of a fine gold stalk, apparently without any visible means of support, yet perfectly secure—to malachite, lapis lazuli and iron pyrites. His showroom is a mineralogist's dream, his themes at once modern and timeless.

David Thomas has designed some of the most brilliant of the contemporary jewels, but one might perhaps pick out a piece which, while not strictly speaking a jewel at all, is in the age-old jeweller-goldsmith tradition. This is the nautilus cup commissioned as a retirement gift from Lord Boyd, former Prime Warden of the Worshipful Company of Goldsmiths, and a noted conchologist, to the Company. Nautilus cups were made by many of the Renaissance masters, the nautilus shell being most beautifully set, lapped in gold and studded with gems. Thomas's, however, gave the old tradition a new twist for he based his design on meticulous study of the living creature's actual appearance: finding that the living nautilus has hundreds of tiny fronds coming from its mouth, he designed a stand made up of a multiplicity of waving golden fronds with slender sinuous arms to hold the polished shell.

OTHER MODERN JEWELLERS

Present-day jewels are so personal that it is impossible to consider them without taking into account their makers and designers—and there is such a crowd of gifted contemporary people that it is also impossible to make anything but a random selection. So many of them are contributing to the excellence of present-day work; so many of them are shaping the future, with its new adaptations of techniques and designs.

Ernest Blyth and **Frances Beck** (Fig. 65) were in their twenties when they opened a joint London workshop in 1966; he had studied at the Central School, she at the great Glasgow School of Art, and both had been awarded travelling scholarships. Their work has been shown all over the world, from Scandinavia to Japan, and several of their pieces have been bought by the Worshipful Company of Goldsmiths for their permanent collection. Both have won De Beers Diamonds-International Awards—the scheme is described more fully in a later section—and other competitions, including the Engagement Ring competitions; in 1972 Blyth won the Goldsmiths' Topham Trophy Award; and in 1973 another Diamonds-International Award for a magnificent choker necklace of gold and diamonds.

Lawrence Wheaton (Fig. 62) is a designer who has dedicated much of his time to teaching others. He was born in 1944; trained first at the Central School of Arts and Crafts and then at the Sir John Cass College of Art; worked for three years with the Swedish Crown Jewellers in Stockholm; and then returned to England to serve as a part-time lecturer at the Hornsey College of Art as well as running his own studio-workshop. Some of his jewels were exhibited in the Collingwood showrooms, and at the end of 1972 he was appointed their resident designer, with a staff of craftsmen, and was thus given the opportunity to promote his own work and ideas and to sell his pieces on their premises: a relationship clearly of great benefit to them both. His style is gently reminiscent of the art nouveau, for he uses beautiful sculptural lines carved in low relief, a continual flow of movement which makes even the largest gemstone seem graceful. He created, for instance, one brooch whose soft fluid gold tendrils cupped a big dark polished piece of lapis lazuli, some of them being tipped with small diamonds.

Among Wheaton's Hornsey pupils were **Richard Bonehill** and **Lynne Bradshaw** (Fig. 64), now in business together. They have tried their hand at every branch of the jeweller's craft, won a good many competitions, exhibited at special shows in Britain and Canada, and worked up a business combining a consistently high standard of design and workmanship with an exemplary commercial sense. Even in the quietest trading times they have been swamped with commissions for personal jewellery, plate, medals and trophies. They won, for example, the commission for designs for the gold, silver and bronze medallions awarded at the 1970 Commonwealth Games, held in Scotland. Their prize-winning design, created according to the terms of the brief, showed classically elegant motifs: on the one side a linked chain, on the other Edinburgh Castle in low relief and the traditional wreath of laurel. They are also experts in enamelling, often working with contrasting colours on, for instance, a solid silver ring.

Gerda Flockinger also lectured at the Hornsey College of Art, and was the first jeweller in Britain to be honoured with a special show at the Victoria and Albert Museum, where her jewels were displayed together with Sam Herman's glass. Although of Austrian origin, she came to Britain in the late nineteen-thirties, when still a child, and opened her own studio-workshop in 1956. Her style is supremely individual and unmistakeably her own creation. She uses both gold and silver, and a wide range of the less well-known gemstones, both rough and polished, particularly those which have a luminous glow suiting the delicate and moon-world quality of her work. Every piece of her jewellery is made by hand. "To watch her work is almost like seeing a Japanese craftsman," John Houston observed. "You can see the mists gathering." She evolves her ideas in the very act of making her piece at the workbench, winding the silver threads this way and that, adding pearls or precious gems as the fancy strikes her. (Among other commissions, she made Mary Quant's wedding ring.) A feature of her style is that nothing ever matches exactly—take a pair of Flockinger earrings, for example, and although they are patently designed to be worn together, one might centre on a moonstone, the other on a pearl, or the left dangle slightly lower than the right. Everything is hand-made, finely delicate, and feminine.

One can compare Gerda Flockinger's fragile-looking jewels with **Wendy**

Ramshaw's finger-rings, bold and spiky, looking as if they were machine-turned. Each has a thin gold shank from which protrudes a metal stalk—different lengths, different shapes—topped by a gemstone cut *en cabochon*. One may wear as many as nine of these, all on the same finger-joint, with the jewelled stalks thrusting out like a fragment of some miniature atomium. These are jewels in the Space Age idiom, crisp and clean and linear.

Like David Thomas with his twentieth-century nautilus cup, **Jocelyn Burton** has adapted Renaissance forms to the modern age and to her own individual style. She has made a speciality of hand-wrought drinking goblets studded with gemstones. There are other splendid Burton pieces too, functional but encrusted with swirls of gold and silver set with precious stones; her unique talent gives her work a quality that is immediately recognizable, each design, no matter how rich and dramatic the materials in which it is made up, still retaining the mysterious fantasy look that is her own "hallmark".

Then too there is **William Tolliday** at Garrards, who creates precious collages, each individually signed and numbered, so versatile that they range from the "Adoration of the Magi" at one end of the scale to "Scissor-Tailed Flycatchers" at the other. The owner of a Tolliday piece can be sure of artistic and aesthetic pleasure, married to the comfortable recollection that this is not only a work of art, but a creation of such intrinsic value that it could, if one were absolutely forced to it, be turned into hard cash—a truly Wittelsbach conception of being able to back one's investment both ways. However, only the greatest despair would prompt such an action.

There are still more people one should mention—all the brilliant new award-winners, for example, who are named, all too briefly, in the next section; and a fascinating trio of opposites, **Nevin Holmes**, **Charlotte de Syllas** and **Ingeborg Bratman**, all of them doing totally original work; and **Stuart Devlin**, whom many experts consider the greatest goldsmith in the world today, as great a twentieth-century metalworker as Paul de Lamerie, the premier goldsmith of the eighteenth century. Devlin is an Australian, born in 1931, who now has showrooms in London; he has won just about every prize there is for design and silversmithing—it is difficult to know whether he is supremely a goldsmith, a silversmith or a jeweller—and has exhibited regularly in every continent and a whole string of the world's capitals. His work is surpassingly rich; if you are paying for gold, he says, you do not want to be sold something that looks like stainless steel. Devlin makes annually a limited collection of precious Easter eggs, translating the Fabergé tradition into a modern idiom and creating these jewelled surprises in his own marvellously inventive and energetically rich style. The golden eggs, many of which look as though they are meshed in a clinging golden net, open to show some jewelled fantasy of a yolk: perhaps an enamelled flower with a bee hovering above, perhaps a huge amethyst crystal surrounded by spikes of gold—the possibilities are endless.

The De Beers Competitions

De Beers Consolidated Mines Limited have done a gigantic amount on behalf of jewellery design and the world-wide jewellery trade, exemplified by their annual competitions, which began in America in 1954, when thirty-one Americans submitted entries, but which are now truly international—in 1972, for example, there were 1,289 designers submitting entries from thirty-five countries. The adjudicators—usually four experts from four different countries—spend about two weeks sifting through the hundreds of entries, each of which bears only an anonymous number, and pick out about thirty, which are then made up; the awards, presented publicly at a glittering annual prize-giving, are the acknowledged Oscars of the jewellery trade. The designs must feature diamonds; this apart, the judges consider the use of materials, and the beauty, originality and wearability of the piece.

Andrew Grima alone has so far won eleven awards. **Gilian Packard** won in 1963 and 1964, one of her pieces being an inspired design: a pyramid of rose-quartz set in gold, diamond-tipped—seen one way up, it looks like some strange flower, seen the other way, like a pale-pink crystal caught in a golden cage (Fig. 61). **David Morris** also won in the same years; his diamond jewellery is beautifully rich, and, interestingly, much of his new work features corals. In 1967 twenty-five prizes were awarded, nine of them going to British designers; **Terence Waldron**, who was amongst those nine, won again in 1972, his third award, for a really beautiful and unusual gold bracelet made in diamond-shaped sections of tiny gold wires, springing from a smaller central mass of individually mounted round stones. The honours are, in general, evenly divided between the sexes, and many of them go to designers who are still very young—**Susan Barfield**, for instance, was still a student at the Hornsey College of Art when she won an award for her fluid gold-and-diamond necklace, its rippling strands flowing closely about the throat and spreading out like a bib of sculptured gold across the breast (Fig. 67). She won again, the very next year, still a student; among her fellow-prize-winners were **Jean Johnstone**, whose brooch was inspired by light pouring through an old stained glass window—small diamonds, closely placed, set on shapes of textured gold in a framework of smooth polished gold, bringing in that "extra dimension" which sets apart exceptional present-day jewels; and **Thelma Robinson** with a jewelled collar: a bold intricate design in gold, studded with diamonds and hung with coloured enamel tendrils—this revived use of enamels again giving the work the sense of an "extra dimension". Three men won that same year: **David Robinson** from Liverpool (his second win), **John Gilchrist**, a Scot from Motherwell, and **John Willmin**, who is an exemplar of the designer who, thoroughly grounded in the basic techniques, enjoys working in a variety of fields—in his time he has made jewelled animals, a chess set, an extraordinary and elegant radio, beautiful silverware, jewels, and a range of marvellously inventive industrial designs. In 1971 one of the awards went to **Jane Allen** (Fig. 66) for a fragile cobweb of a necklace, its gold strands interwoven with diamond rosettes.

So many award-winners, so many prize-winning pieces: it is impossible to include them all, impossible to evaluate them properly, lacking the perspective of time and later work, but two things are notable: first, that as many girls win as men—the jewellery craft is one in which they excel—and secondly, that the winners who seem to go on immediately to further successes are those designer-craftsmen who not only design their work but make it up as well.

Even apart from their Diamonds-International Awards, De Beers do an enormous amount to publicize the jewellery trade. They arrange for articles and booklets, lend prepared lectures with or without slides, commission the finest photographers available to take photographs of their diamond jewellery, loan fine diamonds for special shows— Johnson Matthey similarly loan gold and platinum—see there is adequate press coverage for the award prize-givings, organize national competitions, such as the British Engagement Ring Competition, on various prize-levels, the winning pieces being exhibited at the Design Centre—no organization could work harder for the good of the diamond trade.

Exhibitions and Showrooms

Like De Beers Limited, the Worshipful Company of Goldsmiths does a great deal to help the jewellery trade; and their encouragement includes the staging of exhibitions— large set-pieces, like the *International Modern Jewellery Exhibition 1890–1961* which was staged as long ago as 1961; one-man shows at Goldsmiths Hall which often feature the work of well-established modern jewellers from overseas, stimulating the interest, even the fury, of contemporary British designers who come to look and learn, perhaps to argue, but never to ignore; exhibitions abroad featuring the work of groups of leading English designer-craftsmen. Their help, on the quiet personal level, is unparalleled.

Jewellers who do not have showrooms of their own sometimes show their work, or at least pieces of it, in commercial galleries, or at the showrooms which are under the aegis of the British Crafts Centre, backed by a small government grant, whose aim is to show the best work of leading British craftsmen in any field; exhibits are always for sale.

The Design Council (set up in 1944, and previously known as the Council of Industrial Design), again government-sponsored, also sets out to assist the jewellery trade, with its displays at the Design Centre. Its influence is considerable, especially in the export field, and its experts informative and helpful.

The Years to Come

What lies ahead? Fresh developments, changing styles, new techniques, all flowering afresh from the long traditions of a craft that dates back over five thousand years, all shaped by the discoveries of each new era. But not, one hopes, development in a closed-off world where the creative artist is set apart from the rest of us. It is our duty, it is our privilege, to study the work of our own time as well as the treasures of the past; not to be put off by a strangling beanstalk of mystique which grows up all too quickly, overnight almost, if art is left to the professional critic alone; to demand more financial help if the grants given are disgracefully little, as they so often are; to accept that conventions are only the loose and fluid meshes that cling about a living craft which is forever surging and bursting through them to fresh creation—not a series of arbitrary rules imposed externally upon it, but the shape of its own past achievements from which the new can grow; to communicate with our own creative artists; to encourage, to buy, to patronise; to show our pride in the brilliant designer-craftsmen of our own present day.

The Era of the Salesman

The twentieth century is the era of the salesman; whether one likes it or not, this is an inescapable fact. The power of professional selling is absolute. It has penetrated every area of modern life. Selling is done by word of mouth, by sound, by sight, by radio and television, by the written word, and by commercial advertising. For over fifty years people have been working on the psychological approach to selling and have evolved brilliant means of doing so—not simply selling goods or marketing an idea, but putting forward a public "image", creating confidence. The quirks that lie behind the choosing of a red-wrapped tin of meat rather than a blue one, the importance of its position on the supermarket shelves and its nearness to the check-out point, the appeal of the name it carries: all these have been researched in the most minute detail. Yards of clever books have been written on the art of advertising: they act as bibles to the salesman.

The salesman today is a professional: and a professional approach to selling is absolutely essential. The most important factor in selling is the creation of a bond of confidence between the public and the vendor. Whether we realize it or not, we almost always buy from firms we feel are intrinsically trustworthy and reliable, rarely from a firm we do not "know". Publicity, properly handled, with real commercial integrity, creates an atmosphere in which buyer and seller can, as it were, relate to one another. It is, of course, expensive, but can, if organized by the dedicated professional, be truly worth while.

Publicity is desperately needed for the silversmiths and goldsmiths and jewellers of Britain. During the eighteenth and nineteenth centuries her jewellery trade was at a peak: her craftsmen were superb, her machines the finest in the world, the general public had confidence in both, and patrons never considered buying from abroad—British was Best and Britain was Great and Britain exported British all over the world; the whole country then was proud of its craftsmen, their work and their standards.

During the twentieth century, advertising has come to be a force of tremendous importance, affecting almost the whole world—especially America, for so long the richest and most influential country. The public now buys almost everything over the counter; and generally speaking, it is guided, even manipulated, in its choice by the psychological cleverness of the advertising used by the various sales companies, organizations, and so on.

British students and craftsmen have won as many, or more, international competitions for design and craftsmanship as those of any other country in the world; yet the general public knows little or nothing of these successes. The media seem to publicize the art students' squabbles with authority, the length of their hair and the style of their clothes; not their achievements, not their successes. The ability—and it is riveting in the arts—is all here; year after year the art colleges turn out brilliant youngsters with originality, skill, craftsmanship, enthusiasm; and then comes the sad reckoning when they try to find a place in the commercial world, which is wary, even unwelcoming, feeling that to take in a student is asking for some uncomfortable type of disruption; when they try, too, to find patrons among a general public which has lost confidence in its craftsmen. Patrons need not be rich—it is often cheaper to commission a new piece than to buy over the counter—but they do need to be interested; above all, they need to be informed.

Who can help? Individual craftsmen cannot afford to back a steady publicity campaign for themselves. But they do have their parent body: the Worshipful Company of Goldsmiths, the "guardians of the craft", its name so solid, its reputation so flawless that it can establish confidence in anything it cares to promote. The Worshipful Company of Goldsmiths sets out to do many things, and most of them it does very quietly—quietest of all is the way that it deals with its charities, specializing in helping the least glamorous people, the needy who will neither hit the headlines nor conveniently die, the old, the sick, the addicts, the poor, the blind, the homeless, the maimed servicemen, giving away about £100,000 a year in charities and educational grants and gifts—and it is giving its own money, not the tax-payers'. The list of its gifts would fill volumes, and to each is attached a permanent and benign interest. Its collection of historic plate is unrivalled, and is added to regularly. (Because of insurance problems, it is impossible to mount a permanent display of the finest exhibits, or to admit visitors at will; but the Hall is open to the public six days a year, mainly in the summer, when those interested can, by appointment, join a public party and view the buildings at least.) Its library is magnificent, its collection of photographs unrivalled, its slides—loaned for lectures—superb, its officers charming and helpful. It gives technical advice and assistance. It arranges exhibitions, both in Britain and abroad. It sets up competitions. It helps students, it helps teachers, it helps the independent designer-craftsman. Since 1960 it has had a public relations officer—it seems extraordinary that so great an institution waited so long before employing one, but one is apt to think that a venerable and supremely reputable organization has no need of publicity; sadly, this is no longer so. Since 1960, too, it has had a dynamic art director, Graham Hughes, who has taken matters in hand, travelling world-wide to publicize the beauty and craftsmanship of present-day British work, mounting exhibitions, writing books on silver and jewels.

It is our loss that we still know so little about the company. Ask the average man in the street what the Goldsmiths Company does, and he may venture a guess that they hallmark metals—or he may confuse them with a commercial firm; if the street is in any town or city but London, he may not even have heard of their Hall and the exhibitions mounted there.

It is our loss too that we know so little about our craftsmen-designers, our students and their successes; and we need guidance over what is good design, good craftsmanship rather than merely clever styling. The craft needs publicity now more than ever before in its history, and valiant efforts are being made on its behalf; but the publicity it is getting is still on a very modest scale when compared with that expended, say, on selling a can of beans. The public is often amazed and delighted to learn that there are so many award-winning artists about; it had simply no idea that they existed. Could we not try out some of the new publicity methods? What is wrong with promoting silversmiths and jewellers through the personality cult? Film stars sell cigarettes, football stars sell shirts; there are a good many young designer-craftsmen of both sexes who are as glamorous as any film star and who have twice the personality. Why not a television competition—a "Jewel for Europe" instead of a "Song for Europe"? Why not a campaign staged by the most professional advertising firm available to educate the public in what is happening in the craft, to establish names and firms, to build up the careers of brilliant craftsmen, to give people a chance to be proud of their own fellow-nationals?

The ability is there. All that is needed is for some body to promote and publicize the brilliance of our young people; to take up and expand the efforts of the Worshipful Company of Goldsmiths and the various commercial companies; to act as a searchlight into the future, guiding and leading the modern craftsmen as surely as the "guardians of the craft" guided their fellows in the past six and a half centuries. This is no time to hide our light under a bushel. If we do, it may one day go out altogether. The most brilliant of artists cannot exist in a vacuum. It is our duty to help, to find out, to encourage, to press for better grants and more publicity. This is the era of the salesman, and there is no point in trying to avoid the fact or to pretend that the climate of the age is other than it is. This is the time to spread a rightful pride.

N.J.A.
March, 1973

A: On Caring for Jewels

In order to care for one's jewels properly, one must understand the nature of the gemstones with which they are set, and of the setting material. Caring falls into three general categories: housing, cleaning and checking.

Each jewel should be housed in a separate container—those beautiful jewel-cases are splendid for costume jewellery, but no good for precious jewels. When one buys a piece of modern jewellery, one should keep it in the case supplied by the jeweller; when one buys an antique piece, the original case may be missing but a good jeweller will always supply a substitute. Very small jewels—personal gifts from relatives, for instance—can be kept in individual chamois leather bags—*each piece in a separate pouch*. Jewels *must* be housed separately because of the danger that one stone can be scratched by another which is harder (Mohs' Scale in Appendix D sets out the order of hardness).

Jewels should be checked for cleanliness every six months. Examine them under a magnifying glass (this can be a revelation); if they are obviously filthy, take them to a professional jeweller for cleaning. Mildly dirty jewels—and there is no reason at all for them to be worse than this—can usually be cleaned at home. The basic formula is very simple—*but should not be used without first checking the list of exceptions which is given below*. Prepare a small bowl of soap suds with very hot water. Leave the jewel in the suds for about half an hour, then remove it and let it stand under hot running water for a few minutes. Shake away the drips, then dip it into a small bowl of surgical spirit (gin will do). Rinse again under hot water; then put the jewel in a small box of warm sawdust (a few penceworth from the local pet shop lasts a lifetime; keep it in the airing cupboard and it will always be warm and ready) and leave it for another half-hour, so that the sawdust can absorb the damp. Then brush the jewel gently with a complexion brush. *Never* pick at it with a sharp tool for this loosens the setting.

At this six-monthly cleaning, one should also check that the setting and catches are secure; if they are not, take the jewel to a jeweller at once.

It is best to examine a piece of jewellery after each wearing, and clean it if need be before putting it away, either in its own case or, if that is lost, in a small plastic bag. Nothing is more indicative of a slovenly woman than dirty jewellery. Remember its value: a jewel can sometimes cost as much as a house, but it is a fair assumption that the house gets better overall care. Even if it only costs as much as the gas stove, the stove will probably be attended to far more often.

There is no real ruling by which one can assess the value of a gemstone, but eight different factors can generally be taken into account: (1) the cut, (2) flaws, (3) beauty,

(4) durability, (5) scarcity value, (6) portability, (7) personal superstitions and associations, (8) current fashions. If it has any value at all, even if it does not rate ten points on each of these counts, it deserves to be taken care of properly.

Gemstone exceptions to the basic cleaning method are listed below. Most setting materials will respond satisfactorily to the basic method given above, but one should be careful with pinchbeck which, if dipped into a proprietary cleaner, may turn black.

Amber is very easily scratched, so it is best simply to polish it with a clean soft cloth. Alternatively, if the surface is dull, one can buy some powdered pumice from the chemist's or the drugstore, mix this with water and apply it to the surface; leave it for a short time only, and then polish it off with a clean soft dry cloth.

Coral is a soft stone and should be carefully washed with warm soapy water and equally carefully rinsed afterwards. A coral necklace needs frequent re-stringing.

Diamonds: when one washes **natural** diamonds with soap suds, it is essential to rinse away every trace of grease afterwards; otherwise a thin film will obscure the fire. Grease clings to diamonds very easily (when they are being separated from the gravelly ore at a diamond mine, they are spread on a conveyor belt which is thickly coated with grease; water washes continually over the belt, carrying away the grit while the diamonds stick to the grease). **Synthetic** diamonds may be cleaned by the basic method, but, like all synthetics, need more frequent care. When in doubt, take them to a professional.

Enamelled Jewels can be dipped into a mild solution of pure soap suds mixed with a few drops of household ammonia. Dry by the sawdust method and polish with a soft cloth.

Iron Pyrites: see under **Marcasite**

Jade: buy some black emery powder or graphite powder from the chemist's or the drugstore, and use a little on a soft cloth to polish the jade.

Marcasite or iron pyrites should never be washed, nor coated with oil, but rubbed with a soft brush and then polished with a soft metal-cleaner-impregnated cloth.

Mother-of-Pearl should never be washed, or worn when washing-up, cooking, etc.; clean it with a little machine-oil and polish with a soft cloth. Mother-of-pearl can become very brittle and flaky, and should always be wrapped in a soft cloth when not in use.

Opal is slightly porous and should *never* be washed, or worn when washing-up, cooking, etc., as it will absorb the dirt from the water. Like mother-of-pearl, it should be cleaned with a little machine-oil and then polished with a soft cloth.

Paste is ruined if any damp gets into it; the section on pages 164–168 goes into more detail about this.

Pearls are very absorbent and readily destructible. Chemically speaking, they are made of calcium carbonate and calcium albuminate. Seen under a very strong microscope, a pearl looks like a brick wall joined together with mortar. Unfortunately they will readily dissolve in acid (because calcium carbonate predominates in their composition), and their lovely sheen and lustre can be blurred by chemicals in the atmosphere. They are very soft (2 to 3 Mohs' Scale) and must be kept away from all other gemstones as any faceted stone can scratch them. If a pearl necklace has a jewelled clasp, a separate wrapping of protective material should be tucked around this—unless one is keeping the necklace, as of course one should, in a properly designed case to guard against this danger.

The average life of a string of pearls is about a hundred and fifty years, provided that they are re-strung on silk by a professional every six months *however little they have been worn*. Silk thread helps to protect them by absorbing the acid from the wearer's perspiration; nylon, which absorbs nothing, should not be used. The pearls should be cleaned every time they are worn, either with a soft chamois leather, or by rubbing them gently with warm bran; polish them with a soft cloth. The greatest dangers are scent, soap and hair lacquer; but pearls can also be damaged by a lack of oxygen if kept in a safe deposit, for instance. They really are extraordinarily fragile and need great care.

Cultured pearls should be treated in exactly the same way as "real" ones. They can on occasion be even more valuable.

Turquoise should be treated exactly like opal.

B: A Career in the Jewellery Trade

There are many worthwhile opportunities for men and women in the retail jewellery trade. As with every career, the more you put into it, the more satisfaction you get out of it; and here the most rewarding part is voluntarily becoming properly trained.

Most memorable events in a person's life are marked by a gift of precious metal or jewellery, from a silver christening mug, via an engagement ring and a wedding ring, to an anniversary or retirement clock. The person buying the present may have saved for a very long time to purchase it, and has to rely entirely on the integrity of the jeweller.

The general standards of the retail jewellery trade are higher in Great Britain than in any other country in the world. The foundations of these standards were cemented by the Worshipful Company of Goldsmiths, and during the last hundred years the National Association of Goldsmiths, which helps to oversee the retail trade, has also played its part. Whereas in other countries one visits one is well advised to check whether a jeweller is reliable, in the British Isles one can go along to any jeweller, large or small, town or country, and be confident of his integrity. The British public trusts the retail jeweller, realizing that he is a skilled person, professional in his approach, and knowledgeable about his trade.

In order to keep up this very high standard, most firms insist that their staff does not merely consist of trained salesmen, but includes qualified gemmologists.

There are several courses in gemmology which are open to people of either sex and of any age, which can be attended at night school. There are also correspondence courses, though these are mainly for the first year's study. Information about the centres of instruction and the examination syllabus can be obtained from the National Association of Gemmologists.

It was in 1908 that the Educational Committee of the National Association of Gold-smiths first realized the great need to standardize the training of gemmologists and started such a scheme. In 1931 the Gemmological Association was founded, and after the war, in 1947, this was given a new title—The Gemmological Association of Great Britain. It is affiliated to or liaises with all the other sister associations in the world, and is a purely educational and scientific organization which is non-profit-making. It promotes the serious study of gemmology and organizes the qualifying examinations by which one can become a Fellow. The present examination is in two parts, the preliminary and the diploma. This generally takes two years of reasonably intensive study.

Once one has passed the examinations and attained the status of a Fellow, one can meet to hear regular lectures, have the use of an excellent library, and receive the quarterly journal which has a world-wide circulation. One can also obtain specialized textbooks, instruments, and samples of gem specimens; and use the special laboratory facilities for testing pearls and other gems.

All this apart, qualification should ensure a better salary, and a much better chance of guaranteed employment.

Should a teenager of modest means wish to become a retail jeweller, he or she need not worry over money for training, or specialized academic qualifications; they can start work at once in a jeweller's establishment and take their gemmological training at night school. Alternatively they can enter into an apprenticeship. Details of apprenticeship schemes are available from the National Association of Goldsmiths, which also runs an apprenticeship scheme for watch and clock repairers.

There are various other certificates which can be obtained and which are helpful in making a career as a retail jeweller: the National Retail Distribution Certificate, for example, the Retail Trades Junior Certificate, and the Certificate in Retail Management Principles. All these qualifications are well worth having and would stand one in good stead if living and working abroad.

The thoroughness of the training is indicated by a brief glance at the summary of the present preliminary examination for gemmology, which is divided into five separate parts, these being again subdivided. It begins with elementary crystallography, and moves on to physical and optical properties such as distinguishing refractive indices, hardness and specific gravity. In Section Three are the elementary uses of apparatus, such as a dichroscope; in Section Four the exact descriptions of gem materials including—"only"!—four types of garnets, synthetic stones and organic products; and in the last section, the styles of cutting most gemstones. The present Final Diploma is divided into a theoretical examination and a practical, on much the same lines as the preliminary examination but at a much more sophisticated level.

The ideal training for a student would be to combine taking a Diploma in the History of Art and becoming a Fellow of the Gemmological Association. This would train him to recognize the artistic and aesthetic qualities of jewellery and silver, as well as giving him a superb technical knowledge; it could not be bettered. (The Diploma in the History of Art can also be obtained through studying at night school; there are a great many centres in the British Isles where one can undertake such a course; details are usually available from one's nearest university.)

Further details about the jewellery trade as a whole can be garnered from the Jewellery Information Centre, an organization set up to propagate information about British jewellery firms through the media of press and radio, and through general lectures. Their work is strictly on a commercial basis. Artistic appreciation can be forwarded by attending lectures such as those held at the Victoria and Albert Museum in South Kensington, London.

C: Valuations

Valuations can be obtained, for a small fee, through most commercial firms. Alternatively one can go to the big salesrooms, such as Christie's and Sotheby's.

A proper valuation of one's jewels should be obtained every two or three years. Values alter very quickly nowadays, and realistic insurance is a safeguard.

It is also possible to take an item of jewellery to the Victoria and Albert Museum on a weekday afternoon to be advised about its historical and artistic character.

D: Mohs' Scale

Frederick Mohs (A.D. 1773–1839) worked out a scaling of stones according to their hardness, in about 1820, and this is still in use. Any stone can cut or scratch the stones which are softer than itself. The "pecking order" of gemstones is as follows:

10. Diamond
9. Corundum—rubies and sapphires
8. Beryl—emeralds, aquamarines, topazes
7. Quartz—amethysts, cairngorms, tourmalines, zircons
6. Orthoclase
5. Apatite
4. Fluorite
3. Calcite
2. Gypsum
1. Talc

Generally speaking, stones ranging from 7 to 10 on the Mohs' Scale are transparent, and those from 1 to 7 opaque.

Many gemstones in the 1 to 6 range are very beautiful, even though they were not much used in earlier jewellery. Some are almost too soft to be used for jewels, those in categories 1 and 2 being, relatively speaking, about as hard as a finger-nail.

A number of organic stones are grouped among the gemstones: coral, for instance, is categorized at $3\frac{1}{2}$, amber at $2\frac{1}{2}$, pearls also at $2\frac{1}{2}$. Others used in jewellery are lapis lazuli (5 to $5\frac{1}{2}$), opal ($5\frac{1}{2}$ to $6\frac{1}{2}$), turquoise (5 to 6) and jade (either nephrite, a silicate of calcium and magnesium, which is categorized at $6\frac{1}{2}$, or jadeite, a silicate of aluminium and sodium, categorized at 7).

E: The National Art Collections Fund

Throughout the twentieth century the National Art Collections Fund has concerned itself with buying for the public treasures the government cannot afford to purchase, ensuring the country is not artistically impoverished. It will, when approached, step in quietly and try to raise enough to keep essentially national treasures in their country of origin, not merely buying paintings but also furniture, glass, silver—to furnish the museums and galleries, both in the capital and in the provinces. The annual fee is very small, but it goes towards preserving a heritage of fine art and craftsmanship. If people would just help the fund a little, or leave something in their will (no sum is too small), it would help so much. Some of us are afraid that pieces we have treasured, loved and looked after will be sold at some impersonal auction sale after our death; pieces such as these can be willed to the fund, providing that they are of high quality, and will be placed in some museum or stately home open to the public where they can still be cared for and admired, and give pleasure to so many people.

F: The National Association of Decorative and Fine Arts Societies

NADFAS is a splendid organization which has brought enormous pleasure and satisfaction to thousands of people all over the British Isles. The first society was founded in 1965, and the movement has snowballed, with societies springing up all over the country. Each manages its own affairs and arranges its own lectures and outings, secure in the knowledge that in any difficulty it can get advice from fellow-societies and the central committee.

These are not just cultural societies providing lectures of the highest possible quality. They have another aim: to stimulate interest in, and give aid to, the preservation of the national heritage. Interested members are trained in such straightforward but responsible tasks as mending fabrics, cleaning old books, cataloguing silver, and learning to act as guides in museums and country houses. In addition, a vigorous programme of foreign tours, impeccably organized, non-profit-making, and often including visits to private houses and private collections, is arranged annually.

NADFAS is now a registered charity, and should forge ahead yet more strongly, satisfying many people's longing to enjoy and care for the decorative arts. Especially grateful are those who live farthest from city museums and galleries.

G: List of Addresses

Any winner of a Diamonds-International Award can be contacted by writing to *De Beers Consolidated Mines Ltd.,* whose address is given below.

Susan Barfield, c/o Mappin & Webb, 106 Regent St., London W.1.

Frances Beck and Ernest Blyth, 2 White Horse St., London W.1.

Richard Bonehill and Lynne Bradshaw, 623 Eccleshall Rd., Sheffield S11 8PT.

British Crafts Centre, 12 Waterloo Place, Lower Regent St., London W.1, *and* 43 Earlham St., London W.C.2.

Jocelyn Burton, 50c Red Lion St., London W.C.1.

Messrs Cairncross of Perth, 18 St. John's St., Perth, Scotland.

Cameo Corner Ltd., 26 Museum St., London W.C.1.

Christie's, Fine Art Auctioneers, 8 King St., London S.W.1.

Collingwood of Conduit Street Ltd., 46 Conduit St., London W.1.

De Beers Consolidated Mines Ltd., 40 Holborn Viaduct, London E.C.1.

The Design Council, The Haymarket, London S.W.1, *and* St. Vincent's St., Glasgow, Scotland.

Stuart Devlin, 90/92 St. John's St., London E.C.2.

John Donald, 120 Cheapside, London E.C.2.

Garrard & Co. Ltd., Crown Jewellers, 112 Regent St., London W.1.

Goldsmiths, The Worshipful Company of, Goldsmiths Hall, Foster Lane, London E.C.2.

Andrew Grima, 80 Jermyn St., London W.1.

Jewellery Information Centre, 44 Fleet St., London E.C.4.

Johnson Matthey & Co. Ltd., 73 Hatton Garden, London E.C.1.

National Art Collections Fund, Hertford House, Manchester Square, London W1M 6BN.

National Association of Decorative and Fine Arts Societies, c/o The Secretary, Woodland, College Farm End, Loosley Row, Aylesbury, Bucks.

National Association of Gemmologists, St. Dunstan's House, Carey Lane, London EC2V 8AB.

National Association of Goldsmiths, as for *National Association of Gemmologists,* above.

Gilian Packard, Ramillies House, 1 Ramillies St., London W.1.

Wendy Ramshaw, 35 Leighton Rd., London N.W.5.

Sotheby & Co., Auctioneers, 34 New Bond St., London W.1.

David Thomas, 48 Old Church St., London S.W.3.

Wartski Jewellers Ltd, 138 Regent St., London W.1.

Lawrence Wheaton, c/o *Collingwood of Conduit St.,* above.

H: A Book List

Selected Bibliography

Akrigg, G. P. V., *Jacobean Pageant*, Hamilton (Hamish) Ltd., London, 1962

Blakemore, K., *The Book of Gold*, Deutsch, André, Ltd., London, 1971

Bradford, E. D. S., *English Victorian Jewellery*, Spring Books, Feltham, 1968

—— *Four Centuries of European Jewellery*, Spring Books, Feltham, 1967

Bruton, E., *Diamonds*, NAG Press Ltd., London, 1971

Bryant, Sir Arthur, *Makers of the Realm*, Collins (William), Sons & Co., Ltd., London, 1953

Clifford, Anne, *Cut-Steel and Berlin Iron Jewellery*, Adams & Dart, Bath, 1971

Clifford-Smith, H., *Jewellery*, Methuen & Co. Ltd., London, 1908

Copplestone, Trewin, and Myers, Bernard S. (General editors), *Landmarks of the World's Art*, The Hamlyn Publishing Group Ltd., London, 1966

Craig, Sir John, *The Mint*, Cambridge University Press, Cambridge, 1953

Edwards, Ralph, and Ramsey, L. G. G. (Eds.), *The Connoisseur's Complete Period Guides*, The Connoisseur, London, 1956, 1957, 1958

Evans, Joan, *English Jewellery from the Fifth Century A.D. to 1800*, Methuen & Co. Ltd., London, 1921

—— *English Posies and Posy Rings*, Oxford University Press, London, 1931/2

—— *History of Jewellery, 1100–1870*, Faber & Faber Ltd. (rev. ed.), London, 1970

—— *Magical Jewels of the Middle Ages and the Renaissance*, Oxford University Press, 1923

Faulkiner, Richard, *Investing in Antique Jewellery*, Barrie and Jenkins, London, 1968

Gere, Charlotte, *Victorian Jewellery Design*, Kimber & Co. Ltd., London, 1972

Gilchrist, James, *Anglican Church Plate*, The Connoisseur & Joseph (Michael) Ltd., London, 1967

Good, Edward, *Cameos and Inspirational Jewellery*, 1914

Gregorietti, Guido, *Jewellery Through The Ages*, The Hamlyn Publishing Group Ltd., London & Sydney, 1970

Hughes, Graham, *Modern Jewellery*, Studio Vista Ltd., London, 1968

—— *The Art of Jewellery*, Studio Vista Ltd., London, 1972

Huizinga, J., *The Waning of the Middle Ages*, Penguin Books Ltd., London, 1955

James, Bill, *Collecting Australian Gemstones*, K. G. Murray, Sydney and Melbourne, 1972

Jenkins, Elizabeth, *Elizabeth the Great*, Gollancz (Victor) Ltd., London, 1958

Jessup, R., *Anglo-Saxon Jewellery*, Faber & Faber Ltd., London, 1950

Kendall, Hugh P., *The Story of Whitby Jet*, Whitby, 1936

Kotker, Norman (Ed.), *The Horizon Book of the Elizabethan World*, The Hamlyn Publishing Group Ltd., London, and the American Heritage Publishing Co. Inc., New York, 1967

Kybalova, Herbenova, Lamorova, (Eds.), *The Pictorial Encyclopaedia of Fashion*, The Hamlyn Publishing Group Ltd., London, 1969

Laver, James, *A Concise History of Costume*, Thames and Hudson Ltd., London, 1969

Lewis, M. D. S., *Antique Paste Jewellery*, Faber & Faber Ltd., London, 1970

Lister, Raymond, *The Craftsman in Metal*, Bell (G.) & Sons, Ltd., London, 1966

Longford, Elizabeth, *Victoria R. I.*, Weidenfeld & Nicolson Ltd., London, 1964

Meen, V. B., and Tushingham, A. D., *Crown Jewels of Iran*, Oxford University Press, 1969

Millar, Oliver, *Tudor, Stuart and Early Georgian Pictures in the Royal Collection*, Phaidon Press Ltd., 1963

Mitchell, R. J., and Leys, M. D. R., *A History of London Life*, Longman Group Ltd., London, 1958
Murray, Peter and Murray, Linda, *Dictionary of Art and Artists*, Thames and Hudson Ltd., London, 1965.
Norman, P., *Nicholas Hilliard*, Walpole Society Transactions, 1911–12.
Oved, S., *The Book of Necklaces*, Barker (Arthur) Ltd., London, 1953
Peter, Mary, *Collecting Victorian Jewellery*, MacGibbon & Kee Ltd., London, 1970
Plumb, J. H., *England in the Eighteenth Century*, Penguin Books Ltd., London, 1950
Ritchie, C. I. A., *Carving Shells and Cameos*, Barker (Arthur) Ltd., 1970
Scott Thomson, Gladys, *Life in a Noble Household, 1641–1700*, Cape (Jonathan) Ltd., London, 1937 (re-issued 1940, 1950)
Sitwell, Edith, *The Queens and The Hive*, Macmillan & Co. Ltd., London, 1962
Steingraber, E., *Antique Jewellery*, Thames and Hudson Ltd., London, 1963
—— *Royal Treasures*, Weidenfeld & Nicolson Ltd., London, 1968
Strong, Roy, and Trevelyan Oman, Julia, *Mary Queen of Scots* Secker (Martin) & Warburg Ltd., London, 1972
Tanner, Lawrence E., *The Story of Westminster Abbey*, Raphael Tuck & Sons Ltd., London, 1952
Taylor, Gerald, *Continental Gold and Silver*, The Connoisseur & Joseph (Michael) Ltd., 1967
—— *Silver through the Ages*, Penguin Books Ltd., Harmondsworth, 1956 (re-issued, Cassell & Co. Ltd., 1964)
Toynbee, Margaret, *King Charles I*, International Textbook Co. Ltd., 1968
Trevelyan, G. M., *Illustrated English Social History*, Longman Group Limited, 1944
Wheatley, William, *Isaac Le Gooch*, Hammersmith Local History Group, 1964
Williams, Raymond, *The Long Revolution*, Chatto & Windus Ltd., London, 1961
Wilson, Henry, *Silverwork and Jewellery*, John Hogg, London, 1903 (also later Pitman edition)
Younger Dickinson, Joan, *The Book of Diamonds*, Muller (Frederick) Ltd., London, 1965
Younghusband, Sir George J., *The Jewel House*, Jenkins, 1929

Selected List of Inventories, Papers, etc.

Bower, J. S., *Letters and Papers, Foreign and Domestic, of the Reign of Henry VIII*, Public Records Office, London, 1867
Collins, A. J. (Ed.), *Jewels and Plate of Queen Elizabeth I: the Inventory of 1574*, London, 1955
Cox, J., *A descriptive inventory of several exquisite and magnificent pieces of mechanism and jewellery*, London, 1773
Nichols, J., *The Progresses and Public Processions of Queen Elizabeth*, London, 1788–1821
Palgrave, F., *The Antient Kalendars and Inventories of the Treasury of His Majesty's Exchequer*, London, 1836

Selected List of Historical Sources

Bornemann, Wilhelm, *Einblicke in England und London in Jahre 1818*, Berlin, 1818
Castellani, A., *Antique Jewellery and its Revival*, London, 1862
Chardin, Jean, *Journal du Voyage*, 1686
Dickinson Brothers, *Comprehensive Pictures of the Great Exhibition of 1851*, (2 vols), London, 1854
Flach, Thomas, *A Book of Jeweller's Work*, London, 1736
Hakluyt Society, *The World Encompassed . . . carefully collected out of the notes of Master Francis Fletcher, preacher in this employment and divers others his followers in the same*, 1854 (original edition printed 1628)
Herbst, *A Book of Severall Jewelers Work*, London, 1710
Hilliard, Nicholas, *The Arte of Limning*, 1598
La Belle Assemblée (magazine)
Pepys, Samuel, *Diary*, 1660–1669
The World of Fashion (magazine)

Selected List of Booklets and Catalogues

Great Exhibition of 1851, Official Descriptive and Illustrated Catalogue, London, 1851
Halford, William, and Young, Charles, *The Jeweller's Book of Patterns in Hair Work*, London, 1864
London Museum (Catalogue), *The Cheapside Hoard of Elizabethan and Jacobean Jewellery*, 1928
Raspe, R. E. (Ed.), *Descriptive Catalogue* of James Tassie's Work, Edinburgh, 1790–1
Read, C. H., *The Waddesden Bequest*, The British Museum, London, 1899
Strong, Roy, *The Elizabethan Image*, Tate Gallery, London, 1969
Victoria and Albert Museum (Catalogue), *Victorian Church Art*, London, 1971
Wedgwood and Bentley, *A Catalogue of Cameos Etc.*, London, 1773

Index

A number of abbreviations have been used in index entries, the most common of these being Ch. H. for Cheapside Hoard (*c.* 1600), d. for daughter, Edw. for Edwardian, Fig. for Figure, j. and J. for jewel and Jewel, Mary Q. of S. for Mary Queen of Scots, med. for medieval, pl. f. for plate facing, S. Hoo for Sutton Hoo treasure, Vic. for Victorian and w. for wife.

When numerals appear in alphabetically arranged lists of design periods, etc., they are placed as if spelt out: e.g. *1900–1920*=nineteen-hundred to nineteen-twenty.

All monarchs are English/British monarchs unless otherwise stated.

73998